PRAISE FOR
TWENTY-SIX SECONDS

"Zapruder is a gifted writer and storyteller who delicately unravels a minor mystery few people know or care about, but that she makes human, complex, and quite interesting."
—*New York Times Book Review*

"The fifty-year saga of the most important witness to the JFK assassination—a home movie shot by Abraham Zapruder—is a high-stakes morality tale, suspenseful, thought-provoking, and at times nasty. Zapruder's embattled descendants defend their claim to the film, while researchers, conspiracy theorists, disapproving editorial writers, and the federal government swirl around them, and millions of dollars hang in the balance."
—John Berendt, *New York Times* bestselling author of *Midnight in the Garden of Good and Evil*

"Enlightening…an intelligent blend of memoir and cultural criticism that breaks fresh ground in the crowded field of JFK assassination studies."
—*San Francisco Chronicle*

"It is rare to find a book like TWENTY-SIX SECONDS that uncovers new information about one of the most tragic events in American history...an intelligent examination of the changing media landscape, sudden notoriety, and its aftermath."

—*The Washington Times*

"A wholly unique family memoir and a fascinating monograph about one of the most consequential artifacts in recorded history...So much has been written and said about the Kennedy assassination that a reader might wonder what is left to be said. In the pages of TWENTY-SIX SECONDS, Alexandra Zapruder says it."

—*Jewish Journal*

"A fascinating history." —*Men's Journal*

"Zapruder evokes the tension and horror of the assassination. Scrupulous facts are woven into an intensely personal, sometimes painful, family history...TWENTY-SIX SECONDS is an important contribution to our understanding of history on a grand scale, and to the personal history of a private family reluctantly thrust into history's spotlight." —*Lone Star Literary Life*

Also by Alexandra Zapruder

Salvaged Pages: Young Writers' Diaries of the Holocaust

TWENTY-SIX SECONDS

■ ■ ■ ■ ■ ■ ■

A PERSONAL HISTORY OF
THE ZAPRUDER FILM

ALEXANDRA ZAPRUDER

TWELVE

NEW YORK BOSTON

Twelve
Hachette Book Group
1290 Avenue of the Americas, New York, NY 10104
twelvebooks.com
twitter.com/twelvebooks

Originally published in hardcover and ebook by Twelve in November 2016.

First Trade Paperback Edition: September 2017

Twelve is an imprint of Grand Central Publishing.
The Twelve name and logo are trademarks of Hachette Book Group, Inc.

The publisher is not responsible for websites (or their content) that are not owned by the publisher.

The Hachette Speakers Bureau provides a wide range of authors for speaking events. To find out more, go to www.hachettespeakersbureau.com or call (866) 376-6591.

Unless otherwise noted, photos are courtesy of the Zapruder family.

Library of Congress Cataloging-in-Publication Data

Names: Zapruder, Alexandra, author.
Title: Twenty-six seconds : a personal history of the Zapruder film / Alexandra Zapruder.
Other titles: Personal history of the Zapruder film
Description: First edition. | New York : Twelve, [2016] | Includes bibliographical references and index.
Identifiers: LCCN 2016025786 | ISBN 9781455574810 (hardcover) | ISBN 9781455541690 (large print) | ISBN 9781478924159 (audio download) | ISBN 9781478924166 (audio book) | ISBN 9781455574803 (ebook)
Subjects: LCSH: Kennedy, John F. (John Fitzgerald), 1917–1963—Assassination. | Kennedy, John F. (John Fitzgerald), 1917–1963—In motion pictures. | Zapruder, Abraham. | Amateur films—Texas—Dallas—History—20th century. | Memory—Political aspects—United States. | Motion pictures and history.
Classification: LCC E842.9 .Z37 2016 | DDC 973.922092—dc23 LC record available at https://lccn.loc.gov/2016025786.

ISBNs: 978-1-4555-7482-7 (trade pbk.), 978-1-4555-7480-3 (ebook)

Printed in the United States of America

LSC-C

10 9 8 7 6 5 4 3 2 1

In memory of our grandfather, Abraham, and our beloved father, Henry

To my immediate and extended family with love and gratitude

With special love to Hannah, Toby, Levi, Sam, and Simon, who carry our name into the next generation and in whose hands it is rightly entrusted

CONTENTS

Introduction   1

Prologue: Home Movie   19

CHAPTER 1: Assassination   27

CHAPTER 2: Exposure   48

CHAPTER 3: First Glimpses   75

CHAPTER 4: All Rights to *LIFE*   104

CHAPTER 5: Images in Print   129

CHAPTER 6: Mounting Pressure   158

CHAPTER 7: Court Cases and Bootlegs   189

CHAPTER 8: *LIFE*'s Dilemma   223

CHAPTER 9: *The Eternal Frame* and the Endless
  Debates   254

CHAPTER 10: The Floodgates Open   276

CHAPTER 11: *JFK*: The Movie and the Assassination
  Records Act   299

CHAPTER 12: To Take or Not to Take the Film   319

CHAPTER 13: A Final Firestorm   348

CHAPTER 14: Arbitration and Resolution   381

Epilogue: Public and Private Legacy   413

Acknowledgments   423
Notes   433
Reading Group Guide   457
Index   469

INTRODUCTION

When I was eleven years old, I went looking for my grandfather in William Manchester's book *The Death of a President*. I'm not sure how I knew that I would find him there. I found the book by looking it up in the old card catalog in my elementary school library. I pulled the thick, black-covered volume off the shelf and sat on the floor between the stacks to read it. I vividly recall flipping to the index, turning the leaves until I reached the last page, and scanning the Ys and Zs until I landed on the words I sought: *Zapruder, Abraham.* It was thrilling to see my own last name in print and in the satisfyingly long list of pages on which my grandfather was mentioned. I read the pages stealthily, consuming the few details about his personality and about what happened to him just before, during, and after President John F. Kennedy was killed.

I had no occasion to revisit those pages until more than thirty years later, when I was writing this book. When I did, I was shocked to see his story embedded in an incredibly gory account of the assassination, which I must have read at the same time. I don't remember that at all. Neither do I remember reading the short paragraph in which Manchester described Jackie Kennedy and my grandfather in the same sentence, though that is the sort of proximity to fame and pathos that would normally have attracted my attention. What impressed itself on my memory was the image of my grandfather, crying and screaming over and over, "They killed him! They killed him!" I remember the description of him at his office, anguished and in shock, slamming the door and kicking "every object that would move" in rage and fury. I read that he was, in Manchester's words, "a casualty, one of the weekend's walking wounded," so traumatized that, unlike nearly everyone else, he shunned the TV news coverage of the assassination and the funeral. I remember reading these pages over and over again, drawn to and horrified by the idea of my grandfather so broken and filled with sorrow. And I distinctly remember wishing there was more to read, feeling that these tantalizing fragments of his story were not enough.

I never knew my grandfather. Papa Abe, as he was known in our family, had died when my twin brother, Michael, and I were ten months old and our older brother, Matthew, was not yet three. Unlike my three living grandparents, who were a big part of my life, Papa Abe existed for me in his absence, as if our family were a great big smile with one giant missing front tooth. My sense of him came mostly from the stories my parents told and his one-liners that became stock phrases in our family's private language. Our dad loved to tell how Papa Abe would drop him off at school and always say the same thing: "Got any money?" Our dad would say yes. Papa would hold out his hand, palm up, and shoot back, "Then gimme some," and laugh at his own joke. He was endlessly curious about how things worked and terrific with his hands, rigging up gadgets and rewiring the electrical systems around the house, frequently with hilarious results. The family's longtime friend Ada Lynn used to say that he tinkered with the wiring so much that she was afraid she would ring the doorbell one day and the house would blow up. He loved to talk, equally happy debating politics and world events as he was discussing philosophical or existential matters. He was a born musician who never had a lesson and could play by ear; he came home from work every day and sat down to play the piano before even taking off his hat. He was a keen observer and social commentator, predicting, for example, that people were getting so used to doing things by pushing buttons that, in the future, babies would be born with only one finger. I can still see the wistful smile that crossed my dad's face when Papa Abe came up in conversation, and hear his laugh, laced with regret and grief from a too-early loss. I loved when my father remembered him aloud at the dinner table, and I wanted the night to stretch on long in the telling.

Of course, I also knew that he had taken a home movie of President Kennedy's assassination in Dallas. I have no memory of learning this fact; it seems to me that I always knew it. I also knew his movie was called the Zapruder film, and Zapruder was my name, too, which in my childhood brain meant that I was famous, although I definitely knew I wasn't supposed to think that. This part of his life never came up at the dinner table. "The film"—as it was always called in our family vernacular—was almost completely compartmentalized from our family identity, our stories, and our sense of ourselves. It's extremely difficult to describe what I mean by this or even to fully untangle it in my memory. It's not that the topic was forbidden or suppressed or that the film's existence was denied or ignored. That is a too-blunt way to describe something far more subtle. But I knew—we all knew—that the grown-ups really didn't want to talk about it. Why was another story. I'm sure I never thought to ask. It simply existed somewhere offstage, there and not there, fascinating and a little bit scary.

When I was very young, I accepted this without question, as children tend to do. The film generally only came up when a stranger in a bookstore, at the grocery, or in the airport would recognize our name and ask my parents: Isn't that a famous name? Wasn't that the guy who...? Are you related? And I remember with a visceral clarity how they responded. I would watch as my father deflected the question, smiling graciously and offering a firmly closed-ended response, so different from his usual warm, embracing enthusiasm. I saw how my mother, unfailingly charming in other public situations, would tense slightly, and she would say, "Yes, it is a famous name." Even I understood that this polite but noncommittal answer telegraphed a resistance to further discussion, buying her enough time to finish signing the slip, smile, and escape the shop without getting embroiled in a conversation.

In addition to what I absorbed from our family culture and watching my parents, I remember a few very clear messages that were conveyed to me—to all of us, I think—about the Zapruder film. First and foremost, whatever the rest of the world thought, Papa Abe was remembered in our family for his true self, not for anything having to do with the film. I must have heard my mother say a hundred times, "Your grandfather should have been famous for who he was, for being a good person and a funny, wonderful man, and not for the film." Surely this feeling came naturally to my parents, but it was handed down as an imperative to us. Second, we don't brag about the film. It is a gruesome, horrible record of President Kennedy's assassination, which was a tragic event for the country and the Kennedy family. It is nothing to be proud of. Third, we are tied to the film by chance and coincidence. It was an accident of fate. It happened to be taken by our grandfather and it happened to be called by our name. Apart from that, it has nothing to do with us. Now, as an adult with children of my own who bear my last name and who have innocently bragged about it just as I did, I understand and even appreciate the wisdom of this guidance. Well, the first two parts at least. That third one—it has nothing to do with us—would turn out to be more of a wish than a fact. But I didn't know that at the time.

When I think back on it now, I imagine our family identity as a Venn diagram in which the overlap between the Zapruder family and the Zapruder film was neither clear nor fixed. When viewed from inside our family, the film was marginal, of little significance compared to the memory of a beloved patriarch who died too young. But strangers' curiosity and prying calls from the media had a way of pushing it into view, emphasizing our family's connection to the film in ways that were hard to ignore. If, in childhood, family identity is primarily defined by the tastes, interests, and values of parents, adolescence brings about questions and change. As I got older, I must have wondered about this thing called the Zapruder film: Why did people keep bringing it up if it wasn't all that important, and what did other people know about it that I didn't? On the other hand, my parents had already told me where the film stood in relation to our grandfather and how we should regard it, so I hesitated to ask them again. Eventually, caught between my own curiosity and my sense that a conversation with my parents would never fully satisfy me, I went rogue in the school library with William Manchester instead.

My parents and my brothers and I used to travel to Dallas to see my father's family once or twice a year. I adored our grandmother and my aunt (my uncle died when I was very young, so I have only a few sweet memories of him), but the best part was being with my four older cousins—Jeffrey, Adam, David, and Aaron—who were always known collectively as "the boys." Since I was the last grandchild and the only girl on that side of the family, they spoiled me, constantly hugging and kissing me, playing with me, teaching me to play pool, and giving me Juicy Fruit gum. It was heaven.

My memories of our time together as a family in Dallas remind me that there are two families who make up the descendants of Abraham Zapruder. Abe and Lil had two children—Myrna and Henry. Myrna changed her name when she married Myron Hauser, so their four boys are Hausers, as well. My father, Henry, married Marjorie Seiger, who became Marjorie Zapruder, and my brothers and I grew up as Zapruders. This otherwise innocuous fact matters because this is not just a story about family but about the inheritance of names, and how it shapes identity and life experiences. Since our grandfather's film very quickly became known as the Zapruder film (to distinguish it from the other films taken that day), and the name is, by coincidence, nearly unique in America, the five of us who bore the name were linked to the unique record of the Kennedy assassination in a way that was different from that of our Dallas family.

For this reason, there is no singular experience of our family's relationship to the Zapruder film. Throughout this book, when I refer to "our family," I generally mean the immediate family and descendants of Abraham Zapruder, whether they are named Zapruder or Hauser. This is because we are a close family with a shared fate, and what happens to one of us happens to all of us. Nevertheless, there are other times when I have written about the particular experience of my immediate family, which is unique not just because of our name but because it was our father, Henry, who handled the film for twenty-five years and who bore the primary emotional, intellectual, and logistical responsibility for it. Finally, and most frequently, I have written from my own perspective, endeavoring to recall my experiences and memories of growing up with the film as truthfully and accurately as I could. Some of my memories or feelings may echo those of my siblings or other family members, while others may be completely different. In the end, we each experienced the film and its effect on our lives uniquely, as all members of a family do with their respective pasts.

I did not end up nurturing a secret interest in the Zapruder film after my clandestine reading of *The Death of a President*. Far from it. My curiosity must have been more or less satisfied, because I rarely thought about the film through most of my teens, in college, and after. It was not because I suppressed it; to the contrary, it genuinely didn't occur to me to dwell on it. Of course, strangers still sometimes asked about the film, or the media would suddenly seize upon it, but this no longer intrigued me. By the time I was in my teens, I found myself more surprised by this than anything else. I suppose by then I had absorbed my parents' feelings about it—I took it for granted as a part of our family's history but I did not see it as a defining element of my life or identity. For this reason, when strangers asked about the film, I often felt they were imposing their curiosity on me in a way that could be intrusive or even embarrassing. In this regard, the association of our name with the film felt a bit like having an unsightly birthmark—it was something we were born with, but it didn't define us. I was used to it and no longer particularly noticed it. But I didn't expect people to point it out, either.

It became increasingly difficult to avoid the topic of the film in the 1990s, when events pushed it more into the news and the public eye than it had been at any other time in my life. First there was Oliver

Stone's movie *JFK*, and then the film was parodied on *Seinfeld*. There followed a long public period (examined at length in this book) during which our family and the federal government tussled over the ownership of the Zapruder film, its copyright, and its monetary value. There were routinely articles about our family in the *Washington Post* and the *New York Times*. While some of the media coverage was balanced and reasonable, I also heard my family's motives and morality casually critiqued on NPR and by idols of mine like Doris Kearns Goodwin. Closer to home, a mean-spirited article in our local *Washington City Paper* accused my grandfather, my father, and our family of shamelessly profiting from the president's murder. A professional colleague at the United States Holocaust Memorial Museum, where I was working at the time, challenged me on our family's policy regarding permissions to use the film, coldly pointing out that "we" charged high fees for its use. Stung and embarrassed, I tried to defend my father but realized that I had no idea what I was talking about. When our family and the government at last reached a resolution on the ownership of the film in 1999, I opened Yahoo to check my e-mail and found a poll question on the home page in which the public was invited to vote on whether they felt the Zapruder family deserved the amount of money awarded for the film. At the time I saw it, 18,000 people had already weighed in. The news of the decision aired on every network and on shows such as *Entertainment Tonight*, and my father was deluged with media wanting interviews. As much as I cringe at the memory, I now know that what I read in the paper and experienced for myself was, in fact, only the tip of an iceberg that my father was trying to steer us around.

And then, in the way that such things happen, it was over. The controversy died down and, mercifully, the media went on to other news and the public forgot about the whole thing. My brothers and I began our careers—mine in nonfiction, my twin brother Michael's in music, and our older brother Matthew's in poetry. I got married. Our parents worked, traveled, hosted evenings with friends talking politics, laughing, and drinking wine, and pursued their own interests: my father sailing and playing guitar, my mother taking photographs. We spent holidays and vacations together as a family. We went back to being the Zapruders, as we had always been. And if we didn't have to think much about the Zapruder film anymore, so much the better.

In September 2004, days after my husband and I learned that I was pregnant with our first child, my father underwent a biopsy that showed that he had a malignant brain tumor. We had known since the previous April that he was ill, but nothing compared to the crushing blow of his diagnosis. The shock sent reverberating shudders through our family and our wide circle of friends. He was just sixty-five at the time.

At some point early in his illness, he told me that someone should interview him about the history of the film. I suppose he realized that he was very sick and that, since he had been the primary actor on our family's behalf for everything that had to do with the film for so many years, he felt he should record his vast knowledge of it before it was too late. But it was a pipe dream; the idea reflected the wishful belief that life was going to continue as it always had, that his illness was an abstraction that would not actually have implications for our lives. As his cancer progressed with shocking rapidity, whatever fleeting thoughts I had of recording his memories regarding the film receded into the background. For one thing, to interview him at all was to face the fact of his impending death. It seemed impossible to accept it myself, let alone to ask him to acknowledge it so openly, to tell me things that he would not be alive to say later. Beyond that, the most articulate, precise, gifted talker I ever met lost his language incredibly quickly, and while his memory might have been intact inside his diseased brain, the cancer took from him his greatest intellectual gift, which was to translate his ideas into spoken language. Most of all, his illness and death—and, simultaneously, my first pregnancy and the birth of our daughter—occupied every cell of my being during that time. I was far too wrapped up in trying to soak up every minute I could with him—and eventually, helping him die with dignity—to give a thought to the Zapruder film. Luckily for our family, the cancer never robbed him of his gentleness and sweetness, of his love and generosity. But it did take his life far too early, like his father before him, and with it, among many other things, a vast personal and intellectual understanding of the history of the Zapruder film.

In the years following my father's death, I was periodically visited by the idea that I should do something to capture and record the history of the film from our family's standpoint. Surely it was his death—the sense that so much had slipped away—that gave rise to this impulse to collect what I could and to put some order to this narrative in whatever way was possible without him. I knew there were family papers about the film, voluminous legal documentation, and family and friends who had been involved in its history but who had never spoken publicly about it—and probably never would unless one of us asked them to.

My father's sister, Myrna, her son Adam (also an attorney, who had worked with my father on the conflict with the government), and my mother all shared this sense of responsibility. Periodically, one of us would raise the subject and all would agree that we should gather the family's papers, catalog them, and make sure they were stored somewhere safe. I would resolve to take it on, but somehow, the forward momentum always stalled and stasis would set in. Then, months later, I would wake in the night with a sudden panic: The documents were scattered, there were materials in my mother's attic, what if something got lost or damaged? Who was going to interview my father's personal secretary, the intellectual property attorney who had represented our family for more than a decade, and my father's friends, not to mention my mother and my aunt and all the others?

I would plan to begin again. But before I got very far, I would realize once more the logistical complications of this effort and the massive, daunting nature of the subject matter. I would quickly get overwhelmed and lose heart, and then the whole thing would drift away from me. Along the way, our daughter turned three and our son was born. Life was full and busy. It was not the time, I told myself. I didn't have the mental wherewithal to organize my refrigerator, let alone the Zapruder family's history of the Zapruder film, even if it was only for our family and for posterity.

Which I already knew it wouldn't be.

If I'm being truly honest with myself, I have to admit that on some level, I felt that taking even the smallest step in this direction meant taking on more than just organizing the family's papers. I'm a writer. I am drawn to the study of history and I am especially curious about how simple narratives conceal much deeper, more complicated and interesting truths. It was hard to see how inviting this subject into my life *wasn't* going to end in my wanting to write a book about it. I had no idea what kind of book it would be or what I would find if I dug into this history; I just knew that there would be questions and that I would want to find answers. At the same time, the thought of publishing a book—that most public of actions—flew in the face of at least one central life principle about the Zapruder film, which was that we did not invite conversation about it. I could see the conflict looming from a hundred miles away.

As if that weren't enough of a deterrent, along the way I was going to have to study the history of the Kennedy assassination—a subject I had avoided my entire life—and confront the immense, unspoken complexities of the Zapruder film. People spend their lives on this topic. I hardly knew a thing. Not only that, but my father and my memory of him were imprinted on every part of this story; in order to learn and tell it, I would also have to invite him back in, only to endure his loss again, to face my unanswered questions, and to risk the grief that still sometimes brought me to my knees. And so it would go. I would run through all the reasons that this was a terrible idea. I would parse out all the ways that I didn't want to do this. I would push the thought aside and leave it all for another day. And it would always come back.

My brothers—both of them gifted artists—have been the staunchest supporters of my writing. They encouraged me in my earliest thinking about this book, though they understood better than anyone the inherent problems that it raised. In 2010, my twin brother, Michael, sent me a quote from José Saramago's novel *The Cave*.

Begin at the beginning, as if beginning were the clearly visible point of a loosely wound thread and all we had to do was to keep pulling until we reached the other end, and as if, between the former and the latter, we had held in our hands a smooth, continuous thread with no knots to untie, no snarls to untangle, a complete impossibility in the life of a skein, or indeed, if we may be permitted one more stock phrase, in the skein of life... These are the delusions of the pure and the unprepared, the beginning is never the clear, precise end of a thread, the beginning is a long, painfully slow process that requires time and patience in order to find out in which direction it is heading, a process that feels its way along the path ahead like a blind man, the beginning is just the beginning.

I taped this quote up above my desk where I could see it every day. And somewhere along the way, I found myself pulling the end of the thread, telling myself not to worry about the knots and tangles but just to follow it along for as long as I could. I began gathering the material records of the film—requesting copies of documents from our attorneys and going through my father's old files in our attic, bringing home papers, letters, and photos from my aunt's home in Dallas. I went to the National Archives and began wading through the government papers about the film. I also began reading the seminal books about the Kennedy assassination to get some purchase on the events of November 22, 1963, and its aftermath and poring over the handful of books and hundreds of articles about the Zapruder film. I started to interview close family friends, my father's colleagues, and others from our inner circle who could offer insight into the life of the film. I had lunch with my father's friends and asked them my questions. I see now that I was practicing the act of talking about the film—such an unfamiliar and uncomfortable experience—with the people I trusted, trying to locate and follow the strands that I knew ran through its history.

Immersing myself in this material was anything but simple. It was an exercise in learning, calibrating, and interpreting at the same time. As I read, I was amazed at how much I didn't know—the sheer breadth of the life the film had had without my realizing it. It was not just my grandfather's story, or even that of our family, but the centrality of the film's place in the Kennedy assassination debates, how it had challenged norms around the public representation of violence, how it triggered new debates about the media's role in protecting personal privacy or providing access to information, not to mention who should own and control the public dissemination of personal but historically relevant information. Added to this were all the ways the film had touched American culture, influencing some of the century's greatest and most provocative filmmakers, artists, and writers.

And then there was our name. Zapruder. The Zapruder film. Abraham Zapruder. Mr. Zee. The Z-Film. Henry Zapruder. The Zapruder family. Zaprudered. The Zapruder Quotient. The Zapruder Curve. I could not get over my astonishment at seeing it in print so often. The experience was distinctly different than it would have been if our name had been comfortably ambiguous, like "Smith" or "Cohen," shared with hundreds of thousands of others. But no. It was actually, literally our name, worn only by those who are descended from the man who shot the film. When people used the name Zapruder, there was no mistake about it. They were talking about us.

I often became overwhelmed by the implications of this research. I would find myself staring off into space, spinning out various strands of thought, trying out alternative narratives and struggling to wrap my mind around the immense significance of this object that bore my name but that I knew so little about. Sometimes, I could tolerate only a few pages of reading at a time. Sometimes, I had to abandon the books altogether and try again later. I frequently stumbled over information that I found upsetting. Sometimes, my reading illuminated aspects of the film's history I had felt but not known, or sensed but not understood. Sometimes, I found myself forced to think differently about parts of the past I thought I knew. And many times, more often than I liked, I faced characterizations of our family and interpretations of our actions that didn't tally at all with my knowledge and understanding of who we are.

This latter part was certainly the most difficult. I had an impending sense of dread each time I began reading about our family—a feeling that criticism was waiting in the wings. It usually was. As I turned the pages, I noticed how my body tensed and my jaw clenched. And when I realized that the topic had shifted to something else, I would find myself relaxing and breathing again. It took work to overcome my natural defensiveness about my family. Most frustrating of all, I didn't know our own story well enough to counter points of view that seemed wrong or unfair. It was very hard to stay present in the face of it all.

Over the course of this work, I began to see how our family's insistence on dignity and restraint when it came to talking publicly about the film had left a vacuum in the public story. Everyone but us seemed to own this narrative; each writer told the story and interpreted its meaning with his own facts, information, and perspective. But there was so much they didn't know. They did not know who my grandfather was and how his life experiences and personality shaped how he handled the film. They did not understand the deeply personal relationship between our grandfather and Richard Stolley, the *LIFE* reporter who bought the film from him the morning after the assassination, and how that relationship shaped *LIFE*'s handling of it over the next twelve years. They did not understand why *LIFE* returned the film to our family in 1975 and the internal family dynamic that brought that about.

They did not understand how our father thought about the film, and how he struggled to balance the public interest with his own private feelings about it, and how much our grandfather's wishes and imperatives shaped everything that followed. They did not know what took place behind the scenes during the 1990s when our family was negotiating with the government about the film. They could not fathom what it was like to be in my father's place, a Zapruder trying to strike the right balance between personal legacy and public responsibility for the Zapruder film. I might not know very much about the Zapruder film, but I knew a lot about the Zapruders. And I knew that no history of the film was complete without these threads woven into the story.

Gradually, and with some degree of shock and even dismay, I began to realize that it wasn't true that the Zapruder film had nothing to do with us. My family might have wished that was the case, but the gaps, distortions, and simplifications in the public story revealed just how much was missing and just how much it mattered. This was the substance of the book whose content I had not been able to imagine years before.

Now what kept me up at night was not the worry that the materials would be scattered but what would happen when I brought them together and shaped them for myself, imposed my own narrative and interpretation on them. Through contentious times, high-stakes negotiations with plenty of money at stake, not to mention our name and reputation, our family had stuck together. What if, in spite of my best efforts, this book caused conflicts among us? What if it brought about outcomes that I would regret? There were other worries. I could not write a paean to my father or grandfather, but I did not relish the thought of judging their actions, either. Most of all, I knew that our grandfather and father had not welcomed attention about the film; it was difficult not to wonder if the mere act of writing this book would go against their unspoken wishes. As I worked, I struggled to reconcile the personal and historical imperative I felt to write this book with the worry that it would bring unintended and unwelcome consequences.

These were real fears and they made the early years of this work difficult. But time helped. I mostly focused on tracing the life of the Zapruder film, endeavoring to understand how its public and private strands intersected and influenced each other. I sought to grapple with the complex problems that the film raised for so many people—not just our family but also the media, the federal government, assassination researchers, artists, filmmakers, and the public—and to untangle the vastly different and often conflicting points of view. I wanted to do more than tell "our side" of the story; I wanted to see it from as many sides as I could and to capture the truly maddening contradictions that the film embodies. In time, I began to see that although our relationship to the film was integral to an understanding of it, it was only a part of it. There was a story that was bigger than ours, and there were intrinsic questions that superseded my doubts and worries.

Along the way, I inevitably had to revisit my own history with the Zapruder film, as well. Although in my growing-up years I did not experience our family's silence around the film as particularly unusual, I grew to wonder what it was all about. Why *didn't* we ever talk about it? Why *didn't* I know more about this when I was growing up? Was there something that I needed to understand in order to make sense of the film's place in our family's life? Was there a personal legacy of the Zapruder film and, if so, what was it?

These questions—individual and collective, public and private—are the ones I've tried to answer in this book. As in all creative work, it required faith: in the legitimacy of my questions, in the idea that the public story of the film was more complex and meaningful than it seemed, and in the belief that there were new contributions to make even to a topic as well traveled as the Zapruder film. It also demanded faith in my family—in the conviction that no matter how morally complex the situations of the past or how risky it might be to ask questions in the present, we were capable of coming to terms with this part of our legacy. I had to believe that challenging the prevailing culture of silence around the film was a reflection of our values, not a contradiction of them, and that we would be better for incorporating this part of our past into our understanding of our family legacy.

But when it came to writing about my grandfather and father, whose stories are, after all, at the heart of this book, I found myself facing an entirely new challenge. Before learning the history of the film, without fully knowing the details of my grandfather's and father's handling of it, I knew there was a risk that I would run into facts, details, or decisions that might run counter to what I expected or undermine my fierce tendency to defend them against criticism. For this, I had to draw upon convictions that ran deeper than knowledge—never a comfortable position for a writer of history. Still, I felt sure that each of them had wrestled in their own time with the private and public problems that the Zapruder film raised, that they had confronted the hard decisions, weighed their conflicting desires, tested their values, and faced the consequences of their mistakes. This is who they were in every other part of their lives; how could it be different when it came to the film? Whatever else the story might reveal, I believed that it was their humanity, above all, that shaped how they bore the burdens of the Zapruder film. This is why there is a story to tell, one that offers us all a deeper understanding of the film's dilemmas and its place in American life. That faith was entirely borne out in the writing of this book.

▪ ▪ ▪ ▪ ▪ ▪ ▪

HOME MOVIE

It was past ten p.m. when Abe Zapruder pulled up in the driveway of his house on Marquette Street in the Highland Park suburb of Dallas. Exhausted and agitated, he turned the key in the ignition and pulled it out, sat for a moment in the darkened car, images of the day passing before his eyes. He dropped his head, disbelief washing over him yet again. His eyes felt dry and raw, his throat sore from screaming, his head aching. He had to go in. They had been waiting for him for hours. He reached over to the passenger side of the car and pulled the camera case by its long shoulder strap, the weight of it bumping across the seat, the silver buckle clattering. He reached for the bright yellow Kodak boxes in which the 8mm film reel and one duplicate had been hastily stashed. He suddenly remembered the technician handing them to him. "There'll be no charge, Mr. Zapruder." Had he even thanked him? He couldn't remember. He grabbed his hat and put it on as he slid from the car, then slung the camera over his shoulder, cradled the films in his arm, and slammed the car door.

His wife, Lillian, met him at the door. "Oh, Abe," she said, her eyes filling with tears. He looked at her face for a moment and shook his head. There were no words. Passing through the family room, he crossed the hallway, with his wife following behind. In the dining room, the table wasn't set for dinner. Normally, his daughter, Myrna, and her husband, Myron, would have brought their three children for Friday night dinner. Lil would say the blessings over the candles and he would recite the words of thanksgiving over the wine and bread. He wasn't a religious man, but tradition mattered. They would eat Lil's broiled chicken, or a brisket, or maybe both, and they would discuss politics, arguing and laughing, talking over each other. But not tonight. Tonight—as in homes all across the darkened landscape of America—this was a house of mourning.

Now Abe moved about the house quickly. Where was the projector? Turning right, he darted into the den, where Myrna and Myron were sitting, still in shock. He saw confusion, grief, and a trace of rage on his daughter's face as she stood up and came toward him. He didn't stop to talk; all he could think about was the film. He dug around in the closet until he found the projector and the screen. He yanked them out and began setting them up. Lillian stood nearby, uncharacteristically silent, reading her husband of thirty years, the man she had loved since she was a teenager in Brooklyn. Now was not the time to push him. After a pause, Myrna said, "What are you doing?" He still did not answer. He began threading the film through the projector and onto the take-up reel. Myrna's face registered comprehension. "I can't watch that," she said. "I don't want to see it." He didn't blame her. But he had to do it. He didn't know when the thought had come to him.

He just knew that all during the long, incomprehensible day, he had been thinking that he needed to get home, to see his family. He needed to show them his film.

A few minutes later, they were ready: Abe at the projector, Lil and Myron seated nervously on the couch. Myrna retreated to the living room, weeping, her head buried in the couch pillows. The den had been his son Henry's room, and it was here that Abe always showed the home movies, projected against the stand-up screen. He had been taking home movies for nearly thirty years—Myrna as a baby in Brooklyn, his wife and family at the beach in Far Rockaway, Henry toddling on a city sidewalk, then, later, the children riding bikes in Dallas, a visit to Fair Park. Hours of unexceptional films spanning the thirties, forties, and fifties. Home movies that caught the past—their parents now dead, the streets of Jewish Brooklyn changed, his young children grown and married—saving at least a bit of it for his own memory and for the grandchildren who would come after him. Only this time, he and his family weren't telling stories and talking and remembering. The room was completely silent but for the clicking of the film running through the projector.

The first frames appear: two of his grandchildren playing in a backyard suburban scene—green grass and a small white patio with a lounge chair in the background. There is the baby, David, in blue gingham overall shorts, toddling toward the camera with his mischievous smile and eyes that crinkle into half crescents when he laughs. The film is silent but his mouth forms the word "Papa." Then there is Jeff, the eldest, long and lean, digging in the grass. He does not look up or wave, so absorbed is he in his task. The scene changes. Abe is inside Jennifer Juniors, his dress manufacturing company. Lillian Rogers, his longtime assistant and trusted friend, is fooling around, talking on the phone and pretending to make him wait. *I'll be with you in a minute, Mr. Zee.* Everyone at work calls him that. Seconds later, he zooms slowly in on her face and catches her in an unguarded moment, smiling girlishly at him. Then the image fades out.

He stands, agitated.

The screen flickers again and they are in bright sunshine, outside on Dealey Plaza. He remembers making some test shots and adjusting the settings. How he loved that camera. He loved the mechanism and the beautiful, clean way it operated, and the elegant design of the case. He loved anything that ran efficiently and well. In another life, he would have been an engineer instead of a dressmaker. Maybe if he had been born here instead of in Czarist Russia. Maybe if he had gotten a proper education instead of going to night school in America to learn English and getting by on his brains and wits. But such was life and chance.

There are his employees, Charles and Beatrice Hester, seated at the pergola at Dealey Plaza, and his receptionist, Marilyn Sitzman. He had tried a number of spots before she turned up and noticed a four-foot wall that he could stand on. It would be perfect, offering him just the vantage point he wanted, looking down on Elm Street, able to follow the motorcade perfectly from left to right as it sailed past him.

Here are the first frames, the lead motorcycles rounding the corner of Houston onto Elm. He remembers again that his heart had skipped a beat when they came into view but that he had stopped filming when he realized that it wasn't the motorcade yet. He wanted to save the film, to make sure he got it all. He would capture the president's beaming smile and a glimpse of his glamorous wife, whose style the women in his own family tried to emulate. One day, he would show it to his grandchildren. "That's Jack Kennedy," he would say. "There's Jackie. Look at them smiling and waving. Aren't they beautiful? We loved them. We thought of them like our own family."

Finally, the long dark cars came into view. He remembers the moment, lifting the camera to his eye and pressing the button. No more fiddling. He gripped his forearm, steadying the hand holding the camera, and trained his eye on the open limousine. There they were. He was going to get the whole thing from his perch above Elm Street. They were going to pass right in front of him. The light was excellent—the green grass behind the black car, the first lady in a pink hat. They came closer, and he could see them perfectly.

It had all happened so fast; now he couldn't fully match up the sounds he had heard with what he saw. The president was smiling and waving; then Abe lost sight of him for a second or two behind a street sign. When he came out the other side, something seemed wrong. His wrists were up around his throat, and then he slumped over to the side, toward the first lady. Abe didn't understand what he was seeing—he was paralyzed, watching through the lens. Had he heard a firecracker? Was the president joking—"Oh, he got me"? No, he wouldn't. But then, what—? As he struggled to focus, there was another sharp *crack* and, inside the car, an explosion. It couldn't be. But it was. It was the president—his blood, his brains, everywhere inside the car, on his wife. It was the most horrific thing he had ever seen, more so than anything he could ever have imagined. He was utterly frozen, his mind trying to register what had happened. There was a pink streak on the back of the car—the first lady in her suit—what was she doing? She was shoved back inside, back into that bloody horror. And then they were gone.

This was how he had known before anyone else; he had seen it magnified through the zoom lens. There was no way the president could have survived. He was as sure of his death as he had ever been of anything in his life. And yet it seemed like hours before everyone else knew. It was like being in a nightmare, trying to scream but finding that you couldn't make a sound. He would try to tell someone that the president was dead, and they would reassure him—they thought he was hysterical. *No, he's been shot,* they said. *He's been taken to Parkland. We don't know anything yet.* But he knew. He was alone with his certainty, shaken to his core, shocked and horrified that such a thing could happen in America. In Russia, where he had come from, yes. There, anyone could be pulled off a train and beaten to death or shot on the street. That was why his family had come here, to escape that barbaric violence and find a place in a democratic country, a society of progress. How could this have happened here? In America in the twentieth century? This event flew in the face of everything he believed about his beloved adopted country.

His stunned wife and son-in-law sat numbly on the couch, unable to speak.

The silence was interrupted by the ringing of the phone. Who could it be at this hour? He had already talked to his son, Henry, moments after the shooting, and the rest of the family was here. Reporters again? He had been given several hasty offers to buy the film but had refused, saying that he needed to make sure it reached the federal authorities. He had seen to that—it had taken all day, but the Secret Service had a copy and another one was on a plane heading to Washington. No one had asked for the original—or the camera, for that matter—so he had brought them home with him. But now what? The press was not going to give up, not when they realized that he was in possession of his pictures and at liberty to sell them. It was only going to get worse.

The phone kept ringing, insistent. "Abe?" Lillian asked. "Should I answer?" His heart sank again, for the hundredth time, thinking of Jackie Kennedy and imagining the footage crossing her path. Would he be the cause of further pain and suffering for her and her family? But how would he prevent it? It was too late. The film existed, and there was no way to undo it now. But one thing was for certain; he wouldn't keep it. He never wanted to see it again, though see it he would, nearly every night for years to come, in his nightmares. Should he sell it? To whom? He could already imagine the images splashed all over the news, on the television. The thought was sickening. Choices upon choices, none of them good. He was exhausted; it didn't seem like so much could have happened in a single day. And he was going to have to make more decisions tomorrow, and the day after that.

He should let the phone ring. He should wait and deal with whatever it was tomorrow. But he didn't. He walked into the kitchen, dazed, and picked up the receiver.

CHAPTER 1

ASSASSINATION

When Abe woke on the morning of November 22, the weather was overcast and drizzly, a disappointing beginning to the day of the president's visit to Dallas. A few days earlier, the papers had published the details of the motorcade route. After landing at Love Field, Mr. and Mrs. Kennedy, together with Texas governor John Connally and his wife, Nellie, would travel in an open-top limousine downtown to Main Street, greeting spectators and fans before turning right on Houston and then making a quick left on Elm heading for the Trade Mart, where the president would address a gathering of business leaders. Abe must have been delighted when he realized that the motorcade was going to pass directly in front of 501 Elm Street, where Jennifer Juniors was located. A short walk to Dealey Plaza and he would have a splendid view of the president and first lady as they passed by.

In spite of the rain, Abe left home early, as usual, and by the time he arrived at Jennifer, the plant was up and running. He and his assistant, Lillian Rogers, began every day the same way, walking around to be sure everyone was at work and all was going smoothly. Abe was considered a tough but fair boss, one with meticulous taste and high standards for efficiency and excellence but who also cultivated a sense of warmth and informality in the plant. Everyone was family, from the office staff to the salesmen, cutters, pattern makers, designers, and seamstresses.

After they finished their morning check, they would leave the fifth floor of the building and head down to Abe's office for coffee. It was November, which meant that the company would be preparing its spring line. As Abe and Lillian sat drinking their coffee, they were surely going over one aspect of the business or another, maybe looking over some dresses or tweaking a design.

To make their inexpensive knockoffs, they had to buy couture and other sample dresses, which they kept on racks in the factory while they were using them to create the patterns. They would often go to Neiman Marcus and consult with Helen Kessler, a thirty-year veteran of the Haute Couture Department, to choose dresses that they would put on his wife Lil's Neiman's charge and bring back to the shop. There they would take photos of them, mock them up, and then—in an impressive act of *chutzpah*—return the dresses for a refund before finishing the knockoffs to sell. Still, getting the dresses wasn't the whole story. There was a lot more to it. Lillian, who gave an interview with my mother and aunt in the nineties, described what set Abe apart. "A lot of pattern makers are clumps, schlumps; they just don't have any idea of fit," Lillian said, but Abe "could see if something had a ridge across the back or didn't fit quite right. There would be a little dress that was not just right and he'd lift it up here, and he'd say they'd have to adjust the pattern and take that little bit out to correct it."

Abe had learned the needle trades together with hundreds of thousands of Jewish immigrants who had arrived in New York from Eastern Europe, taking a job as a pattern maker in a factory on Seventh Avenue when he was still a teenager. He stayed in the New York garment industry until 1941, when he and Lil moved to Dallas for the opportunity to work for an up-and-coming sportswear line called Nardis. By 1963, he had been in the business for four decades.

But his success in the business was not just a result of experience. From his earliest days in America, he had an innate sense of style, dressing like a gentleman in a crisp white shirt and well-pressed trousers, or a perfectly cut suit and hat. It was surely part of what caught the eye of his future bride, Lil, who also dressed with a flair that belied her family's poverty. Street smart and savvy, she knew how to shop carefully, getting expensive clothing for a fraction of the cost by buying samples. In pictures of them from the late twenties and thirties, they are a glamorous couple, Abe grinning with his hat tilted rakishly on his head, and Lil, tall and slim in a tailored suit or a long skirt with a silk blouse. She, too, wore fashionable hats that framed her heart-shaped face and her radiant smile. They were a young, modern American couple and they dressed the part. In later years, Abe would joke that there was nothing to dressmaking: All you needed was "a front, a back, and two sleeves." But the truth was that he knew from his own experience how the right clothing—and careful attention to style, fabric, cut, and fit—could transform a person.

At some point over coffee that morning, Lillian asked Abe if he had brought his movie camera from home, as he had said he was planning to do a few days before. Well, no, actually, he hadn't. He had given up on the idea at the last minute, thinking that with the crowds packing the motorcade route, he would never get near enough to see, let alone film the president. I can picture Lillian's reaction—a sigh, a shake of the head. She knew as well as anyone how he operated. She had been working with him for seven years by then. He was practical almost to the point of being pessimistic. Not only that, but in spite of his many talents and sharp mind, he could be uncertain of himself. It wasn't his style to put himself forward.

So when Lillian heard that he had left the camera at home, she wasn't about to let it lie. "You ought to go home," she told him firmly. He quibbled with her, telling her she should go get her camera, even though she preferred still photos and wasn't nearly the avid photographer that he was. "You're the one that makes the beautiful movies," she protested. It was true. Abe loved photography. He had started with stills, taking many photographs of Lil in the early 1930s, developing them in a darkroom he set up for himself in the basement of the family's apartment building on Park Place. Soon he became interested in home movies, catching on to the first wave of amateur filmmaking. By 1963, it had been a favorite hobby for three decades; he had bought himself a brand-new camera the year before. Those who knew him well, like Lillian, knew that he would regret it if he let this once-in-a-lifetime opportunity to film President Kennedy and the first lady slip through his fingers.

At some point in the back-and-forth, Abe's receptionist Marilyn Sitzman and his young business partner Erwin Schwartz—the son of his original partner, Abe Schwartz—came in and joined the conversation. Marilyn tried to encourage him to get the camera, remembering that the only way to get Abe to do something was to cajole him into it. Erwin, on the other hand, scoffed, "You're crazy... When he comes around that corner, makes that run onto Elm off of Houston, they'll be going over a hundred miles an hour. You won't get to see anything. I mean, the parade's over." But Lillian pleaded, "Oh, Mr. Zee, go home and get the camera. Don't listen to him."

Eventually, however, Lillian gave up and went back to work. She knew he would have to make up his own mind. When she returned to the fourth floor later in the morning, she realized that Abe was nowhere to be found. "Where had he gone?" Lillian rhetorically asked my mother and aunt in her interview with them. "Home to get the camera, of course."

This story of a near miss with history—Abe Zapruder leaving his camera at home on the morning of JFK's assassination—has been told many times before. It's been said that he forgot it, or that it was overcast and that he feared rain, or that he was afraid he was too short to get a good enough view to take the pictures. Any of these explanations could be true, but they fail to take into account just how predictable it was that he would leave the camera at home and that Lillian would talk him into going back to get it. In a certain way, that's the least unlikely bit of it; he had Lillian in his life exactly for this reason. Unlike Abe, she carried the innate confidence of a Midwestern American who had never known the traumas and instability that he had. She saw when he hesitated but never let him give in to his insecurities, encouraging him to trust his instincts and take risks. In return, he taught her everything he knew about business and about people, ideas, and the wider world.

It is true that Abe Zapruder's intersection with history is laced with coincidence and chance. Any number of things could have gone differently that day. But Lillian letting Abe get away with not filming the president when he was passing a hundred yards away from Jennifer Juniors was not one of them.

While Abe was out, Lillian made an announcement over the company's PA system giving the employees permission to take an extra-long lunch to watch the president's motorcade. "This is your captain," she said, "and we don't care what your religion is or your politics. You could be Baptist or Republican...We don't care, but today the president of the United States is coming down here and we have a chance to see him, and it doesn't make any difference whether you agree with him or not. He's still the president."

Her words hint at the political tensions that sharply divided the city of Dallas at the time and had raised serious concerns for the president's safety. In fact, Dallas—more than any other American city—had become ground zero for a reactionary political movement that bitterly opposed President Kennedy. They were led by a small knot of ultraconservatives, including Ted Dealey of the *Dallas Morning News*; H. L. Hunt, the oil tycoon and the wealthiest man in the world; Rev. W. A. Criswell, pastor of the First Baptist Church in Dallas; and retired Army General Edwin Walker, together with the fiercely right-wing Texas representative to Congress, Bruce Alger. Gripped by an ironclad conviction that the United States faced the threat of an imminent Communist takeover, they believed that Kennedy's international policies and his support of the United Nations amounted to a betrayal of the United States.

There was simply no way to live in Dallas and avoid this climate. The *Dallas Morning News* (which Abe referred to as "that rag") was filled, day after day, with editorials excoriating the president. In 1960, Myrna and Myron had been appalled to witness Lyndon and Lady Bird Johnson being physically harassed at the Adolphus Hotel in Dallas by a group of high-society women led by Representative Bruce Alger and called the "Mink Coat Mob" by onlookers to the protest. Then, just a month before the president's visit, protesters spat on Adlai Stevenson, American ambassador to the United Nations, when he spoke in Dallas. Myrna wrote him a personal letter of apology.

Far from quieting down in advance of the president's visit, conservative agitators papered the city days before his arrival with five thousand leaflets showing a mug shot of President Kennedy and the words "WANTED FOR TREASON" beneath it. They accused him of betraying the US Constitution and turning the sovereignty of the government over to the "Communist-controlled United Nations." Then, the very morning of his arrival, the *Dallas Morning News* ran an inflammatory ad by the so-called American Fact-Finding Committee that read, in part: "Welcome Mr. Kennedy to Dallas...A City that rejected your philosophy and policies in 1960 and will do so again in 1964—even more emphatically than before."

Abe returned to Jennifer around 11:30 a.m. with his camera. First he filmed a few minutes of Lillian to fill up side A of the reel of film already in the camera and then flipped it over so he could start with a fresh side for the motorcade. There was a big discussion among the staff about where they should stand to get the best view. Several decided to congregate on Dealey Plaza, along the stretch of Elm Street that would mark the last leg of the motorcade. Compared to Main Street, where spectators were five deep, cheering and waving, the crowds along Elm were fairly thin. There was a mass exodus from Jennifer shortly after noon, with nearly everybody "hitting the elevator," in Lillian's words, on the way down to the street, except for a handful of people who went out on the fire escape to watch from there. *Nearly* everybody: Marilyn, who wasn't a supporter of the president, decided to go open her first bank account instead. Erwin, too, left the office to attend a meeting at North

Park Inn just as the staff began to filter out around 11:45. As the office emptied out, Abe realized that someone had to stay back to keep an eye on the place. He gallantly offered to stay instead of Lillian. Years later, she remembered, "Mr. Zee was telling me to take the camera and I could go and he would stay, but he didn't really mean it. But anyway, he said it. So he went on but I stayed there and I could see. I had the window open. It was a warm day, beautiful day, the sun was shining."

Camera in hand, Abe went down to Dealey Plaza to scout out a location. He tried a few places, walking all along the curb on Elm Street, but could not find solid footing there. Another spot was blocked by a tree. After a while, Marilyn Sitzman came walking up the hill. All the banks had been closed because of the president's visit, so she gave up and walked back to the plaza, where she encountered Abe taking some test shots of his payroll clerk Beatrice Hester and her husband, Charles, sitting on the pergola at the back of the plaza. As Abe continued to look for a place to stand, Marilyn suggested a four-foot-high concrete abutment. It was a perfect location—high above the street, giving him a clear view of the length of Elm; the president and Mrs. Kennedy would ride right past him in the open-top limousine. There was a risk, however: He would need to set the telephoto lens on full zoom in order to get a clear view of them, and he worried that he would get dizzy standing up on the ledge while following them through the lens as they passed by. Since he suffered from vertigo, this was a real possibility. So, as Abe climbed up on the ledge and found his bearings, he asked Marilyn to stand behind him and steady him if he started to lose his balance.

Abe Zapruder wasn't the only photographer on the scene. In fact, there were no fewer than twenty-two photographers on Dealey

Plaza, most of them amateurs, positioned along the last part of the motorcade route. Some were shooting black-and-white or color stills, Polaroids, or 35mm slides, while several others had movie cameras loaded with color film. It seemed everyone had the same idea. Mary Moorman and James Altgens, their cameras loaded with black-and-white film, were positioned near the curb across the street from where Abe was standing. Farther up the street, near the hairpin turn from Houston to Elm, Phillip Willis stood ready with color film in his camera. Marie Muchmore was standing on the opposite side of Elm from Abe, on a grassy area set back from the street, her movie camera loaded with color film. Over on Main, Orville Nix was waiting with a movie camera and color film, as well.

Up on the concrete ledge, Abe looked out for the motorcade. When the lead motorcycles rounded Houston to Elm Street, he started filming, only to stop when he realized that it was not the president's car yet. He re-cranked the mechanism of the camera to "full wind" so that it would run for the maximum amount of time. He didn't start filming again until he could see the president and the first lady coming toward him in the car. Years later, in an interview she gave with my mother, Marilyn remembered, "When they started to make their first turn, turning into the street, he said, 'OK, here we go.'"

Those first few seconds of the film are perfect: The sun is shining and you can clearly see the unmistakable, handsome face of the president as he brushes his hair from his face, lowering his arm as he turns toward the crowds on his right, smiling, and raising his hand again to wave briefly. For an instant, the back of a freeway sign obscures the limousine, and then the Kennedys reappear. "As it came in line with my camera, I heard a shot," Abe later recalled. The president's elbows fly up, his face distorted in pain, and he suddenly hunches forward as his wife looks at Governor Connally, sitting in the jump seat across from them, before turning back to her husband with visible confusion on her face. "I saw the president lean over to Jacqueline. I didn't realize what had happened," Abe remembered.

The next part of the sequence always feels agonizingly long to me, even though it took place in seconds. The car dips into the lower part of the camera frame, and as the president's body sinks down in the car toward his wife, the fatal shot strikes him. "And then I realized," Abe said. "I saw his head open up and I started yelling, 'They killed him! They killed him!'" Jackie recoils, her mouth open in horror, and suddenly she is climbing out of the open-top car, scrambling on the back hood of the limousine, met by Secret Service agent Clint Hill, who pushes her back down into the seat.

For an instant, Abe and Marilyn stood stunned on the concrete stump, paralyzed by what had just happened. Then someone behind them dropped a soda bottle, which made a loud crack and shattered on the concrete. Marilyn recalled that the noise woke them out of their shocked trance. "Some people were screaming," she said. "I mean, it was utter chaos by that time. But the first thing I remember is after that bottle hit and I looked down...everybody was laying flat on the ground almost. There might have been one or two people still standing but I would say that ninety-eight percent of the people were still laying flat on the side of the hill."

Abe never remembered getting down from the ledge or anything that happened in the immediate aftermath of the shooting except for his own anguished screams. A still photo taken by James Altgens of the Associated Press shows Marilyn and Abe in his hat and bow tie, holding the camera; they are faintly visible in the far background, having just gotten down from their perch. They moved toward the pergola where the Hesters had been standing during the motorcade, but in the panic and chaos, Abe soon got separated from the rest of them. He was by himself on the plaza, distraught and in a daze, with the camera still in his hand and the case slung over his shoulder, when he encountered Harry McCormick, a reporter from the *Dallas Morning News*. McCormick had been at the Trade Mart waiting for the president to arrive when he heard of the shooting. He rushed over to Dealey Plaza, where he spotted Abe holding his camera and immediately approached him to find out if he had caught the shooting on film. Abe answered that he would not speak about the film with anyone but the federal authorities. In Harry's account, it was he who told Abe that the Secret Service would want to see the film, and he offered to get Dallas Secret Service chief Forrest Sorrels and bring him to Jennifer Juniors.

Somehow Abe got back to the office. Lillian remembered that "Everybody was going nuts, turning on the television. There was nothing and you couldn't get anything on television...So anyway, he walked in, and he handed me the camera. He says, 'I've got it all on there.'" Abe later tried to piece together his memory of the traumatic first moments after the assassination. "Well, I was in a state of shock when I got back," he said, "and I was kicking and banging the desk. I couldn't understand how a thing like this could happen. I personally have never seen anybody killed in my life, and to see something like this, shooting a man down like a dog, I just couldn't believe."

His first instinct was to call his son, Henry. In his confusion, he dialed the home phone number and reached his daughter-in-law, Margie, instead, who had been home waiting for a furniture delivery and listening to the radio when the news broke. She knew that the president had been shot, but like everyone else in the nation, she did not know yet that he was dead. This was one of the few stories I remember hearing from my childhood, perhaps because the innate awfulness of it impressed me. When I asked her to tell me the story, my mother recalled, "Papa called the house and said, 'Is Henry there?' and I said, 'He's at his office.'...He said the president had been killed. And I said, 'Well, he's been shot. He's been taken to Parkland Hospital.'" He was distracted and rushing, she said, very anxious to reach Henry, never stopping to explain what he knew or that he had a film of the shooting. Like many others during that long hour between the shooting and the announcement that the president was dead, she tried to reassure him that the president was being treated at Parkland and might yet survive. But Abe insisted that the president was dead. "He knew," she said, and even fifty years later, I hear the sadness and resignation in her voice.

Abe was able to reach Henry at his office at the Justice Department shortly before the phone lines got jammed. "He was crying," Henry recalled in an account he wrote thirty-five years later. "He said that the president was dead. I protested that this was not true, that the radio had reported that he had been taken to Parkland, the emergency hospital in Dallas. There was no way, my father said, that the president could have survived. He told me that he had seen the president's head 'explode.' He kept saying how horrible it was that Mrs. Kennedy had been there when this happened to her husband and expressing his own horror at having seen the president 'shot down in the street.' [He] told me that he had a film of the assassination and discussed with me what he should do with it...He kept saying that the president was dead, asking me how this could happen in America."

By the time he got off the phone with his son, Abe was resolved to get the film into the hands of federal authorities. Meanwhile, Marilyn Sitzman and the Hesters were heading back toward the office through streets suddenly jammed with police: detectives and officers from the Dallas Police and the sheriff's office, all trying to collect clues and eyewitness testimony. On their way, they ran into Darwin Payne, a young reporter for the *Dallas Times Herald*, at the corner of Houston and Elm. He had been working on a story about Jacqueline Kennedy when he got word of the shooting. He rushed to the Book Depository Building where, he later recalled, "There were some women who worked at the next building for Abraham Zapruder who said, 'Our boss took pictures of it. He has a movie camera.' And that, of course, was of great interest to me, so . . . they led me to him, in the building next door. We went up to the fifth or sixth floor, whichever floor he was on. There he was in an office. He was a dress manufacturer, and I saw him and talked to him."

Payne said that Abe was in tears and that he knew for certain that the president was dead, even though the TV was on in the office and the national news hadn't reported it yet. Payne's fragmentary notes, scrawled in a blue spiral-bound notebook, survive to this day. They read: "I got film. I saw it hit in head. They were going so fast. [Illegible] Slumped over with first shot. Second shot hit him in head. It opened up. Couldn't be alive. She was beside him. After last shot, she crawled over back of car."

Payne wasted no time trying to acquire the film for his paper. "I was trying to get Zapruder to let us take the . . . to go with me to the *Times Herald* with his film and see about having it developed," he remembered. "To see if he had anything. And I told him I felt certain that we'd pay him for the film. He said he didn't want to do that. He said he wanted to give it to the Secret Service or the FBI."

When that approach failed, Payne enlisted the help of the paper's publisher. "So I got [James] Chambers on the telephone," he said, "and we had a three-way conversation...Chambers, myself, and Zapruder. And he told Zapruder that he was very interested in the film. He would pay him for it, you know, if it were good." But still Abe refused. He insisted that he was going to get it to the Secret Service.

In an oral-history interview nearly forty years later, Payne remembers a flash of an idea and relays it with a smile: "The camera was on top of a filing cabinet right there. And in a fleeting moment, I thought, 'Well, I could grab it. Nobody would stop me. I could grab the camera and run.' Of course, I didn't." It wouldn't be the last time that members of the media lost their heads for a minute or two over what they thought might be the scoop of the century.

Minutes later, the phone rang. It was Erwin, calling from a friend's house where he had been following the news of the shooting. In an interview, he recalled: "I picked up the phone and I called the office and I hear screaming, turmoil, and I said to the girl, 'What's going on?' She said, 'Oh, Mr. Schwartz, the police are here with shotguns.' I said, 'What are you talking about?' And she said, 'Oh, Mr. Zee has the films and they want the films and he told me to put it in the safe.'...And I said, 'Where's Mr. Zee?' She said, 'He's in his office, crying.' And she went and got him, and he picked up the phone and said, 'Erwin, Erwin, it was terrible. I saw his head come off.' I said, 'I'll be right there.' I said, 'Just stay there. I'll be there as quick as I can.'"

When Erwin arrived at Jennifer and got off the elevator on the fourth floor, he found two uniformed Dallas police officers with shotguns standing in the outer vestibule. When he asked them why they were there, he recalled that they said, "We came to get the film." Abe had declined to give it to them as well; he was waiting for the federal authorities. Erwin brushed past them and went straight to Abe's office, where he found him still in shock, still saying over and over that the president's head had exploded and how horrific it had been. Erwin said, "Who...why do they want this film? Why are they after the film?" And Abe answered, "I told them I'd give it to them but only to someone in authority."

All this time, Harry McCormick had been looking for Dallas Secret Service chief Forrest Sorrels. Sorrels had been in the lead car of the motorcade and had ridden to Parkland in advance of the president's limousine. At Parkland, he commandeered a police car and rode back to the area of the Texas School Book Depository (TSBD) Building to start trying to piece together what had happened. He brought two witnesses to the sheriff's office just across the street to have their testimony taken. While there, he ran into McCormick. Sorrels described their meeting in an official affidavit: "At that time Mr. Harry McCormack [*sic*], who is a reporter for the Dallas Morning News, and whom I have known for many years, came to me and says, 'Forrest, I have something over here you ought to know about.' I said, 'What have you got here?' He said, 'I have a man over here that got pictures of this whole thing.' I said, 'Let's go see him.' So we went on to a building at the corner of Elm and Houston, on the east side of Houston, and across the street from the court house building there, up to the office of a Mr. Zapruder."

Payne remembered their arrival. "A group of people came in... ties, coats, and all that. And they were Secret Service... With them was Harry McCormick, the police reporter for the *Dallas Morning News*. They had come to get the film... They went into an office and shut the door. Harry McCormick went with them as they shut the door. I went in, decided I was going to go in, too...I mean, I was a reporter, as well. They said nope, no reporters admitted. And there I saw that Harry McCormick was already in the room. He was at the opposition paper...And so I said, 'I've got to be in there. If McCormick's in there, you've got to let me in there.' So they kicked McCormick out." But not before Harry could offer $1,000 for the film, which Abe again refused.

While the two frustrated reporters waited outside, Abe, Erwin, and Sorrels discussed matters in the office. Sorrels described the meeting in his Warren Commission testimony the following May. "Mr. Zapruder was real shook up," he recalled. "He said that he didn't know how in the world he had taken these pictures...and he says, 'My God, I saw the whole thing. I saw the man's brains come out of his head.' And so I asked Mr. Zapruder would it be possible for us to get a copy of those films. He said yes." Erwin remembered it this way: "Forrest Sorrels identified himself and Zapruder said, 'I'll give you the film. I'd like to.' [Sorrels] said, 'Well, let's see if we can't get it developed.'"

Getting the film developed was not as easy as one might think. At some point, Harry McCormick had suggested that they might have luck at the *Dallas Morning News*. So the group decided to go over there to try. They retrieved the camera from the company safe and left with the two police officers who had been waiting in the vestibule. The officers escorted Abe, Erwin, Forrest Sorrels, and Harry McCormick in a squad car with its siren blaring, while Darwin Payne resumed his investigation by heading over to the Texas School Book Depository. They arrived at the *Dallas Morning News* and inquired about processing the film, but, as Forrest Sorrels later put it in his Warren Commission testimony, "There was no one there that would tackle the job." Perhaps unwilling to let the film out of his sight, McCormick suggested they try the ABC affiliate WFAA-TV, which was located right next door.

When they arrived, program director Jay Watson was already on the air, having interrupted the station's regular programming to cover the shooting. He was interviewing eyewitnesses from the scene and trying to report the news as it came in. It wasn't long before the producers nabbed Abe and put him on the air while Erwin stood off to the side, holding the camera inside its leather case. In retrospect, it's another strange twist in a story of coincidences that the man who caught the moment on film was himself caught on film almost immediately afterward, preserving his first, fresh impressions of the event that changed his life.

In the grainy black-and-white image, Abe is neatly dressed in a dark suit, with a white shirt, a small dark bow tie, and just the hint of a white pocket square. He is wearing glasses, the classic 1960s browline style framed in dark plastic along the top and rimless on the bottom. He is obviously agitated and upset, moving around uncomfortably in his chair and repeatedly clearing his throat as he speaks. Meanwhile, Watson is smoking and looks slightly bored, holding an on-set phone to his ear and distractedly adjusting the microphone as Abe describes finding a place to shoot the pictures and what happened until the motorcade came into view. "As the president was coming down…I heard a shot, and he slumped to the side like this," he said, slumping over. Still no reaction from Watson, who has the phone to his ear, looking off camera. "Then I heard another shot or two, I couldn't say whether it was one or two, and I saw his head practically open up"—Watson suddenly swivels around, leaning in and locking on as Abe raises his hand to his head, gesturing to show the explosion of the president's skull—"all blood and everything, and I just kept on shooting." Watson is staring at him now, completely motionless. "That's about all," he says, deflated, and then there is a momentary pause, just the slightest shake of the head and exhale of breath as he struggles for composure. He looks down, shaking his head again, and I can almost see the adrenaline coursing through him, his disbelief and revulsion. Still shaking his head, he pushes himself to speak. "I'm just sick, I can't . . . terrible, terrible."

It is one of the very few interviews that exist of my grandfather. I remember the first time I saw it. I was watching TV and I happened to pass by it as I was changing channels. I never knew the interview existed, and I remember the moment of shock and confusion as I realized I was seeing my own grandfather on TV, and I tried to absorb the fact, searching for a trace of familiarity that would connect me to him. I noticed his slight accent—not a pronounced Russian one but a kind of thickness or weight in his voice and a clipped way of speaking—as well as his breathlessness and agitation.

The full interview is longer than the bit I first saw. There's a second part where Abe speaks very little, referring first to the "sickening scene" and trying to make sense of his position relative to the shooting. I can see the wheels turning in his head. Then Watson interrupts him to start talking about himself and carry on with the business of broadcasting. There is a minute or two when Abe is not "on"; he is just sitting at the desk next to Jay Watson, biting his lips, shifting around, twitching his shoulder slightly. The first part of the interview has been dissected and examined ad infinitum for clues about what Abe Zapruder, the quintessential eyewitness, recalled seeing. But I am mining the second part, too. I'm looking for gestures, facial expressions, his voice and accent, the emotions and thoughts going on inside his head and heart. I'm looking for my father, my brothers and cousins, looking for the bloodline that links us to this missing member of our family.

I remember excitedly calling my father to tell him that Papa Abe was on TV and asking him if he knew about this interview. I wish I could remember the entire exchange, but I only recall realizing that this information was not a revelation to my father. I might have been momentarily surprised that he didn't seem particularly impressed, but thinking of it now, I understand that this little clip would never have the importance for him that it did for me. After all, he had a lifetime of experiences with his father to recall. I had only snippets and fragments. More than that, for me there was no clean way to untangle the memories that came from our family from those that came from his public identity. This was one of those times—like digging around in *The Death of a President* when I was eleven—when it occurred to me that there was an access route to my grandfather through the Zapruder film and the assassination. I understood, if vaguely, that his experience held not only information about the assassination but also clues about Abe Zapruder, clues that no one else would notice or look for but that were substance for the mental picture I wanted to create of him.

My periodic ache for my grandfather is hard to explain. I don't know if it's because of the film—because I felt somehow that he was public property and it didn't seem fair, in that most basic and elemental childhood way, to have to share him with strangers. Or if it was because my three living grandparents were such a big part of my life and his absence made the picture feel especially incomplete. Or because his death so clearly pained my father, which in turn pained me enough that I wanted to try to undo it. Or maybe it wasn't about him at all, but the way I first grappled with the finality of death, railed against it as all children must, and wanted to cheat it by cobbling together a picture that would bring him back to life.

While Abe shifted under the hot studio lights and breathed in Jay Watson's secondhand smoke, business was being conducted off-screen. McCormick and Sorrels were consulting with Bert Shipp, the assistant news director at WFAA-TV, about what could be done with the film. They told him they might have something showing the assassination of the president taken by "some clothing manufacturer over here." When Shipp asked them what kind of film it was, they told him, "Just film." But it wasn't just film. It was double 8mm color film, which was complicated and laborious to process. WFAA could process black-and-white film, and they could process 16mm, but this was way out of their league. Bert told them in no uncertain terms, "Let me tell you something. If you think you have in here what I think you have, don't you be running around to any Bert Shipps or anybody else trying to get them to develop this film. You call Kodak. You get them to open that lab. Don't you let anybody but an expert process this 8mm film."

Sorrels was convinced. Shipp called the Eastman Kodak lab near Love Field to see if they might be able to process the film that afternoon, but he couldn't get anyone on the line. As was the case everywhere, the staff at Kodak were in a state of shock over the president's murder. Phil Chamberlain, who was the production supervisor at Kodak, recalled: "When the news came that the president indeed had died, I cried, and had the receptionist announce it over the PA system. And then we planned to shut down the operations the rest of the afternoon. So we shut down the processing machines and people just...people just stood around in little groups crying and talking and commiserating." When Shipp couldn't get through via the regular channels, he called the emergency number instead and reached Jack Harrison, the staff supervisor on duty that day. Shipp put Agent Sorrels on the phone, who conveyed the urgency of the situation, saying, "We want to have you to process our film. We want you to shut your machines down and process the film we have here. How long will it take you to do it?" When he learned it would be about an hour and fifteen minutes, he told Harrison that they would be right over. "There'll be a lot of us so just leave it open for us, and no other film to be run."

The group piled into a police car to ride the five miles to the Eastman Kodak processing lab at 3131 Manor Way. It was just blocks from Love Field. At around the same time, Lyndon Johnson was sworn in as the thirty-sixth president of the United States. At the very moment the police car approached the Kodak plant, Air Force One could be seen taking off from Love Field, ascending steeply into the blue for the terrible trip home to Washington with the casketed body of President Kennedy and his widow on board.

CHAPTER 2

■ ■ ■ ■ ■ ■ ■

EXPOSURE

The Eastman Kodak lab was located in an unadorned salmon-brick building with a double-height tinted-glass entryway. The group hustled up the steps into the nondescript lobby, where they were met by production supervisor Phil Chamberlain and Richard "Dick" Blair of the Customer Service Department. Harrison recalled later, "You could hear them like a bunch of cattle coming. All these people coming up there, talking among themselves... well-dressed men and a couple of policemen and just two or three 'civilians.' And one of them was Zapruder."

They wasted no time getting to work. Blair went with Abe into the darkroom, where they ran the unexposed portion of the film through to the end of the reel and took out the spool. The film was handed off to Kathryn Kirby, who was in the Special Handling Department. She stamped it with a processing identification code that would forever identify the film as the in-camera original. The perforated number, located on the edge print of the film, is 0183. The original was then given to Bobby Davis at machine #2 for processing. The machine had been cleared and certified by John Kenny Anderson, the production foreman, shortly after the call came in from Forrest Sorrels to make a machine ready. Bobby Davis had loaded the machine with new leader, a strong tape that is affixed to the unexposed film and literally "leads" it through the processing. According to Blair, Forrest Sorrels remained in the darkroom while processing took place, and Abe watched through a small window. He periodically called home to check in, and apparently spoke with an attorney who advised him about having affidavits made to certify the safe handling and processing of the film and the duplicates. Meanwhile, Harry McCormick of the *Dallas Morning News* never let up trying to get the film. "I spent over four hours with this man, trying to get prints for the paper. We made large cash offers, which he refused... When I could not get them for the paper, I tried to get them for myself, thinking I could then get something for the paper. I told him he did not know the markets and how to handle this and that if he would turn it over to me, I would give him all but twenty-five percent. I later went down to ten percent but still had no luck."

Meanwhile, the hunt for the president's killer was closing in on Lee Harvey Oswald. Just forty-five minutes after the assassination, thirty-nine-year-old Dallas police officer J. D. Tippit, a World War II veteran and member of the force for eleven years, spotted a man who fit the physical description of the suspect in the Oak Cliff section of Dallas. Tippit stopped to question him through the window of his police cruiser, and when he got out of his car to approach him, Oswald shot him three times at point-blank range before delivering a fatal gunshot to the head. Oswald fled to a nearby movie theater, where he was arrested and brought into custody. Forrest Sorrels got the call while he was at Kodak. He urgently needed to return to the Dallas Police Department, where Oswald was being questioned, but before he did, Erwin recalled that he said to Abe, "If [the pictures] come out all right, get me a copy. Would you do that for me?" "Sure," Abe replied.

Here I have to take a break for a brief technical explanation about the Bell and Howell movie camera and the development and duplication of double 8mm film. It's the kind of section that I, as a reader, would normally skip. But it turns out that this matters a lot to the story later.

Abe bought his Bell and Howell 414 PD Director Series camera the year before, in 1962, from Peacock Jewelry on Elm Street in downtown Dallas. The camera had gotten excellent reviews in *Modern Photography*, where it was described as "undoubtedly one of the finest 8mm motion picture cameras we have ever seen. The Zoomatic is an 8mm camera that has been beautifully thought out and designed along clean, functional lines." That sounds like the kind of review that would have gotten Abe's attention. Not only that, but it came with a sleek, elegant carrying case of hard black leather with a shiny silver buckle and trim. Everything about the design of the camera and the case suited him and his sense of style.

Now for the particulars: The body of the camera is black with silver fittings and buttons. It has a flush-mounted crank on the right side of the camera's body that the filmmaker pops out by pushing a button. You have to be careful doing this because the crank snaps out hard, and if it hits your hand, it will smart. I know this because I've done it. It takes thirty-five revolutions of the crank to fully wind the camera for filming. It seems obvious enough to go without saying, but there are no batteries or other power sources. The power comes only from the mechanism inside the camera that the operator winds to make it ready to film. When set at "full wind" (shown in a small "reserve power indicator" window), the camera runs uninterrupted for seventy-three seconds, exposing about fifteen feet of film.

The camera has both a wide-angle and a zoom or telephoto setting, which can be set using a button on top of the camera or manually by adjusting a metal zoom lever on the lens. Most importantly, on the right side of the camera, there is another small window with the buttons to run the camera: ANIMATION, STOP, RUN, and SLOW MOTION. The button rests at the STOP position. ANIMATION is a single-stop setting, essentially to take still photos, which is accomplished by pushing the button up and then releasing it each time the filmmaker wants to capture an image. To film at normal speed, the filmmaker presses the button down to the RUN setting. And for slow motion, he pushes down to the very bottom setting. At normal speed, the camera should run at sixteen frames per second, though later tests, which were of critical importance to establishing the time clock of the assassination, showed that Abe's camera was actually running at 18.3 frames per second.

The 414 PD camera takes double 8mm film, which, confusingly, is sometimes just referred to as "8mm" (the forerunner to Super 8). Double 8mm film actually starts out as 16mm-wide unexposed film stock with perforations (or sprocket holes) on both edges of the film. When the filmmaker wants to make a movie, he opens the door on the left side of the camera, loads the unexposed film reel (in low light) onto the spool, and then closes the door and runs off a few feet of film to get to the start position. He has about twenty-five feet available for shooting, with a few feet of leader. He winds the mechanism (remember that "full wind" allows the camera to run about fifteen feet uninterrupted) and begins filming. When he is finished, he will have a strip of 8mm-wide images running along the left half of the 16mm reel of film. This is side A. To continue filming, he needs to take out the reel, flip it over to the other side, and reload it before rewinding the mechanism. Then he can shoot side B, whose images will occupy the right half of the film strip. So, when it comes out of the developing machine, still in its 16mm-wide form, the images on side A are on the left, running in one direction on half of the exposed film, and the images on side B are on the right, running in the opposite direction. At this point, there are perforated holes on each edge of the film strip. Then, in the normal course of processing, technicians slit the film strip down the middle, making two 8mm strands of film, which are then spliced together so that it can be watched as one continuous reel with all the images going in the same direction on the right, and the perforated holes along the left.

We aren't quite done. When the film spool is loaded into the camera, it's held in place by a spindle in the middle and sprockets that fit into the perforations, or sprocket holes, along both edges of the camera roll. The original film captured the images all the way to the edge of the film, including in between those tiny holes. Duplicates of the film do not include what is sometimes called the "inter-sprocket" material. This became very important in later years when assassination researchers sought to mine every millimeter of the film for clues about the shooting.

The reel of film that was loaded in the camera on November 22, 1963, was Kodachrome II safety film, a color film that was less grainy and produced a more saturated color image than other films on the market. The downside was that it was not easy to develop and had to be sent to a Kodak lab for processing. Decades later, I would find a box containing many small yellow boxes with my grandfather's name and address hand-lettered on them from years of having films developed at Kodak and sent back to him. The assassination sequence that he caught on film is only twenty-six seconds long and is composed of 486 individual frames.

All my life I heard people say that it was amazing that he kept shooting when the shots were fired and that he didn't drop the camera, fall to the ground, or lose his balance or his composure during the whole sequence. Apart from a few infinitesimal flinches, his hand remained remarkably steady. I never paid much attention to this when I was a child; it seemed like the kind of boring thing that adults were always saying. But now I have the replica camera that Bell and Howell sent him after the original camera was taken for testing and eventually ended up in the National Archives. When I hold it in my hand, feel its weight and the pressure of holding down the button, try to focus through that tiny viewfinder while the camera is in motion, I think it is more amazing than I ever realized. Add to this the trauma of witnessing the murder of the president of the United States, and there's really no accounting for it. I think my grandfather would say the same. He was asked over and over again but he could never explain how he did it.

It took an hour to finish developing the film. The first step was to review it using the standard quality-control method. According to Phil Chamberlain, they watched the unslit 16mm film on a Kodak processing inspection projector, which ran at four times normal speed, just to check for scratches or other physical problems. The assassination sequence, on side B, ran along the right side of the film—right-side up, fortunately—while the family shots ran along the left side of the film strip and appeared upside down. Chamberlain remembered, "He started out...apologizing that he didn't really know what was on the rest of the film, that he wasn't much of a photographer...First thing we saw were pictures of his family, even as I recall, a couple of children...And then all of a sudden we're seeing the motorcade coming down...You could tell that he definitely had pictures of what had happened. And we saw...the one frame where Kennedy's head literally exploded."

"My God," someone said after the film ended, breaking the long silence in the room. Jack Harrison, who was in the room, remembered it as "needle sharp," and Erwin described the first images as "the clearest, most beautiful picture you ever saw." He went on, "That last shot, you see his head come off, and I mean, you could see it so clear...[It] was an absolute shock."

Abe asked Chamberlain if they could see it again, but he handed the reel back, saying that he didn't want to risk it getting damaged. When Abe asked about making copies for the Secret Service, Chamberlain told him that the Kodak lab in Dallas couldn't make duplicates; for that, they sent films to Kodak headquarters in Rochester, New York. Someone suggested that a local motion picture company called Jamieson Film Company might do it, provided that the original was kept in the unslit 16mm form so that they could run it on their 16mm duplicating printer. Pat Pattist, Kodak's quality-control supervisor, got on the phone with Bruce Jamieson to discuss the situation. The first problem was that neither Kodak nor Jamieson had duplicating film stock for 8mm on hand. Kodak could provide three rolls of 8mm camera film but that wasn't the same as duplicating film; the Jamieson technicians would have to guess what exposure to use to get the right color and light level in the duplicate. In a later interview, Jamieson described it this way: "We could use our best estimate of what the exposure should be and print all three of them that way. Or we could print the first one at the optimum calculated exposure and then print the next two, one somewhat overexposed, the other one somewhat underexposed. And this way we could be assured that we had one optimum copy."

With a plan in place, the group prepared to leave Kodak. Before they did, Phil Chamberlain signed an affidavit attesting to the fact that he had developed the original film, that it had been given the perforation identification number 0183, and that it had not been damaged in any way during processing. It was witnessed and dated by Richard Blair. Then the two Dallas police officers drove Abe and Erwin, with the unslit 16mm original film, back to the Jennifer Juniors factory and dropped McCormick off at the *Dallas Morning News* offices. According to Erwin, when they went upstairs, "there was not a soul. Everybody had left, and that never happened before. The place was left completely alone. We couldn't believe it." He recalls that they were still "in a daze," but they closed up the plant and had a drink before Abe said that they had better get over to Jamieson. Erwin drove them. He remembers that it was dark by the time they arrived, and as they approached Jamieson, someone from the *Dallas Morning News* "came out of the shadows" offering to pay $200 a frame for several frames of the film. Erwin later said, "Zapruder said, 'No. I don't even want to talk about it.' And [he] did not really want to sell it. He wasn't looking, I think, to benefit. He was trying to help out the Secret Service."

The technicians at Jamieson produced three copies of the film, as agreed on the phone with Kodak. When asked in an interview whether there was any possibility that additional copies were made that afternoon, Bruce Jamieson laughed. "There were absolutely only three copies made and that's the only possible way they could be made. There was no way anybody could, could do all that. And I'll tell you: Zapruder—Zapruder would not let that film out of his sight. Zapruder went in the darkroom with the printer operator while he made the three copies and it never left his...never left his possession." As at Kodak, and presumably at the direction of the attorney who was advising him, Abe had Frank Sloan at Jamieson sign an affidavit attesting to the fact that only three duplicates had been made.

At that point, Abe and Erwin got back in the car and drove from Bryan Street back to the Kodak plant so that the duplicates could be processed and printed. At Kodak, the three duplicates—Copy 1, stamped 0185 (one notch below optimum), Copy 2, stamped 0186 (optimum), and Copy 3, stamped 0187 (one notch above optimum)—were processed. None of them contained the visual information between the sprocket holes. The original film seems to have remained unslit, while the three duplicates were slit into 8mm strips that were spliced together. This time, production foreman Tom Nulty signed three affidavits to guarantee that the copies had been processed and were not "cut, mutilated or altered in any manner during processing." But he wanted to show the film to his colleagues. Erwin later recalled "standing at Kodak, and we were eating from a huge vending machine where they had chili and beans and stuff like that in cans. And we stood there in the back and watched them show it to those people...I mean...everybody went *gasp*, like that, when the final shot came."

By the time they were finished at Kodak, it was nine o'clock at night. In keeping with his promise, Abe and Erwin drove to the Dallas Police Department on Harwood Street with the original film and the three duplicates, which would come to be called the "first-day" copies. When they arrived, it was chaos in the station. Erwin described the scene as being "like a zoo. People were yelling and screaming and standing on the desks, and they were moving Oswald from one room to another, so we jumped up on the desks and watched. And there I saw Forrest Sorrels." Perhaps because he had his hands full with Oswald, Sorrels did not accept the film himself but asked them to bring it to Agent Max Phillips at the Secret Service offices on Ervay Street. They did. Although no one in the Secret Service had seen the film yet, and no one knew what it might contain, the Secret Service retained Copy 1 in Dallas, while Copy 3 was put on a plane that very night, bound for Chief James Rowley at Secret Service headquarters in Washington, DC.

Erwin drove Abe to his car, which was parked in a lot in downtown Dallas, and dropped him off there. When Erwin reached home, he found three men, whom he later described as "the scruffiest-looking people I've ever seen, cameras hanging all over them, beards," at his door. They turned out to be photographers from the *Saturday Evening Post*. They offered him $10,000 cash to take them over to the Zapruder home to make an introduction that night, pressing him insistently until he made them leave.

Abe, meanwhile, got in his car and drove back through the deserted streets of downtown Dallas, the city he loved and his adopted home. He was finally alone: One by one, all the people who had surrounded him that day—Lillian and Marilyn, Darwin Payne and Harry McCormick, Forrest Sorrels, the Dallas police officers, all the technicians at Kodak and Jamieson, and even Erwin—had gone back to their lives, their official responsibilities, or their own private grief. And the hubbub—the debate over how to process the film and what to do with it, and the first hints of the media frenzy that would become deafening over the next several days—had died down to silence. As he drove, his camera, the original copy of his film, and one duplicate sat quietly on the seat beside him.

When he had woken that morning, Abe Zapruder had every reason to believe he knew where his life was headed. But in a matter of seconds, the fate of the Kennedy family and the nation had veered wildly off course, and his own life intersected with both, never to be untangled again. Now he found himself responsible for a home movie of the assassination of the president of the United States. I am sure it was a burden that he felt keenly in that moment. It was already a profoundly personal situation, fraught with grief over the president's death, anxiety for the Kennedy family, revulsion at the film's violence, discomfort with the prospect of financial gain, and deep uncertainty about what to do with it. When I think about Abe Zapruder at that moment, I am aware of how his formative experiences, his interests and values, his family life and his politics must have influenced the way he thought about that burden and the decisions he made about it from that time forward.

Abraham Zapruder's early life was shaped in large measure by the forces that shook Imperial Russia in the first two decades of the twentieth century. Born on May 15, 1905, he was the last of Chana and Israel Zapruder's four children. He grew up in the town of Kovel, district capital of Volhynia in Ukraine, part of the vast Russian empire ruled by Czar Nicholas II and Empress Alexandra. His father was a carpenter, remembered as an exceptionally difficult person who couldn't get along with anyone. His mother was a very beautiful woman with a bad heart—small wonder, when the particulars of her life come into focus. She was married off to Israel

Zapruder—almost certainly under the auspices of a matchmaker, as such things were done in those days—and gave birth to her first child, Sarah Ida, when she was just fourteen years old. In 1900, their first son, Morris, was born; three years later, Fannie came into the world, followed by Abraham. Israel left the family in 1909 to establish himself in America, leaving Chana alone to care for four children under the age of twelve.

World War I broke out in 1914, when Abraham was nine. Major battles were fought in and around Kovel, devastating the city's infrastructure and bringing chaos and economic uncertainty. As frightening as the war must have been, the repeated and vicious anti-Semitic pogroms—hundreds of which took place in Ukraine between 1905 and 1920—must have been still more terrifying. At any time, on any pretext, Russian gangs could sweep through the villages and towns, assaulting and murdering at random and with impunity. They carried out mass rapes, sometimes in public, and other unspeakable acts against Jews. No one who endured such searing hatred and unpredictable violence could ever forget it.

In spite of this, when in later years Abe told his daughter, Myrna, about Russia, he did not talk about war or pogroms. Perhaps he suppressed those memories. Instead, he told her about the family's poverty and his own relentless hunger. He and his siblings had little to eat, sharing soup made from a single potato and fighting for the skin that rose to the top of a pot of boiled milk. Abe remembered another form of deprivation, as well. He yearned for an education but found himself shut out due to quotas limiting Jewish enroll-ment in Russian schools. Instead, he was sent to cheder, the tradi-tional Hebrew school for religious instruction, known for its strict teachers and agonizing days sitting on hard benches studying Torah and Talmud. This was not the education he wanted. He was curious and inquisitive, fascinated by how things worked. He did not want to prepare himself for a lifetime of study and prayer, immersed in Jewish law and religious dialectic; to the contrary, he wanted to escape his parochial circumstances by investigating everything he could about the wider world. He had a creative side, too, which found expression in his longing to play music. I grew up hearing the story of how he would stand underneath the window of a wealthy little girl, listening to her music lessons and dreaming of learning to play an instrument. His curiosity and ambitions could never be satisfied within the confines of his life as a Jew in Imperial Russia.

Meanwhile, Israel Zapruder was naturalized as a US citizen in 1915; by 1918, he had dutifully registered for the draft and also to vote. Finally, nine years after he left Russia, he sent for his family. There is no clear, coherent story about how Chana and the children made it to America or the tragedy that befell them before they reached the United States. I remember being told when I was a child that my grandfather had a brother, whose name no one seemed to know, and that he had died before the family left Russia. He was described as sickly, with a club foot, so I assumed he died of illness before they tried to emigrate. Later, I learned that Abe told Erwin that his brother had been murdered. "The Polish guard killed his brother," Erwin said. "Took him off a train and killed him right in front of his eyes." Lillian's remembered version of the story was both more and less specific: that "they"—it is not clear who—seized Morris because he looked Jewish, but that Abraham, being fair-skinned and blond, was left alone. However, Myrna remembers Abe telling her that *he* was the one pulled off the train, right in front of his sisters, who were hysterical with terror, but that somehow he was allowed back on. Perhaps some combination of all these stories is true. And while I am constitutionally inclined to want exact details and historical verification, such an impulse will never be satisfied. The times were far too chaotic for that.

Piecing together the scant surviving documents and the historical record, it seems that Morris was killed sometime between 1915 and 1918, when the family left Kovel. Israel had listed him with the other three children on his 1915 US naturalization certificate but, years later, when my grandfather's first cousin Herschel Czyzyk wrote a letter to Abe, he recalled only three siblings leaving with their mother for America. "Your mother, Chana, my aunt Chana, left Kovel at the end of World War I with her three children," he wrote, "two girls, Ida the eldest, the younger one Fannie and a little boy, Avreml. [They] went to our [Israel] in Brooklyn." There is no mention of Morris. Given the history of the time, he was almost certainly a casualty either of the war or, more likely, one of the many anti-Semitic pogroms in Ukraine.

Another story I remember from my childhood is that after leaving Kovel in 1918, the family was "thrown from the train" in Warsaw and remained there for two years. The train, as the locus for so many terrible events in the family history, seems to stand for all the precariousness of their circumstances and the inherent dangers of trying to leave. Even if they were headed for a better future, the journey was far from simple and the outcome not assured. I don't know why they remained in Warsaw for two years or what they did during that time. I know only that in 1920, Chana presented herself at the US Consulate in Warsaw to fill out papers for an emergency American passport, to which she was entitled as the wife of a naturalized citizen and which would ensure her safe passage through Ellis Island. In the picture attached to the passport, she is thin and gaunt, hollow eyed and exhausted, wearing the haunted expression of a mother who has been through war, pogroms, displacement, the loss of a son, and God knows what else. Scrutinizing the page, I notice three Xs on the line where her signature should have been. I realize with a jolt that on top of everything else, she could neither read nor write.

Chana, with Ida, Fannie, and Abraham, finally boarded the SS *Rotterdam* on the Holland America Line—with her emergency passport—on July 3, 1920. Morris remains the brother who did not get away. It took nine sickening days at sea, crammed into the steerage of the boat with 2,500 other passengers, before they steamed into New York Harbor on July 12, 1920. Abe remembered the journey as a terrible trial, with people constantly vomiting and no fresh air. They were herded through the immigration screening ordeal at Ellis Island and somehow were reunited with the father and husband they had not seen in eleven years. From there, he led his family through the chokingly crowded streets of Jewish Brooklyn to their new home.

Abraham Zapruder had escaped the violence, discrimination, and limitations of Russia, although its imprint on his psyche would never entirely fade. As he faced a new life in America—even with the uncertainty and challenges ahead—the horizon of possibility stretched out in front of him. It was his right to cast off humiliation and poverty and to claim a better life for himself. As family lore has it, he wasted no time exercising that right. With his first paycheck, he went out and bought himself his first musical instrument, a beautiful violin.

When I wanted to know what Abe was like as a young man and hear stories about my grandparents' early courtship, there was really only one person to ask. Alice Feld is a tiny, wiry New Yorker in her nineties who still takes the bus to Lincoln Center to hear concerts and has no patience for stupid questions. She is funny and frank, and generous beneath her tough New York shell, sitting with me for several hours, reaching back in her memory to recall the past and share it with me. I began our talk by asking her to introduce herself, for the record. "I don't hear so well," she tells me. "All right," I say, speaking up, "I'll talk loud." "Well, not so loud," she says firmly.

Alice and my grandmother Lil were best friends from childhood, living in adjacent tenements on Beaver Street in the heart of Jewish Brooklyn. Lilly Schapovnik, born in 1912, was the middle daughter of three, between elder sister, Anne, and younger brother, Morris. Her father, Samuel—slim with a dark mustache and round wire-rimmed glasses—was a quiet, gentle bookbinder and not, as it turned out, much of a breadwinner. His wife, Esther, was short and stout, with a firm but kind expression, her hair pulled back into a coil behind her head. She was a "balabosta," an excellent cook and impeccable homemaker who worked as the building custodian to make the rent. After Esther cleaned the building, she would return to the family apartment on the lowest level of the building, change her dress, sit in her rocker, and listen while Alice read poems to her. "And like a jerky kid, I was delighted," Alice told me.

Soon after arriving in the United States, Abe and his family came to live in the same tenement as Lilly at 84 Beaver Street. Alice remembered him vividly from this time, standing on the street with a small group of friends, talking politics. Unlike many Jews of this period, he was politically progressive but no left-leaning Marxist. As much as he hated the Czarist regime under which he grew up, he equally loathed socialism and communism, equating them both with Russia and all the ignorance, violence, and repression he had experienced there. Later in his life, when people would extol the virtues of communism, he would shout, "You don't know what you are talking about! I lived there. I know!" At the same time, he was not much of a Zionist. While he was deeply attached to his Jewish identity, he did not see his future in Palestine. He wanted to be an American through and through, and he loved his adopted home, embracing all that it had to offer. Alice saw him as a "respected gentleman," and he and his friends were the "elite." "They were not well educated but they were cerebral," she says.

Pictures from the midtwenties, some five years after he arrived, show him surrounded by friends in the country in Ferndale, in the Catskills, where they camped, canoed, climbed trees, and dressed in silly costumes. He is smiling, holding a banjo on a ferry-boat, arms slung around two bobbed-haired women dressed in knickers, and grinning at the bottom of a pyramid of friends. He had clearly embraced his new life with gusto. Still, Alice remembered that the scars of his early life remained with him. "He had a struggle without an education because he had a brain, but there was no going to school," Alice says. "He was past the age where you go to school. So here was this man that was caught between two cultures. It was a wonder that he stayed as calm and cool and pleasant as he did. It must have been very hard for him."

Like Alice, Lil must have seen Abe on the street, standing and talking politics with his friends. But, unlike Alice, Lil did not keep her distance. "By the time she was fifteen, there was no one in the world but Abe," Alice tells me with a knowing smile. Photos of their courtship in the early thirties show them in a canoe together, embracing on a campground, smiling for the camera. It is clear that they suited each other. Theirs was a big love that endured for the thirty-seven years of their marriage.

By 1930, Israel had purchased a four-unit apartment building at 1522 Park Place, where he and Chana lived with their children and families. Ida had married Joe Feld and they lived in one of the apartments, and Fannie and her husband, Sam, were in another. When Abe and Lil married, they would occupy the fourth one. Also in 1930, a *New York Times* reporter wrote an article poking fun at Israel Zabruder's [*sic*] excessive use of the city's ambulance service, titled, TAKEN TO HOSPITAL 13 TIMES; SETS AMBULANCE-RIDING RECORD. According to doctors at Bellevue, who provided a helpfully detailed list of his ailments and dates of his visits, Israel suffered from neuritis, vertigo, fainting, epileptic seizures, hemiparalysis, hypertension encephalopathy, transitory confusion, and psychosis. No wonder he was described as "difficult." He was obviously physically and psychologically sick, the latter of which surely went untreated, leaving him to suffer and inflict his suffering on his family and others. I am equally pained for his son, Abe, thinking of what he had to endure with a frail mother gradually succumbing to heart disease and a father whose problems were likely only dimly understood.

Still, life moved forward, and Abe and Lil were married in her parents' apartment in June 1933. They took their honeymoon at Niagara Falls, where a photograph shows Lil dressed in a slim white frock with a ribbon at the waist and flat walking shoes, while Abe is, as always, in a suit and hat. They also visited the Chicago World's Fair ("A Century of Progress"), where they are pictured in raincoats and galoshes, smiling broadly at the camera, ready to go spelunking. How Abe must have loved all the evidence of inventions, technology, and ways of improving the lot of the common person.

The birth of his daughter, Myrna, may have been the catalyst for his switch from still photography to home movies, since his earliest reels date from about mid-1934, when she was four or five months old. Like all new parents, he wanted to capture every millisecond on film, no matter how uneventful it might be. He filmed her lying in a pram outside, squinting at the sun. He filmed her having a bottle, having a bath, and being fed in her wooden high chair by twenty-one-year-old Lil. He filmed her as she crawled, then cruised, then walked. On Myrna's fourth birthday, her little brother, Henry, entered the picture. Soon Abe was filming him, too, a hugely round baby grinning toothlessly in his carriage; later, he follows his toddler son around the playground as he plays in the shadow of his adoring big sister.

Myrna and Henry grow up in these home movies. And I see in them not only my family—so many of them gone now—but the world they inhabited back then. Abe was a devoted amateur, carrying his camera everywhere, taking pains to capture not just the big moments but all of it—the Brooklyn city scenes with the children on tricycles and roller skates in front of their home on Park Place; the broad paved avenue of Eastern Parkway, lined with park benches where the old people sat and talked and where the children would fly down the street, stopping just short of their father, squinting and smiling at him through the camera; the birthday parties with children in silly hats and a mother slicking down her son's hair, forcing him to smile for the camera; the crowded beach at Far Rockaway, the grown-ups sitting around laughing, tossing a ball, dipping the children in the water. There is Lil's younger brother, Morris, before he went off to fight in the war, and a young, beaming Alice smiling and waving.

From time to time, Abe steps out from behind the camera. In the thirties, he is young and handsome—fit in his swim trunks, bare-headed and wearing wire-rimmed round glasses. He grins; he talks to his daughter; he points at the camera; *say hello*, he tells her, *wave to the camera.* At the beach, he carries Myrna on one shoulder, then sits on the sand next to Lil, talking with friends, gesticulating wildly with his hands, emphatic, enthusiastic, full of energy and life.

At the same time, life was not as perfectly idyllic as it appeared in the home movies. In 1936, Chana's frail heart gave out when she was just fifty-four years old. It was a terrible loss for Abe. On top of that, America was in the grip of the Great Depression, and Abe lost his job and then got very sick with pneumonia, having to be carried off to the hospital on a stretcher. After he recovered, he got a job in Bridgeport, Connecticut, and lived there for a year, while Lil held down the fort in Brooklyn. She was not happy living in such close quarters with her husband's family. Unlike Abe and Lil, his father and sisters were greenhorns, using Yiddish with one another and speaking English with a thick, recognizably Jewish inflection. Abe would chide his elder sister about her English pronunciation, telling her, "Don't say 'heggs,' Ida. It's 'eggs'!" But it was more than just a crowded family life and a clash of cultures. Abe's father and sisters' worldview had been forged in Imperial Russia; it would always reflect the confines of that time and place. Lil, in particular, wanted a different environment for her children.

Her chance to escape came in 1940. A redheaded dress designer named Elroy, whom Abe had known from a factory in New York, called him from Dallas. She had gone out there to work for a women's apparel company called Nardis, owned by brothers Irving and Ben Gold. Ben, formerly a taxi driver in New York, was a visionary, coming up with the idea of dressy garments that were washable, and pushing the business toward polyester knits, which were a novelty in those days. They became well known for manufacturing dresses from botany wool—a wool from merino sheep—during the war years. Elroy said, "Abe, come to Texas. We need a good inside man." Lil immediately saw her way out and urged him to go look into the possibility. So he did, riding the train three days to Dallas and three days back. But when he returned, he told his wife that he didn't think it was for them. He later said that when he saw the crestfallen look on Lil's face, he knew he had made a terrible mistake. Luckily, Elroy didn't give up. When she called back about a month later to see if he'd visit again to reconsider, Abe told her, "I don't need to visit again. We'll come."

It was the second time in his life that a strong woman paved his way to a new frontier and new possibilities. In August 1940, Abe and Lil, with six-year-old Myrna and two-year-old Henry, loaded trunks packed with their earthly possessions on the train that was to carry them on the three-day ride to Dallas, the land of cowboys and the flat-land prairie. Sleeping in a Pullman car and stopping in St. Louis, the family arrived at Union Station in Dallas on a blazing hundred-degree Sunday. My grandmother was dressed to kill in gloves and a hat, heels and hose, and a fabulous suit cut from yellow shantung. For his part, Abe wore his customary three-piece suit, tie, and hat.

At first, Ben Gold got Abe and Lil situated in an apartment in Oak Cliff, which was just over the bridge from downtown Dallas and decidedly unfashionable in those days. It was brutally hot and, while there was no air-conditioning, there were Texas-sized bugs—thousand-leggers, crickets, June bugs, and scorpions—the likes of which the family had never seen before. Life in the Southwest was strange and unfamiliar. Abe used to tell the story of leaving a store as the sales clerk called after him, "Y'all come back!" Puzzled by the phrase, he turned around and went back in.

It didn't take long for the family to move to the heart of the Jewish community of South Dallas, first on Park Row and then on South Boulevard. Years later, Myrna would remember it fondly:

"It was a small city and all the Jewish community knew each other and it was just a wonderful, wonderful place to live. It wasn't a metropolis of millions then." The children attended Brown Elementary during the week and saw Hopalong Cassidy movies at the White Theater every Saturday, buying a kosher pickle at the deli next door. Soon, they joined the big reform congregation at Temple Emanu-El, located at that time in South Dallas. Back home in New York, Abe didn't like the crowded, loud neighborhood shul. It probably reminded him too much of the childhood he wanted to forget. But Abe loved Temple Emanu-El. Meanwhile, Abe and Lil were busy with a nearly constant stream of parties, picnics, game nights, and other gatherings with the social circle of Nardis. Ben's brother Irving had a farm, and everyone would go up on Sundays. Pictures from the time show Abe and Lil with Myrna and Henry smiling and windblown in a heap of people. While Abe worked at Nardis, Lil occupied herself with the domestic sphere. She developed a reputation for her excellence in the kitchen, but when people complimented her, Abe would joke, "No, no, I'm the one! I'm the one who told her: Too much salt, Lil. Not enough salt!"

The Zapruders were dyed-in-the-wool Roosevelt Democrats and patriotic to the core. When America entered World War II, Lil's brother, Morris, went off to fight, as did her sister Anna's husband, Isadore. In photos taken during those years, the children are dressed in little soldier's uniforms, ones that Abe made for them himself. At the same time, they were embracing their new identity as Texans. Pictures show Henry dressed in full cowboy getup, complete with a fringed shirt, chaps, and boots, smiling under a cowboy hat and toting a silver toy gun. Later, Abe and Lil bought shares in oil, and the whole family would go "visit the oil lease," as Lil described it on the back of several snapshots, smiling broadly before a giant oil tank on the barren prairie. Myrna remembers that they also occasionally went to check on Abe's investment in a small herd of cattle; he would dress in cowboy boots and a ten-gallon hat, and they called him Abie the Cowboy. It had taken only two decades for Abe Zapruder to transform himself from Russian immigrant to American patriot to Texan Jew.

Life had its ups and downs in the 1950s, but the overall trajectory was upward, toward the middle class. Like many in the Jewish community, the Zapruders left South Dallas and moved out to a rambler on Marquette Street in the serene northern suburb of Highland Park in 1950. By this time, Abe had left Nardis and opened a new business called Chalet with Irving Gold. The business struggled to get off the ground and, in 1953, there was a labor dispute that resulted in a strike against Chalet and serious harassment of the family at the hands of the International Ladies' Garment Workers' Union. The conflict was eventually resolved, and Abe was entirely exonerated of any wrongdoing, according to the National Labor Relations Board report. But the damage was done and the business folded.

Before long, Abe was ready to take another run at it. This time, he partnered with Abe Schwartz to start Jennifer Juniors, which ultimately became known as Jennifer of Dallas. They started making their knockoff couture dresses in a loft on Jackson Street in downtown Dallas around 1954–55. Abe was later proud to say that, in the beginning, he cleaned the toilets and swept the floors himself. Abe Schwartz's son Erwin came back from serving in the army in the Korean War and started working in sales, and in 1956, Lillian Rogers came on board. When Abe Schwartz died, Erwin took over his part of the business. They grew it enough to move from the narrow, cramped loft to a bigger space at 501 Elm Street, where they initially had only the fourth floor. Eventually, they took the fifth floor as well and put the sewing rooms upstairs, increasing their revenue threefold over time. Even as the staff grew, Abe continued to have a big hand in the designs, overseeing the management of the plant and nearly everything to do with the business.

In the late fifties, Abe began training Lillian in every aspect of the business, teaching her the ins and outs, entrusting her with more and more responsibility. He had worked relentlessly for four decades, overcoming obstacles and setbacks and always pushing to build the life that he had dreamed he would have when he left Russia. He was looking forward to slowing down a little. He told her that he and Lil wanted to travel and he wanted to devote more time to his hobbies: tinkering around the house, playing his piano and organ, perfecting his pool game, playing golf, experimenting with his passion for home moviemaking.

Given the Zapruders' progressive outlook and liberal politics, it was no surprise that they supported Jack Kennedy when he announced his candidacy for the presidency in 1960. Abe admired the young senator and shared his political values, but I also have to believe that he liked the idea of the descendant of Irish Catholic immigrants ascending to the highest office in the land. It was not just that he could imagine a similar path for his own grandchildren and great-grandchildren, but also because, as a Catholic, Jack Kennedy was in a position to understand the experience of being in a minority, an outsider, discriminated against and misunderstood.

He was not the only Kennedy fan in the family. In fact, the women in his family dressed exactly like Jackie, from the tailored suits and high-heeled pumps right down to the dark curled hair and the pearls. But their enthusiasm for the Kennedys was more about substance than style. During the Kennedy campaign in Dallas, Myrna had worked as a volunteer, and before the election she had gone down to South Dallas (by then no longer a Jewish neighborhood but a predominantly black one) to sell poll tax as part of the Democrats' efforts to increase minority voter turnout.

Henry, meanwhile, wrote a letter to Senator Kennedy in September 1960, ostensibly to ask a campaign question but clearly also to express his enthusiasm and support. In his short letter, he inquired about whether the senator supported the idea of a school for diplomats that would be funded and run by the federal government. In closing, he added this: "Just a note. I am an avid supporter of yours, from Dallas, Texas, and if there is anything I can do for you now, I would be more than happy to do it." He went on to say that he could be reached at Harvard Law School, where he would be starting in the fall. He concludes by wishing young Jack Kennedy "good luck."

Years after reading that first letter, I stumbled on a second one while I was corresponding with the Kennedy Presidential Library in Boston. By this time, Henry was getting ready to graduate from Harvard Law and Jack Kennedy was president of the United States. He wrote:

Dear President Kennedy:

My boundless energy must be directed toward meeting the exciting challenges of the Sixties. On May 25th, 1962, I will be graduated from the Harvard Law School. From that time forth I want to engage in the opportunities and activities that you are directing. I deeply sense the crises confronting this Nation; I want to devote my energy and talent toward meeting these crises.

You spoke of "... the edge of a New Frontier—the frontier of the 1960s—a frontier of unknown opportunities and perils—a

*frontier of unfulfilled hopes and threats." You asked, "not what
I intend to offer the American people, but what I intend to ask
of them." I am part of that New Frontier, and I ask you, what
can I do for America?*

*I will be in Washington, D.C. on Monday and Tuesday of
February 26th and 27th. Who can I see and what can I do?*

I was always told how much our family loved the Kennedys and
how much my father admired the president. But it was not until
I came upon these letters that I realized I had always heard those
words in relation to JFK's assassination and our family's connection to it. It was as if the Zapruders had to apologize for the film by
saying how much they had loved the president. These letters take
me back to a moment when being a Zapruder meant nothing at all
in relation to John F. Kennedy, offering independent evidence of
what my parents had always told me. But there's more to it than
that. My father—so idealistic, so urgently hopeful—was twenty
years younger than I am now when he wrote this letter. What it
captures is his voice—his earnest wish to use his skills as a lawyer
to work for the common good in the Kennedy administration. In
this, the letters also give me a deeper sense of what he must have felt
when our family's fate got intertwined with Kennedy's assassination, and what it meant for him when the film eventually became
his burden to bear.

Henry got a kind letter back from Lawrence O'Brien, who was
a very influential and important aide to the president, but there
was no job for Henry at the time. Instead, he traveled to England
to do a postdoctoral year at Oxford University, leaving behind his
girlfriend, Margie, who had completed her degree at Smith College
and her master's in Art History at Radcliffe by then. She spent a

summer working at an ad agency on Madison Avenue ("with all the Mad Men," she told me, "only I didn't know it then") and then she took a job in the registrar's office at the Metropolitan Museum of Art. As Henry made plans to return from England, he wrote to Margie and asked her to meet him at the pier. That very day at lunch, he proposed, she accepted, and they traveled down to Dallas soon after for an engagement party for which my grandmother cooked every last bite of food herself.

For a while, it looked as if they might settle in Dallas. Then, shortly before their wedding, Henry and Margie were elated when he was offered a position in the Tax Division at the Justice Department in the Kennedy administration. He jumped at the chance.

Henry and Margie were married on October 31, 1963, at the St. Regis Hotel in New York City. The bride's father, Ben, worked for the government, and her aunt Sue was a famous New York voice coach. Her mother, also named Lil, was petite and incredibly lovely, with huge eyes, dark hair, and a reserved, mysterious smile. I remember poring over their wedding album when I was a child, taking in every detail of my mother's white dress, the guests dressed in pink and red, and my aunts and uncles, so young and happy. Myrna stood up for my mother as matron of honor; her husband, Myron, and Margie's brother Joe were groomsmen. Abe was best man, wearing a fine tuxedo. Margie's going-away suit was an Italian couture outfit, a black-and-white houndstooth with a matching cape that she got from the samples rack at Jennifer.

The young couple took a short honeymoon after the wedding and then settled into an apartment on G Street in Washington, DC, so that Henry could begin his new job. When the president and first lady came to Dallas, Henry was just three weeks into the job of his dreams, working for the Kennedy administration.

CHAPTER 3

FIRST GLIMPSES

All through the afternoon and into the evening of November 22, as the horrified citizens of Dallas absorbed the news of the president's murder, Lillian, Myrna, and Myron waited at the house on Marquette Street for Abe to return. They knew from his phone calls that he had taken a film and he was getting it processed, but they were so wrapped up in the events of the moment that they had not begun to grasp the implications of this fact. They just wanted him to come home so that they could grieve and comfort each other.

The morning had begun for Myrna when she and her best friend Ruth Andres went to Love Field to join the packed and frenzied supporters of the president and first lady, hoping to catch a glimpse of them as they stepped off the plane. Her husband, Myron, a stockbroker, was watching for the motorcade from his office window at the Praetorian Building on Main Street. Myrna had been euphoric after seeing them. ("She was gorgeous but he, oh God, he was so handsome. And that smile. He was just a knockout.") Afterward, she had gone with Ruth to a nearby luncheonette but no sooner did they enter than they heard screaming and commotion, people yelling that shots had been fired at the president. Myrna immediately found a pay phone in the back of the restaurant to call Myron. "Oh my God, is it true?" she asked him. "Yes, it's true," he answered her. "I just saw him and turned around and a few minutes later on the ticker tape… 'President Kennedy was shot.'" Myron, in disbelief, had called his headquarters in New York, saying, "It's not possible, I just saw him."

Myrna told me this story in February 2013 when I traveled to Dallas to spend a few days with her and to interview her about the assassination and its aftermath. As soon as I arrived, we went to lunch at North Park, where I'm sure my grandmother's spirit still roams the racks at Neiman's, and then settled down at her home for the first session in what would turn out to be a marathon interview.

Like her mother, Myrna is tall and has always been beautiful, with short, lightened hair, large, wide-set eyes, and high cheekbones. She dresses with style and has cultivated, elegant taste—her home is filled with artwork, glassware, pottery, and trinkets collected from travels to Israel, Africa, and Europe. She is passionate about politics and ideas, reads widely, and does not shrink from sharing her opinions. I think of her as a combination of her parents: strong-minded and strong-willed like her mother and cautious, reserved, skeptical, and analytical like her father. Like most of the family, she is quick to laugh, though she has had more than her share of sorrows.

I asked her to tell me what else she remembered from that day. She said that she and Ruth were nearly hysterical as they headed toward home, not knowing the president's condition or what had happened. Like many in Dallas, Myrna first assumed that the shooting had to be the work of the conservative anti-Kennedy forces in Dallas. She was at her house, having been dropped off by Ruth, when the president's death was announced, and she flew into a rage, kicking the tires of her car, then marching next door to yell at her conservative neighbor, and calling the *Dallas Morning News* to scream at them for the hateful anti-Kennedy ad they had run that morning. "Oh, I chewed them out! That they were responsible. Oh, I gave them hell!" In a parting shot, she canceled her subscription. When she tells the story now, she laughs a little at herself but she remembers that then, she was completely wrapped up in the most intense grief she had ever known. When I ask her for details, she says, "I don't remember. I was so emotional. I was just totally—I was just nuts. I was just nuts. I was angry. I was furious. I was crying. I just couldn't deal with the fact that our president, who I loved so much, was killed in Dallas. It was horrible. It was horrible."

Abe finally got home around ten or eleven at night. "And he had the film," Myrna says. "He had a copy of the film and he showed it on his projector in the den. I remember I sat in the living room. I could not watch it. But Mother and Myron and Dad watched that film."

As it turned out, the day wasn't quite over. Before Abe could fall into bed, the phone rang. On the other end was a young Richard Stolley, who had been trying to reach Abe all evening from a suite in the Adolphus Hotel, which was humming with newsmen, photographers, and writers scrambling to cover the rapidly unfolding events in Dallas. The conversation that followed eventually rescued Abe from his terrible internal dilemma about what to do with the film and, at the same time, put events in motion that would later raise deeply contentious questions about the film's disposition and fate.

Dick Stolley is a seventy-year veteran of the news industry, handsome, with a beaming smile, an easy, warm manner, and a great sense of humor. He is eighty-seven years old now, a bit stooped, but he still has the mischievous glint and sharp energy of a gumshoe reporter. Although I had known about him all my life, we never spoke or met until 2013, when he asked me, on behalf of *LIFE* Books, to write a piece about my grandfather for a book about the assassination. When we finally met in person in New York, I felt an immediate sense of familiarity and affection for him.

In November 1963, Dick was the Los Angeles bureau chief for *LIFE* magazine. He had learned about the shooting from a correspondent in the office, Tommy Thompson, who saw it coming over the AP wire at just about the same time that my uncle Myron saw it on the Dow Jones ticker tape. Dick immediately called New York headquarters, where he reached assistant magazine editor Roy Rowan. Henry Luce and the other managing editors from his magazine empire had just heard the news during their weekly lunch at the Time & Life Building. Everyone sprang into action: At *LIFE*, managing editor George Hunt headed downstairs to face the inevitable. Production of the current issue of the magazine, due out on November 29, was already under way in Chicago. In fact, 200,000 copies had been printed, dried, bound, and sent to various distribution points. There was no way around it; they would have to stop the presses and completely remake the magazine in a matter of hours. A crack editorial team, including Rowan, associate art director David Stech, and a writer, layout man, and researcher flew to Chicago to the R.R. Donnelley plant where *LIFE* was printed. Teams in New York, Dallas, and Washington would report, gather photos, and prepare the content, which they would send to Chicago for assembly on the spot. Time was of the essence, not only to capture the breaking news in Dallas but also to close the issue and print the magazine's enormous run in time for the November 29 publication date.

Meanwhile, Rowan asked Stolley, "How fast can you get to Dallas?" Stolley and Tommy Thompson nabbed two photographers who happened to be in the office with their equipment and dashed to the Los Angeles airport. Stolley remembered, "No bags, no nothing, I mean, not even a notebook. And just outside the airport the announcer came on the radio and said that Kennedy was dead. Tommy, a Texan, let out a groan that I will never forget." On the plane, they found themselves cheek by jowl with packs of other newsmen, many of them carrying camera equipment on their laps. "Television cameramen were getting on with those huge cameras... There wasn't time to put them down in the baggage carrier, so they were carrying them into the plane and putting them in the aisle...I mean, everyone had a seat but equipment was everywhere and the pilot said, 'Let's go, let's go.'"

As soon as they landed in Dallas, Stolley went downtown to the Adolphus Hotel, where he got a suite and began setting up a headquarters for the *LIFE* staff who would be covering the story. Tommy Thompson left with one of the photographers for the Dallas jail to see what they could get on Oswald's family, since Oswald himself was by then in custody. Soon, Stolley got a call from Patsy Swank, a stringer (part-time local correspondent) for *LIFE*, who had a juicy tidbit to share. "She said, 'I just got a call from a reporter friend of mine who...tells me that a cop told him that a businessman with an 8mm home movie camera was in Dealey Plaza and photographed the assassination.' I said, 'Well, who is he? What's his name?'... She sounded out three syllables—'Zah-pruh-der'—and no first name, and I said, 'OK. Patsy, that's not a hell of a lot to go on.'...I'd never been in Dallas before, so I thought the best place to start would be the phone book...and I flipped over to the Zs and literally ran my finger down the Zs...and, by God, there was the name, exactly, phonetically, as it had been pronounced to me. I mean, spelled out: *Zapruder, Abraham.*"

Stolley immediately started calling the house, but it was hours before he finally got Abe on the phone. When I asked him if he felt any apprehension about calling Abe at home, he said, "Oh, not the least. I mean, that's what reporters do. You intrude on perfect strangers." When at last Abe answered, Stolley introduced himself as a reporter with *LIFE* magazine and got straight to the point.

"Mr. Zapruder, is it true that you photographed the assassination?"

"Yes."

"Did you get the entire sequence from beginning to end?"

"Yes."

"Have you seen the film?"

"Yes."

"Mr. Zapruder, can I come out now and see it?"

(*Pause*)

"No."

Stolley remembered Abe saying that he adored the president, that he was devastated by having witnessed his murder, and that he couldn't deal with anything more that day. It was too much. Stolley added, "I felt genuinely sorry for the man. He was truly grieving. You could hear it in his voice." As much as he felt compassion for Abe, he was also a reporter through and through. He had enough experience to know that sometimes you need to push to get what you want, and sometimes you need to back off. Not because it's the kind thing to do—though in this case it was—but because pushing too far can sometimes backfire. His instincts told him to let it lie. But just for one night. Before he hung up, Abe told the reporter that he could meet him at Jennifer Juniors at nine o'clock the following morning.

LIFE was undoubtedly in a league of its own as a pictorial magazine in those days. My grandparents had a subscription to the magazine, as did everyone else in the family. *LIFE* had a reputation for bringing images of the most important events of the day to the public—political events, natural disasters, profiles of world leaders, cultural affairs, and a sizable number of frivolous or entertaining stories, too. Moreover, the magazine had a special relationship with the Kennedy family, publishing color photographs of the gorgeous first family that fed the public's fascination and cemented the Kennedy mystique. When there was breaking news, *LIFE* could not always compete with other news media for speed and breadth of coverage, so the editorial staff focused on special angles, striving to uncover a part of the story that would otherwise go undiscovered. In many cases, the key to their uniqueness lay in the photography; it was the powerful image—poignant or revelatory, emotional or insightful—that moved the story past the facts and the words to make readers feel that they were there. Sometimes, these photos came from their own staff photographers, but just as often, *LIFE* reporters went in search of photos taken by amateurs. Loudon Wainwright described it clearly in his book, *The Great American Magazine: An Inside History of LIFE*: "The questions *LIFE* reporters always asked themselves as they arrived at the scene were: 'Who might have taken photographs that no one knows about?' 'How can we go about finding them?'"

When Patsy Swank called Stolley with a tip about an amateur film, it was exactly what he was there to find. Before eight o'clock the next morning, Stolley left the Adolphus and took the short taxi ride through the deserted streets of downtown Dallas to Jennifer Juniors. Though he had been instructed to arrive at 9:00 a.m., *LIFE* reporters didn't get the scoop by showing up on time. They came early. Not only that, but he was properly dressed in a suit and tie, and he carried himself with the authority of a representative of one of the leading magazines in the world. It may seem trivial now, but in this and other important ways, Dick Stolley separated himself from the outset from the roughneck, clamoring pack of reporters who would soon throng the offices of Jennifer Juniors. I asked him what was on his mind as he made his way to this meeting with Abe Zapruder. "You have to remember, you know, I had done this before. After one of the hurricanes that hit New England, I was a young reporter…and I was sent up to Cape Cod to get people who had taken pictures of the hurricane to give us pictures. So, in some ways, this was just like that."

As he prepared himself for the meeting, he was thinking only of seeing the film and, if it turned out to be good, procuring the print rights for his magazine. The previous night, after he got off the phone with Abe, he had called Dick Pollard, director of photography, in New York. "I said, 'What are the parameters? I mean, I hope I am going to see that film first thing in the morning, and I have no idea who else is going to show up, but I need to know what I can offer.' And the answer was, 'You can go up to fifty thousand dollars, but then call us.'" When I interviewed Stolley in 2013, I asked him if that seemed like a lot of money to him then. "Yeah," he said. "That was a fair amount of money for still photos." It never occurred to him in that moment to consider the moving picture rights. For one thing, *LIFE* had no television outlet and no way to use moving images even if they wanted them. That wasn't how they delivered the news. Not only that, but print still dominated the news in those days. TV news was relatively new, and evening broadcasts had only recently expanded from fifteen to thirty minutes a night. In fact, it was the round-the-clock coverage of the assassination that marked a turning point in the history of television news. But Dick Stolley was a print journalist. He was focused entirely on finding the still images he needed to bring the shocking news of the assassination to the American public in the pages of *LIFE* magazine.

Before Abe could deal with the media, he had the painful duty of screening the film for two Secret Service agents who had come to the office for that purpose. Stolley thought Abe seemed slightly annoyed when he showed up early, but Abe just looked at him for a moment and then said, "Well, you might as well come and see this." Stolley recalled that Abe had brought his projector from home and that he set it up on top of a rickety table in a small, windowless room on the fourth floor, preparing to project the images against the white wall. He ran the projector while Stolley and the Secret Service agents stood against the far wall. With no sound but the rhythmic clicking of the old movie projector, they watched the film in silence, until the moment of impact when the president's head exploded in a shower of red. "And at that point...the three of us just went *ugh*, as if we had all been gut-punched, literally," Stolley recalled. "I mean, we knew what had happened, but we had no idea what it looked like, and...it was the most dramatic moment of my career in journalism, seeing that unbelievable thing for the first time."

It was suddenly crystal clear to Dick Stolley that this was not, in fact, like getting photos taken by an amateur on the scene during a hurricane in Cape Cod. There would be nothing routine about this one. As he put it in his interview with me, "I thought, at that instant, there is no fucking way I am going to walk out of this building without that film."

Abe screened the film once or twice more for the Secret Service, who asked him a few questions about where he was standing and what he heard at the time the shots were fired. Stolley stayed quietly in the background, his mind racing, thinking that no one else in the media had yet seen the film and trying to calculate how he could use this to his advantage to convince Abe Zapruder to sell him the film. Meanwhile, it was almost 9:00 a.m., and reporters were beginning to gather in the outer vestibule at Jennifer. Eventually, nearly two dozen reporters turned up, representatives from the Associated Press, the *Saturday Evening Post*, *Movietone News*, and United Press International, but no one, at that time, from the national TV networks. Many of them had likely been up all night, and they were under enormous pressure to get whatever they could in the way of a scoop. Still, Erwin and Lillian, who were there at the time, remembered them as unkempt, brash, and rude, as far in temperament and style from Abe as people could be.

Stolley took pains to separate himself from the other reporters, asking politely if he might use an office while the other news media screened the film. Abe showed him to a desk in what Stolley described as a "bull-pen" area of the office, where the staff usually worked. That's probably how he started talking with Lillian, winning her over with his politeness and charm, which was just about the smartest thing he could have done. It turned out that they were both from Illinois and they shared the state's passion for high school basketball. Stolley had been the sports editor of his hometown newspaper, and he knew all about her favorite team, the Taylorville Tornadoes, who had won hearts for their 1943–44 season, in which they made Illinois history by becoming the first high-school basketball team to win the state championship with an undefeated record. While they traded notes about sports, Abe showed the film over and over to the assembled reporters and responded to requests to show it each time a new journalist turned up.

Stolley says that the strain of showing the film over and over again got to Abe. He had started the morning in a subdued but calm frame of mind, very courteous but also businesslike. But after repeatedly screening the film, he had become more emotional and upset. After about an hour, he came out to where Stolley was sitting, not failing to notice that he was chatting sociably with Lillian. "I've shown the film to everybody who has come," Abe said, "and I'm ready to talk." Stolley followed him to the hall, where the reporters were assembled, and Abe addressed the group. He politely thanked everyone for coming and acknowledged that they all wanted to speak with him, but firmly said that since Mr. Stolley had been the first to contact him the previous night, he was obligated to speak with him first.

Of course, Dick Stolley wasn't the first reporter to have reached him at all. There had been Harry McCormick the day before, and Darwin Payne, and various others at the Jamieson Film Company and at Erwin's house. They had all made offers for the film, hoping that by being the first, or the most persistent, they would convince him. But Abe had one thing on his mind on Friday, November 22, and that was to get the film processed, duplicated, and safely deposited with the Secret Service. That had taken all day. Still, if

Stolley was not the first reporter to reach Abe, he was the first one to reach him after he had discharged his civic responsibility to get the film into the hands of the federal authorities. Depending on how you look at it, when Stolley reached Abe at the end of the day, he was either finally free to sell the film or still burdened with the problem of what to do with it.

Either way, I suspect that the call from Stolley came as an enormous relief to my grandfather. He—like millions of others—knew and trusted *LIFE* magazine. It offered the best way to get the film out of his hands and into those of an organization he felt would not sensationalize the president's murder. Although he went through the motions of showing the film to all the reporters who showed up, it doesn't appear that he seriously entertained the possibility of selling the print rights to any of them. At the same time, it's impossible to overstate the role that Stolley himself played in the final decision. As the morning wore on, and as the gulf widened between Stolley on the one hand and the pack of rude, pushy, aggressive reporters on the other—and the character of the publications they represented—there can have been little doubt in Abe's mind that he wanted to deal with Dick Stolley and *LIFE* magazine and no one else.

Stolley remembers the reaction in the room when Abe finished speaking. "Well, the others went berserk at that and began screaming at him," he said. " 'Promise me you'll sign nothing, Mr. Zapruder!' 'Don't sign anything!' 'Talk to us!' 'You've got to promise us!' . . . And poor Abe was just . . . he was stunned. That day, with all these reporters screaming at him, he just looked shell-shocked." Nothing in his life could have prepared him for this. It wasn't just the connection of the film to the money that was painful to him. It was the reporters' lack of sensitivity about what the film actually showed. These weren't agents from the Secret Service or FBI, who obviously needed access to the information on the film. This was the media up close, hungry to pay any price and disseminate at any cost images that he felt no decent person would want to see. They were treating the purchase of these images exactly as they would any other "scoop," not as if they showed the gruesome murder of a man, the making of a widow, the felling of a young leader who had promised so much to a nation hungry for change. Or—even worse—it was exactly because they showed all those things that they were desperate to get the images.

He had known almost immediately that this would be the dilemma of the film. The very night after the assassination he was visited by nightmares, some of which would haunt him for the rest of his life. But the one that pressed in on his dreams the most that night was not about the murder of the president but about the film. He dreamed he was walking in Times Square in New York, surrounded by the theaters and the flashing marquee lights. There, on the street corner, in front of a sleazy theater, stood a man in "a sharp double-breasted suit" hawking tickets to his home movie, shouting to all those who passed by, "Come inside to see the president murdered on the big screen!" From deep inside his subconscious, it was his anxiety about what to do with the film that rose most prominently to the surface. The worst-case scenario was not failing to sell the film, or not selling it for enough money, but successfully selling it and somehow unleashing consequences that he could never take back or control. It was not only being witness to the murder itself, but the hideous possibility of unscrupulous people exploiting that murder over and over again. It was that he would collude with the media to feed a voyeuristic fascination with the president's murder. The crux of the dream's horror, in my mind, is that he would become the hawker on the street himself.

Richard Stolley and *LIFE* magazine offered him a safe harbor in a sea of sharks. No one was going to come out of this a saint, but maybe there was a way to come out whole, moral fiber intact, liberated from the film, and maybe a little better off financially than he had been before. But he would have to get through the negotiations first. Once settled in his office, Stolley began by testing the waters. He remembered that he wanted to see if Abe knew what he had, and to get a sense of how this was going to go. "That's a very unusual piece of film," he said carefully, in what was perhaps the understatement of the century. He went on to explain that when *LIFE* magazine encountered such unusual images, they occasionally paid more than their usual "space rates." They would certainly consider paying as much as $5,000. In his recollection, Stolley said, "He looked at me and gave me this half smile, which indicated to me that he knew what he had and he knew that I knew what he had, so, kind of, let's get on with it."

For the next half hour or more, the two men sat together. I asked Stolley what they discussed. He said they talked a lot about the assassination and everything that was happening in Dallas, and in between they made small talk. Periodically, Stolley would raise his bid and Abe would let the figure hang out in the air, without saying no but not really saying anything, and they would start talking again. At one point in the conversation, Abe confessed that he was embarrassed that he, a middle-aged garment manufacturer, an amateur, had taken these pictures and not one of the world-famous photographers whose job it was to travel and capture every minute of the president's life. Stolley also remembered that Abe told him about the vivid nightmare he had had the night before, and he repeatedly asked for assurances that *LIFE* would not "exploit" the film, that they would treat the images tastefully and respectfully. Stolley repeatedly reassured him that they would.

Meanwhile, the frenzy outside the office was reaching a fever pitch. Every few minutes, one of the reporters would slip a note under the door or bang on the door and shout, "Don't sign anything!" or "You promised!" Some went down to the street and used a pay phone to call the office, trying to interrupt the meeting in order to avert what looked like its inexorable outcome. Other reporters were verbally abusive and rude to Lillian, accusing her of keeping them from her boss. Erwin said that a reporter from the AP yelled at him, "I'm offering your boss a hundred thousand dollars!" Erwin shot back, "He's not my boss!"

The tension inside the office rose with the chaos outside. Stolley recalled that each bang on the door made Abe flinch and surely increased his desire to get the negotiations over with. "And I kept going up, and I finally got to fifty thousand, and I didn't even wait for a reaction," Stolley says. "I just said, 'Mr. Zapruder, this is as high as I was authorized to go.'...And I think at that point we trusted each other—or he trusted me, which is the most important thing." There is no question that Dick Stolley wanted the film every bit as much as any of the other reporters there. But he also clearly saw Abe Zapruder, understood his distress and shock, and regarded him as more than a human body standing between himself and the scoop of the century. "I mean, you have to keep remembering," he wrote decades later: "We had all seen the film. But Abe Zapruder saw the actual murder." Stolley rose to call his editor, but at just that moment, another reporter pounded loudly on the office door, demanding to be let in and have his chance at the negotiation. "And he just kind of winced," Stolley wrote. "At that point, he just said, 'Let's do it,' very quietly, very simply. 'Let's do it.'"

They typed up a short contract and Stolley took possession of the original film. Abe kept the duplicate that had been made at

Jamieson the night before. Thinking of the mob of reporters out-side, Stolley asked him, "Mr. Zapruder, is there a back door to this place?" There was. Richard Stolley quietly made his way out of the building's rear exit, while Abe was left to face the furious, howling crowd of reporters alone.

As early as Saturday morning, November 23, there was no single life of "the Zapruder film." There were four versions—the original and three duplicates—each of which traveled its own path, creating its own reverberations and consequences for our family, the media, the federal authorities, and the public.

While the media was clamoring around Abe at Jennifer Juniors on Saturday morning, a group of FBI agents from the Dallas field office arrived at Kodak to examine the images on one of the duplicate copies. For this purpose, they had borrowed Copy 1 (number 0185) from the Dallas Secret Service. It's important to keep the FBI and the Secret Service separate—even though people routinely use the names of the agencies interchangeably in their recollections—because they each carried on their own investigations and undertook entirely separate analyses of the film during that first weekend.

The Dallas FBI agents remained at Kodak for an hour or two, watching the film over and over again, using an 8mm projector that allowed freeze-frame stopping to analyze it, trying to determine what it showed and how the information fit with the developing investigation. When they left, it would seem that they returned the film to the Secret Service and did not immediately report their findings to FBI headquarters in Washington. Instead, senior officials at the FBI learned about the existence of the film on Saturday afternoon from disgruntled media who could not get access to it from Abe Zapruder.

Cartha DeLoach, assistant director in charge of the Crime Records Division, a high-ranking operative and close confidant of J. Edgar Hoover, wrote two memos on that day that help piece together the Bureau's efforts to get the film. In the first one, he documented his initial awareness of the film and several calls to Dallas about it. He wrote, "We have received inquiries from 'Time' magazine, 'Telenews,' 'The New York Times' and a number of other communications outlets relative to several minutes of 8 millimeter color film which was reportedly taken at the scene of the assassination by one Abraham Zapruber [sic]." Apparently, other agents in the Bureau had received similar calls. DeLoach called Special Agent Gordon Shanklin in the Dallas FBI field office to find out more. DeLoach reported that Shanklin "knew that we had this film and [he] was having it processed at the present time at a commercial shop in Dallas. Shanklin stated he did not believe the film would be of any evidentiary value; however, he first had to take a look at the film to determine this factor." Either Shanklin was confused or he was covering his rear, because the FBI agents had returned the film to the Secret Service earlier that morning.

In the same memo, DeLoach notes that he further instructed Shanklin to ignore the media, to proceed with processing the film to determine what value it might have, and to get back in touch when he had seen it. He was clearly unaware that it had already been developed and viewed at length—by his own local Dallas agents, no less. He also believed Shanklin was in possession of the original film, writing at the very end that "despite the pressure that was being put on [sic] by the news outlets this matter would have to be treated strictly as evidence and later on a determination would be made as to whether the film would be given back to Zapruber [sic] or not." This seems like an entirely reasonable thing to think, under the circumstances, and it raises the question of why the Secret Service hadn't, in fact, taken the original film in the first place. Unfortunately for the federal agencies, that ship had sailed. Richard Stolley had carried the original out of Jennifer Juniors and had it sent via courier to Chicago so that the *LIFE* editors could include it in the special JFK assassination issue for November 29.

Without the original, the Secret Service had only the two first-generation copies to use for analysis. If the FBI wanted copies to be made from these versions, they would be second generation. The visual clarity would deteriorate with each version. And none of the copies of the film included the visual information between the sprocket holes of the film. But with no other option, the Dallas FBI field office borrowed Copy 1 of the film from the Secret Service in Dallas for a second time that day. Inspector Thomas Kelley of the Secret Service lent it to Special Agent James Bookhout in the Dallas field office of the FBI, who handed it to Special Agent Robert Barrett, also in the FBI field office, to make a duplicate. Here they ran into a bit of a snag. Apparently, Barrett was totally unable to find a way to make a duplicate of the copy. Nowhere in the entire city of Dallas—not at any of the television stations, nor at Kodak, nor at Jamieson—could anyone be found who could duplicate the film. Within hours, Barrett gave up and returned it to Shanklin. Someone else would have to figure out what to do with it.

In DeLoach's second memo, written later that day, it is clear that Shanklin had called and given his boss the bad news. First of all, DeLoach knew by then that "Mr. Zapruder," as he repeatedly referred to him, had sold the film to "Time and Life" (though the memo is not clear about the difference between the original and the copies) and that the FBI would be working with a duplicate. Also, Shanklin reported that local film companies had been unable to duplicate the film. Apparently, the Dallas field office didn't even have a movie projector on which they could watch the borrowed copy, nor could they seem to find one in the whole of the city of Dallas. But, Shanklin added helpfully, when he held the thin strip up to the light, he could clearly see the color images, tiny as they were, showing the president and Governor Connally being hit by the sniper's bullet. I don't know what DeLoach's response was to this report of hapless incompetence, but I can only imagine it was laced with expletives. Neither the Secret Service nor the FBI in Dallas had obtained the original film or the camera when they had the chance. Further, Shanklin had failed to grasp the film's importance, even after his own agents reviewed it for hours. Finally, his agents could not even find a way to have it duplicated. Instead, the FBI would have to use a copy to make a second-generation copy in order to analyze what was turning out to be a critical piece of visual evidence of the president's assassination.

In the written record, however, DeLoach simply ordered Shanklin to "immediately" put the film on a commercial flight to Washington. The matter would henceforth be handled in the capital. So Copy 1 was flown from Dallas to DC on American Airlines flight 20, which left at 5:20 that evening. DeLoach instructed that the film be picked up from the airport and brought into town to be "processed either by our own photographic lab or by a commercial lab with whom we do business here in Washington." But here again, and in spite of DeLoach's impatience to get the film, the momentum stalled. The FBI's state-of-the-art photography lab didn't have the capability to duplicate the film, and the company with whom they did business in Washington was apparently closed for the weekend. Somehow, the FBI could not find a way around these problems, so the agency waited until Monday, November 25, three full days after the assassination, for the commercial lab to open its doors and make the three duplicates they required. Finally, on Tuesday morning—after much consternation from the Secret Service in Dallas, who urgently wanted their copy back—the FBI returned Copy 1 and one of the duplicates to the Secret Service in Dallas. In a cover memo, the FBI director sternly reminded them that these copies were for official use only and that they were to be treated with the utmost confidence. Never mind that in just a few days, millions of copies of *LIFE* magazine with images from the film would be flooding into living rooms across America.

During the day on Saturday, Richard Stolley had dispatched the in-camera original of the film to Chicago, where *LIFE*'s printing plant, R.R. Donnelley, was located. *LIFE*'s skeleton crew had all been there since the day before, working under the guidance of Roy Rowan to tear up the original issue of the magazine and remake it under enormous time and emotional pressure. The work was well under way when word reached Rowan that an amateur movie was on its way to Chicago for inclusion in the new issue. It arrived by courier and Rowan set up a hand-cranked Moviola projector to allow his team to study the film frame by frame and to decide which images they wanted to have enlarged and printed for further editorial review. There was absolutely no question of printing in color; there was simply not enough time, at least not in this first issue. Rowan later remembered how painful it was to watch the film over and over, seeing the "animated young president happily waving to the crowds just before his life was suddenly extinguished."

But there was no opportunity to dwell on these sorts of thoughts; the time crunch was too great. Rowan sent the film to their photo lab, which produced over one hundred 8 x 10-inch black-and-white prints that Rowan and associate art director David Stech laid out all over the floor of an office in the printing plant. Rowan recalled that they agonized over whether to publish frame 313, the gruesome image of the bullet's impact on the president's head. I don't know if Rowan was aware of Abe's plea for respect and dignity for the president, nor do I know if Stolley had the time or forethought to convey it to him. I doubt it. But either way, Rowan decided against using the image in this issue. The debate would be taken up again by members of the editorial and art direction staff for the later memorial edition, published the following month. But for the moment, the public was spared this appalling visual. As it was, the thirty-one images printed in black and white clearly showed the basic sequence of events and were plenty horrifying. Most upsetting were the images of Mrs. Kennedy clambering on the back of the limousine after her husband was fatally wounded.

During this frantic day, while the prints were being made, six frames of the original film were damaged. Four frames were removed, and large splices appear on the original. In later years, in the context of growing fears of a government cover-up of a conspiracy and suspicion that *LIFE* was in collusion with it, rumors of these missing frames took on enormous importance. It didn't help that *LIFE* did not publicly disclose this information until much later. By that time, there was such mistrust of the government and resentment of *LIFE* that any inconsistency having to do with the film could get pulled in by the gravitational force of the various conspiracy theories. For the moment, however, no one outside *LIFE* knew that the original film had been damaged. By midmorning on Sunday, the *LIFE* magazine issue was wrapped up and ready to print.

*   *   *

Back in Dallas, Police Chief Jesse Curry had decided to move Lee Harvey Oswald on Sunday morning from the city jail located in the Dallas Municipal Building on Main and Harwood Streets to the Dallas County Jail. There were considerable concerns for Oswald's physical safety: The FBI and the sheriff's office had received calls from a man claiming that "a committee" planned to kill the president's murderer. Further, on Friday night and Saturday, the building had been mobbed with reporters and cameramen trying to ask questions and photograph or film Oswald as he went back and forth between the homicide office for questioning and the elevator leading to the jail.

On Sunday morning, Curry's police officers took steps to secure the basement of the building and got into position for Oswald's transfer to the county jail. He exited the jail office handcuffed to Detective J. R. Leavelle, and witnesses recalled a surge of media with microphones and cameras with flashbulbs pushing forward as he appeared. About ten feet from the exit, at just about 11:20 a.m., Dallas nightclub owner Jack Ruby slipped between a news reporter and a detective standing on the ramp leading from the basement of the building up to Main Street. His right arm was already extended by the time anyone noticed him. He fired one fatal shot with his .38 revolver into Oswald's abdomen.

There are many reasons why Oswald's murder is important to this story, not the least of which is that it must have seemed to those witnessing it on television at the time, or hearing about it in the immediate aftermath, as if the United States was coming completely unglued. It certainly had major ramifications for the subsequent investigations into the president's assassination, since the accused assassin's murderer was a shady Dallas nightclub owner with cozy relationships to law enforcement and rumored ties to the Mafia, details that made many wonder if Ruby's act had been less an act of vigilante justice than a calculated silencing. Oswald's killing had unintended consequences for the Zapruder film, too. Journalist Max Holland articulated this idea in his 2014 *Newsweek* article "The Truth Behind JFK's Assassination," writing, "In the absence of a cathartic, public trial in Dallas, the Zapruder film displaced Oswald's view from the sixth-floor window; a partial but mesmerizing visual record had to stand in for seeing the assassination through Oswald's eyes and hearing it described in his words." Who knows what role the Zapruder film might have played in history had Jack Ruby not murdered Lee Harvey Oswald, leaving a massive vacuum of information and perspective in his wake?

When *LIFE*'s weary editorial staff learned of Oswald's shooting, they managed to pull themselves together for long enough to update the issue with the new information—changing a headline, adding a few lines of text, and inserting a photo of Oswald just before Ruby fired—before collapsing in total exhaustion. Also on Sunday afternoon, senior staff at *LIFE*, including Dick Pollard and publisher C. D. Jackson, had gathered in New York to screen a copy of the film that had been made in Chicago and sent to their office. Like everyone who saw the film that weekend, the editorial staff were stunned and appalled. C. D. Jackson in particular was personally upset by the film, and he expressed his strong feelings that the public should not see the images, at least until enough time had passed for the initial grief over the president's death to subside. For this reason, he urged *LIFE* to acquire all rights to the film. Although Jackson was not on the editorial staff and, as such, did not make content decisions for the magazine, he seems to have convinced the editors that acquiring the film rights was the best thing to do. Pollard reached out to Stolley, who was still in Dallas. Stolley was to call Abe and inquire about purchasing all rights to the film.

C. D. Jackson's effort to protect the public from images that he considered too violent made sense at the time, even if it reflects what many would consider a paternalistic attitude by today's standards. To understand that moment and the actions of those who decided what to do with the film, we have to go beyond platitudes about the innocence of the sixties and actually imagine a time before people were routinely bombarded with moving footage of violence multiple times a day, at any time, without warning. We have to scroll back and erase the most shocking, watershed images from our collective consciousness: No black civilians being beaten and killed by the police. No beheadings of reporters by ISIS. No slow-motion implosion of the Twin Towers into the streets of Lower Manhattan, no people jumping out of the burning buildings, no planes crashing into the towers. No *Challenger* exploding in flames in the Florida sky. No scenes of the Vietnam War, no dead bodies of Martin Luther King and Bobby Kennedy. In many ways, it's impossible to understand the history of the Zapruder film without traveling back in time to see it through the eyes of those who saw it when there had never been anything like it before.

For Abe Zapruder first, and for *LIFE* magazine and the federal authorities next, there was no map to direct them on how to handle it or what to do with it. In this, it was like Lewis and Clark standing on the edge of a new American wilderness. Which way to go? How to get there? What would they find? What consequences might flow from the path they charted? In the earliest days, when Abe was trying to decide what to do with his film and journalists at *LIFE* were trying to figure out how to represent the assassination, there was no choice but to rely on past experiences and contemporary values to make those decisions. It is worth remembering that—ironically enough—those values were forged in a world before the Kennedy assassination and the Zapruder film. So Abe Zapruder sold the film to *LIFE* because he felt he could trust them, and C. D. Jackson wanted to take possession of it because he felt that, as publisher of *LIFE*, he was responsible to an extent for the images that reached the public. Certainly, their personal feelings carried a disproportionate weight in the decision-making process, but, more than that, their choices reflected an American climate and sensibility that were soon to be challenged by the consequences of the JFK assassination itself.

In retrospect, it can be hard to understand why Forrest Sorrels and the other Secret Service agents failed to seize the camera and the original film from Abe Zapruder after the assassination. There can be no question that if asked to turn them over, he would have done so. Being only human, he might have had a flicker of regret about the film's financial value, but he surely would also have been grateful not to be the one to have to decide what to do with the footage. It's pretty clear from Cartha DeLoach's memo that he assumed the Secret Service had taken the obvious step of securing the original film. But the FBI memoranda from that day show a picture of disarray and chaos in the local field offices instead. This fumble, in combination with the technical problems that the agencies had in reviewing, duplicating, and analyzing the film, makes the government appear wildly unprepared for what had befallen them.

Meanwhile, in his affidavit written in January 1964, Forrest Sorrels had this to say on the subject: "Mr. Zapruder agreed to furnish me with a copy of this film with the understanding that it was strictly for official use of the Secret Service and that it would not be shown or given to any newspapers or magazines as he expected to sell the film for as high a price as he could get for it." When I first encountered this statement, I will admit that I was instantly defensive. It seemed like an impossible thing for my grandfather to have said. For one thing, it doesn't tally with the recollections of Harry McCormick, Darwin Payne, Erwin Schwartz, or Dick Stolley. Each of them independently said that Abe refused to even discuss the sale of the film that day and repeatedly turned down offers from media desperate to buy it. The following morning, at Jennifer Juniors, he had ample opportunities to create a bidding war to raise the sale price of the film, but he didn't. Clearly, financial gain was not his only motivation; finding the news outlet that would treat the images with discretion and dignity was every bit as important. It occurred to me to wonder if Sorrels had his own reasons for reporting the story that way. By January 1964, when Sorrels wrote his report, he may have realized the grave error in judgment he had made by not taking the camera with the film in it at the time. Perhaps he was trying to cover himself after the fact by implying that it was Abe's financial interest in the film that determined the course of events. It is also possible that my reaction to Sorrels's statement has to do with our extreme sensitivity to criticism about our financial motives more than anything else. This is always the nerve that is touched in our family, on our grandfather's behalf and on our own.

Cartha DeLoach and the FBI agents in Washington, needless to say, would not have let the film slip out of their hands. It could only have happened in small-town Dallas, which was totally unprepared for the disastrous events of November 22. In an interview with William Manchester, my grandfather later said, "The Police Department here didn't even have a projector. That shows you what kind of Police Department we have. They had to come to my office to see [it]." Here, there's also a sharp contrast with how the media in general, and *LIFE* in particular, grasped the importance of the film and set about obtaining it. Their concerns and responsibilities were radically different: The media was focused strictly on reporting the story, while the Feds were trying to cope with the loss of the head of the government, the confusing and rapidly changing criminal investigation, and all the evidence pouring in, trying to distinguish what was most important in any given moment. All the more reason, of course, that the government should have seized the original film. Instead, while the Secret Service and FBI were fumbling to get second-generation copies made in Dallas and Washington, DC, *LIFE* had no trouble making prints in Chicago, and was sending a duplicate copy of the film to New York the very next day.

While it's tempting to poke fun at the Feds, there is a common thread that runs through the very different responses of all the people who were dealing with the film, whether it was my grandfather's actions, *LIFE*'s editorial decisions, or the government's delays. The film in Abe Zapruder's camera was not the famous, iconic "Zapruder film" on November 22, 1963. It only became so over time, as a consequence of all the things that happened to it. On the first day, and in the years that followed, the film would always be out of its time, always opening new questions and posing problems that individuals and organizations were unprepared to handle.

In 2013, I interviewed my mother about our family's history with the Zapruder film. When we sat down in the living room of the house I grew up in, she said, "Honestly, I was never interested in the film, so I'm not going to be much help. It's so sad you can't talk to Dad about all this, but I didn't want to have anything to do with it." When I asked her why not, she said, "Because it was just sad. It was a reminder of a terrible thing." My mother is petite, with short, dark, wavy hair that she has worn in the same style for as long as I can remember, and big hazel eyes. She has a slightly crooked smile. Trained in art history as a medievalist and as a museum registrar, she blends her knowledge of the arts with a propensity to carefully document nearly everything. She has produced an astonishing photographic record of our family life and has also captured unforgettable images from her travels with my father that hang on the walls of her home. She tends to dismiss her own creative abilities, but she has illustrated her calendars with lovely tiny drawings and cutouts that represent important events in her life. She is very charming in public, but those who know her best know that there is a deeply sensitive and emotional current running under her polished surface. I know it wasn't easy for her to talk about the film, and that it was still more painful to discuss my father, whose death was her loss more than anyone else's.

I asked her to tell me what happened after my grandfather called and told her that the president was dead and she tried to tell him that he was at Parkland Hospital. "I was just in a state of shock," she said, "and I was listening to the radio. I mean, I just kept listening and listening, and then Dad came home. And the two of us just sat there. You know, it kind of got dark, and we were—we were devastated. It was like someone in your life—someone you knew had been shot." They probably would have sat there alone all night but for Blanche Barbrow, a relative and close friend of my mother's parents, who called and asked them what they were doing. They had only been in the city for three weeks and didn't know anyone yet. It was not a night to be alone. "You come right over here," she said, "and have dinner with us."

Two days later, on Sunday, the president's flag-draped casket was borne from the White House to the Capitol Rotunda on a horse-drawn caisson. My parents were among the 300,000 people who lined the broad avenue that day as the cortege went by. My mother recalled how the news of Oswald's murder reached them. "It was a sunny day, it was very cold, and someone had a transistor radio...and said, 'Oh my God, Oswald's been shot.'"

As the sun began to set on Sunday, hundreds of thousands of people formed a huge line, ten deep, miles long, walking to the Capitol Rotunda to pay their personal respects to the president, whose body was lying in state. My parents and my mother's younger brother, Joe Seiger, who had driven down from Pittsburgh, returned to take their places in line. Although the Capitol was supposed to close at 9:00 p.m. on Sunday and reopen for a short time on Monday morning before the funeral at Arlington Cemetery, officials decided to allow the building to remain open all night so the mourners could file past.

My mother remembered it as a very cold November night, as they slowly made their way on foot along Pennsylvania Avenue toward the Capitol. When I asked her what it was like, and were people talking to each other, she said, "We were devastated. We were there because the president we loved had been killed, and—I mean, this just wasn't part of what I thought of as American history. A president assassinated? We felt like—and I think Dad felt similarly—like it was a personal loss." I can almost see the set of my father's face in that moment, the crushing disappointment he must have felt not only at the president's death but also at the implications for his own life. All those plans, that hard work, that letter to the president pleading for a way to work in his administration—all of it dashed in a matter of seconds. It took them until past dawn the next morning to make their way out of the freezing weather into the brief warmth of the Capitol Building and to momentarily file by the closed casket to say goodbye to their president, and with him, all those hopes and dreams.

CHAPTER 4

ALL RIGHTS TO *LIFE*

Abe's experience over the weekend was different in nearly every way from the rest of the public's and his own family's. He had the responsibility of the film hanging over his head, but it barely registered with his children, so wrapped up were they in their own grief about the assassination. My mother always emphasized this point, that the film had absolutely no significance to them at the time. Myrna agreed. "I absolutely shut the whole thing out. All I could think about was Kennedy and that he'd been shot. I didn't understand the implications of my dad taking the pictures and the press...nothing...My focus was on the loss of Kennedy, not on the film."

But Abe had no choice. "For him, it became the total point," Myrna reflected, "because the phones never stopped ringing." I think now how isolating, even alienating, that must have been for him. He was utterly besieged by the media, who were calling the house at all hours of the day and night, unrelenting in their pursuit of the moving picture rights to the film. It surely didn't take him long to understand that they would not let up until the rights were no longer available for sale.

Against this backdrop, Abe reached out to attorney Sam Passman, who was a partner at Passman & Jones in Dallas. His regular attorney was out of town, but Sam was a family friend and relative through his son-in-law, Myron. I never met Sam but my parents interviewed him in 1994. During their conversation, Sam recalled that Myron called him first, and then he heard directly from Abe. At first, Abe wanted to know if Sam's friend Bill Barnard from the Associated Press might be interested in acquiring the film. It must have been later in the day on Sunday that Stolley reached Abe at home, inquiring for the second time in as many days about purchasing rights to the film. Stolley remembers that Abe sounded "relieved" to hear from him. He told Stolley to meet him the next day, not at Jennifer Juniors this time but at the office of Passman & Jones.

Heartsick and conflicted, Abe arrived at Sam's office on Monday to meet the reporters and media representatives who wanted to purchase the film rights. Although he was surely leaning strongly toward making a deal with Stolley for *LIFE*—for all the same reasons that he had sold the print rights to him two days before—Abe was prepared to meet with the other representatives who were there, including Bill Barnard from the AP, Felix McKnight from the *Dallas Times Herald*, Mike Shapiro from the *Dallas Morning News*, and a very young Dan Rather from CBS. Dan Rather has famously written in his memoir *The Camera Never Blinks* that his heart sank when he saw Richard Stolley walk into the lobby, knowing that *LIFE* had, in his words, "a reputation for paying big." Stolley says he had more or less the same reaction when he saw Dan

Rather, knowing that he was an aggressive young reporter and that he would do whatever he could to get the film for his network.

The camera might not blink but memory definitely falters, and there is no way to tell this part of the film's history without revisiting Dan Rather's role in these events, which reveals a great deal about the media climate that my grandfather faced. Rather, chief of the New Orleans bureau of CBS at the time, had been sent to Dallas prior to the president's visit to organize coverage of the event. Given the hostility in Dallas, and the aggressive Kennedy-haters who had harassed and spit on Adlai Stevenson just weeks before, CBS planned to be prepared in the event of an ugly or embarrassing incident. Working with Eddie Barker, the news director at local Dallas TV station KRLD, Rather saw to it that CBS was ready for anything that might happen, setting up "film drops" all along the motorcade route through Dallas. With coverage of the visit in the capable hands of the local media, Rather traveled to Uvalde, Texas, on Friday morning to do a light piece on the ninety-fifth birthday of John Nance Garner, a former vice president to FDR who had famously compared that office to "a pitcher of warm spit."

When Rather returned to Dallas before noon, he realized that they were missing a film drop at the very end of the presidential motorcade route just at the end of Elm Street past Dealey Plaza, where the motorcade was due to go under the triple underpass en route to the Dallas Trade Mart. That is how, just after 12:30 p.m., he found himself standing on the far side of the underpass, where instead of seeing the motorcade roll by on its way to the Trade Mart, he suddenly saw a police car speed past, followed by two limousines, and take an unexpected route up the Stemmons Freeway. It didn't take him long to realize that something had happened, but what it was he wasn't sure. In his book, Rather fully describes how he learned about the president's death and his early reporting of it on CBS. While that part isn't what interests me, it's worth noting that his nearly single-minded focus on being first to get information, the exclusive holder of it, and the fastest to deliver it—consequences be damned—comes through vividly. It's a set of imperatives that defined his actions when it came to the film, as well.

His account of his early dealings with the film (as reported in his 1977 book and later repeated in his 2003 interview with the JFK Presidential Library, among others) does not, unfortunately, tally with the historical record. He begins by describing how Eddie Barker and his people began calling around Dallas to see if there was any film of the shooting. There was nothing unusual in this; everyone else was doing the same. He writes, "Slowly we picked up a trail. Someone had seen a man standing at a certain spot…We ran our leads through the FBI and the Dallas police. Finally we had a name: Abraham Zapruder. This heavyset man, in his fifties, kind face with skin the color of oatmeal, was to become one of history's great accidents."

My grandfather, kind face or not, did not have skin the color of oatmeal, nor was he particularly heavyset, but fine. Let's let that go. And while I'm desperately trying to keep my eye on the ball here, I have to admit I'm not crazy about Abe Zapruder being described as "one of history's great accidents." Aside from the obvious observation that we are all historical accidents, few of us would choose to have the immense complexity of our lives summed up that way. He goes on, "When we reached him Zapruder did not know what he had. We didn't either, but we helped arrange for Eastman Kodak to process the film. This job had to be done by the best equipment. It had to be done fast. And it had to be kept confidential." In a number of later interviews, including his interview with the JFK

Library in 2003, this story had become calcified in his memory. "Finding the Zapruder tape [*sic*] and getting it, you say, well, you got lucky," he said. "Also we got it processed. That, by the way, is a good story."

I'll say it is.

While it is difficult to account for this assertion, the other mistakes in this part of his book—mixing up days and collapsing the timeline of events—are entirely understandable given the chaos of the moment and the years that had passed. He remembered it as Saturday when Zapruder "put himself in the hands of a lawyer," but here he must mean Monday, because we know that Dan Rather wasn't at Jennifer Juniors on Saturday when Stolley acquired the print rights, and there was no lawyer present. At some point over the weekend, Rather, like Stolley, got in touch with his New York office and pressed the necessity of getting the film, a goal that the executives at CBS apparently shared.

In fact, much later, Don Hewitt of CBS News recounted in his book *Tell Me a Story* the fever that gripped him when he learned about the film. "In my desire to get a hold of what was probably the most dramatic piece of news footage ever shot I told [Dan] Rather to go to Zapruder's house, sock him in the jaw, take his film to our affiliate in Dallas, copy it onto videotape [*sic*], and let the CBS lawyers decide whether it could be sold or whether it was in the public domain. And then take the film back to Zapruder's house and give it back to him. That way, the only thing they could get [Rather] for was assault because he would have returned Zapruder's property." According to Hewitt, Rather enthusiastically agreed to this plan. Then Hewitt came to his senses a few minutes later and called him back, saying, "For Christ's sake, don't do what I just told you to. I think this day has gotten to me and thank God I caught you before you left."

Rather, in his 2003 interview with the JFK Library, questions the veracity of this account, saying, "It makes a nice story," though in his own memory of the events, the same basic elements are there. Recalling his walk to Passman & Jones on Monday morning, he wrote: "All sorts of crude ideas rushed through my mind. What if he gave it to NBC? What if he sold it to someone else?...For a moment I thought, if I have to, I'll just knock him down and grab the film, run back to the station, show it one time and then let him sue us." Darwin Payne had had a similar thought a few days before, minus the part about knocking Abe down. Hewitt and Rather were in a league all their own. However, the fact that Rather was beside himself to acquire the film, and that he recounted that feeling with all the drama of a news reporter in later years, is not surprising. It speaks to the way that media attention had crystallized around the film over the weekend. Even the fact that, despite all evidence to the contrary, he aggrandized his own role in finding the film and getting it developed can be explained by tricks of memory combined with an all-too-human ego. In time, Dan Rather would come to believe this story so fully that he would use it to justify a proprietary right to own the film. In his own words, "Our office—that mixture of CBS and KRLD crews—had done the legwork that turned up Zapruder. We had helped get the film processed. I felt we had at least a claim to it."

In fact, Rather and CBS had no claim to it. If anyone did, it was *LIFE*, since it was Richard Stolley who had learned about the film in the early evening on Friday, reached Abe that night, and behaved with compassion in that moment, throughout the next morning, and in every interaction they had over the weekend. Nevertheless, Abe and Sam Passman apparently entertained bids from parties other than *LIFE*. Perhaps they were using the other reporters' interest as leverage in the negotiations, or perhaps they felt they had to give everyone a fair chance to bid for it. Either way, once everyone was assembled, Sam laid out a few basic ground rules for the proceedings. Both Richard Stolley and Sam Passman recall this part vividly.

The reporters were instructed that they were not to report on what they had seen on the film unless they were the ones to acquire it. In the closed system of media ethics, it wouldn't be "fair" to the reporter or network that acquired the film for what would surely be a substantial amount of money if the competition left the office and blew their exclusive. In Sam Passman's files, I found several copies of the confidentiality agreement that he must have drafted. They are marked up by hand and written in legalese but nevertheless totally clear. The key parts read as follows: "The undersigned will not reveal or disclose to anyone any information or the scenes therein depicted, except to members of the organization which he represents for the purposes of appraising the value thereof... Furthermore, no stories, news casts, commentary or otherwise shall reveal or disclose the scenes depicted therein."

The confidentiality agreements in the file are not signed or executed, perhaps because everyone felt that, under the circumstances, a gentleman's agreement would be enough to guarantee a measure of discretion among the competing reporters. That turned out to be naive. Again, from Rather's memoir:

> The lawyer laid out the ground rules for us: He had set up a projector in a private room. You went in, looked at the film one time, took no notes, came out and gave him your bid. I was already saying to myself, the bid comes second. The first thing I am going to do is look at the film, then knock the hinges off the door getting back to the station and describe what I had just seen. Then, and only then, would we get into the bidding.

And that is precisely what Dan Rather did. On his way out the door, he told Sam that he needed to consult with executives at CBS before he could make an offer. And then, in an act of breathtaking *chutzpah*, he went a step further, extracting a promise from Sam that they would not settle on the sale of the film rights until he got back. Got back from where? From rushing to KRLD to deliver the first description of the assassination to the public, in direct violation of the confidentiality ground rules. "Within seconds after I walked into the studio," he wrote, "I was on the air, describing what I had just observed."

Rather's rush to get the exclusive on the film ended up having an unintended consequence—as rash and ill-considered actions often do—in the later conspiracy debates. Rather, who had seen the film only once, described the president's head as jerking slightly forward at the moment of impact and didn't mention the far more obvious backward motion that followed. This description later fed the interests of a number of different conspiracy theorists, especially the so-called alterationists, who relied on this detail to "prove" that Rather had seen the "real" version of the film as compared to the later ones in circulation that must have been altered because they didn't conform to his spoken recollection. For his part, Rather defends his misrepresentation of what was on the film not by acknowledging that it was irresponsible to give an account after having seen it only once, but as follows: "At the risk of sounding too defensive, I challenge anyone to watch for the first time a twenty-two-second film [*sic*] of devastating impact, run several blocks, then describe what they had seen in its entirety, without notes. Perhaps someone can do so better than I did that day. I only know that I did it as well and as honestly as I could under the conditions."

Maybe that's why it would have been a good idea not to do it in the first place. After all, while Rather surely was trying to be honest about what he saw, he was doing so under inherently dishonest conditions, having disregarded the ground rules established by the sellers of the film. It's true that those restrictions were put in place not to protect the public from rushing to conclusions about the shooting but to prevent one reporter from scooping all the others. Still, his fault in that moment was not a humble failure of memory; it was self-interested professional ambition. And while this may not be new in the annals of media history, Rather's single-minded focus on "the get" throws Stolley's sensitivity into sharp relief and explains, to some extent, the climate that gave rise to Abe's conflicting and complicated feelings about selling the film to begin with.

After getting off the air, Rather consulted with his bosses in New York about what they could offer to acquire the film legitimately. They threw together a proposal ($10,000 for one broadcast) and sent Don Hamilton from the business office at CBS to the airport to fly to Dallas and help negotiate. Rather was told to stall for time—but it was much too late. While Rather was on the air, Abe and Stolley had settled on an agreement with *LIFE*. Sam Passman remembers that there was some back-and-forth with offers from AP until finally Stolley came out with it: "Look. We want to buy the darn thing. Let's quit fooling around with it." They certainly offered a significant sum of money, but there were additional factors: Abe already knew and trusted Stolley; he felt confident that *LIFE* was a responsible choice; and they already had the print rights, anyway. Everything about it made sense. They settled on $150,000 for all rights (a figure that included the $50,000 they had already paid for print rights), with an arrangement to pay in six annual installments of $25,000. Abe and Stolley shook hands, signed a second contract giving all rights to *LIFE*, and Abe turned over the remaining first-day duplicate of the film. He would never possess a copy of his home movie again.

When Dan Rather returned to the office, he was shocked and furious to discover that he had missed his chance to bid on the film. He wrote that Sam Passman told him *LIFE* had made a "preemptive" bid (a detail not corroborated either by Sam or Stolley). In response, Rather shouted at Passman that CBS hadn't put in their bid yet. Apparently, Passman was supposed to wait for Rather to finish breaking the confidentiality ground rules before he closed any deal, just in case Rather—who had not discovered or developed the film but somehow believed that he had and therefore felt a proprietary right to the film—wanted to bid on it. Rather concludes with this: "I tried in an act of desperation to talk tough, which meant I raised my voice and paced back and forth and kept saying things to imply no deal existed since our bid wasn't heard. I remember, clearly, crying out there was an ethical problem here. Both Zapruder and his lawyer ignored me. *LIFE* had the film."

Dan Rather was right about one thing: There definitely was an ethical problem. But it had nothing to do with Abe, Sam Passman, or Dick Stolley. In later years, *LIFE* and CBS would fight it out over the Zapruder film again, and sometimes it was *LIFE* that would get the black eye. But this time, amid all the chaos and the ugliness and the frenzied desire for the film, Abe continued to find a safe harbor in Dick Stolley, and Dan Rather was just another shark he had to fend off as best he could.

Abe's internal conflict over the film did not let up over the course of the weekend; to the contrary, it seems to have become an increasingly agonizing problem for him as they neared closing the deal with *LIFE*. "Abe was really concerned about whether he should sell it or not, whether he should take the money and so on," Sam told my parents in 1994. "[He] was concerned that the Kennedy family might be harmed in some way...or that certain portions of the pictures would be terribly distasteful. He just didn't want to do anything that might harm them. He was really crazy about the Kennedys, he really was...Right up until the end, I wasn't sure he was going to do it."

It was essentially a repeat of the dilemma from two days before, only for more money and more exposure. He had something that the media wanted, and it was clearly worth a lot of money. There was a certain temptation inherent in the prospect of a sudden and unexpected financial windfall that would bring with it security for him and his family. On the other hand, what an awful way to make money. It carried with it not only the ugliness of profiting from a national tragedy but also the equally ugly possibility that the images would bring further pain to the grieving Kennedy family and would bring out public censure or judgment.

Against the backdrop of all his other worries, his Jewish background made him especially self-conscious about the financial aspect of the film's sale. His childhood experiences of anti-Semitism had taught him that those who hated Jews could turn anything into a reason to attack, humiliate, and shame. What was easier for an anti-Semite than accusing a Jew of profiteering? He never liked calling attention to himself, even in benign circumstances; this was, after all, part of why he had hesitated to bring his camera along to film the president to begin with. And now he was going to get rich off the president's murder, and everyone would know it. He sensed that the public would not concern itself with the complexities and pressures of the moment; instead, it would simply see him as a crass and unscrupulous "money grabber." His fears on this score were not solely a reflection of his upbringing and background.

This was Dallas, after all, which had come to be called the City of Hate. It would be bad enough if he or his family were judged for his actions, but what if they caused a backlash against the Jewish community that had welcomed him here, that he loved, that had been his home for more than twenty years?

Abe Zapruder was, in this moment, like many people who face a moral dilemma. The choice is not a binary one—to be a saint who doesn't care about the money or to be an opportunist who only cares about the money. Instead, he was a human being with conflicting feelings, opposing desires, and moral imperatives that clashed with practical realities. He had gotten where he was in life by working hard, conducting himself ethically, and traveling the most American path to success. But, in an irony that no one could have predicted, he would gain financial security not in this uncomplicated way but in a situation fraught with moral compromise.

In the end, as most people do when they are faced with complicated circumstances, he walked the line. He made a deal that contributed to his financial security ($150,000 was a lot of money, especially in those days), but he made it with *LIFE* magazine, because at least that way he could feel that his choice was a responsible one. It was not just the financial terms of the deal that speak to his concerns: He insisted on a clause in the contract guaranteeing that *LIFE* would "present the film in a manner consonant with good taste and dignity." In addition, *LIFE* agreed to defend the copyright of the film. While it was in *LIFE*'s business interest to do this, I believe Abe's reasons had more to do with controlling how widely the film was disseminated and how it was used.

There was one other noteworthy clause in the agreement. Abe retained rights to gross revenues over $150,000, meaning that after *LIFE* recouped its initial investment, they would share future income with him. Abe's continuing financial interest in the film provided him with an ongoing relationship to it and a sense that his wishes and concerns for it would not easily be disregarded. Although there was never any additional income from the deal, this clause would have enormous significance for our family when *LIFE* wanted to get rid of the film twelve years later.

But even this was not quite enough. Sam Passman recollected that in the course of these difficult conversations, he suggested that Abe might donate part of the money from the sale of the film to a charity. "Abe thought that was a great idea. He really wanted to do that," Sam Passman said. It was Bill Barnard from the AP who came up with the idea to give the money to the family of J. D. Tippit, the police officer gunned down by Oswald. Clearly, Abe was relieved to have a way not only to do something positive with his financial gain but also to offset the guilt and anxiety he felt about making money from the film. He acted on that suggestion immediately, turning over his first check for $25,000 from *LIFE* magazine to the Policemen's and Firemen's Welfare Fund for the family of Patrolman J. D. Tippit.

The very next day, Tuesday, November 27, the Associated Press reported the donation in a small news item. Abe is quoted as saying, "I had intended for these films to be home movies for the future enjoyment of my family and friends. Now, from the revenue that has been offered for such a significant film, I wish to contribute to the well-being and future of the family that lost a very brave and gallant husband and father. It is the saddest moment in my life. Normally, I would not be able to give so generously, but I am deeply gratified that I can be of assistance to such a wonderful, worthy family."

I don't know how much Felix McKnight, the reporter, Sam, and my grandfather labored over this quote, but—surely by accident—it captures very well the ambivalence inherent in the taking and selling of the film. He never meant to create something important or great. It was just a home movie, like the dozens he had taken over thirty years. And it was just a hobby, like playing piano or fixing the sprinklers or playing pool. Suddenly, what was meant to be merely enjoyable turned out to be "significant" and, as a result, valuable. Using passive and slightly euphemistic language ("the revenue that has been offered"), the group no doubt hoped to deflect accusations of greed or profiteering. In contrast, the line that sounds the most true to me is this: "It is the saddest moment in my life." Far from exulting in his financial windfall, Abe would always associate the moment with grief.

Perhaps editors were especially in need of a piece of positive news to brighten the heartbreaking coverage of the president's death; otherwise, it is hard to explain why this small tidbit was picked up and distributed as widely as it was, especially since the pictures had not been published yet and few people realized what they showed or how important they would turn out to be. But the article appeared not only in Dallas and throughout Texas but also in small and large newspapers all over the country and abroad, and then the story was broadcast to millions over the radio around the world. Among the many articles, the *Chicago Sun-Times* may have summed it up best: "Abraham Zapruder, the Dallas garment manufacturer, won the nation's heart—and helped regain some of Dallas' lost prestige—with his $25,000 donation to the widow of the slain Dallas policeman J. D. Tippit."

Within hours, telegrams began arriving addressed to Abe at his home in Dallas. The first were warm expressions of pride from friends and acquaintances. One reads, "Congratulations, Abe. LA is cheering you. We're proud to know you," and from another, "You have a heart of gold. We are proud of you." A few strangers wrote messages of thanks for restoring the pride of Dallas: "Dear Abe, you made us proud of Dallas again, what a wonderful thing to do for Mrs. Tippit."

Republican Congressman Bruce Alger, who had orchestrated the Adolphus Hotel protest against the Johnsons in 1960 that turned ugly, was quick to add his voice to the chorus, writing, "Please accept my heartfelt gratitude and appreciation for your unselfish and magnificent action toward Mrs. Tippit the widow of our valiant Dallas Police officer...You are the kind of person most representative of our city, of the great people who have made our community what it is, a truly American community motivated by the God-given attitude of neighborliness and love for our fellow-man." Little could Bruce Alger have imagined how much the Zapruder family despised him and everything he stood for.

Over the next several weeks, the letters poured in from across the United States and around the world. They came in the form of handwritten letters, notes jotted on printed cards, and letters typed on business stationery and airmail paper. They came from nearly every state in the Union, from a Denver housewife and a Florida truck driver, from a private investigator in Chicago and a Boy Scout in Illinois, a chapter regent of the Daughters of the American Revolution, an El Paso turf farmer and a scholar from the Library of Living Philosophers in Chicago, from an entire fourth-grade class at a Catholic school, and a young boy who wrote simply, "Thank you for being nice to the police-widow." There are letters from high-ranking members of the military, including a chief master sergeant in the air force and a brigadier general in the army, and from a navy officer stationed abroad. A few letters were anonymous.

There are letters from mayors and congressmen, from bankers and businessmen, including prominent Dallas leaders like Stanley Marcus (of Neiman Marcus fame), and a great many from people in the garment industry in New York who knew Abe personally and who wrote very touching letters expressing pride that one of their own had done something so fine. "Dear Mr. Zapruder," one began, "you are the nicest thing to happen to the garment industry since Adam and Eve grabbed their first fig leaves." There are letters from Jewish organizations and individuals expressing hope that this action might counteract the embarrassment of Jack (Rubenstein) Ruby's act of vigilante justice in the murder of Oswald. Letters came from Hawaii, Costa Rica, Germany, Austria, Australia, Canada, England, Japan, and the Philippines. They were mostly written in English, though there are a handful in German and at least two in Yiddish. Many were addressed simply to Abraham Zapruder, Garment Manufacturer, Dallas, TX, and were delivered with no street address and no zip code. One envelope reads, "Abraham Zapruder, Philanthropist," and another one, "Mr. Zapruder, the hero of the Kennedy Film." In one, a note is scrawled on the envelope, reading "Please to own hands!"

Nearly all expressed their deep sense of loss and grief for President Kennedy, their sorrow for Mrs. Kennedy, and their compassion for Mrs. Tippit and her children. And nearly all expressed admiration and good wishes to Abe and his family. A man from St. Petersburg, Florida, wrote: "Thank God there are Americans like you... In the eyes of the millions who have read and heard about your kindness to the Tippit family, you stand taller than the tallest Texan; your heart is larger than all Texas. May you and your children and children's children to the end of time enjoy God's blessings."

But inasmuch as many wrote to thank him for his donation, a much deeper chord ran through them, too. President Kennedy's assassination and its immediate aftermath had shattered something in America, leaving people vulnerable, insecure, and afraid. Many wrote to thank him not only for doing something kind for Mrs. Tippit but also for restoring their faith in the basic decency of people, for reminding them that there were still good people out there, for reassuring them that the world was not completely off its orbit.

Inevitably, there were letters that didn't fit the general mold. A few wrote to plead for money or to ask for a job or, in the case of a six-page handwritten letter from the psychiatric ward at Parkland Hospital, to unburden a troubled mind and to beg for help of an uncertain nature. One writer hoped that the film would finally restore 8mm to what he felt was its rightful place among filmmakers. And one anonymous woman wrote:

> I wonder what is the matter with people like you. Mrs. Tippit is receiving all kinds of help. My husband contributed to a fund for her at his company. But in your _flashy_ show of generosity, did you stop to think of the other widow of two small children left by this terrible tragedy? Mr. Kennedy was a fine president and I judge a wonderful man. I'm sure Mr. Tippit was equally well thought of. But it wasn't the saddest day of my life and I doubt if it was of yours...Again I say, your generosity was only for show. God help you.
>
> Signed, A Reader.

Nearly a decade after my grandfather died, my grandmother hired a friend to organize the letters alphabetically by the state each came from and to carefully preserve them in albums. She also had three bound books put together of newspaper clippings related to the film, which barely scratch the surface of the media coverage of the film over the decades. Each album opens with a heading written in black calligraphy: "Compiled by Lillian Zapruder in loving memory of Abraham Zapruder for their children and grandchildren." We are all listed by name—the small band of eleven who were the original heirs to the complicated legacy of the Zapruder film.

Throughout my childhood, the albums sat in my grandmother's living room. From time to time, when we were visiting Dallas, I would choose one to take in my lap so I could look through it. Each time, I remember being a little confused. I always expected the letters to be about the film—thanking my grandfather, perhaps, for capturing the moment on film, or expressing awe, amazement, or admiration that he did—but they weren't. They weren't really about the assassination at all. I suppose that, as a child, there were a few too many steps to follow from the death of the president to the taking of the film, the sale of the film to *LIFE*, the donation to Mrs. Tippit, and the letters themselves. So, in the perfect logic of my young mind, they seemed to totally miss the point.

I forgot about the letters until I started working on this book. For decades after my grandmother's death, they sat in a closet in the guest room in my aunt's home in Dallas, together with boxes of family papers and files, old photo albums, and an exact replica of the Bell and Howell Director Series Zoomatic camera Abe had used to shoot the film. For a few years, while the idea to write this book percolated in my mind, I would go into the closet in my aunt's house whenever I visited her. I remember the feeling of standing there, with the albums glaring at me on the left, willing me to finally pay attention to them. The camera sat just above them.

There were drawers with old photos and files and papers. There were also more benign closet inhabitants—suitcases, framed pictures, clothes—mingling with the neglected history of our family.

One year, for reasons that I don't recall, I finally took out one of the albums and sat down with it on the bed. I let my eyes run over the pages, not trying too hard to absorb anything but just taking in the overall feeling of the letters. And almost immediately, I noticed something that triggered a vague memory, an old but familiar sense of confusion and discomfort. I read a little more closely. In a good many of the letters, though not all of them, I could see that the writers were under the impression that my grandfather had donated *all* the money he received from *LIFE* magazine to the Tippit family. For this act of selfless generosity, the letter writers praised him as a hero and thanked him for redeeming humanity for the evil that took President Kennedy's life. On and on the letters went, one after the other. I remember turning the pages and feeling a little flutter of unrest, a feeling that something wasn't right. He hadn't given away all the money. I knew that. He had sold the film for $150,000. He gave away the first $25,000 and kept the rest.

This was confusing. Why did they think he gave away all the money? Would they have been equally moved to write if they had known that he had given away only a part of it? I had always thought of my grandfather's gesture toward Mrs. Tippit as a truly generous one—it never occurred to me that he had fallen short in any way. And, in absolute terms, he hadn't. But somehow, the letters seemed to define what the gesture should have been, setting the bar higher than it was and making anything less seem, well, less. If it felt that way to me, did it feel that way to him? I imagine him opening the letters and reading them, so many of them expressing admiration for something he hadn't quite done. If the donation was meant, in part, to ease his discomfort and shame about making money from the sale of the film, did this confusion just add a different kind of sting to the whole episode? I closed the album and sat for a long time on the bed. Here I was, reading these letters, thinking these thoughts, and my grandfather wasn't here to explain how it happened or answer my questions himself. I remember thinking that this was exactly the kind of conversation I was not sure I wanted to have with myself, let alone with anyone else.

Years later, when I interviewed my aunt, I asked her about this. She was characteristically frank. "It was always rather uncomfortable," she said. "We received [letters] from all over the world commending my dad for giving the money to Mrs. Tippit, and it was obvious that people thought that was all he received." It wasn't until I was going through Sam Passman's legal files and I came upon the full statement written by Texas journalist Felix McKnight for distribution via the Associated Press that I was able to trace the confusion to its origins. The statement is both scrupulously honest and ambiguous at the same time. It reads: "Mr. Abraham Zapruder, Dallas garment manufacturer, gave the Times Herald a $25,000 commitment to the surging Dallas Policemen's and Firemen's Welfare Fund. It represented payment he had received for publication rights to the historic film." Looking back at the original AP article about the donation, I found the subtle but significant change. It read: "A man who received $25,000 for his color movie films of President John F. Kennedy's assassination gave that entire sum Wednesday to the widow and children of Police Patrolman J. D. Tippit, slain by the man accused as the assassin of the President." But where had "that entire sum" come from? It didn't say that anywhere in the original statement. Then again, it did say that the $25,000 "represented payment" for the film, and since the statement didn't address the overall purchase price, it was an easy enough mistake to make. In fact, Abe had specifically asked *LIFE* not to disclose the purchase price of the film, a request they honored for the entire time they owned it. As a result, there was much speculation—ranging from $40,000 to $500,000—regarding its cost.

What Abe soon found was that, best intentions notwithstanding, no one can control how the media communicates a story and what the public eventually understands. Articles reporting that he had donated all the money from *LIFE* appeared in newspapers across the country, including the *New York Times*, the *New York Daily News*, the *Kansas City Star*, the *Denver Post*, and the *Rocky Mountain News*, to name just a few. The Baton Rouge *Morning Advocate* published a laudatory editorial titled "Abraham Zapruder's Fine Gesture." Clearly, Abe, Sam, and Felix wanted to publicize the donation in hopes of deflecting negative attention from the uncomfortable details of his deal with *LIFE* magazine. That had worked. But if the media mercifully did not characterize him as a profiteering Jew, they turned him instead into a selfless hero who redeemed humanity for the evil of President Kennedy's murder by giving away the money he earned from the sale of the film to the bereaved young widow.

Under these circumstances, this round of media attention—focused not on the assassination but on his donation—exacerbated the conflicted feelings he already had. His ambivalence comes through in a few articles that survive from the time. One from the *Houston Chronicle* is titled "Generosity Forces Gentle Abe Into Hiding." In another widely syndicated Associated Press article from November 30, picked up by the *Reading Eagle*: "Garment manufacturer Abraham Zapruder doesn't want to talk any more about the $25,000 he gave to the family of slain policeman J. D. Tippit. He donated the money from the sale of his motion pictures of President Kennedy's assassination. Zapruder, an amateur photographer, is taking no telephone calls and giving no information about the sale of the film or the gift, his wife said yesterday."

In late December 1963, when my grandparents tried to escape Dallas for a few days in Miami, a reporter even found him there. The headline reads, "He's Sorry He Filmed Assassination." It's clear from the article that Abe resisted every aspect of the interview. "He doesn't like to talk about it," the reporter wrote, pressing on. "His conversation is hesitant, halting. He spoke reluctantly Friday in Room 704, at the Americana Hotel, his bare feet stuck under the bedspread." According to the article, he refused to discuss the gift to Mrs. Tippit, and the reporter repeats the claim that his $25,000 donation was the full amount of his payment from *LIFE*. I can imagine that at this point, after those news clippings and broadcasts and the hundreds of letters, it was difficult, if not emotionally impossible, to correct the record. When asked about shooting the film, Abe said, "There was no reason, no logic, no plan. I was just there. An amateur. I wish I wasn't."

For the rest of his life, Lil respected Abe's wish to avoid talking about the assassination, the donation, and everything connected to it. After he died, however, it would be another story. She was fiercely proud of him—as she was of everyone in her family—and she made sure to attend to his memory and legacy for the benefit of posterity.

Nana from Texas—as my brothers and I called her—was a force of nature. To this day, I cannot arrive in Dallas without looking for her as I get off the plane. She would hover at the gate, peering down the ramp, impatient for the first sight of us. She had short, thick, bright-white hair and a wide smile with a gap between her front teeth. If it was winter, she would be wrapped in a black cape and fur hat; if it was summer, her face would be framed by giant white-rimmed glasses; in any season, she wore huge gold earrings and bracelets clattering on her wrists. She smelled like powder and her jubilant, joyful laugh bubbled up from somewhere deep inside her, her boundless love for us spilling out all over the place. As we rounded the corridor, she would start waving and calling to us—as if she could possibly be missed. When we finally made contact, she would smother us in hugs, wonder over how we'd grown, rejoicing at being with us and lamenting that we didn't live in Dallas all in the same breath. If possible, she would immediately begin feeding us homemade rugelach or strudel or chocolate turtles or whatever she had packed in her bag to bring to the airport.

She hadn't finished high school and she wasn't cerebral like Abe, but she was practical and street smart. I vividly remember playing Trivial Pursuit on vacation with my cousins and brothers, and there she was, yelling out all the right answers from the kitchen to our great exasperation. She was shamelessly proud of her family and utterly devoted to her husband, children, and grandchildren. Once, when my older brother, Matthew, told her that he had bantered with a college friend about whose grandmother made the best chopped liver, she convinced her sweet, gentle younger brother, Morris, to drive her from New York to Amherst College in Massachusetts for the sole purpose of bringing Matthew a batch. She stayed just long enough to drop off the plastic container and to tell everyone in his dorm how lucky they were to live with him.

She was brazenly confident, almost fearless, in many areas of her life. No sooner did she move with my grandfather to Dallas, knowing no one, than she taught herself mah-jongg and bridge and proceeded to beat everyone who played with her. One summer, when she was visiting us in Martha's Vineyard, she decided to make her homemade challah for Friday night. Then, on a whim, she decided to enter it in the bread-baking competition at the State Fair. Who even heard of challah in the Protestant bastion of Martha's Vineyard? Naturally, she brought home the blue ribbon.

There was, of course, a darker side to her personality—she could be overbearing and strong-willed, trying the patience of her more reserved loved ones. I was the last of her grandchildren, and the only girl, so I never saw any of her faults. I only cared that I got to sleep in her bed with her when we visited, sit on the toilet watching her put on her makeup while she offered detailed tutorials on how to apply powder and mascara, and rummage around in her jewelry box to play with her gold bangles, long strands of pearls, and diamond-studded pins.

As strong-minded as she was, the quotes she gave news reporters on behalf of her husband show both her pride in him and her deference to his wish for discretion. "It's embarrassing but it's also wonderful," Lil is quoted as saying. "We didn't want publicity and we want none now. He's a wonderful man but he just doesn't want to talk to anyone." It follows, then, that if Abe wanted to ignore the hundreds of admiring letters he received after the assassination, she would not push him. But she certainly was not going to even tacitly endorse the idea that he should be *ashamed* of his gift to Mrs. Tippit.

After he died, she made sure that his family would know exactly who Abe Zapruder really was and how generous he had been by making the letters accessible and visible. And when it came time to decide on the albums in which she would display the letters, did she choose discreet black leather for the cover, or an understated navy? Perhaps a traditional dark red, like the books my mother used for our family photos? No. She had them bound in the brightest, loudest golden yellow she could find, a color that shamelessly called attention to itself and would not be ignored.

The letters—in Abe's conflicted hands, then bound and given pride of place in Lil's apartment, and then stored away in Myrna's closet—seem to reflect all the contradictory feelings that the film evoked in our family from the very beginning. As I sifted through them as an adult, I came upon one letter that seemed to simplify the matter beautifully. I dearly hope my grandfather read it and remembered these words. "Dear Mr. Zapruder," the stranger wrote, "I do not know how much you received for your film…but I want to add my voice to the voices of countless Americans who say, 'God bless you, and thank you for your great gesture in making this gift.' Acts such as yours reaffirm our faith in the inherent goodness of human nature. It would have been terribly easy to keep all that money."

CHAPTER 5

■■■■■■■

IMAGES IN PRINT

One day in early March 2013, I walked the short half block from my cousin Joanne's apartment in midtown Manhattan to Sixth Avenue and down to Fiftieth Street, where the iconic art deco Radio City Music Hall sits on the corner. It was the perfect morning for a walk: The city streets were just waking up and my boots hit the pavement in the satisfying, rhythmic way they seem to do only in New York City. I waited at the light, Radio City behind me, briefly remembering my parents taking me to see the Rockettes when I was a kid, and looked across the Avenue of the Americas to the broad sweeping plaza that lies in front of the towering forty-eight-story Time & Life Building. As I crossed the plaza and entered the building, I did not realize that I was retracing the steps that my grandfather and father had taken in 1968 and that my grandmother and father took again a few years after that. I was greeted warmly by my friend Ali Zelenko, who was then senior vice president of communications for Time Inc. We went immediately to meet a small group of editors who were putting together a *LIFE* book on the Kennedy assassination for which I was going to contribute an essay. At the end of the following day I was due to meet the legendary Dick Stolley for the first time. But before that, I had two days to go through the Zapruder film records in the *LIFE* archives.

Bill Hooper, the chief archivist of the Time Inc. archives, which contain more than six million items and have rightly been called "America's attic," is slim, with close-cropped gray hair, a subtle white goatee, round tortoiseshell glasses, and a bow tie. He is soft-spoken and gentle, and when he smiles, which is often, his mouth turns down in a wry, knowing way. He was, like everyone I met at *LIFE* that day and since, warmly welcoming to me, treating me with a sort of familial kindness and deference that I had neither expected nor particularly understood until later. I have done a lot of research in a lot of archives. Usually, there's a kind of businesslike formality, even in institutions with the friendliest and most helpful archivists. The work is essentially contractual—you are there to see something and they are there to provide it for you. It was nothing like that at *LIFE*. For me, it was less like doing research in an archive than it was like showing up at the home of a long-lost relative who's been saving a lot of stuff for you and wondering when you'd take an interest and turn up. After all, *LIFE* was the guardian of the Zapruder film for its first twelve years and weathered its own share of media, legal, and public firestorms because of it. The film is an important part of *LIFE*'s history and its identity, and it exists on the cellular level in the cultural memory of the institution. Those who were there at the time, and those who are knowledgeable about the Kennedy years and the assassination coverage, show an attachment—almost an affection—for the film that is difficult to describe. So when I arrived, it was as if that familiarity and affection were extended to me, as if I was already part of the family somehow. For my part, as with so much related to the film and the research for this book, I was a little late to the party, finding myself catching up and backfilling my confused impressions and questions with information after the fact.

Bill set me up in an office and left me with a few gray archival boxes packed with hundreds of documents, some typed on bright blue and pink memo paper, others on pages yellowing with age—handwritten notes, clippings, and letters. As I opened the first box and pulled out a stack of pages, I was vaguely aware that these papers had been sitting in boxes for many decades and that they were private to *LIFE* magazine in exactly the way that our family papers are private to us. I couldn't help but feel like I was getting away with something.

For the next two days, I sat poring over the hundreds of pages, compulsively snapping photos of the documents even though Bill had made it clear to me that his office would provide copies of anything I wanted. Somehow it seemed hard to believe—like the papers might vanish if I let them out of my sight. As I read, I began to see the narrative of the film's life at *LIFE* unfold: the early elation at having acquired it, the immediate problems of how to use it, the public responses to it, the growing frenzy to see it, and the internal pressure at *LIFE* to respond to that curiosity and still maintain the institutional values that defined the magazine.

There were letters between my grandfather and *LIFE*'s director of photography, Dick Pollard, who had the primary responsibility of dealing with the film and whom I never met because he died many years before I began this work. Then came the documents about the bootleg copies, the articles about unauthorized use, the lawsuits, and the headaches. Some of the documents referred to larger historical events that I knew about—like the Josiah Thompson/Bernard Geis lawsuit, the 1967 Clay Shaw trial in New Orleans, and the first showing of the film on Geraldo's program *Good Night America* in 1975.

But in between, there was a deep connective tissue of memos and letters that formed a much more nuanced and complicated story of how the editors at *LIFE* had tried to deal with this object and the unprecedented problems it posed. This was what I wanted to know. After all, what *LIFE* did or didn't do was a chapter in the story that lay between my grandfather's experience over the weekend of the assassination and my father's after 1975, when the film came back to our family. In the strange, disembodied way of such things with the Zapruder film, the documents told a story that was integral to ours, even though we had not controlled it, had little to do with it, and knew almost nothing about it.

On the second afternoon, I was talking logistics with Bill. I was flagging the pages I wanted to have copied—essentially everything—and I was trying to figure out if I was being entirely unrealistic in my request. Also, I suspected that the *LIFE* records had been sealed until this time, but I wasn't entirely sure. Was I really the first outsider to gain access to them? In my most casual manner, I asked Bill if other researchers had gone through these records before. He looked at me quizzically for a moment. Then he said, "No." I nodded and didn't say anything. I remember it as a long moment, in which I understood that something big was happening but I didn't understand why and I couldn't bring myself to ask. On some level, I think I felt that if I called too much attention to it, the spell would be broken. When he left, I kept snapping photos. Just in case.

*　　*　　*

One of the first things that becomes clear in the *LIFE* records is that while Abe was coping with the emotional aftermath of the assassination and his sudden exposure in the public eye, the practical burden of responsibility for the film had shifted to the executives and editors at *LIFE* magazine. The November 29 edition of *LIFE* covering the death of President Kennedy appeared on newsstands on Tuesday, November 26. The cover showed a somber black-bordered portrait of JFK, chin perched thoughtfully in one hand, his green-hazel eyes looking off into the distance, the slightest smile playing around his lips. The editors replaced the traditional red of the *LIFE* logo with black. The issue opens with a letter from George Hunt, managing editor of *LIFE*, and an editorial mourning the president's shocking and untimely death. The assassination coverage is tucked between the regular pages of the magazine, which included an article about the comeback of the Tarzan series in paperback, the use of teepees in fighting fires, and the second article in a series titled "Negro in the North." There are also ads touting the conveniences of the long-distance telephone ("Try it yourself and see"), the GE Mobile Maid dishwasher ("Give her more time with you and the family") and Winston cigarettes ("Winston tastes good like a cigarette should!"). Just in case there was a temptation to read the coverage through twenty-first-century eyes, the ads and articles situate me back in a time when cigarettes didn't kill and long-distance calls were a novelty and we still used the word "Negro."

The assassination segment begins with a full-page photo of radiant Jackie in her pink suit, her arms full of red roses, with the president beside her, just after disembarking from Air Force One at Love Field in Dallas. This is how they looked when my aunt saw them from behind the chain-link fence—what would turn out to be the last perfect moment. Turning the page, the reader encounters a series of small, somewhat grainy black-and-white photos. The images are hard to make out at first, but after a while the events come into focus and the story of the president's death unfolds across the pages. Abe is not mentioned by name; instead, a text box titled SPLIT-SECOND SEQUENCE AS THE BULLETS STRUCK captions the events shown in the images. The editors had chosen to omit the gruesome sequence of the final shot to the president's head. Nevertheless, it is clear that the president is alive in the first frames, then he is in distress, and by the time the eye reaches the last frames on the page, he is slumped over toward his wife. Turning the page again, the second spread shows Jackie crawling out of the back of the open car and on to the trunk, where, in a huge black-and-white image, she is clearly seen reaching forward as Secret Service agent Clint Hill leaps on to the back bumper. One can barely make out the lifeless body of the president in contrast to Jackie's frantic and confusing scramble, which seems to capture not only the panic of the moment but also the collapse of all sense and order in the world.

The assassination sequence is followed by the now famous photo of a woman in New York with her mouth open in horror as she absorbs the news, as well as pages showing the swearing-in of Lyndon Johnson aboard Air Force One with a stricken Jackie by his side, the president's body being returned to the White House, and global reaction to the news of the assassination. The issue ends with a somber piece by Theodore White and an extraordinary series of photos of the young president and his family in happy times, ending with an almost unbearable image of his slender, youthful figure walking on the dunes, his back to the viewer.

No one at *LIFE* or anywhere else could have been fully prepared for the public response to this issue of the magazine. On the first morning that the magazine hit newsstands, the sales office wrote to C. D. Jackson: "The situation here is incredible as far as sales have gone—they were sold the very first morning. We have been deluged by calls. Last night, a TV station spoke for about three minutes on the subject of *LIFE*'s coverage and the film strip." The frenzy to get newsstand copies rose in the following days; internal memos from *LIFE* report copies being scalped for a dollar, and then within days, for ten dollars, and on December 2, a Los Angeles distributor of *LIFE* reported that "five dollar bids for the Kennedy issue are common as dirt, and now the $15 bids are coming in." This for a magazine that normally sold for twenty-five cents.

The following week's issue covered the president's funeral and included the now iconic images of Mrs. Kennedy, veiled in black, walking stoically down Pennsylvania Avenue between the president's grieving brothers, and three-year-old John in his short coat saluting his father's casket. Amid the onslaught of visual images that helped shape the public story of those days, the film took its place in the collective narrative of the assassination.

The *LIFE* offices were flooded with letters requesting copies of the magazine and reprints of the cover photograph of the president, or offering heartfelt words of praise and gratitude for the magazine. One writer wrote: "Amongst all the posthumous tributes, dedications and memorials...you, gentlemen, have succeeded beyond expectations in creating a literary shrine of our times, in honor of our late President." Of the hundreds of letters, almost none mentioned the film. This is an important reminder of a fact that is easily lost in retrospect: The film was but one small element in the vast, overwhelming coverage of the president's death. In later years, as the grief for the president waned and questions remained about his death, the film would grow and change in significance until it would become almost one with the assassination itself. But that was a long way off. In the weeks immediately after the president's death, coverage of the Zapruder film in *LIFE* was not privileged; to the contrary, its still frames simply took their place alongside the many confounding and emotionally bruising images to surface from the assassination, the aftermath, and the funeral.

The colossal demand for the assassination and funeral editions of *LIFE* could not be met. The initial print run sold out instantly. People started calling the New York office in such large numbers that the sales office set up a telephone crew to answer the phones around the clock over the Thanksgiving weekend. They logged 4,500 calls. Subscribers complained that their copies were being stolen, while the prices for scalped copies continued to rise. Within days, editors and others at *LIFE* began talking about putting together a memorial edition of the magazine that would combine the assassination and funeral coverage and would include additional material. A memo from the Chicago office read: "We know the New York office is dragging. The Chicago bureau volunteers to come in overnight and feed you folks Benzedrine—or do something even more useful—on behalf of a JFK Memorial book. We'll bring the turkey." Richard Stolley weighed in two days later: "We would, I think, be doing a great service, not only in terms of our economics, but in this case, more importantly, in terms of preserving the image of a slain president. People want to know, read, see, feel right now…All have said they hope a book is done and that it is published fast for the preservation of memories of a fine man in themselves and even more poignantly in their children. I join them in urging: Let's do it. And fast."

Work began on the memorial edition. In addition to combining the two previous issues, some of the coverage was to be expanded and some features added, but all advertisements were to be removed. In this context, the question arose of whether to print the film's images in color and whether to include frame 313, later hideously and all too casually referred to as the "head shot." I might not have known that there was an internal debate but for the fact that Bernard Quint, art director at *LIFE*, wrote an impassioned memo to George Hunt on November 26, just after seeing the film for the first time. He began by noting that the black-and-white images in *LIFE* omitted the frames that showed the "shot which took away part of Kennedy's head and left him a bloody mess, and also showed part of his head and brain flying through the air." He had heard that the editors were considering using that sequence of images in color. The following paragraphs in his memo echo Abe's fears and presage the later conflicts that would arise over the use of the film. "It seems to me that this must surely involve an element of propriety and good taste and the reputation of *LIFE* and its editors. I can't see how revealing any of the morbid details in color could serve any scientific or educational purpose... If we have anything to add to police knowledge, then it is a matter for the police and not the public. I am firmly convinced that the momentary opportunism displayed in the use of these details in color will be to our everlasting discredit." So strongly did Quint feel about this issue that he threatened to leave the magazine over it, stating: "I could not permit my name to remain associated in any way with *LIFE* magazine and I would be forced to resign and to state so publicly."

I don't know who might have been on the other side of the debate and what their argument might have been, because there is nothing further in the *LIFE* files on the subject. In the end, the editors chose to publish nine frames in the memorial edition, each of which is large in scale and printed in rich, saturated color. They excluded the images that showed the bullet's impact and the moment of the president's death. Even without them, the images tell the shocking, devastating story in a way that the small black-and-white frames could not. In lieu of the most graphic frames, the editors chose a frame showing the first lady leaning toward her husband, clearly trying to help, and in the next frame, a part of his gray suit is just visible in front of her as she rises from her seat, turning toward the back of the limousine, her elbow braced against the backseat, her hair swinging over her face. The resolution is much higher than in the November 29 issue, revealing much more detail, and the composition is intensely compelling—the grassy green backdrop, the shiny black car reflecting the light, the pink of the first lady's suit, Mrs. Connally's bright yellow roses, and the small American flag fluttering helplessly in the wind. It is no wonder that the millions of people who saw these images absorbed them as their own personal memory of the assassination, and that so many later believed they had seen the film on television that weekend, and not just the color stills in *LIFE*.

In the flood of mail that *LIFE* received about the memorial edition, I did not see any letters explicitly protesting the use of the images in color. But *LIFE* was prepared just in case, crafting a careful response in defense of both the purchase of the film and the publication of its images:

> We are concerned by your reaction to LIFE's purchase and publication of the pictures of President Kennedy's assassination and by your distress... The tragic death of President Kennedy will bring painful memories to all of us who have lived through it. But we feel the event—in its totality—is inescapably a part

of our history. As editors of LIFE, our assignment and duty is to report this history as it is and as it happens, however painful and terrible it may be. And for this reason, we gave the most complete coverage we could to the events of November 22nd and the sorrow-filled days that followed.

The letter goes on to mention Abe's donation to Mrs. Tippit and informs the reader that Mrs. Kennedy, Robert Kennedy, and other members of the family "warmly admired and appreciated" the issue.

It's worth noting that the internal memos from the *LIFE* archives clearly show that the staff viewed the publication of the memorial edition as a public service and the fulfillment of their responsibility not only to their subscribers and readers who could not get the previous two issues but also to the nation. As George Hunt put it, "It fell to LIFE to do what LIFE has always done best; to bring memorable events into sharp focus; to show with force and clarity the faces and hearts of people caught up in the news; to paint with swift, broad strokes the look and feel of the events that will stand for many years as a permanent record of the day, to make all who shared in it agree, this week or a decade from now, 'yes, that's how it was.'" To this end, *LIFE* did not seek to make a profit from the memorial edition. They sold it nearly at cost, for fifty cents, and when it nevertheless made a profit, they donated all proceeds to the Kennedy Library. A beautiful, hand-signed letter from Mrs. Kennedy remains in the archives. "Your memorial issue was an appropriate tribute to President Kennedy and the desire of so many people to have a copy was another touching tribute to him," she wrote. "I am most grateful that you gave the proceeds to the cause that is closest to my heart—his Library."

*　　*　　*

At the same time that the editors of *LIFE* were looking at the film to decide how and what to publish for the edification of the public, the federal government was organizing itself to begin an inquiry into the assassination of the president, which would necessitate scrutiny of the film as evidence in the murder. The life of the Zapruder film was, from the beginning, splintered in this way—viewed and used by different segments of society for their own purposes, sometimes alongside and sometimes in direct conflict with each other.

President Lyndon Johnson established the President's Commission on the Assassination of President Kennedy on November 29, appointing seven members with Chief Justice Earl Warren as chairman. The Secret Service and the FBI had already put forward the theory that Lee Harvey Oswald had fired all three shots from the sixth-floor window of the Texas School Book Depository and had been the sole assassin. In the lengthy reports they compiled from the early days of the investigation, these agencies postulated that the first shot had hit President Kennedy in the back of the neck; the second hit Governor Connally; and the third caused the fatal wound to the president's head. Governor John Connally agreed with these findings based on his recollections of what happened inside the motorcade. So when the editors at *LIFE* crafted their written description of the events shown on the film images for the November 29 issue and later in the memorial issue, they held to that basic narrative.

In spite of the official explanation, many in the public wondered if the murder had been the work of a conspiracy, a possibility that seemed even more likely after Jack Ruby shot and killed Oswald just two days after the assassination. The following week, associate editor Paul Mandel wrote an article in *LIFE*, optimistically titled END TO NAGGING RUMORS: THE SIX CRITICAL SECONDS, in which he attributes the rumors to the fact that "the best evidence which could dissolve them, the contents of Oswald's mind, was now irretrievable." He went on to challenge the main arguments against the single shooter, though some of his facts are mistaken, and restated the description from the previous issue that two bullets hit the president and one hit Governor Connally. He also made the case for the use of the 8mm film of the assassination to establish a time clock of the events in question, arguing that the whole sequence took place in 6.8 seconds, enough time for Oswald to have fired three times—a mathematical contention that would be calculated and recalculated countless times in the decades to come.

Meanwhile, it appears that at some point in early December, the Secret Service in Washington enlisted the help of the CIA in analyzing the film. This part of the story turns out to be maddeningly confusing: There is scant official documentation and conflicting, sometimes unreliable testimonies from those involved, often given decades after the fact. As a result, there are wildly divergent conclusions about what happened and the implications. Trying to isolate the hard evidence and write an account based upon it is hampered by conspiracy theorists who have commingled facts and speculation to form narratives that proliferate in print and on the Internet. After getting lost in this labyrinth more times than I could count, I eventually found a guide in Richard Trask, author of *National Nightmare on Six Feet of Film: Mr. Zapruder's Home Movie and the Murder of President Kennedy*, and a measured and reliable historian of these events.

According to Trask, the likely scenario is as follows: As we know, the Secret Service had flown Copy 3 of the film from Dallas to Washington on Friday night, November 22. The agency then urgently enlisted the help of the CIA to make copies of certain frames of the film. Late on Saturday (or possibly Sunday) night, Ben Hunter and Homer McMahon, two employees of the CIA's National Photographic Interpretation Center (NPIC), were called in to the lab. The NPIC was a little-known office charged with solving national intelligence problems by using photo interpretation and imagery analysis. Since the lab had the necessary state-of-the-art enlarging equipment, Hunter and McMahon were put to work making enlargements of the film, a task that was described as "above top secret." Trask, who gleaned this information from careful scrutiny of interviews conducted in the 1990s with Hunter and McMahon, described the technical process: "The work done on the film was accomplished using the special '10-20-40 processing enlarger' with a full-immersion 'wet-gate' used to create internegative prints forty times the original size. These internegatives were then utilized to produce multiple color prints of selected frames."

It's not clear what, if anything, the Secret Service did with these reproductions of the film until early December, when they—again in conjunction with the CIA and NPIC—seem to have analyzed the film more thoroughly. Nearly nothing was known about the NPIC handling of the Zapruder film until the midseventies, when first-generation assassination researcher Paul Hoch came across CIA Document 450 among other materials he had received in response to a Freedom of Information Act request. This record confirms that the NPIC analysis took place and establishes that two sets of four large briefing boards with enlargements of the film were created, though the document does not state when or by whom. Much later, NPIC photo analyst Dino Brugioni would state that he made two of these briefing boards, although it appears that his memory of the timing and other details was not accurate.

In Document 450, there is a prominent reference to *LIFE*'s report that Abe's camera was running at 18 frames per second—an important fact for establishing a time clock of the assassination. This information had first appeared in Paul Mandel's December 6 *LIFE* magazine article, which makes it even more likely that the in-depth analysis of the film at NPIC happened several weeks after the assassination. As Trask suggests, it seems that Hunter and McMahon's efforts to create enlargements of the film took place urgently, over the weekend of the assassination, so that the Secret Service and CIA could clearly see the images on the film. Then, weeks later, amid rising questions about whether the early FBI and Secret Service accounts of the assassination were correct, the CIA and NPIC undertook a more comprehensive analysis of the enlargements from the film in order to try to establish the timing and impact of the shots fired at the motorcade.

Who cares when it happened? After all, a report of two security agencies working together to glean as much information as they could about the president's assassination seems innocuous enough. But don't be fooled. Decades later, this link between the film and the CIA would become fodder for elaborate conspiracy theories whose proof, in many cases, rested on very different readings of the testimonies provided by these aging former NPIC personnel.

At approximately the same time, in early December, the Warren Commission requested access to a copy of the Zapruder film from *LIFE* magazine. In the simplest of terms, their main focus in examining the film was to try to determine, in the words of assistant counsel Howard Willens, "which of the bullets hit whom and when." To this end, general manager Art Keylor at *LIFE* had a copy of the film couriered to Washington, DC, on December 10 for their use. That same day, Keylor sent the original film to his colleague, senior editor John Jenkisson, with a cover memo: "Here is the original of the Zapruder assassination film for salting away in a vault. Because of the hazard of damaging the film, this one should not be used for projection."

Within a month, Keylor wrote another memo expressing the first concerns about the film prints and how they were being circulated. It was just the beginning of an issue that would preoccupy *LIFE* magazine for the full term of its ownership of the film. "I think we are all agreed we ought to be careful about the prints that are in existence on the Kennedy assassination film," he wrote, going on to document the status and location of the various copies of the film. He proposed a plan to keep track of them, and, as for the copies in the possession of the federal government, he suggested that he "write a letter to the Secret Service in both Dallas and Washington and the Warren Commission officially requesting the return of the material when no further use is required by these organizations." In early February, Secret Service chief James Rowley wrote to *LIFE*'s Washington bureau chief, Henry Suydam, with his response. It was an unequivocal no. He explained that Abraham Zapruder had duplicates of the film made expressly for the "official use" of the Secret Service before he sold the original to *LIFE* and that since that deal was made after the fact, it was of no concern to the Secret Service. "Please be assured," he concluded, "that it will not be shown by us to anyone outside the Government unless for official investigative purposes. However, we consider it part of the official Secret Service file of the investigation of the assassination of President Kennedy."

Members of the commission staff, the FBI, and a photographic expert from the FBI laboratory named Lyndal Shaneyfelt examined the film seven times between January and April. At first, they worked from a second-generation copy of the film, but Shaneyfelt believed it was necessary to review the original because it would show much more detail. On February 11, Jenkisson drafted another memo, which began "Assassination film again." He had just learned that the Warren Commission planned to request access to the original film because "the FBI [was] having trouble determining the trajectories of the shots" and they thought that "a look at the original film might help." It is clear from the memo that *LIFE* was perfectly willing to help the Warren Commission; at the same time, executives were very concerned for the film's safety. It is not stated explicitly in any of the memos, but I can't help remembering those six frames of the original film that had been damaged in Chicago. The senior executives and editors at *LIFE* were among the few who understood not only how valuable and precious this film was turning out to be, but also how fragile.

Herbert Orth, assistant chief of *LIFE*'s photographic laboratory, personally brought the camera-original film from New York to Washington for the commission to review on February 25. They watched it through several times, though they did not stop to examine it for fear of damaging it. At this time, Orth offered to make 35mm transparencies of key frames of the film (frames 171–434) so that the commission could study them more thoroughly. Shaneyfelt explained how they used their duplicate copy of the film in his testimony before the commission:

In each case we would take the film and run it through regular speed, slow motion, we would stop it on individual frames and study it frame by frame, trying to see in the photographs anything that would give any indication of a shot hitting its mark, a reaction of the president, a reaction of Mr. Connally or Mrs. Connally, reaction of the Secret Service agents, reaction of people in the crowd, relating it to all the facts that we felt were important. When we obtained the slides from *LIFE* magazine, we went through those very thoroughly, because they gave so much more detail and were so much clearer.

For the Warren Commission, the film's main value was in establishing a time clock of the assassination. By determining the precise speed of the camera (how many frames elapsed per second) and correlating the timing with the visual evidence of the bullets' impacts on the president and Governor Connally, they sought to establish a reliable sequence of events, including how many bullets were fired into the car, which ones hit the president and Governor Connally, and, among other things, whether Oswald could have worked the bolt action on his Mannlicher-Carcano rifle fast enough to fire all the shots.

In addition to looking at the film, the commission needed to conduct some tests on the Bell and Howell camera, as well. It had, in fact, already been tested by the time the Warren Commission began its work. In *National Nightmare,* Trask wrote that on December 4, a local agent of the FBI got the camera from Abe to send on to Washington for testing. Sure enough, I later found the receipt for that loan amid some unsorted papers that were turned over to me by my mother and my aunt. Handwritten on yellowing lined paper, the note reads: "Received this date, from Mr. Abraham Zapruder, one Bell and Howell 8 mm movie camera (and case) which will be returned upon completion of its use to FBI." It was signed by Special Agent Robert Barrett of the FBI, the same Dallas field agent who had been assigned (and failed) to get the Secret Service copy of the film duplicated the day after the assassination.

When they were finished using it, the camera was returned to Abe (he had received a request to donate it to the Bell and Howell archives), but then the Warren Commission requested it. They wanted to check the speed of the camera when it was fully spring-loaded and as it ran down during the course of filming, to ensure that the frames-per-second rate was accurate. The testing showed that 18.3 fps was still an accurate calculation. As the commission reviewed the evidence, they saw significant problems with the initial scenario described by the FBI and the Secret Service. In Max Holland's 2014 *Newsweek* article, he neatly explains the problem:

[The commission] came to realize that the president and the governor had been wounded in such a brief time span that Oswald could not have worked the bolt action on his Mannlicher-Carcano rifle to fire two shots so quickly and accurately. Consequently, the staff theorized that there were either two shooters, or one of the bullets hit both men. The latter seemed more plausible, in part because Oswald had used military ammunition designed to pass through people. Besides, there was another insurmountable problem with the Life-FBI scenario: If a bullet, traveling at an entrance velocity of 1,900 feet per second, penetrated the president's upper back, where did it go after exiting his throat at a velocity of 1,800 feet per second? Only one other person or object in the limousine was struck by a bullet, and that was Connally.

Where, indeed, did that bullet land? If it didn't hit Connally, they argued, it would have damaged the interior of the limousine, and there was no evidence of that. Sometime in March, Arlen Specter is credited with articulating a new theory for the first time: The first bullet hit the president, passed through the back of his neck and exited his throat, and then hit Governor Connally in the back, exited his chest, shattered his wrist, and lodged itself in his thigh. The second bullet missed. The third bullet caused the fatal head wound to the president. Thus was born the "single bullet" or "magic bullet" theory, which would cause no end of controversy—and even ridicule—for decades to come.

The members of the staff were well aware that it sounded implausible at first blush. Not only that, but it directly contradicted Connally's own beliefs about what had happened; he believed that he had been struck by a second bullet and that it was not the same bullet that had hit the president. Mrs. Connally and another Secret Service agent corroborated the governor's opinion. To test the single-bullet hypothesis, the commission staff decided to reenact the assassination in situ in Dallas. In spite of resistance from the Secret Service and the FBI—who, along with other concerns, did not want their initial conclusions to be proven incorrect—the commission staff carried out this complicated and elaborate plan on a Sunday morning, May 24, 1964. Using the film as a time clock of the assassination, they proceeded with certain assumptions, namely: that a shot, which they believed was the first one, hit the president sometime between frames 210 and 225; that the governor was wounded by the same bullet; and that the final shot came at frame 313. They positioned agents in crucial locations: standing in for Oswald in his "sniper's nest," sitting in for each of the occupants of the limousine, and standing where three key photographers had stood along the motorcade route—Abe Zapruder, Orville Nix, and Marie Muchmore. They marked the spots along Elm Street that represented where the car was when the shots were fired and took into account the various landmarks that they believed would have been a factor (a large tree obstructing Oswald's view and a large freeway sign obstructing Abe's view). By the end of the day, they were satisfied that the scenario they had proposed was indeed plausible.

*   *   *

Just about two months later, on July 22, 1964, Abe walked a little less than a mile from his office at 501 Elm Street to the Post Office and Courthouse Building on North Ervay Street in downtown Dallas. It was the hottest month of the year, with the mercury climbing day after day to a blistering 99 degrees. He entered the handsome limestone building through the formal colonnaded entry and made his way to the US attorney's office, where he was met by a young staff lawyer for the Warren Commission, assistant counsel Wesley J. Liebeler. Abe had been called to give his testimony as an eyewitness, as had hundreds of others who were present on Dealey Plaza on the day of the president's assassination. Liebeler had a slightly round baby face, dark hair, and thin lips, and he wore browline glasses. From the beginning of his testimony, Abe sounds a little nervous, explaining that he had been out of town when he was summoned and that his secretary had made the appointment for him. The first part of the interview is fairly routine—there is some back-and-forth about where he was standing, and his position is established in a photograph from a series shot by Phil Willis, who was standing on the opposite side of Elm Street, but closer to Houston Street, at the time of the assassination. Then Liebeler asks him to describe how the film was taken.

> MR. ZAPRUDER: Well, as the car came in line almost—I believe it was almost in line. I was standing up here and I was shooting through a telephoto lens, which is a zoom lens. And as it reached about—I imagine it was around here—I heard the first shot and I saw the president lean over and grab himself like this (*holding his left chest area*).
>
> MR. LIEBELER: Grab himself on the front of his chest?

MR. ZAPRUDER: Right—something like that. In other words, he was sitting like this and waving and then after the shot he just went like that.

MR. LIEBELER: He was sitting upright in the car and you heard the shot and you saw the president slump over?

MR. ZAPRUDER: Leaning—leaning toward the side of Jacqueline. For a moment I thought it was, you know, like you say "Oh, he got me" when you hear a shot—you've heard these expressions—and then I saw. I don't believe the president is going to make jokes like this, but before I had a chance to organize my mind, I heard a second shot and then I saw his head opened up and the blood and everything came out and I started—I can hardly talk about it (*the witness crying*).

MR. LIEBELER: That's all right, Mr. Zapruder, would you like a drink of water? Why don't you step out and have a drink of water?

MR. ZAPRUDER: I'm sorry—I'm ashamed of myself really, but I couldn't help it.

MR. LIEBELER: Nobody should ever be ashamed of feeling that way, Mr. Zapruder. I feel the same way myself. It was a terrible thing.

After Abe composed himself, Liebeler asked him to verify various frames of the film and asked him some questions about where he thought the shots were coming from. Interestingly, he always said that he heard only two shots, even after he learned that there were, in fact, three shots fired. Liebeler also asked him where he thought the shots were coming from. At first he said that at the time he thought the shots were coming from behind him, but he almost immediately qualified his statement, saying that he wasn't sure what he heard, and given the circumstances, he had "no way of determining what direction the bullet was going." Mr. Liebeler then asked him, "Did you form any opinion about the direction from which the shots came by the sound, or were you just upset by the thing you had seen?" "No, there was too much reverberation," Abe answered. "There was an echo which gave me a sound all over. In other words, that square [Dealey Plaza] is kind of—it had a sound all over."

What I notice in my grandfather's testimony, beyond his obviously emotional state, is how hesitant and faltering his English seems to be and how careful he is to avoid making any kind of declarative statement or seeming to have any authority about what happened by virtue of having taken the film. In fact, in the very beginning, when Liebeler asked him to describe what he saw that day, Abe said, "Well, of course, what I saw you have on film." This is something that I'm told he often said. It is not that he didn't think about what had happened, or that he didn't read about the various theories and try to understand them. Apparently, he did. He knew the film well, and he understood about the camera speed, the critical frames, the time required to fire the rifle, and how all those elements related to the time clock of the assassination. In fact, according to his daughter, Myrna, he talked so much about it in the months after the assassination that there was eventually a blowup at the dinner table, when she and her husband, Myron, told him he had to stop obsessing about it. Although she deeply regretted those words in retrospect, at the time they felt that the family needed to move on and that talking about the assassination was both painful and unproductive. While it's clear now that he had been traumatized by what he had experienced, it's not surprising in the context of the era that he did not get the psychological or emotional support he needed in order to process the events and move on. Still, whatever he said within our family, he was aware that he had to be careful not to be drawn into making the case for anyone's pet theory. He was generally consistent in his accounts, even when he knew that his memory was wrong (as in the case of the two shots), and when he was unsure, he preferred to defer to the film.

Toward the end of the interview, Liebeler entered deeply uncomfortable territory. He asked Abe about what happened to the original film and the copies, and then said, "The commission is interested in one aspect of this and I would like to ask you if you would mind telling me how much they paid you for that film." Abe deflected the question, saying, "I just wonder whether I should answer it or not, because it involves a lot of things and it's not one price—it's a question of how they are going to use it, are they going to use it or are they not going to use it, so I will say I really don't know how to answer that." Of course, it really wasn't a hard question to answer—there was a figure he could have cited—but I hear the emotional truth under the deflection: It was a terribly difficult question for *him* to answer. So he didn't. Mr. Liebeler went on to say that he would not pressure Abe to answer but that the commission thought it would be helpful. I can't help but wonder why. How would the purchase price for the film have had anything at all to do with the question of who shot the president, how, when, and why?

In response to this pushback, Abe mentioned the $25,000 payment and the donation to the fund for the Tippit family. "I didn't know that—you received $25,000?" Liebeler said. "$25,000 was paid and I have given it to the Firemen's and Policemen's Fund," Abe answered.

"You gave the whole 25,000?"

"Yes. This was all over the world. I got letters from all over the world and newspapers—I mean letters from all over the world. It was all over the world—I am surprised that you don't know it—I don't like to talk about it too much."

"We appreciate your answer very much."

"I haven't done anything, the way I have given it, at a time like this."

Again, Abe's internal conflict is written all over this exchange. He wanted to avoid the question, but if pressed, he would deflect it; and if pressed further, he would make it seem that he had given away the money; but then when he was acknowledged for his generosity, he certainly wouldn't accept any praise. It is a study in emotional complexity and ethical uncertainty.

As it turned out, the commission was not prepared to let it lie. A few weeks after his testimony, in August, Abe told his attorney, Sam Passman, that Mr. Liebeler had called him wanting more information about the sale of the film to *LIFE* magazine. Sam advised him to tell the commission attorney that it was a private matter and he did not want publicity about it. In an internal memo that Sam wrote to the file, he noted: "Mr. Liebeler indicated that he might take additional depositions but we'll just have to take that risk. Of course, Liebeler could get this information from *LIFE* magazine, if he wanted to, but maybe we can get away with it."

A few days later, Sam wrote a longer memo to the file, after having received a call from Liebeler himself. During their phone conversation, Sam had repeatedly explained to Liebeler that "it would be very harmful to Mr. Zapruder to have this come out here" and that "it would result in some unfavorable comment here." It's clear that Sam is referring not just to a general desire to keep the financial terms of the deal private but to Abe's very real anxiety about the reactionary climate in Dallas and the possibility of an anti-Semitic response. Liebeler pressed on, pointing out that there was some confusion within the commission about how much money Abe had made on the deal and that, based on his testimony, it appeared that he had earned only $25,000. Sam pressed back, repeatedly asking what this had to do with the work of the commission and why Abe's privacy couldn't be respected.

Finally, Liebeler provided what, at least from the written memo, appears to be a confused explanation having to do with evidence being sold to people who would suppress it or fail to provide it to the authorities or use it for their own purposes. Of course, as Sam pointed out, this was not at issue in this instance, since Abe had ensured that the federal government had copies of the film before he sold it. Finally, in one last effort, Liebeler asked Sam if he would advise Abe to refuse to turn over the *LIFE* contract if the commission issued a subpoena for it. Sam noted in the file, "I replied that this would put us in a position of publicly refusing to do something which the commission requested, but asked what would be the purpose of that, as then the only purpose would be that we'd be placed in an embarrassing position of explaining publicly why we would not do it in the first place. That any type of publicity would be just as bad, one as the other, and agreed that he does have the power to harm us." Liebeler assured Sam that he did not want to embarrass them publicly and that he would take the matter under advisement. Again, Sam said that if the information were "important in any way that would help the true purpose of the commission," to please let him know. The matter was left there and the commission dropped it.

As Abe concluded his testimony for the Warren Commission, Mr. Liebeler told him how extraordinarily helpful the film had been to the work of the commission and thanked him for coming to give his testimony. "Well, I am ashamed of myself," Abe says. "I didn't know I was going to break down and for a man to—but it was a tragic thing, and when you started asking me that, and I saw the thing all over again, and it was an awful thing. I know very few people who had seen it like that—it was an awful thing and I loved the president, and to see that happen before my eyes—his head just opened up and shot down like a dog—it leaves a very, very deep sentimental impression with you; it's terrible."

In June 1964, a letter arrived in the mail at Abe's home. It was from a man named William Manchester, who had been invited by the Kennedy family to write an authorized account of the president's assassination. Abe was still reluctant to speak with anyone publicly about the assassination. Lillian recalled, "He talked to Manchester because of the Kennedys. Mrs. Kennedy okayed it. That's the reason he talked." And indeed, years later, as I was sifting through my grandfather's few remaining personal papers, I came upon not only the original letters from William Manchester but also a typed note from Jackie Kennedy's personal secretary requesting that Abe cooperate with Mr. Manchester. On the envelope is Jacqueline Kennedy's original signature. If he'd had any hesitation, this alone would have been enough to persuade him. He would never have said no to anything that Mrs. Kennedy asked him to do, no matter how remotely the request was made.

Abe's interview with William Manchester took place in September 1964. Manchester's few pages of notes still exist, and they are strangely scattered and not very satisfying. Nevertheless, in the interview, Manchester captured the basic outlines of the story that Abe had already recounted on television on the day of the assassination and again for the Warren Commission. He mentioned how much he loved Kennedy, and he told Manchester that his son was a "young lawyer" in the Justice Department. He remembered that when he got back to the office after the assassination, he kept saying, "They shot him down like a dog"—reiterating the deep impression of disgrace, humiliation, and shame that reminded him of the Russian lawlessness that he never expected to see in America. As for Dallas, he recalled an episode that captured some of the right-wing flavor of the place. "In a Dallas department store, I met a young man who was arguing with me about civil rights. He said, 'God made little people and small people and Colt made the .45 to even things out.' 'People like you we don't need,' I said." In the short two-page interview, there is one line that seems to capture the essence of his feelings: "I am not a great man," he said. "I just happened to be in the wrong place at the wrong time."

Years later, when Manchester's book came out, Abe was horrified to see himself described as "stubby" with "short legs." Lillian Rogers recalled in her interview that "Mr. Zee was furious. He was furious. So time went on, and the book laid there in the office, and it laid there, and it laid there." While I suspect that Manchester intended his brief portrait of Abe Zapruder to be comically affectionate, he portrayed him as a bit of a Jewish caricature, hapless and henpecked by his secretary. I can see why it touched a nerve, especially for our grandfather, who was self-conscious about having been an immigrant to this country and not having a proper education. Moreover, he had worked hard to establish the very opposite identity: not a greenhorn but a successful American businessman. If his reaction seems overblown, consider that it is the peril of anyone who gets unwillingly thrust into the public eye. In such moments, we risk being exposed or presented in ways that do not conform to our sense of ourselves, which is not only internally jarring and unsettling, but potentially humiliating.

How he was represented to the public remained a sensitive topic even after he died. In 1973, when my grandmother was interviewed by Richard Stolley for a piece he was writing for the tenth anniversary of the assassination, she made sure that her husband's posthumous image was protected. "Now, I understand that you're going to describe him as a short, pudgy man. He was not short and he was not pudgy," she said. Stolley laughed. My grandmother went on, "I don't want him described that way." Stolley tried to speak but she cut him off. "My husband was about five foot eight and a half, five foot nine." Stolley tried to speak again, saying only "He was—" before my grandmother stepped in once more, this time with the last word on the subject. "He was not pudgy," she said firmly. "I thought he made a nice appearance, as a matter of fact," she added, laughing a little at herself. Toward the end of the conversation, when she was thoroughly finished contradicting him on every last point, Stolley gently pointed out, "You might be slightly prejudiced, Mrs. Zapruder." And she finally agreed. "Well, yes, I think I must be because…he absolutely, honest to God, my husband was a man of integrity. I've never met anybody like him yet."

While my grandmother was there to defend not only Abe's height but also his character after he died, there was no one to correct the record when Henry was misrepresented and his character assailed far more seriously by the media decades later. It was one of the many burdens and responsibilities of dealing with the film that he quietly bore and about which he never complained. I don't know if it hurt him the way it hurt his father. He never said. But I know that it hurt me.

CHAPTER 6

■■■■■■■

MOUNTING PRESSURE

The Warren Report was published on September 24, 1964. The commission found no evidence of a conspiracy to kill the president and found that Lee Harvey Oswald alone was responsible for firing all three shots from the Texas Book Depository Building. While they concluded that one bullet hit both the president and Governor Connally and another bullet caused the president's fatal head wound, they could never firmly assert which bullet missed the motorcade, nor could they establish with absolute certainty what the time frame was for the shooting. The vagaries and inconsistencies in the report caused widespread skepticism among an already disturbed public about its accuracy and veracity.

LIFE devoted its October 2, 1964, issue to an examination of the Warren Report. On the magazine's cover, running vertically as in the original 8mm strip, were a series of images from the film in color—clearly after the president was wounded but before the fatal shot to the head. The cover remains arresting and powerful to this day. What was published on the inside was a little more complicated. As a member of the commission, Gerald Ford was invited to write an article describing its work, explaining, in the words of the editors, "how the Commission pieced together the evidence." Accompanying the article, the editors ran eight large color frames from the Zapruder film. In the initial print run, they used frame 323, taken just a half second after the fatal shot to the president's head, as image number six. In it, the viewer can clearly see the huge bloody crater on the right front of the president's head as he fell toward his wife. The caption described the president having been shot from the rear, causing a massive wound and causing his head to snap to one side. Since the wound is clearly visible in the front of his head, and there is no text explaining that entry wounds are small whereas exit wounds are much larger and more damaging, the image seemed to directly contradict the caption or vice versa. At some point during the run, the editors decided to replace this image with a different one. They broke and reset the plate—a disruptive and expensive procedure— using instead the even more controversial frame 313, in which the president's head virtually explodes. They did not change the caption. This was a confusing editorial decision, since the replacement image corresponded even less convincingly to the caption than the previous one. Finally, a third version of the issue was printed with frame 313 but with a clarifying caption that conspiracy theorists the nation over would deride. It read: "The direction from which shots came was established by this picture taken at instant bullet struck the rear of the President's head and, passing through, caused the front part of his skull to explode forward."

For the general public, most of whom were not scrutinizing each frame and questioning how closely the captions matched the images, the publication of these graphic frames touched a cultural nerve that had little to do with questions of evidentiary interpretation. While only a small sample of letters survive in the archives, they speak clearly to how jarring these images were in the context of 1964 America. One reader wrote: "The repeat printing of the motorcade photos are [sic] completely unnecessary and are extremely inconsiderate; the use of color further emphasizes your desire to sensationalize. Granted, it was important to report on the findings of the Warren Commission, but your terrible approach to bring the public's attention to your report is repulsive and uncalled for. What are you trying to prove?" Another writer chimed in: "The pictures of President Kennedy's assassination in gore color rank equally with the life-like or death-like pictures of the Ugly War in Vietnam . . . I begin to believe that we all love violence and death more than life." "I was astounded and disgusted to see the last moments of our President so exposed," wrote another reader.

The broad outlines of this argument—that decency and good taste should prevail over the public's right to knowledge—had been drawn in 1963 when Bernard Quint threatened to resign if the editors used frame 313, and the editors drafted a preemptive letter to defend their (much tamer) use of the images. But if they had previously dodged an outcry, they walked right into the thick of it this time. It is not clear whether they believed that the public was ready to see the images or if they genuinely believed that it was necessary to show them for the purposes of the report. Either way, their decision and the public response to it speak to the taboo nature of the film's images and the painful, complex way in which they would gradually make their way into the collective American psyche.

Most would agree that the film broke a social and cultural barrier not only by its violence but also because it witnessed the instant shattering of the physical person of the president, the institution of the presidency, and the image of perfection and power that the Kennedys projected. This was, of course, a modern problem, linked to technological progress and the ability to capture and share information that was previously either fleeting or socially unacceptable. For many, this was exactly why people shouldn't see it; to show it was to normalize visual images that should remain taboo, or to cross that boundary publicly and permanently. Others asked what could possibly be learned or contributed by publishing such violent pictures. Wasn't it just satisfying a voyeuristic desire to see the otherwise forbidden?

On the other side of the debate, there were those—particularly those in the media—who justified dissemination under the broader rubric of the public's "right to know." Proponents of this point of view held that what happened belonged to the world and that no federal, corporate, or private entity should decide for the public what they should or shouldn't see. Ultimately, the question was whether to cross that barrier and face the social consequences or hold back and hope to protect social norms in the process. At different times, *LIFE* did both.

For the subset of the public that was looking at the film for the clues it contained about the assassination, and comparing their own interpretations with what was written in the Warren Report, this issue of *LIFE* magazine raised a completely different set of concerns. Why had the editors printed two different images in the magazine, and why were the captions changed? Could *LIFE* be colluding with the members of the Warren Commission to deceive the public about what had happened during the assassination? After all, resetting the magazine plates was elaborate and costly. Why would they do that unless the president's head wounds in the first printed photo (frame 323) did not support the Warren Commission's assertion that the president was shot from the rear? Perhaps, the thinking went, *LIFE*'s editors were scrambling to do a sort of visual damage control during the course of the run.

I found nothing in the *LIFE* archives about this very unusual situation, but it seems certain that this was an editorial and not a political decision. From a purely practical standpoint, of course the editors wanted the images in the magazine to match the narrative of the Warren Commission; after all, they were writing an issue reporting on its findings. The problem wasn't that *LIFE* magazine had to turn itself inside out to find frames of the film that matched the Warren Commission's findings. The problem was that the film didn't clearly and unequivocally show a single narrative upon which everyone could agree. No matter which frames they used, or how they described them, or which experts they consulted, the "unimpeachable witness"—the universally agreed-upon most valuable, most meaningful, most significant film of the assassination—did not convincingly answer the fundamental question that everyone asked of it.

In November 1964, those who wanted to see more of the film got their wish. For seventy-six dollars, they could purchase the full set of twenty-six volumes of the Warren Report, including testimony, documents, and other supporting material that the commission used in their investigation. Volume 18 contained 160 images from the Zapruder film, made by *LIFE* technicians from a set of 35mm transparencies created from the camera-original film. It was far from seeing the film in motion, and it was only part of the 486 frames that compose the entire twenty-six-second sequence, but for the small and growing band of assassination researchers who were already conducting their own investigations into the president's murder—and, in many cases, compiling evidence and building a case against the findings of the government—it was certainly more useful than the select frames that had thus far appeared in *LIFE* and a handful of other publications. Richard Trask described in *National Nightmare* how "more than one researcher quickly made crude filmstrips of the printed portion of the film utilizing motion picture cameras that had the capacity for single frame exposures." He was among them. After he shot each frame from the film in the Warren Report with 8mm color Kodachrome, he wrote in the introduction to *National Nightmare*, "the result was a short, muddy and bumpy movie that crudely displayed several copies of the Zapruder film in motion!"

There had, of course, been many who suspected a conspiracy in the president's murder from the very beginning. With the publication of the Warren Report, these early critics had an extraordinary wealth of evidence to review, consider, and criticize. Ranging in temperament from contentious and aggressive to sober and methodical, they pored over every word and image in the report, scrutinizing and questioning everything from procedural problems to inconsistencies in the medical, ballistics, pictorial, and testimonial evidence.

Harold Weisberg was among these first critics. He wrote a scathing condemnation of the Warren Report, accusing the commission of deliberately covering up the evidence of a conspiracy. As part of his broader case, he focused on inconsistencies that he found in Abe's Warren Commission testimony and in the publication of the images in the Warren Report. Perhaps most significantly, he called attention to an issue that would become increasingly important over the next few years, pointing out that four frames (208–211) were missing from the sequence published in Volume 18 and that published frames 207 and 212 had visible splices running through them.

He was not the only one to have noticed this omission, and since there was no note or explanation in the report of the hearings to explain the missing frames, researchers grew suspicious. As we know now, the reality was more embarrassing than nefarious; *LIFE* had damaged those frames on the original film in Chicago during the first hours of its ownership. But this was not public knowledge at the time, and it would be several years before *LIFE* would offer an explanation. In addition, two critical frames following the mortal shot to the president's head (frames 314 and 315) were transposed. This was not helpful, given the brewing controversy over the direction in which the president's head went after the shot. In a nutshell: Forward = Book Depository, Lee Harvey Oswald, and single shooter vs. Backward = Grassy Knoll, multiple shooters, and conspiracy. Some interpreted the transposed frames as an attempt by the government to make it look like the president's head went forward instead of back, in order to support its single-shooter theory, though others felt that the mistake was so obvious that they made nothing of it.

Those who wanted to see the evidence for themselves, to pore over it and reach their own conclusions, faced a maddening paradox when it came to the Zapruder film. They believed it was impossible to fully understand what had happened without seeing it, and yet they felt repeatedly obstructed when they tried to do so. Not only that, but when it did appear, it seemed to cry out for attention with its inconsistencies and gaps. After all, why were there four key frames missing from the Warren Report with no explanation? How could an editorial error really be to blame for transposing two critical frames of the film when to show them correctly would seem to contradict the report's conclusions? And what of the multiple images and confusing captions in *LIFE*'s Warren Report issue? Seen through this prism, it's no surprise that many became very suspicious indeed.

In fact, the film was more accessible than people realized. The Warren Commission had deposited all the material from the investigation at the National Archives, which held at least one 8mm copy of the film and several sets of the 35mm color transparencies that *LIFE* had made for the commission's use. It was possible, though certainly not easy, to come to Washington and request access to the film and the transparencies for study. However, reproducing the images or showing the film on television was another story.

Another early critic of the Warren Report, and a vehement defender of Lee Harvey Oswald, was Mark Lane. He was one of many who reached out to Abe to ask him about the film. Lillian, Abe's longtime assistant, recalled that, in general, he did not want to speak with any of these researchers, concerned as he was about his words being twisted or taken out of context. "I think Lane bullied him," Lillian recalled. "Something about 'Who do you think you are, not giving any interviews?'" Abe eventually agreed to the interview, but according to Lillian, it did not go well. Lane grew frustrated when he felt he was not getting answers—or perhaps the answers he wanted—and things turned ugly. Abe accused Lane of being in it for the money, to which Lane responded, "You've made millions!" That's all Abe needed to hear to be done with *that* interview. According to Lillian, affable, mild-mannered Abe got up, grabbed Lane by the shoulder, and shoved him right out the door.

Lane published his book *Rush to Judgment* in 1966 and it quickly shot to number one on the *New York Times* best-seller list. It was very much a sign of the times, as the American public appeared more and more skeptical of the single-bullet theory and questioned the plausibility of the Warren Commission's theory. The conversation was changing, and with this change came louder and louder clamors for access to the Zapruder film.

By 1966, the Zapruder film had taken its place among assassination researchers and investigators—governmental and otherwise—as a central piece of visual evidence in the murder of the president. For the wider public, its appearance as stills in *LIFE* could be either horribly fascinating or tastelessly disrespectful. In that same year, filmmaker Michelangelo Antonioni released his first English-language movie, *Blow-Up*, to international acclaim and box-office success. Although the film was inspired by a short story by Julio Cortázar titled "Las babas del diablo" ("The Devil's Drool") from 1959, and the filmmaker never made an explicit link to the Zapruder film, it is impossible not to see in key scenes of the movie a social commentary on the questions that the film raised.

The movie is set in 1960s London and follows the story of Thomas (David Hemmings), a young high-fashion photographer whose wealth, sexual encounters, and fame leave him bored and disaffected. Walking in a park one day, he takes a series of photographs of a pair of lovers embracing; the woman (Vanessa Redgrave) protests and follows him, trying in vain to get the film back. When he develops the pictures in his studio, he thinks he notices something in the woods, in the direction of the woman's gaze. We see him from the back, looking at the photo, when he suddenly cocks his head and moves in for closer examination. Suddenly animated, he jumps up and rushes to the darkroom to develop the image in an enlarged format, focusing on the area in question, pinning the image up in his studio alongside the others. In the photograph he deciphers a man behind a fence, pointing a gun at the couple. He sees again that the woman, an anxious expression on her face, seems to be looking in the direction of the gunman. Thomas continues to develop images, pin them up, examine them, enlarge them, and pin them up again in an effort to make out what has happened. In a later image from the series he believes he sees a corpse, perhaps the woman's lover. But the more he enlarges the photographs, the more the image dissolves into abstract forms that he cannot make out. It becomes impossible to tell whether the shape is a dead body or a benign part of the landscape. He returns to the park that night and finds the dead body under a tree, but he does not tell anyone or notify the police. The next morning, when he goes again to look for the body, it is gone, and he finds that someone has entered his studio, torn it apart, and removed all the photographs and negatives of the crime except for the extremely enlarged, essentially unreadable image of the corpse.

In his book *Shooting Kennedy*, art historian David Lubin writes that "Thomas's step-by-step investigation of his still photographs, recapitulates the meticulous close analysis of Zapruder's footage performed by forensic experts and conspiracy theorists alike in the months preceding the making of Antonioni's film." Although the film addressed many other themes, this particular scene (which Lubin describes as a "set piece," twelve minutes long, without any dialogue) asks the same questions that many could ask about the Zapruder film. Is there a difference between visual representation and visual truth? We can see that something has happened—the president is murdered, or a man is pointing a gun—but we do not know who the actors are, what exactly occurred, or why. We are witnesses to something whose visual representation does not bring clear answers or universal consensus. Instead, we have fragments of information and sequential moments in time that can be stitched together to create a narrative explanation, but it is subject to interpretation, and what one person sees is not what another person sees.

In this way, the photograph, a modern technological invention that allows us to document events, preserve memory, and share experiences, can perhaps provide information but it cannot always give us what we really seek: knowledge and, more important, understanding. Scientific methods and technological inventions can get us only so far. In Antonioni's film, there is clearly a murder, and Thomas has captured some evidence concerning it, but in the end, he is left only with an image that he has himself rendered useless by having placed too much faith in it. He enlarged it so much in his search for clues that it not only fails to deliver the information but also mocks the viewer by confusing him as to whether what he thinks he sees is even there. Antonioni was the first but far from the last to raise these questions, implicitly or explicitly, in relation to the Zapruder film. The conspiracy theorists were likely in no mood in 1966 to entertain such abstract thoughts about the film or consider their relevance to the assassination, but the conversation that Antonioni started continued in various forms in the world of arts and letters for many decades.

In the fall of 1966, a new researcher came on the scene. Josiah Thompson was an assistant professor in philosophy at Haverford College, holding both his BA and PhD from Yale. His area of expertise was Kierkegaard, and he had served in the navy and lived in Denmark before returning to the States to complete his PhD. Like many of the early critics who preceded him and paved his way, he found himself drawn into the subject matter by a combination of innate curiosity, passion, and intellect. In an article by Calvin Trillin for the *New Yorker* in 1967, titled "The Buffs," Thompson describes the unorthodox nature of the scholars and the study of the assassination: "The marvelous thing about it is that there are no credentials. There's no PhD in the assassination. It's pure scholarship. You have to make your own credentials." This leveling, democratic quality reflected a truly American spirit: a dogged refusal to accept the crushing of the Kennedy dream and the idealistic faith that the raw evidence of the case could be assembled and reassembled like a jigsaw puzzle until the truth was revealed. No one was excluded from trying their hand at it, as long as they had an idea, the passion for it, and access to the material. And when they didn't gain access to the material? Well, they were not about to let it lie.

Thompson had become interested in the assassination at the time it occurred, and had even visited the local FBI office in New Haven to point out an inconsistency he noticed between a statement made by one of the Dallas doctors regarding the president's wounds and what he saw in the frames of the Zapruder film. "I'm sure they must have died laughing after I left," he said in the Trillin article. He was critical of the Warren Report, dabbling in research until he crossed paths with first-generation assassination scholar Vincent Salandria in 1965. He became seriously interested at that time, visiting the National Archives with Salandria to review the Zapruder film and working on a draft of a long article. In September 1966, he traveled to New York to meet with an editor at *Harper's* to see if he could place the article. While he waited to meet the editor, he met up with an old friend, Don Preston, who was the executive editor of Bernard Geis Associates. They talked about Thompson's work, which Preston found intensely compelling, and then went out to eat with Geis himself. In the bygone way in which things were apparently done in the sixties, he had a book contract by the time they had finished lunch.

Things had changed in America when it came to the Kennedy assassination. Conversations about conspiracy and the legitimacy of the Warren Commission were no longer the purview of outliers or fringe elements; to the contrary, they were increasingly being taken up among mainstream news media and respected voices across a number of disciplines. *LIFE* magazine was well aware of the change in the air. Given the magazine's centrality both as America's beloved print magazine and as the holder of a vital piece of visual evidence, the editors of *LIFE* decided in 1966 that it was time to urge the reopening of the investigation into the Kennedy assassination. On October 7, Loudon Wainwright wrote an editorial for *LIFE* that precisely captures the mainstream perspective on the question. He described his own feelings at the publication of the Warren Report in the fall of 1964, his inclination to accept its conclusions based on its exhaustive scope and the prestige of its members, and his sense of relief that there might be an end to the "monstrous" grief shadow of the previous year. He acknowledges that there were always those who saw conspiracy and admits that he felt that much of this seemed "shady" and repellent to him. But now, books and articles had begun to appear that he could not ignore, indeed that had "shaken badly" his comfortable confidence in the Warren Report. "If they haven't entirely swung me over to their view," he wrote, "I, like many others, am beginning to wish very much for further clarification." Wainwright made the case for a new investigation, arguing that this matter was far too important to be left to "individuals acting on their own initiative" or "historians of future generations." Serious doubts had been legitimately

raised, he says, and it would not do to ignore them. He concluded
the editorial with this:

Recently I saw again the amateur movie film which is the best
record of the moment of the assassination. I had not seen it
since the weeks immediately following President Kennedy's
death, and that mounting sense of horror came right back as
soon as the leading motorcycles came into view on the little
screen. The old incredulity persisted as the gleaming caravan
approached down Elm Street. The open car went behind the
road sign, it reappeared, and the President's hands were at his
throat, Governor Connally turned and then fell backward,
and then—as the projector whirred in time and space so far
removed from Dallas on November 22, 1963—there was the
ghastly impact of the killing shot against the President's head.
It is too much, too much. Yet we must look at it, reverse it and
run it again, slow it and stop it and find out everything about
it, because it happened.

Sometime in October, Bernard Geis arranged a meeting between
Josiah Thompson, Loudon Wainwright, and members of the editorial staff of *LIFE* who were working on an issue revisiting the Warren
Commission and the question of conspiracy. The way Thompson
explained it in a later interview is that *LIFE* wanted and needed
to be ahead of the curve on their investigation and reporting, and
that it would take too long for any single person to familiarize
himself with the vast amount of material that had already been
accumulated on the assassination. But here was Josiah Thompson,
a respectable scholar with a book contract, who could codirect the
project as a consultant. Everyone's interests and abilities seemed to

align perfectly: Thompson desperately wanted access to the copies of the Zapruder film at *LIFE* (which were far better than either the second-generation copies at the National Archives or the reproductions in the Warren Report), and the magazine's editors would get an expert to write an article, or several articles, that would appear sometime in the first half of 1967. They would begin with an issue for November 1966 about reopening the investigation and go from there. "And within an hour," Thompson said in an interview, smiling, "I was looking at the Zapruder film. Which was brilliant. I mean, the colors were there, the clarity was there. It was really something, really, really something."

Even so, from the very beginning of this arrangement, there was a conflict looming down the road. Thompson knew that he would want to publish frames from the Zapruder film in his book, and *LIFE* editors knew that they would not give him that permission. There is considerable disagreement about who said what and when, but it seems likely that Thompson hoped that after he got into *LIFE*—developed a relationship with the editors, worked on the project, and made his contributions—he would prevail upon them to change their minds. Certainly, he would have a better chance inside *LIFE* than he would under any other circumstances. He worked from home except when he needed to be in the office; a copy of the film and the transparencies were apparently kept in associate editor Edward Kern's office, and Thompson worked there on those occasions when he needed to use the film.

All seemed to be going well until early November 1966, when Thompson grew suspicious that something was not right at *LIFE* when it came to the film. His doubts began when he was on a research trip to Dallas. According to his own account, he showed a full set of the film transparencies to a doctor who had treated Connally, then went to dinner, leaving the transparencies with Miami bureau chief Henry Suydam, who, in his former position as Washington bureau chief, had dealt with the film when it was being used by the Warren Commission. When he returned and asked to see them again, Thompson found several transparencies missing. According to Thompson, Kern and associate editor Richard Billings carried out some kind of distract-and-search maneuver in Suydam's hotel room to see if they could locate the missing transparencies, to no avail. Thompson feared that someone inside *LIFE* might be trying to hide or suppress some frames of the film. As he later explained it, "I suspected there was some power struggle at *LIFE* in motion, but I had not a clue what it was about and who was on what side. I decided that it would be an extremely good idea for a good copy of the relevant frames to exist outside the Time-Life Building." That was when Thompson decided to undertake what would be the first—though far from the last—cloak-and-dagger operation to secretly copy the film.

The November 25 issue of *LIFE*, titled A MATTER OF REASONABLE DOUBT, closed on November 18. As always after a big deadline, the editorial staff were beat, so the place emptied out. Earlier that day, Thompson had traveled from his home in Philadelphia up to New York with a copying stand, a 35mm camera, and fifteen rolls of film wrapped in Christmas paper and stuffed in his briefcase. When Kern left his office at the end of the day, Thompson got to work illegally copying the film. "I set up my copying stand over the light table in Kern's office," he wrote, "and started copying the 4" by 5" transparencies." When Kern returned to the office rather late and found Thompson in flagrante, he demanded to know what he was doing. "I'm copying some frames from the goddamn film," he snapped. He then explained that he couldn't keep coming up to New York every time he wanted to look at the film and he wanted to have copies down in Philadelphia for his work. Oddly, Kern did not stop him. He simply left the office, whereupon Thompson continued copying the frames for another two hours. No one at *LIFE* said anything to him the following day, demanded the return of the images, or fired him for making an unauthorized copy of the film. Not only that, but executives at *LIFE* magazine signed a contract with Thompson after that date, even though the editors knew full well what he had done. At the same time, they gave him no permission to use the images in his book or anywhere else. Years later, in his interview with the Sixth Floor Museum, Thompson said, "So, basically, I stole the film. I stole it because of my concerns about its security." This sort of confused logic would become something of a trend over the next nine years.

In November 1966, Abe granted a rare television interview. I suspect that *LIFE*'s decision to revisit the assassination and the extensive use of frames of the film in the November 25 issue prompted the calls from reporters eager to get his unique viewpoint. Marvin Scott was a reporter working for the Mutual Broadcasting System who was producing a radio documentary about the assassination. As he described it in an article posted on the New York City TV station WPIX website in November 2013, Abraham Zapruder was the "hoped-for prized get" for his documentary, and it took some cajoling, pleading, and good old-fashioned charm to get him to agree. Eventually, he did, and they went down to Dealey Plaza to do the interview.

Abe began speaking: "Well, as I'm standing right here, I believe, I can almost see it as a picture before my eyes…It's almost three years. It's left in my mind like a wound that heals up, and yet there's some pain left as to what happened." He recounted the basic outlines of the story, as he had already done for Jay Watson at WFAA-TV, the Warren Commission, and William Manchester. The story was entirely consistent, with a few additional reflections brought on by the time that had passed. He talked about his disbelief at having been able to capture the whole scene, saying, "I'm amazed with myself how I stood there and continued shooting the film after what I saw... Some tell me they call it [being] 'froze up,' or paralyzed. I don't know what to call it, but I kept on shooting and yelling until he went out of my sight. I don't know where I got the strength but I had it."

Marvin Scott spent a considerable time in the interview asking Abe for his thoughts on the controversies around the assassination, such as the debate about the number, timing, and direction of the shots fired. From the interview, it seems that Abe was well versed in these issues, and he did not hesitate to contradict Scott when he thought he miscalculated the time elapsed between shots or other elements related to the time clock. He had apparently thought about the issues more than anyone in our family realized. He even mentioned that he had gone back to the site and looked at the stockade fence to the right of the wall on which he had been standing, to measure its distance from his position that day and to determine if the shots he heard might have come from that direction. In the end, he felt sure that—even though he heard only two shots and not three—the shots sounded consistent, leading him to conclude that they both came from the same direction. At the time of the assassination, he and his receptionist, Marilyn Sitzman, who had been standing behind him at the time, both believed the gunfire had come from the left, the direction of the Texas School Book Depository.

When questioned by Scott about the various controversies

surrounding the film, he comes across as pragmatic and unflappable. Scott asked him first what he thought about the speculation that frames were missing. In response, he pointed out that "four frames would hardly be a third of a second, and I don't think anything could happen in a third of a second that would amount to anything." Next, Scott asked him about assassination researcher David Lifton's contention that he could detect on the film evidence of shock waves or stress marks from what he thought was a bullet striking the Stemmons Freeway sign, and that this bullet could not have come from Oswald. "Strangely enough," Scott continues, "after the assassination, the sign disappeared." Abe had a practical answer for that, too. First, he pointed out that Dallas was a growing city and signs were constantly being moved to make way for new roads and the like. "As to the distress marks, when you take an eight millimeter and enlarge its size as showed in *LIFE*, a speck of dust will show all kinds of marks, and if you want to elaborate on 'em and pick on 'em you could pick, but I don't believe there was [*sic*] any shots going through the sign." In general, while he acknowledged that anyone could have doubts about anything, he felt that the conspiracy theorists were "looking at the hole instead of the doughnut."

Abe's support for the Warren Commission is not at all surprising. Everything about his worldview and experience led him to have a basic faith in the American government. But it was more than that. I think the best reflection of his viewpoint is expressed in this interview, when Scott asked him what he was feeling as he stood in the spot where it all began:

Well, my thoughts come back as they were almost three years ago. I think we've lost a great man. I loved that man; my family loved that man. There were millions, I'm sure, [who] loved that man. He was an inspiration to the youth of America. I believe he's the first time that in this country we had a president as young as Kennedy was. The loss was great. He was an inspiration, as I said, to the youth, and I believe if our country wasn't what it is—strong—that it could [not] withstand a shock like this. Would this be in another country, where they had a one-man government, [it could be] a terrible tragedy for the whole country, if [we] weren't as strong as we are.

Thinking back on the assassination from the vantage point of three years, he could grieve the murder of John Kennedy and at the same time reiterate his absolute faith in America. For him, the fact that America elected John Kennedy was the purest proof that its people possessed the values, courage, and strength to endure his assassination and prevail. I have to wonder if, somewhere in the back of his mind, he was thinking of the overthrow of Czar Nicholas II and how the Bolshevik Revolution had plunged Russia into chaos and violence. He was just twelve when he lived through those events. But America was not Russia. Even if he saw the fissures that Kennedy's assassination had caused, in his mind they could not threaten the basic foundation of American democracy. For him, and for many of his generation and background, the Warren Commission and its conclusions were part and parcel of that faith.

In December 1966, the editors at *LIFE* clashed with CBS over access to the film. It was not the first time. CBS had asked to use it in June 1964, when they were preparing a program about the

Warren Report, but had been firmly turned down. There is nothing in the internal documents about this, perhaps because the reasons were so entirely obvious. As a print magazine, *LIFE* could only run the images as still frames in their magazine. That had been all well and good in 1963, when C. D. Jackson bought the film to get it off the market and when the editors felt it should not be seen anywhere, but as time went on and the public began to want to see it, *LIFE* faced a very serious practical problem. They simply had no mechanism to show the film as a film, even if they decided that it was appropriate or commercially wise to do so. Meanwhile, television—in the form of CBS, among other networks—was on the rise, competing for advertising dollars and cutting into print profits. The medium, of course, was perfectly suited to the Zapruder film. But in what world would it make sense for *LIFE* to simply hand over the Zapruder film to CBS so that they could be the ones to broadcast it for the first time to a national audience? Not only would they be giving away their exclusive; they would be implicitly acknowledging the supremacy of television in news coverage. No indeed, that would not do. But if it had been only briefly unpleasant to turn down CBS's request to air the film in 1964, it would prove to be far more difficult in 1966, as the cultural context changed and pressure began to build on *LIFE* to make the film accessible both to researchers and to the public at large.

Edward Kern wrote to Dick Stolley and George Hunt to brief them on the latest. "CBS has been putting a lot of pressure on us to either allow them to run the Zapruder film, which I refused, or to let them send over a couple of experts to see a run-through of it for purposes of reporting on a two-hour telecast sometime over the year end." He denied their request to even view the film, and when CBS asked where else they could go to see it, he directed them to the FBI and the Warren Commission. It seems that he hoped this would be the end of the matter. Upon further inquiry, CBS learned that the Warren Commission had given their copies of the film to the National Archives. It was not welcome news at *LIFE*. "We hold journalistic copyright to this film," Kern wrote his colleagues, "and I assured CBS that we would sue the hell out of them if they got it either through the FBI or the Warren Commission, but there is the possibility that their experts could get a run-through." Kern believed that *LIFE* should try to intervene to prevent this possibility, but he left the matter to the Washington bureau to sort out. The following day, Stolley reported that it was too late—CBS had already contacted the National Archives and seen the film, and they were "probably there again this morning viewing the Zapruder film." From this, *LIFE* learned that the National Archives not only had the film, they had a policy to "run it in its entirety for bona-fide researchers but not for the simply curious."

In his memo of response, Stolley raises the thorny problem of what ownership of the film actually meant. While it was clear that *LIFE* had the right to grant permission for reproduction of the film, did it also hold the right to decide who saw it and when? If there were copies in the National Archives that had come there through government channels (from Abe to the Secret Service to the FBI and from *LIFE* to the Warren Commission), what right would *LIFE* have to control them? Did *LIFE* control only the dissemination of the images or access to the images as well? It seemed unclear. The dustup ended that afternoon with the realization that there was nothing *LIFE* could do about CBS seeing the film at the National Archives. *LIFE*'s editor, Ed Thompson, wrote back to Stolley, "It's a very tricky public domain question and I suppose whatever comments go on the air [in the CBS program] could have come out of *LIFE*'s publication of the frames and the Warren Commission report. But if there's a chance, let's try to stop the viewing."

While it seems understandable from a business point of view that the *LIFE* editors did not want to hand over the film to their television competition, it's also understandable that researchers and others resented the magazine's exceptionally tight control over it, especially in the light of Loudon Wainwright's October editorial. After all, who should be able to scrutinize the film—only the executives and editors at *LIFE* and the federal authorities? The assassination researchers also wanted to add their contribution to the public discourse in light of the reopening of the investigation that Loudon Wainwright was advocating. Then again, was it *LIFE*'s duty to share its copies of the film if other copies were available elsewhere? Did *LIFE* have an obligation to let researchers publish those images for the greater good? The underlying question—whether an individual's interest in historically significant images should supersede a corporation's right to control the content that it owned—would plague the film for much of its existence.

For decades, *LIFE* was portrayed as a commercial Goliath with negligible concern for the Zapruder film beyond protecting its financial interest in it. And it's true that, looking through the prism of the post-Kennedy era and the cynicism that arose at that time, it would be easy to reduce the whole story of the Zapruder film at *LIFE* magazine to the now familiar narrative of corporate abuse of power. The reality, however, is far more complex and nuanced. *LIFE*'s resistance to granting access to the film in the midsixties was shaped not only by a desire to protect its exclusive and by the mores of the time but also by the proximity to the assassination and the personal nature of the deal Stolley had struck with Abe Zapruder.

I realized this only because, to my surprise, I came upon a number of letters from Abe to Dick Stolley, and later to Dick Pollard, in the *LIFE* archives. In the years following the assassination, Abe called and wrote from time to time, inquiring about violations of copyright or rumors he had heard or other concerns about the film. That Abe continued to feel an attachment to it, and a concern for how it was being used, is not surprising. What is unexpected is that Stolley and Pollard did not brush him off, or manage him, or treat him like an irritating interloper. To the contrary, they took pains to keep him informed, to follow up on potential rights infractions, and to reassure him of their shared concern for how the film should be made public. In one letter, Stolley wrote to dispel a rumor that the film had been publicly shown, going on to update Abe as follows: "No decisions have yet been made about the film you shot. It is locked up in the company vault until such time as it seems appropriate to make those decisions. Meanwhile, the feeling is that it increases in commercial value. You certainly will be advised of any such decisions…As I explained to you at the time I purchased your film, we are concerned that it be handled in a proper and respectful way. That remains our objective and I'm sure you share our feelings." It is abundantly clear that the relationship they had forged, and the agreement they had made, was not a dusty relic from a distant past. It was, at least in 1966, still current not only for Abe but for the editors at *LIFE*, as well.

In February 1967, *LIFE* decided to suspend its investigation of the assassination and amicably ended their consulting arrangement with Josiah Thompson around the same time. He continued to work on his own investigation with the understanding that he would be allowed to use the material he gathered in the course of his research. Except, that is, for the stills from the Zapruder film, stolen or otherwise.

LIFE had weathered quite a few rocky shoals in 1966. However, by early 1967, the relationship with Josiah Thompson and CBS seemed under control. One matter that would not go away, however, was the pesky problem of the "missing frames." In the wake of the "Matter of Reasonable Doubt" issue, the question came up again. In the *LIFE* files, there is an undated statement—likely written after the magazine came out—sent to them by Wesley Liebeler, the Warren Commission lawyer who had deposed Abe.

I know I'm going to get a laugh when I tell you this, because it is absolutely unbelievable, [but] *LIFE* magazine, who paid almost $500,000 [*sic*] for this picture, for this roll of film, was working with the original in our laboratory [*sic*] and some guy dropped it on the floor, reached to grab it and he crushed those four frames and they cut them out. Now I know you laugh but I put it to you bluntly—I've talked about this to the editors of *LIFE* magazine time and time again and I've said to them—since you had such an interest in the work of the Commission and you published Governor Connally's speculations about this and some of the Zapruder film, why don't you have the moral courage to tell the American people in your editorial column that you broke the film and lost those four frames? Well, they haven't done it yet but I suggest that someday they're going to get their nerve up and they're going to do it and I'm perfectly willing to stake my whole case on that one fact and you can check it out any way you want but it's a fact.

Since the editors had questioned the conclusions of the Warren Report—and by extension Wesley Liebeler's work—in the November issue, I have to wonder if he wrote this and sent it to *LIFE* to

Chana Zapruder and her children in a family portrait taken in Kovel, Russia. She is standing with her arm around her young son Abraham; in front of her, from left, are Fannie, Morris, and Sarah Ida. c. 1906–7.

Chana Zapruder's identification photo from her emergency US passport application, Warsaw, Poland, 1920.

Abraham Zapruder with his violin, New York, c. late 1920s.

Lillian Schapovnik standing in front of the tenement building at 84 Beaver Street in Brooklyn where her family lived and where the Zapruder family had arrived and settled in 1920. This photograph was taken before her marriage to Abraham Zapruder in 1933.

Abraham Zapruder and Lillian Schapovnik in the Catskills, c. 1930–33.

Abraham and Lillian Zapruder on their honeymoon in Niagara Falls, June 1933.

Abraham and Lillian Zapruder with their children, Myrna and Henry, at Fair Park in Dallas, Texas, 1942.

Abraham and Lillian Zapruder, Dallas, Texas, c. 1940s.

Abraham Zapruder with Marilyn Sitzman at Jennifer Juniors, early 1960s.

Henry Zapruder in Dallas, c. 1963.

Back row from left: Henry Zapruder holding his son Matthew and Myron Hauser holding his son Aaron. Front row from left: Marjorie Zapruder, Adam, Jeffrey, Myrna, and David Hauser, c. 1968.

Abraham Zapruder in his office at Jennifer Juniors, late 1960s.

First contract between *LIFE* magazine and Abraham Zapruder for the sale of print rights to the Zapruder film, drafted by Richard Stolley in the office of Jennifer Juniors, Saturday, November 23, 1963. *(Courtesy of Time Inc. Archives)*

Nov. 23, 1963

In consideration of the sum of fifty thousand dollars ($50,000.), I grant LIFE Magazine exclusive world wide print media rights to my original 8 mm color film which shows the shooting of President Kennedy in Dallas on Nov. 22, 1963. I retain all motion picture rights, but agree not to release the film for motion picture, television, newsreel, etc., use until Friday, Nov. 29, 1963. You agree to return to me the original print of that film, and I will then supply you with a copy print.

Abraham Zapruder

Agreed to:

Richard B. Stolley
LIFE Magazine

Witnessed:

Amateur Filmed Bullets' Impact; Sequence Is Sold to Magazine

By RICHARD J. H. JOHNSON

An amateur movie camera enthusiast in Dallas snapped a 15-second close-up sequence showing the actual impact of the assassin's bullets on President Kennedy.

The 8-millimeter film clip in color was sold by the photographer, Abraham Zapruder, for about $40,000 to Time-Life, Inc.

Life magazine will publish the pictures in its issue dated Friday, Nov. 29. The issue will be on the street next Tuesday.

Mr. Zapruder, president of Jennifer Juniors, Inc., a dress shop in downtown Dallas, declined yesterday in a telephone conversation, to discuss the film or the arrangement fir its sale.

A secretary to Mr. Zapruder, speaking from the offices of the dress shop, said that the Secret Service had sent agents to examine Mr. Zapruder's film and had permitted him to keep or sell it.

The film was developed Friday night. Time-Life editors said yesterday that it had been studied by their Dallas representatives, who were authorized to make the purchase. The film was sent by air to the Chicago laboratories of the magazine.

From a description given by the Life representative in Dallas, the editors said, it appeared that the shots had been taken with a telephoto lens.

Mr. Zapruder's secretary said that Mr. Zapruder was "one of hundreds" who were taking pictures of the Presidential motorcade.

Life editors here said that they were unable last night to give precise details as to what the film showed, but that they were assured that it depicted the impact of the bullets that struck Mr. Kennedy.

The photographic department of The Associated Press in New York acknowledged late yesterday that the AP had bid for the pictures but that Mr. Zapruder had sold the film to Time-Life, Inc. A spokesman said he understood the price was in the vicinity of $40,000.

Mr. Zapruder's secretary would neither confirm nor deny the figure, nor would Time-Life spokesmen discuss it. The AP spokesman, however, said the figure was "well over $25,000 and close to $40,000."

"Amateur Filmed Bullets' Impact; Sequence Is Sold to Magazine," *New York Times*, November 24, 1963. *(From The* New York Times, *November 24, 1963, © 2016 The New York Times. All rights reserved.)*

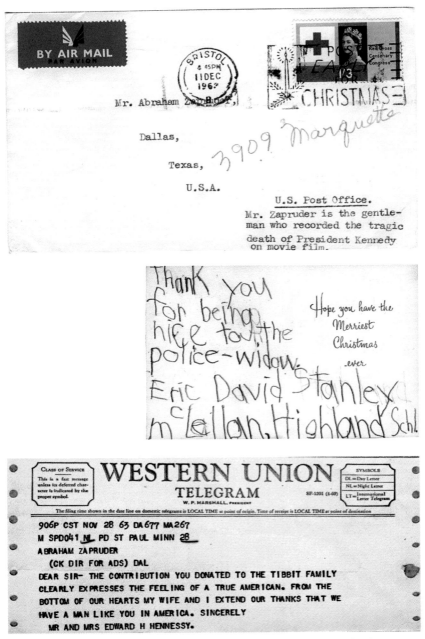

BY AIR MAIL
PAR AVION

BRISTOL
8·45PM
11 DEC
196?

Mr. Abraham Zapruder,

Dallas,

Texas, 3909 Marquette

U.S.A.

U.S. Post Office.
Mr. Zapruder is the gentleman who recorded the tragic
death of President Kennedy
on movie film.

Thank you
for being
nice to the
police-widow.
Eric David Stanley
McLellan, Highland Schl.

Hope you have the
Merriest
Christmas
ever

WESTERN UNION
TELEGRAM

SYMBOLS
DL = Day Letter
NL = Night Letter
LT = International
Letter Telegram

CLASS OF SERVICE
This is a fast message
unless its deferred char-
acter is indicated by the
proper symbol.

W. P. MARSHALL, PRESIDENT

SF-1201 (4-60)

The filing time shown in the date line on domestic telegrams is LOCAL TIME at point of origin. Time of receipt is LOCAL TIME at point of destination

906P CST NOV 28 63 DA677 MA267
M SPD041 NL PD ST PAUL MINN 28
ABRAHAM ZAPRUDER
    (CK DIR FOR ADS) DAL
DEAR SIR- THE CONTRIBUTION YOU DONATED TO THE TIBBIT FAMILY
CLEARLY EXPRESSES THE FEELING OF A TRUE AMERICAN. FROM THE
BOTTOM OF OUR HEARTS MY WIFE AND I EXTEND OUR THANKS THAT WE
HAVE A MAN LIKE YOU IN AMERICA. SINCERELY
    MR AND MRS EDWARD H HENNESSY.

Correspondence sent to Abraham Zapruder after his donation to the Tippit family.

FILMED ASSASSINATION
Generosity Forces Gentle Abe Into Hiding

BY STAN REDDING
Chronicle Reporter

Dallas — Abe Zapruder, a man of modest means and noble heart, is in hiding today, a circumstance brought about by his generosity.

Chance cast Zapruder in the role of recorder of one of history's momentous events—President Kennedy's assassination.

Still and movie film he made of the tragedy last Friday brought him a modest fortune.

Abe, a garment manufacturer, could have used that money—$25,000 for the still pictures bought by Life magazine.

Hero's Family

A gentle heart prompted him to share his bonanza with a fallen hero's family—the family of policeman J. D. Tippit.

Tippit was slain last Friday while attempting to arrest Lee Harvey Oswald as a suspect in the ambush slaying of President Kennedy.

Tippit left a wife, three children, and no insurance.

Zapruder, in making the gift, said Tippit was a "brave and gallant man who literally gave his life for his country."

He wanted to keep his gift a secret, but newspapers ignored his pleas.

"People Are Wonderful"

Now telegrams, letters and wires are flowing into the Zapruder home.

"It's embarrassing, but it's also wonderful," Mrs. Zapruder said. "We never realized people were so kind. We are thrilled at the reaction, in spite of the fact we didn't want publicity, and want none now.

"But it proves people are wonderful, despite the tragic thing that happened.

"It is not a gift, of course, we could have made except under the circumstances."

Other Income?

Zapruder may receive other income from the films.

Several companies are bidding for the motion picture rights. Zapruder will likely receive a handsome sum, far in excess of $25,000, for his pictures.

But today, the modest businessman is in seclusion.

"He's a wonderful man, but he just doesn't want to talk to anyone," his wife said.

"Generosity Forces Gentle Abe Into Hiding," *Houston Chronicle.* (Copyright Houston Chronicle. All rights reserved.)

Mrs. JOHN F. KENNEDY

August 28, 1964

Dear Mr. Zapruder:

This is to advise that Mr. William Manchester has been authorized by Mrs. Kennedy to conduct such interviews as he feels are required to obtain the information necessary for his forthcoming book on the assassination of President Kennedy.

Sincerely,

Nancy Tuckerman

Nancy Tuckerman
Secretary to Mrs. Kennedy

Mr. Abraham Zapruder
501 Elm Street
Dallas, Texas

Letter to Abraham Zapruder from secretary Nancy Tuckerman and envelope signed by Jacqueline Kennedy regarding William Manchester's authorized account of President Kennedy's assassination.

Mr. Abraham Zapruder
501 Elm Street
Dallas, Texas

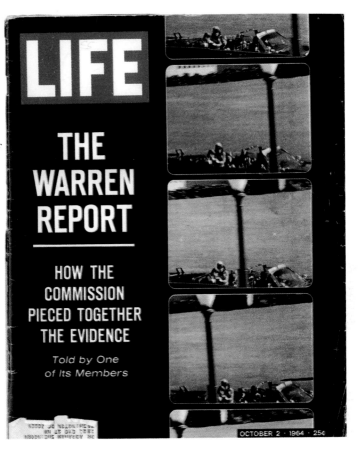

Cover of *LIFE* magazine issue dated October 2, 1964, showing frames from the Zapruder film in color. *(Courtesy of Time Inc. Archives)*

Section C   **SUBPOENA**

#198-059 "C", STATE   THE STATE OF LOUISIANA

Criminal District Court for the Parish of Orleans

To   ABRAHAM ZAPRUDER
      3909 Marquet Drive
      Dallas, Texas

YOU ARE HEREBY COMMANDED to appear in the CRIMINAL DISTRICT COURT, for the Parish of Orleans, SECTION C, on the   12th   day of   February   , in the year of our Lord, 19 69 , at   9   A. M., to testify the truth according to your knowledge, in the case of the STATE OF LOUISIANA, vs.   CLAY L. SHAW   DEFENDANT

And you are not to fail herein, under a penalty of a fine of not more than One Hundred Dollars or by imprisonment of not more than ten days, or both.

BY ORDER OF THE COURT   Edward A. Haggerty, Clerk.

Tulane Avenue and S. Broad Street   Deputy Clerk

Subpoena issued to Abraham Zapruder to testify at the Clay Shaw trial in New Orleans on February 12, 1969.

NEW ORLEANS
STATES-ITEM
FINAL
SPORTS
MARKETS

VOL. 92—NO. 213   THURSDAY, FEBRUARY 13, 1969   PRIC

ZAPRUDER PUT ON STAND, NEW TRIAL PHASE BEGIN'

Abraham Zapruder, the Dallas dress manufacturer who took a color movie of the assassination of President John F. Kennedy, went on the witness stand this afternoon in the trial of Clay L. Shaw.

After a hassle between state and defense attorneys over the relevance of Zapruder's testimony, Judge Edward A. Haggerty Jr. ruled he could testify, thus opening the way for the state to go into the whole question of the assassination itself.

Shaw, 55, is on trial in Criminal District Court on charges of conspiring to kill Kennedy, shot to death in Dallas Nov. 22, 1963.

Garrison Appears at Trial

District Attorney Jim Garrison made one of his rare appearances at the trial of Clay L. Shaw this afternoon as state witness Abraham Zapruder of Dallas was questioned. Garrison took no part in the questioning. It was the DA's third appearance in the courtroom since the trial began Jan. 21.

UNDER LOUISIANA LAW, ALL THE STATE has to prove is that a conspiracy involving Shaw existed and that an overt act necessarily the shooting itself was committed in furtherance of the object of the conspiracy.

But Judge Haggerty ruled today the state "has the right to determine its case, if it so desires."

Chief prosecutor James L. Alcock said the state will show that the actual killing of JFK resulted from a conspiracy.

DEFENSE COUNSEL, F. IRVIN DYMOND argued unsuccessfully that the Zapruder testimony, and all other testimony relating a scene in Dealey Plaza, or "boundaries as to what happened here" in New Orleans, where the court has jurisdiction.

Zapruder testified that on the day of the assassination

he went out to watch the film the president's parad after three attempts found a satisfactory place to stan a four-foot-tall concrete abutment in Dealey Plaza.

He said he had an 8-millimeter movie camera with films and a zoom lens.

AT THIS POINT, THE STATE attempted to intr

Turn to Page 6, Column 1

ASSISTANT DISTRICT ATTORNEY ALVIN V. OSER, second from left, reads into the record testimony of the late Dr. Nicholas J. Chetta, former Orleans Parish coroner. At left is assistant DA JAMES L. ALCOCK; at right, CLAY SHAW.

Front page of the *New Orleans States-Item* o the day that Abraham Zapruder testified in Clay Shaw trial in Ne Orleans. *(Courtesy of: New Orleans States-Ite Advance Media)*

Zapruder, Assassination Photog, Dies

Abraham Zapruder, 65, of 3909 Marquette, who took the historic motion pictures of the assassination of President John F. Kennedy, died in Dallas Sunday.

Zapruder came to the United States from Russia in 1920 and took a job in the dress manufacturing business in New York. He moved to Dalls in 1941 and worked for Nardis of Dallas until 1949, when he went into business for himself with Jennifer of Dallas.

He was a member of Temple Emanu-El, and was a 32nd degree Mason with the Pentagon Masonic Lodge.

Survivors are his wife; a daughter, Mrs. Myrna Hauser of Dallas; a son, Henry Zapruder of Washington, D.C., two sisters, rMs Ida Field of Dallas and Mrs. Fanny Bornstein of New York; and seven grandchildren.

Funeral services have been set for 10 a.m. Tuesday in the Sparkman/Hillcrest Chapel at 7405 W. Northwest Highway.

Obituary of Abraham Zapruder, August 31, 1970.

FILM FRAMES

Frame 162: President Kennedy rests his arm on the open limousine and smiles at onlookers, his wife in her pink suit sitting to his left, just after the motorcade completes the turn from Houston to Elm and enters Dealey Plaza. *(Zapruder Film © 1967 [Renewed 1995] The Sixth Floor Museum at Dealey Plaza)*

Frame 225: The limousine emerges from behind the Stemmons Freeway sign, where it had been momentarily obscured, as President Kennedy suddenly begins to lift his arms up toward his throat. *(Zapruder Film © 1967 [Renewed 1995] The Sixth Floor Museum at Dealey Plaza)*

Frame 230: President Kennedy, reacting to the bullet that hit him in the upper back and exited through his throat, contracts his upper body, pulling his shoulders up and raising his elbows and hands toward his face. *(Zapruder Film ©️ 1967 [Renewed 1995] The Sixth Floor Museum at Dealey Plaza)*

Frame 254: President Kennedy hunches slightly forward as he begins to lower his arms and Jackie Kennedy turns toward him. Governor Connally, also wounded, begins to fall toward his right. *(Zapruder Film ©️ 1967 [Renewed 1995] The Sixth Floor Museum at Dealey Plaza)*

Frame 269: Jackie Kennedy leans toward the president and appears to take his hand as he continues to slump forward; she is looking at Governor Connally, who is turning to his right and falling back toward his wife, Nellie, obscured by the lamppost. *(Zapruder Film © 1967 [Renewed 1995] The Sixth Floor Museum at Dealey Plaza)*

Frame 304: Jackie Kennedy bends her head toward her wounded husband, appearing to embrace him, as Governor Connally falls backward into the lap of his wife, Nellie. *(Zapruder Film © 1967 [Renewed 1995] The Sixth Floor Museum at Dealey Plaza)*

Frames 330 and 335: Jackie Kennedy reacts in horror immediately after her husband suffers the mortal gunshot wound to his head and dies, collapsing into her lap. *(Zapruder Film © 1967 [Renewed 1995] The Sixth Floor Museum at Dealey Plaza)*

Frames 334 and 348: Jackie Kennedy rises from the rear seat, turning toward the back hood of the limousine while the lifeless body of the president falls into the seat. Secret Service Agent Clint Hill can be seen leaping on to the rear of the car. (*Zapruder Film © 1967 [Renewed 1995] The Sixth Floor Museum at Dealey Plaza*)

Frames 366, 371, 375, and 386: Jackie Kennedy climbs out of the backseat and on to the hood of the limousine while Agent Clint Hill jumps on the rear bumper in an attempt to stop her. Nellie Connally's yellow roses can be seen strewn inside the car. *(Zapruder Film © 1967 [Renewed 1995] The Sixth Floor Museum at Dealey Plaza)*

Frame 398: Agent Clint Hill reaches for Jackie Kennedy's arm and forces her back toward the seat of the car as the limousine picks up speed. *(Zapruder Film © 1967 [Renewed 1995] The Sixth Floor Museum at Dealey Plaza)*

Frame 445: The limousine rushes toward the Triple Underpass heading for Parkland Hospital. Jackie Kennedy's pink hat is barely visible in the backseat as the American flag waves over the front headlight. *(Zapruder Film © 1967 [Renewed 1995] The Sixth Floor Museum at Dealey Plaza)*

let them know he planned to publish the information as a response to their issue. Wesley Liebeler never dropped that bombshell, but it may well have been the catalyst for managing editor George Hunt's statement on January 30, 1967, clarifying the matter of the so-called "missing frames." He explained that six of the original frames (207–212) were damaged by *LIFE* but that before that happened, three color copies of the film had already been made. "These are and have always been intact," he stated. When the Warren Commission wanted to make reproductions from the original film, they obviously could not use the missing frames. Hunt explained that those frames were made available to the Warren Commission from the duplicate. Hoping to defuse once and for all what he deemed an "irrelevant discussion," Hunt released for publication the six frames that were left out of the Warren Report.

George Hunt and the editors at *LIFE* barely had time to catch their breath from putting out this fire before two quietly burning embers—CBS and Josiah Thompson—flared up again. Both issues involved the right to use the film. And while one would be tried in the court of public opinion, the other would end in a lawsuit.

In April 1967, Josiah Thompson contacted the editors at *LIFE* to make a formal appeal to use frames from the film in his upcoming book about the assassination, *Six Seconds in Dallas*. In order to reconstruct exactly what had happened in Dealey Plaza that day, he planned to make use of all the photographic materials that existed, as well as schematic drawings, charts, measurements, and highly precise, detailed examinations of every aspect of the material evidence. The crux of his theory was that four shots were fired in Dealey Plaza by three different gunmen: the first from the Book Depository (hitting Kennedy); a second shot one to one-and-a-half seconds later from the Records Building on Houston Street, kitty-corner from the Book Depository (hitting Connally); and then, nearly simultaneously, a third shot from the Book Depository and a fourth shot from an area behind the stockade fence on the grassy knoll behind Abe's location (both of which hit the president in the head).

Thompson's theory was, by definition, a refutation of the Warren Report. He challenged the single-bullet theory, positing that the elapsed time between the president's reaction and that of Governor Connally was too long to be the result of one bullet but too short to allow two bullets fired in succession by the same gunman. A second assassin in another location seemed the answer. But it was his theory about the so-called head shot that was the most original. By scrutinizing the Zapruder film, Thompson theorized that a shot from the Book Depository explained the short forward motion of the president's head but that only another shot, fired at almost the same time from the grassy knoll, could explain how the president's head—and his brain matter and parts of his skull—flew dramatically backward and to the left. Thompson had looked at the Zapruder film and had combed through the forensic and ballistic evidence, reviewed testimonies, and analyzed the autopsy reports. Certainly, there were many who disagreed with his interpretation of the evidence and his findings. But his approach was logical, measured, and thorough; and unlike many who came before him, he was neither strident nor aggressive in the presentation of his case. Most of all, he was the first to offer a clear theory regarding the confusing visual information about the president's fatal head wound on the Zapruder film. In the coming years, the debate over a single assassin versus a conspiracy would center almost entirely on this issue.

For Thompson, there was no way to publish his "micro-study" of the assassination in *Six Seconds in Dallas* without the visual evidence provided by the Zapruder film. "You can't even try to reconstruct this case without the Zapruder film," he said. For this reason, between April and June, Thompson, his editor Don Preston, and Douglas Hamilton, a copyright law professor from Columbia who advised them, made no fewer than five appeals to *LIFE* to allow the use of certain frames of the film in the book. What started off as a plea—explaining that the lack of the film images were "holes" in the book and emphasizing how much Thompson needed them—quickly turned to frustration, as Thompson suggested that *LIFE*'s control over the images came about through a "quirk in the property laws" and that although they might have a legal claim to the film, they had only a "tenuous moral claim" to it. It's a phrase that stops me in my tracks. Is there such a thing as a moral claim that supersedes a legal one? Does an object's content or status (its historical value, emotional impact, importance to a society, a culture, or an individual) determine the legitimacy of private ownership? I can think of examples across the spectrum in which I would answer both yes and no. But we don't have select laws for select objects. Here, as the daughter of a lawyer but also as a writer of history, I see both sides, though I believe—as my father did—in the inherent necessity of the law even when its consequences are infuriating.

LIFE repeatedly denied Thompson's requests, though not without sympathy. In a last-ditch effort to get access to the images, Thompson and his publisher offered to turn over all profits from the book to *LIFE* in exchange for the use of the frames. It was a pretty extraordinary offer. But *LIFE* didn't want Thompson's money. They were not trying to extort him, nor were they trying to prevent him from making his case, though they certainly did want to avoid devaluing the film images until such time that they could use the film themselves. But they were also trying—fruitlessly, as it would turn out—to keep the floodgates closed to requests for the Zapruder film. It didn't take a genius to see that the instant they granted permission to one individual or organization, they would be deluged with requests and would find themselves deciding who should and shouldn't use the film, under what circumstances, and how. As unenviable as *LIFE*'s position was, Thompson's position was frustrating, too. He was left with few avenues to pursue in order to complete the work that he had begun. For any scholar or writer or creative person, there is almost nothing as maddening as having an original idea, believing deeply in it, investing time, emotion, energy, and money, working relentlessly on it, and then finding it impossible to bring it to completion because of something entirely outside of your control.

While *LIFE* was going back and forth with Thompson, CBS made its third appeal to *LIFE* to allow the use of the Zapruder film in a four-part documentary series on the Warren Report that they were planning to air that summer. On June 16, general manager John Watters responded to Gordon Manning, vice president and director of TV News at CBS, with the familiar refrain. "The Zapruder film is owned by Time Inc. and copyrighted in its name. Although Time Inc. gave a print of the film to the Warren Commission to help in its important deliberations, it has been and will continue to be the policy of Time Inc. not to allow anyone to use all or any part of this film in the United States at this time. We consider this film an invaluable asset of Time Inc. and its use is presently limited to Time's publications and its other enterprises." In retrospect, this was perhaps not the absolute best answer to send to CBS, since it failed to capture any of the nuances or complexities inherent in their reasoning, and it left the magazine wide open to criticism for hoarding the film for financial gain.

The four-part series *A CBS News Inquiry: The Warren Report* aired on CBS beginning on June 27, 1967. In it, the reporters deeply analyzed the commission's findings, questioning some aspects of the investigation but for the most part agreeing with its conclusions. Although they did not have the ability to show the film, they did conduct an interview with Abe, a very brief excerpt of which was included in the broadcast. Instead of leaving the film out of its series, CBS repeatedly commented on their inability to show it on the air. At a certain point, Walter Cronkite, America's beloved, trusted newsman, who had delivered the news of the president's death to the nation, handed down a sober and stern rebuke of *LIFE* magazine to millions of viewers:

> There is one further piece of evidence which we feel must now be made available to the entire public: Abraham Zapruder's film of the actual assassination. The original is now the private property of *LIFE* magazine. A *LIFE* executive refused CBS News permission to show you that film at any price on the ground that it is 'an invaluable asset of Time Inc.' ... *LIFE*'s decision means you cannot see the Zapruder film in its proper form, as motion picture film. We believe that the Zapruder film is an invaluable asset, not of Time Inc., but of the people of the United States.

Cronkite's statement immediately had the desired effect. Letters began to pour into the *LIFE* offices, and this time they were not filled with gratitude, accolades, and thanks for a job well done. To the contrary, they were from angry members of the public who demanded an explanation as to why the Zapruder film was being withheld from view. It is utterly clear that every reader was convinced by Cronkite's statement that *LIFE*'s sole reason for withholding the film was to protect its financial interest.

One of the first letters reads, "The [CBS] programs were important. They were tremendously worthwhile. They were marred by just one terrible omission...the Abraham Zapruder film of the actual shooting in Dallas...It has always been my opinion that *LIFE* never had any right to buy this film. It belongs to the nation. And in spite of the money you paid for it...it still isn't yours." Another writer says, "Money cannot buy everything; it certainly should not have bought the Zapruder film." The letters go on and on with rage and fury at *LIFE*'s apparently despicable, profiteering, selfish desire to profit at any cost. A number of letter writers canceled subscriptions or asked *LIFE* to revisit their policy or begged them to turn the film over to the government. One writer from Tacoma, Washington, wrote: "As an American, I feel outraged by your actions. You shrewdly snatched up the film and use it to, I see, help sell your magazines. America, on the whole, is deeply concerned over the assassination. And you know it. So, we see no film. I used to enjoy the integrity you people backed *LIFE* up with. Now I'm sickened, like I am with that senseless Dallas crime. Can you come up with a decent excuse or do you even care? I care. You people obviously don't. Unfortunately, you've lost my lousy 35 cents."

CHAPTER 7

■ ■ ■ ■ ■ ■ ■

COURT CASES AND BOOTLEGS

By the fall of 1967, *LIFE* was mulling over its options regarding the Zapruder film. In an internal memo to general manager John Watters dated November 10, editor Dick Pollard laid the matter out quite clearly:

We will certainly lose the copyright to this film eventually. In the interim a lot of reputable and disreputable people and companies are sniping at us for concealment and possession (for profit) of a film which, they say, should be in the public domain.

In the public interest (and in the interest of getting our money back), I suggest we make a thirty minute movie of the late John F. Kennedy animating [*sic*] from our superb collection of stills, plus amateur film, plus Zapruder...Then give the film, including the Zapruder footage, to the Government or Harvard or someone and let them make the decisions as to who should be allowed to view or use the Zapruder frames.

Before this idea could even make the rounds at *LIFE*, the publication of Josiah Thompson's book *Six Seconds in Dallas* by Bernard Geis Associates stirred up more problems for *LIFE*. Unlike CBS, which had addressed the problem of not being able to use the film by publicly shaming the company on national television and causing a giant public-relations headache, Thompson and Geis dealt with it by coming up with an ingenious, if devious, workaround. They hired an artist to render black-and-white drawings of the film frames that Thompson needed to make his arguments, presumably using the images that Thompson had illegally procured from *LIFE*. In the book, publisher Bernard Geis wrote a prefatory note explaining the circumstances of the sketches and how they had come to be used. He described the great lengths to which they had gone to gain permission for the use of the frames and *LIFE*'s repeated refusals. Then he went on to explain the rationale for their solution. "It seems clear to us that this crucial historical document should not be sequestered from the eye of responsible enquiry through an accident of private ownership; still, by law, the film belongs to *LIFE* and we cannot make use of it without their consent. We have therefore been forced to content ourselves with an artist's rendering of the events depicted on the Zapruder film, since the events themselves are John Kennedy's tragic legacy to us all."

In fact, the film's ownership was not "accidental" at all, nor was it somehow a quirk of the law or a trick perpetrated by *LIFE*. Those who railed against *LIFE*'s ownership of the film either forgot or never knew that the object in question was a home movie made by a private citizen who had first offered it to the government. When the government failed to grasp its importance, the media swept in and did its job, as unsavory as it was, swarming and harassing him to such an extent that he sold it to the news organization he felt was most responsible. There was nothing accidental about it. Had a *LIFE* photographer taken this film, it's hard to imagine that Josiah Thompson or CBS or any researcher would have felt morally entitled to have access to it. So what made this circumstance different? Was it the subject matter itself or the fact that it was a home movie by an amateur photographer?

If those questions seem thorny, they get even more confusing with the rest of the publisher's note. Geis explains at length how accurate the renderings are and asks readers to compare a photographic reproduction of frame 207, released by *LIFE*, with the artist's copy of it. "These charcoal sketches...have been checked rigorously against the original sources and every attempt has been made to ensure that their representation of the events is scrupulously exact." At the same time, he asserts that "the sketches are *not* the Zapruder film." So let's review: The events of the assassination were Kennedy's legacy to the public. The film depicting that event legally belonged to *LIFE* but its content morally belonged to the American public. The artist's drawings of it in the book are precise and accurate enough to use as evidence in Thompson's arguments but they are not so precise and accurate as to be reproductions of the film, which would imply infringement. It was a fine, fine line indeed.

For the editors of *LIFE*, Thompson and Geis had crossed it. On December 1, 1967, Time Inc. sued Bernard Geis for copyright infringement and for engaging in unfair trade and competition practices. While Geis was spoiling for a fight, Random House, which was distributing the book, wasn't so sure. As Thompson later remembered it, smiling, "[They] got cold feet and [were] not going to let any books leave their warehouse. Geis then threatened suit against them for breach of contract and actually hired trucks to go to the Random House warehouse to get the books out." Random House eventually relented and distributed the book as planned. And by going on the offensive to defend their copyright, *LIFE* continued to come out badly. In mid-December, Thompson went on *The Mike Douglas Show* on the ABC network to make his case not only for a conspiracy in the murder of President Kennedy but also against *LIFE* magazine's ownership of the Zapruder film. At a certain point in the broadcast, Thompson urges viewers to act: "I think the first thing that has to be done—and I would invite all your help in this enterprise—is to get *LIFE* magazine to release this film that they've had in their possession for four years. It should never have been in any private person's possession anyhow. Release that film and let the American people judge as to whether what I say is the case."

Even I, who have a lot of sympathy for Josiah Thompson in this situation, think he went a little far here. The film should never have been in any private person's possession? It was made by a private person. To dismiss that foundational fact of the Zapruder film is to pretend that it sprang to life in some collective way that made it by definition the property of the nation. Its status over time might change, and perhaps it should eventually belong to America as a whole, but it did not begin its life that way—so who was to say exactly when and how that transition should happen?

Further, those who called for the film's release to the American people never seemed to bother with any of the practical consequences of such a decision. Release it to whom? The federal government? That didn't seem like a good idea, given the mistrust of the government that came about as a result of the Warren

Report. So who would administrate it? There would need to be a physical place for people to screen it and a mechanism for obtaining copies, including charging fees. Who should govern access to it and on what terms? There would be innumerable requests for its use, not just from reputable researchers but from people wanting to use it in advertising, or to exploit its shock value, or for any number of other unscrupulous reasons. Who would decide when and how it should be used? Unlike Josiah Thompson and the others who criticized from the sidelines, those who actually dealt directly with the Zapruder film felt instinctively that it was akin to the contents of Pandora's box. Its release into the world might be inevitable, but there was no telling what the consequences would be. For this and many other reasons, the editors and executives at *LIFE* were in no hurry to pull off the lid.

Thompson went on to urge the audience to write to *LIFE*'s managing editor, George Hunt, to request the release of certain frames of the film. At that point, Kay Stevens, cohost on the program, helpfully piped up that viewers should perhaps cancel their subscriptions. Apparently, many did, and according to the *LIFE* records, hundreds more letters arrived at the *LIFE* offices expressing displeasure at the information they gleaned from *The Mike Douglas Show*. *LIFE*'s PR battles were far from over.

In 1968, while *LIFE* waited for a judgment in their lawsuit against Josiah Thompson, they continued to try to find a way to bring the film to the public in a respectful way that would restore their reputation (i.e., get them out of the public-relations mess they were in), honor their agreement with Abe, reflect the place *LIFE* magazine occupied in America, and earn back some of the money they had spent on purchasing the film. Then, the thinking went, they would get rid of the damn thing. Dick Pollard, in a letter to Elmer Lower at ABC in February 1968, wrote:

C. D. Jackson bought the copyright to Abraham Zapruder's Kennedy assassination film to keep it from being shown in motion. C. D. had some vague notion of impounding the film for ten or twenty years until it became "history."

Well, it can't work out that way. We spend too much time defending our copyright and defending ourselves against accusations that we are concealing evidence (nonsense). We'd like to make a tasteful documentary about the assassination of an American president wrapped around the Zapruder film. Assuming we could get the film on television or into theaters, we would run it a couple of times and then give it to the Library of Congress.

Is there any way ABC and *LIFE* could get together on such a film?

Pollard wrote to his colleagues a few days later to say that ABC seemed interested but that Lower was away and they should wait for his return before approaching any other networks. "My experience has been that ABC is anxious to work with *LIFE* and Time Inc. While the other two networks are uncooperative if not downright hostile." *LIFE* contacted a few potential scriptwriters and consultants to do treatments, trying to find the right tone, approach, and framing for this very sensitive and difficult piece. At the same time, the editors at *LIFE* began to tackle the technical problems of turning the 8mm original film into a large format that could be used in a motion picture broadcast.

Moses Weitzman was working for a New Jersey film lab called Manhattan Effects when *LIFE* came calling. First, he accomplished the highly difficult task of converting the images on the 8mm camera-original film to 16mm, which pleased the executives at *LIFE* enormously. They then commissioned him to duplicate it in the still larger 35mm format. Weitzman developed a painstaking, technically complicated method to accomplish this, inventing new techniques and jerry-rigging the special equipment he needed for this purpose. His efforts yielded mixed results early in 1968. One copy had bubbles in the blowup images, so it was thrown away. Another copy was unusable because the images were incorrectly printed in the soundtrack area of the film, so Weitzman threw that one into a box in his office and began again. In May 1968, his third try was successful. He was able to deliver to *LIFE* magazine a 35mm print of the film, along with an internegative from which future duplicates could be made, and the camera original.

In May, *LIFE* had in its hands a high-quality 35mm reproduction of the Zapruder film that could be used as the centerpiece of a short documentary about the president's death. But Martin Luther King had been assassinated in April, and then in June Bobby Kennedy was also murdered. By August, the movie discussion was completely over, at least as it appears in the *LIFE* records. It was clearly not the time to make a film about the assassination of an American leader, least of all a Kennedy.

Even as *LIFE* had its hands tied by basic decency, the legal wheels continued to turn on the Thompson case. In September 1968, more than a year after the publication of Thompson's book *Six Seconds in Dallas*, New York Federal District Court judge Inzer B. Wyatt handed down a summary judgment in the case *Time Inc. v. Bernard Geis Associates*. There were two important parts to the case. The first part hinged on whether or not the Zapruder film could be the subject of copyright. While there was a long history of copyright law that protected both still and moving photographs, the defendants had argued that the Zapruder footage was simply a record of what occurred—with no artistic or creative elements—and that it was therefore "news" and, as such, not subject to copyright. The judge dismissed this point, not only on the basis that every photograph reflects some element of choice and design, but on the particulars of this footage, writing, "The Zapruder pictures in fact have many elements of creativity. Among other things, Zapruder selected the kind of camera (movies, not snapshots), the kind of film (color), the kind of lens (telephoto), the area in which the pictures were to be taken, the time they were to be taken, and (after testing several sites), the spot on which the camera would be operated." He also touched, albeit briefly, on something that is central to much of the controversy around the film. After a lengthy justification of photographic copyright in any number of scenarios, including a street scene of the New York Public Library, he wrote: "Thus, if Zapruder had made his pictures at a point in time before the shooting, he would clearly have been entitled to copyright. On what principle can it be denied because of the tragic event it records?" Although the judge said no more here, this is indeed the core of Thompson's claim. For many people, it was exactly the importance of the event, America's need to understand it, the collective tragedy it recorded, and the national pain it captured that undermined *LIFE*'s legal claim to it. While this may satisfy an emotional argument, it does not work as a legal one.

So there was clearly a copyright to the film. The next question was whether the sketches constituted infringement. According to the judge, they did. "The so-called 'sketches' in the Book are in fact copies of the copyrighted film," he wrote. "That they were done in charcoal by an 'artist' is of no moment." In other words, there was no real difference between making an accurate drawing of the film's frames or photographically reproducing them. It was looking good for *LIFE*. But then, there was the slippery matter of "fair use"—a provision that has been called the "most troublesome in the whole law of copyright." To determine whether Thompson's use of the drawings fell within the bounds of fair use, the judge had to consider several factors, including what Thompson's purpose was in using the Zapruder pictures, how much of the whole film they used, and if Thompson's use of it in his book took away any meaningful value from *LIFE* magazine.

The judge acknowledged Thompson's bad behavior in secretly copying the film and publishing the sketches, and acknowledged that this made him reluctant to rule in his favor. However, he argued, there was no injury to *LIFE*, because Thompson's book was not in direct competition with *LIFE* magazine and people did not buy the book to see the Zapruder images but rather to follow Josiah Thompson's argument about the assassination, of which the images were a necessary part to illustrate his points. Most of all, he wrote, "There is a public interest in having the fullest information available on the murder of President Kennedy. Thompson did serious work on the subject and has a theory entitled to public consideration." This was a nod to the public's "right to know" and the author's First Amendment rights of freedom of expression. He ultimately found that the sketches were within the bounds of fair use. The ruling of fair use granted the material's replication within strict bounds, and it certainly didn't dismantle *LIFE*'s proprietary right to the film. This case—deemed by many to be a landmark one—would be cited in copyright cases for decades as an example of how the fair use doctrine could be expanded to allow for copyrighted materials if it was determined that it was in the public's interest for them to be seen.

In media accounts of the case, *LIFE* was said to have lost the suit. Strictly speaking, they did, in that they were not able to halt the publication and distribution of Thompson's book with the Zapruder sketches in it. But for *LIFE*, that outcome was ultimately not very damaging—it probably wasn't nearly as bad as the public smackdown they had gotten from CBS. Although *LIFE* had received another public black eye, the judge had, in fact, reiterated the legitimacy of the film's copyright, which was a victory in and of itself, as their lawyer pointed out in a letter to the magazine's editors. Still, as with everything concerning the film, even this "victory" was a mixed bag. They had the legal standing of the copyright to the film, but the judge's ruling of fair use might gradually erode their exclusive use of it. Their public-relations problems just kept growing, and this small legal victory didn't do a thing to alleviate them. Even more important, all the copyright protections in the world wouldn't stand a chance against the small army of committed conspiracy theorists who were determined to get their hands on the film, bootleg it, and show it to as many people in the United States as possible.

A five-star general in this army set his sights on the Zapruder film in March 1968. This was New Orleans district attorney Jim Garrison, who had the previous year brought formal charges against a local businessman, Clay Shaw, for allegedly having conspired in New Orleans with Lee Harvey Oswald to murder President Kennedy. On the face of it, the charges were totally outrageous and elicited wide criticism from mainstream sources around the United States. Clay Shaw was a respected businessman in New Orleans who had helped found the International Trade Mart and was active in civic affairs throughout the city, especially in the restoration of buildings in the historic French Quarter. He had supported Kennedy in the election and had not so much as an outstanding parking ticket in the way of a criminal record. Nevertheless, Garrison pressed forward, armed with little more than his certainty that the president had been killed as a result of a conspiracy, and a handful of witnesses who claimed that Shaw had been present at a meeting with Oswald and David Ferrie, another local man, in which such plans had been discussed.

Garrison's case rested on convincing a jury first, that there had been a conspiracy to kill the president, and second, that the plotting of it had taken place in New Orleans with Lee Harvey Oswald and David Ferrie (both dead) and Clay Shaw. Garrison maintained that there could be no proof of conspiracy without the Zapruder film, which he believed would convince any sane person that there had been a second shooter on the grassy knoll. On March 13, 1968, in remarks he made to his colleagues at the National District Attorneys Association convention in New Orleans, he publicly denounced LIFE magazine for withholding the film. That was nothing particularly new. But in those same remarks, he also accused LIFE of suppressing it at the direction of the federal government as part of a deliberate conspiracy to cover up the truth of the assassination. Now, *that* was new. For this, LIFE reporter David Chandler accused Garrison of civil contempt of court. Undaunted, two days later Garrison issued a subpoena to LIFE magazine to present the film to the grand jury in the Clay Shaw trial in New Orleans.

LIFE photo lab technician John Francis appeared in the New Orleans courthouse with a copy of the film on March 28, 1968, where it was shown to the grand jury and members of

Garrison's staff. The transcripts of those hearings disappeared in the 1970s—generally thought to have been destroyed on orders from New Orleans district attorney Harry Connick, who succeeded Garrison—and only resurfaced in 1995, and there is no record of the film viewing among the surviving records. However, Mark Lane—a close confidant of Garrison and a constant presence throughout the trial—wrote an editorial in the *Midlothian Mirror* that offers a perspective, though a wildly biased one, about the effect of this showing of the film on Garrison's staff and others.

According to Lane's editorial, *LIFE* provided an "excellent first generation color reprint" for the purposes of the screening, though some disagree with this characterization. But as far as the film was concerned, Lane—and Garrison, for that matter—was interested in just one aspect of it. Since they both believed that the film showed unequivocal evidence that the president was shot from the front (because the president's head appears to snap back and leftward immediately after the explosive shot), they also believed that it proved a conspiracy. If this were so, the visual evidence on the film undermined the credibility of the Warren Report and its authors, and suggested that the government was in on a conspiracy to cover up the truth. To support his point, Lane went on to quote at length five people who viewed the film and interpreted it exactly as he did. He quoted exactly no people who interpreted the film in any other way. In case readers did not fully comprehend the significance of this landmark showing of the film, Lane made sure to spell it out. "What have we learned?" he asked. "That while *LIFE* is an intransigent part of the establishment and in the fact-suppressing and truth-distorting business it is, on occasion, willing to yield a step or two to maintain its image of truth seeking. And we have learned that the monster that inhabits the Time and Life Building is kind, benign, friendly, and thoroughly democratic when contrasted with your own monster who rules from Washington."

The showing of the film to the grand jury was just the beginning. *LIFE* was compelled to leave the copy with Garrison for use in the trial, whose date had not yet been set, with strict provisions stating that it would not be shown to the media, duplicated, reproduced, distributed, or shared in any way except as required by the trial. Having agreed to these conditions, Garrison's office took possession of the film and promptly set about breaking every single one of them. The film remained in Garrison's possession for almost a year, but the full impact of his control over the film on *LIFE* magazine, their copyright, and the larger debate over the conspiracy would not be clear until well after the trial had ended.

For many who were engaged in studying, writing, and arguing about the assassination, the movement of the president's head on the Zapruder film was obvious evidence of a shot from the front and, therefore, a conspiracy. For the most prominent dissenters to the Warren Commission—among them Mark Lane, Josiah Thompson, and Jim Garrison—it was all but an article of faith. As Mark Lane put it in *Rush to Judgment*, "So long as the Commission maintained that the bullet came almost directly from the rear, it implied that the laws of physics vacated in this instance, for the President did not fall forward." In 1969, for the first time, a brilliant Berkeley physicist named Luis Alvarez put that conviction to the test.

It was not his first foray into the assassination debates. Alvarez had read the *LIFE* magazine issue A MATTER OF REASONABLE DOUBT in November 1966 and found himself fascinated by the color images of the Zapruder film reproduced in its pages. Among his many areas of knowledge, he was an expert in photo analysis and had invented a camera stabilizer and several other optical devices. As he scrutinized the frames, he observed that points of glare on the moving limousine caused streaks whose lengths differed from frame to frame. By plotting these streaks, he could detect minute "jerks" that had gone unnoticed by the FBI in their examination. He developed what came to be called the "jiggle theory," positing that the sounds of the rifle firing caused Abe to flinch, which in turn caused minute tremors in the camera's steadiness. It seems like a plausible idea, though when my uncle Myron heard about it for the first time, he shook his head sadly and said, "What that guy doesn't know is that all Abe's movies look like that."

Alvarez had presented these ideas to CBS in 1967 and visited the National Archives with executives from the network and the photo analysts they had hired. Using exhaustive and comprehensive analysis, Alvarez correlated the jiggles on the film to possible gunshots, suggesting a possible missed first shot at frame 177 (when the president and Mrs. Kennedy were still smiling and waving before going behind the freeway sign) and a second shot that hit the president at frame 215, while he was behind the sign. CBS briefly mentioned his theories in their 1967 Warren Commission series, but they had not given them nearly the time and in-depth coverage that Alvarez felt they warranted.

Then, in 1969, Alvarez asked one of his physics students, Paul Hoch, what he thought was the best evidence of a conspiracy to kill President Kennedy. Hoch responded, "The head snap," and gave Alvarez a copy of *Six Seconds in Dallas* by Josiah Thompson. In a 1976 article about his various studies and findings about the JFK assassination, titled "A Physicist Examines the Kennedy Assassination Film," Alvarez wrote that he studied Thompson's book carefully and came to the conclusion that the explanation for the movement of the president's head was that it was "driven backward by some real force" but not necessarily by a bullet from the front. As Hoch put it in an e-mail to me, Alvarez's belief was that "one cannot argue from basic physical principles (as Thompson had done) that the bulk of any target has to move in the same direction as the bullet." Anticipating the limits of my understanding of physics, Hoch added: "Beyond that, it gets complicated."

Hoch is among the lowest-profile first-generation critics of the Warren Commission, credited with decades of serious and methodical work on the case, in particular finding important records at the National Archives and through Freedom of Information Act requests. He was intrigued but not convinced by his professor's initial calculations. They needed to test the theory. So, armed with a rifle, a ruler, and a bunch of melons taped with Scotch glass filament tape "to mock up the tensile strength of a cranium," they set to work testing what would come to be called the jet-effect hypothesis. As Alvarez explained it in his 1976 paper, "The simplest way to see where I differ from most of the critics is to note that they treat the problem as though it involved only two interacting masses: the bullet and the head. My analysis involves three interacting masses: the bullet, the jet of brain matter observable in frame 313, and the remaining part of the head. It will turn out that the jet can carry forward more momentum than was brought in by the bullet, and the head recoils backward, as a rocket recoils when its jet fuel is ejected."

The experiments they conducted bore out the plausibility of Alvarez's theory. Paul Hoch wrote up their findings for the assassination research community, showing the results of the study and, in his words, "got a lot of flak for it." Although it would be several years before Alvarez's theories received wider readership, it was an important example of how scientific analysis, and not political bluster, could be applied to the question of what happened to the president on Dealey Plaza.

The trial of Clay Shaw opened on January 29, 1969, with Judge Edward A. Haggerty presiding. The State was represented by Jim Garrison (famously in attendance only a handful of times during the trial) and Assistant District Attorneys Andrew Sciambra, James Alcock, William Alford, and Alvin Oser. Clay Shaw was represented by Irvin Dymond, brothers Edward and William Wegmann, and Salvatore Panzeca.

On February 10, Abe received a letter from Assistant District Attorney Alvin Oser with an enclosed subpoena to appear in the Criminal District Court for the Parish of Orleans on February 12 to "testify the truth according to your knowledge in the case of the State of Louisiana vs. Clay L. Shaw." Alvin Oser's letter and the original summons, signed by Jay Carlo, deputy clerk of the court, were among the family papers that I came upon in the course of researching this book. I can only imagine the sinking feeling my grandfather must have had upon receiving the summons. He may not have realized it, but his appearance would mark the beginning of the second phase of the trial, the part where Garrison planned to show that the president had been killed by a conspiracy, and where he planned to openly challenge the findings of the Warren Commission and accuse the federal government of colluding in a cover-up.

Although Abe was called to testify, it was really the film itself that was the prosecution's star witness for this phase of the trial. As Garrison put it in his opening statement, "The State will offer an 8mm color motion picture film taken by Abraham Zapruder, commonly known as the Zapruder film. This film, which has not been shown to the public, will clearly show you the effect of the shots striking the president... Thus, you will be able to see—in color motion picture—the president as he is being struck by the various bullets and you will be able to see him fall backwards as the fatal shot strikes him from the front—not the back but the front." With such unequivocal visual evidence, the DA reasoned, the jury would be convinced that there had been multiple shooters, which meant conspiracy.

You might be wondering where Clay Shaw fits into all this. So did a lot of people. Even though there was no hard evidence linking Clay Shaw to any of the material from Dallas, the DA intended first to prove through witness testimony that Shaw had conspired to murder the president, and then to use the Zapruder film and other evidence to prove that the president had been killed by a conspiracy. Then, the DA promised, it would somehow all come together and the two parts of this narrative would merge and make sense. It was a specious legal strategy at best, and it only got off the ground because of Judge Haggerty's permissiveness and inconsistent legal rulings.

On the afternoon of February 12, Abe and Lil Zapruder arrived at the courthouse, and Abe was called to the witness stand. Also present was novelist and reporter James Kirkwood, who had met Clay Shaw in November 1967 and become interested in the trial and the man himself. He wrote a profile for *Esquire* magazine, which appeared in December 1968, and went on to cover the trial in great depth, writing an excellent book titled *American Grotesque*. His account of this day in the trial, together with a few press reports and the transcripts, captures not only this trying experience for Abe but a pivotal moment in the history of the film. "The first witness called was Abraham Zapruder," Kirkwood writes, "a gentle, bespectacled, balding dress manufacturer who went to Dealey Plaza…hoping to get a few shots of Mr. and Mrs. Kennedy as they passed by. He ended up with as gruesome and heartbreaking a piece of film as the world has ever seen. The shock of being witness and recorder to this event has not left Zapruder and doubtless never will. It has left the man humbled, as if he'd been witness to a holy—and terrible—vision." Abe was asked to review a photograph, identify himself on it, and answer a few questions about where he was standing and the type of camera he was using. At this point, the prosecution requested to enter into evidence a number of additional exhibits—photos, a mock-up of Dealey Plaza, and the like—which were draped so that the jury could not see them.

It was a seemingly routine moment but it was, in fact, a crucial one. What was actually at stake was whether the judge was going to allow the prosecution to "go into Dallas"—that is, to bring evidence into the courtroom to make the case that President Kennedy had been killed by a conspiracy, though nothing in this part of the trial had any direct evidentiary link to Clay Shaw. Beyond the question of relevance, the defense feared that the jury, after seeing the violent murder of the president on the Zapruder film and potentially being convinced that it showed evidence of a conspiracy, would direct their rage and helplessness at the only person available to pay for the crime: Clay Shaw.

The defense objected, whereupon the jury was sent out of the room and the two sides fought it out one last time while Abe sat on the witness stand. Irvin Dymond tried his best to dissuade the judge from this disastrous decision, reminding him that in the past he had ruled that he would not allow evidence from the assassination to be brought into the court. "If the Court please, at this time we object to all this testimony concerning Dealey Plaza on the ground of relevancy. Your Honor has ruled many, many times that there is no connection between the happenings at Dealey Plaza and this case."

The prosecution countered, saying that the judge should allow the State to "overprove" its case. In the words of James Alcock, "The State admits, and this Court has acknowledged on numerous occasions, the State does not have to prove, as a matter of law, the president was killed as a result of this alleged conspiratorial meeting. However, the State may call evidence which tends to confirm or corroborate that it was discussed." In other words, the State did not have to show that the alleged meeting between Clay Shaw, Oswald, and David Ferrie had led directly to the assassination of JFK, but it could show what it believed was evidence of a conspiracy to assassinate the president in order to corroborate the possibility that such a meeting had taken place. In the end, as expected, the judge permitted the evidence. As Kirkwood put it, "The door to Texas was flung wide open." In the words of the defense team, it was "their darkest hour."

As the exhibits were unveiled, Abe was momentarily dismissed from the stand so that Robert West, the county surveyor for Dallas, could come and answer questions about the mock-up of Dealey Plaza and the accuracy of the exhibits. When Abe returned to the stand, he was asked to identify his location on the mock-up. Here he seemed slightly confused and shaken up, having some difficulty situating himself, and he was scolded by the judge for not speaking loudly enough—"Unless the jury can hear you, it is no good your giving evidence." At one point, when looking at a photograph, Abe asked if he was looking at an image of the Dal-Tex Building—his own office. The judge snapped, "If you don't know, who would know it?" "Give me some time," Abe answered. He clearly did not want to be there, and he seemed intimidated and uncomfortable about answering a rapid-fire set of questions in the crowded courtroom, thronged with reporters and spectators and under the unsympathetic eye of the judge.

When asked by the prosecution to recount his story, he once again described how he came to film the assassination, and the gruesome details of the shooting and its aftermath. While describing what he saw through the camera lens, Abe referred to Mrs. Kennedy as "Jackie." Kirkwood noted that his "use of [her] first name was not irreverent but gentle and tinged with a sorrowful affection." Meanwhile, a *New York Post* reporter was watching Lil. "His wife nervously sat on the opposite side of the courtroom toward the rear. Her mink coat kept falling from her shoulders, revealing the strand of pearls around her neck. As she reached for the coat, her bracelets and rings glistened in the faint courtroom light. Her silver hair blended with her gray tinseled eyeglass frames."

When I first read this description, I cringed a little. The mink coat, the pearls, the bracelets and rings—she always did have great style, but was she perhaps dressed a little too richly for the circumstances? Was it perhaps a little insensitive? Maybe leave the mink coat in Dallas? Maybe don't wear *all* the bracelets? For a minute, I try to imagine having this conversation with her, explaining to her how it might look or what people might think. I am not halfway into the thought before I realize how badly the conversation would go. I can see her straightening herself up and giving me a very stern lecture in her definitive manner about how she would never dress a certain way just because of what people might think. She was nothing if not authentic; she made no apologies for herself and she would not adjust her image for the benefit of others. This wasn't always easy to take, but I deeply admire it.

I read on. The reporter continued describing my grandmother as she listened to the most difficult part of her husband's testimony.

"Mrs. Zapruder suddenly leaned back," he wrote, "staring at the floor in front of her. She reached for a lavender handkerchief and pushed it under the glasses to wipe her eyes. The tears kept coming." She wept through his entire testimony. It's true that she had style and self-possession. But she was also bighearted, emotional, and compassionate. This was the grandmother that I always knew.

After he finished his account, Abe was cross-examined by Irvin Dymond. Here it became clear that Abe had not brought a copy of the film with him from Dallas—of course, because he no longer had one—but that he had been given a duplicate by the DA's office when he arrived. It was, presumably, the copy that *LIFE* had turned over to the DA's office almost a year before. Dymond objected to the use of the film under these circumstances because it could not be assured that the version the prosecution was preparing to show was, in fact, identical to the original. Once again, the jury was made to leave the room, this time so that Abe could authenticate the film. The courtroom prepared itself for the first-ever public showing of the Zapruder film.

From the vantage point of the present, with the film so completely embedded in the American consciousness, it's difficult, if not impossible, to imagine what it was like when virtually no one had seen it. But Kirkwood's account takes us back in time to that moment, when the film was shrouded in secrecy and most people had no visual image in their minds of what had happened apart from the handful of snapshots that had been published in *LIFE*. I have often thought about how my grandfather's home movie of the Kennedy assassination became the iconic Zapruder film over time, gradually making its way into the American imagination. This first public showing—even though it was to a relatively small group of spectators and members of the press who were not allowed to reproduce it—was a turning point in the process. Kirkwood writes:

As Alvin Oser manned the projector and the courtroom was darkened, those spectators on the right of the room began squeezing and joggling to the left. They were admonished to be quiet and orderly but there was an insistent, almost panicky eagerness not to miss the first public showing of the widely heralded but little seen film. The Ladies of the Court were most distressed; the majority of them were sitting behind the screen. Many crowded to the side of it, spilling over into the aisle and crouching down or kneeling, some on all fours, in their attempts to peer around and up at the white surface... Except for the whir of the machine, the courtroom was deathly quiet.

There came the motorcade, turning onto Elm Street... the President, on the near side of the car to the camera, with Mrs. Kennedy in that now famous pink suit next to him, both of them smiling and waving, with the breeze blowing their hair and the trees in the background...

An intake of breath was heard in the courtroom, then a loud communal gasp when the President is hit a second time and his body jolts as the right side of his head literally explodes, sending a crimson halo of blood and matter spraying up into the air above him. Now short words and phrases filled the court: "Oh, God!" "Jesus!"... Then the President is falling toward his wife, to the left, and disappearing out of sight down in the car. Next the total surprise—one had heard of it but had forgotten—of seeing Mrs. Kennedy rise up, twist around and scramble back across the trunk of the car, only to be grabbed by Special Agent Clint Hill and shoved back into the rear seat.

The first showing was bloodcurdling; one could barely take it in... When the lights were switched on there was complete silence as all of us who had viewed this testament to the savagery of man pulled ourselves together.

Abe Zapruder quietly confirmed that this was his film, though he pointed out that since each frame represented one-eighteenth of a second, there was no way he could ensure that every single frame was there just by watching the film run through. The judge accepted the film as authentic and ordered that the jury be brought back into the courtroom. Abe was dismissed from the witness stand and went to sit with his wife. Over the course of the next few hours, in the presence of the jury, the press, the public, the attorneys for both sides, and the defendant himself, the Zapruder film was shown four more times—once in a careful frame-by-frame analysis that made the twenty-six-second reel last more than half an hour.

In his book, Kirkwood captures the continued frenzy inside the courtroom as the spectators and press shoved, argued, and jockeyed for position to get a better view. Of a moment that would have been comical in its absurdity if it had not been so distressing, he writes, "Three nuns in full habit crouched down in the center aisle, almost stretched out in a prone position on the floor, in an effort to see the film." Likewise, the jury was utterly gripped by what was happening. "The jurors, to a man, were riveted to the screen; never had they appeared so completely fascinated. A few in the back row stood and all leaned forward as the lights were lowered once again." Clay Shaw himself stood to the side smoking cigarettes, clutching one up to his chest in between puffs, as he watched the assassination over and over. With each successive showing, the viewers grew more and more annoyed with each other as they tried to get a better view. The judge ordered the courtroom spectators to settle down, but it appears that he had some trouble controlling his domain that afternoon. At one point, he interrupted the proceedings to say, "I have been advised that a reporter had the gall to ask if he could take a picture of this film while it was being shown in court. Don't they realize all rights are reserved on this picture?...I don't want anybody surreptitiously trying to take pictures of this film."

Kirkwood did not fail to notice my grandparents amid all of this chaos. "Mr. and Mrs. Zapruder sat quietly and virtually alone in the far right section of the courtroom, completely out of viewing range, staring not at the film but gazing rather sadly at the anxious, ill-tempered and, if not bloodthirsty, most definitely morbid craning mob of voyeurs who were glued to the screen." This was exactly what Abe Zapruder had dreaded. But it was under way and there was nothing to be done about it.

During an afternoon recess, Kirkwood found my grandparents and introduced himself. He described them as "a pleasant couple, she more talkative than her husband." During their brief conversation, Kirkwood asked my grandfather how many shots he recalled hearing (two, as he had maintained from the beginning), and my grandfather told him again of the "intense horror" that the film caused in him. According to Kirkwood, my grandmother said she had seen the film only once before the showings in the courtroom. That must have been on the night of the assassination, when my grandfather came home and showed it at the house on Marquette. "It was gruesome, wasn't it?" she said to him, shuddering.

When the session resumed, the judge had to reprimand the press again. "I have been informed," he said, clearly exasperated, "and I believe it, because I noticed it myself, that certain reporters and spectators have seen fit to leave early this afternoon trying to scoop the evidence...This morning, when it was announced Mr. Zapruder was going to be permitted to introduce his film, when we get to it, someone rushed out of the courtroom. If that happens in the future, that person's credentials will be taken away. You have cooperated with me for twenty-three days and I have enough problems of my own without worrying about the reporters and spectators, so I would appreciate cooperation in this matter."

When one of the jurors requested another showing of the film, Kirkwood reported again on the clamor in the courtroom to find the best position; but this time, the eagerness of the crowd began to wear on him. "I focused on those spectators around me and the ladies and nuns hunched in the back and over the far wall. Some of them were all smiles and giggles, nudging one another now that they had managed to get a bird's-eye view. A hungry look of salivating eagerness seemed to draw their faces to a point...I saw one lady arch her neck forward, grasp her companion's arm and, eyes shining, whisper, 'Now, now—here it comes!' This followed shortly by the sucked-in vacuum of a gang gasp. I wanted out of there."

It was evening by the time Abe was able to leave the courtroom. The film continued to play a role in the trial; it was shown several more times the following day and referred to repeatedly during the rest of the proceedings. When the prosecuting attorneys delivered their closing arguments, they again dwelled at length on the details of the assassination to make the case that there had been a conspiracy, even though they still could make no direct connection between those events and Clay Shaw. In his final appeal to the jury, Garrison invoked the Zapruder film again, accusing the government, and implicitly *LIFE* magazine, of perpetrating a fraud on the American people.

You heard in this courtroom in recent weeks, eyewitness after eyewitness after eyewitness and, above all, you saw one eyewitness which was indifferent to power—the Zapruder film. The lens of the camera is totally indifferent to power and it tells what happened as it saw it happen—and that is one of the reasons 200 million Americans have not seen the Zapruder film. They should have seen it many times. They should know exactly what happened. They all should know what you know now. Why hasn't all of this come into being if there hasn't been government fraud? Of course there has been fraud by the government.

In his closing statement, Irvin Dymond tried to mend the damage. He reminded the jury that no matter how horrifying it was, the Zapruder film did not have any bearing on Clay Shaw's innocence or guilt.

The State is going to come back before you and wave the Dallas flag again, gentlemen. They are going to talk about the Zapruder film. That is a horrifying film. That is the reason I squawked about your seeing it ten times. I had never seen it before, and I was shocked and horrified by it. But don't let that prejudice you, gentlemen, don't let it cause you to lose sight of the basic issues in this case.

The closing arguments ended late in the evening, and although the judge offered to allow the jurors to return to their hotel rooms and deliberate in the morning, they wanted to continue. It was after midnight on March 1, 1969, when they left the courtroom to deliberate. They were back within an hour. They found Clay Shaw not guilty and acquitted him of all charges. The trial was over and Clay Shaw was a free man.

The Garrison trial went down in history as a gross abuse of power, a two-year attack on an innocent man, and a waste of government time and resources. And while many came away from the trial believing that there might well have been more than one shooter in Dealey Plaza, Garrison's actions deeply discredited the conspiracy movement and drove it back underground for many years.

If the editors at *LIFE* hoped that the resolution of the Garrison trial would bring an end to their immediate problems related to the film, they were very much mistaken. On Wednesday, November 26, 1969, just about nine months after the end of the trial, an article titled "Texan Pushes Cause: Bootleg Film of JFK Slaying Offered" appeared in the Washington, DC, *Evening Star* newspaper. The reporter explained that Greg Olds, editor of the *Texas Observer*, a liberal Austin newspaper, had an "eighth or tenth generation copy" of the film and was offering to get more copies of it to sell to the public for $2.50 or $5.00 at no profit to himself. If his source for obtaining copies dried up, he went on, he would have duplicates made from his own copy. When the reporter shared this information with Dick Pollard at *LIFE*, Pollard responded unequivocally, "That would be a major lawsuit. I can assure you it is illegal. You can argue public interest, but not the copyright law." The Bernard Geis case had proved it. Then the reporter called Abe, who is quoted simply as saying, "This is the first I've heard of it."

That same day, Greg Olds sent a polite letter with best wishes to Dick Pollard, enclosing two copies of his editorial. The full text of his piece offers a clear explanation of why this ordinary citizen appeared determined to pick a fight with the media colossus. After running through the familiar tropes of conspiracy arguments that came from viewing the film, most notably how it clearly and unequivocally shows the president reacting to a shot from the front, the tone shifts. Suddenly, Olds is writing about something more than just solving the mystery of the assassination; he is expressing an urgency to confront these unanswered questions because something fundamental in the American character depends on it. Whether you consider this idealistic or misguided, Olds's impassioned explanation sheds light on those who made this their cause, even at the risk of legal action or worse. He writes:

> I know you are sick of this subject…But I do not raise it again here out of morbid curiosity or any maudlin longings. I simply believe we as a nation never faced seriously the alternate possibilities that the first Kennedy assassination posed… It conformed more with our sense of what our country is—or is supposed to be—to believe that a single madman, acting alone—had shot the president…
>
> But if we as a nation are to prevail we must face hard questions. Consider all that has happened to our country since that November six years ago. Perhaps it is only a sickness of spirit that has caused the unhappiness this nation has endured since then; a sickness of spirit arising out of our sense of shame and loss, and, more to the point, out of a deep-seated sense, often repressed, that we failed Kennedy, our nation, and ourselves in not looking diligently, intensively, and hard into the assassination—unafraid to face whatever the truth might have been.
>
> …Whatever you believe, you owe it to your country to see the Zapruder film. If you do see it, you won't believe the Warren Report.

Pollard responded with a polite letter of his own, reiterating that the film was protected by copyright and that it would be defended as such. But, he wrote, "From your article, I gather that your purpose is not to use the film for publication or financial gain but rather for investigatory reasons. Assuming that is true, why don't you come to New York and we'll show you a perfect dupe of the original with no frames missing." Greg Olds declined. But he did take *LIFE's* threats seriously, writing a follow-up to his original editorial. In it he addressed those who had ordered copies of the film directly, asking them for patience as he consulted with a lawyer and weighed the implications of violating the copyright, and alluded to a possible legal justification if the public need were sufficient. In thinking through the issues, he suggested that the best option would probably be a showing of the film on national television. In this, he duly considered questions of "taste and purpose," but concluded that these were outweighed by "the importance of this document whose implications must be faced by the nation."

In the article, he casually mentioned that "additional copies of the film, in whatever quantity I need, are available…So, supply is not the problem." It might not have been the problem for Greg Olds, but it most certainly was the problem for *LIFE*. How could this unknown person have unlimited copies of the Zapruder film? Who was supplying them to him? What would this mean for defending the copyright? If they couldn't defend it, would they eventually lose it? What would happen to their investment?

For now, the most pressing matter was figuring out the source of these bootleg copies. They had some suspicions, but to dig deeper they put their Austin stringer, Robin Lloyd, on the case and also hired an investigator (unnamed in the files) who spent a month or more conducting interviews and gathering information, uncovering traces of bootlegs not only in Austin but also in New Orleans, Washington, San Francisco, and Montreal, among other places. What they found was that there was no shortage of people and institutions that were perfectly willing to violate the law in their desire to get their own copies of the Zapruder film.

One creator of bootlegs, according to Lloyd, turned out to be *LIFE*'s erstwhile nemesis, CBS. Lloyd reminded Dick Pollard in a telegram dated December 2, 1969, that *LIFE* had lent a copy of the film to CBS in mid-1966 for background research on their Kennedy assassination documentary series. There is no written account of that loan in the Zapruder film files at *LIFE* from that year, so this information came as something of a surprise to me. According to Lloyd's telegram, the loan had been strictly for study purposes and not for reproduction or broadcast. In a surprise move, CBS made ten copies (though, according to a report by Hugh Aynesworth elsewhere in the file, it was reported to have been thirteen). It's worth noting that CBS, having been entrusted briefly with the film, had not only secretly duplicated it in spite of explicit instructions to the contrary, but had then gone on the air and publicly shamed *LIFE* magazine for refusing to allow it to be broadcast. It occurred to me to wonder if this was Dan Rather's revenge for *LIFE*'s having acquired the film back in 1963 in spite of his belief that he was both entitled to it and swindled out of it.

While there is no indication that CBS shared its copies, one source for the pirated copies allegedly included Bill Turner, an ex–FBI agent who wrote for the antigovernment and antiestablishment magazine *Ramparts*, who was "with Garrison at all times," and who is said to have been the source of the film that was supplied to Olds. But it was really Jim Garrison himself who appeared to be the primary culprit in the flagrant disregard for the copyright of the film and the protective orders issued by the courts against its reproduction and distribution.

None of this was particularly surprising, though it was perhaps alarming and unsettling. But in mid-December, *LIFE*'s investigator reported a story that sounds more like bad genre fiction than the actions of a legitimate district attorney. Investigator William Gurvich, who had worked in Garrison's office but had resigned over the Clay Shaw trial, met with Charles Ray Ward, who had been Garrison's first assistant and had also resigned his post in mid-1969, denouncing Garrison as a fraud and criticizing him for the charges against Clay Shaw. In utmost confidentiality—and only with guarantees that he would be held harmless in the investigation—Charles Ray Ward confessed that he had brought *LIFE* magazine's copy of the Zapruder film to a hotel room on the fourteenth floor of the Pontchartrain Hotel in New Orleans in mid-1968. He delivered the film to a French reporter, referred to by the code name "Inspector No. 3," who wrote for *Paris Match*. As if the story didn't have enough dodgy details, Ward added that one of Garrison's girlfriends was in the hotel room when he arrived, apparently "shacking up" with the Frenchman, at least for the night. Shortly thereafter, the film was allegedly taken from New Orleans to Montreal, where it remained for several weeks while three copies were made. Upon the Frenchman's return to New Orleans, he gave the copies to Garrison. In a report produced for Time Inc., Gurvich recounted the information he had gotten from Ward regarding pirated copies of the film. "One was kept in Garrison's residence and another in the safe in his office," he wrote. "The third was given to Ward to retain. According to Ward, Garrison believed he would be assassinated and wanted copies made 'or else the world will never know the truth.'"

In the spring of 1969, my parents were in New York with friends for the weekend when they got a call. Abe wasn't well. He had been diagnosed with stomach cancer and was going to have surgery. "We just kind of stayed in the hotel," my mother recalled. "We didn't feel like going anywhere." When I ask her if she and my father knew right away how serious it was, she says no. In those days, she tells me, doctors operated and then routinely told patients that they had removed all the cancer, whether or not it was really true.

In September 1969, there is a letter from Dick Pollard, polite as always, responding to what must have been a phone call from Abe, who had heard disturbing news about the film. According to the *New York Times*, a short motion picture called *Mort d'un président* had been scheduled to premiere in Paris at the Théâtre Balzac on the Champs Elysées. Director Hervé Lamarre confirmed to the *Times* that it included the Zapruder film and said that it was the first time that the film would be seen in full in public. It was, of course, an entirely unauthorized use of the film and a clear violation of *LIFE*'s copyright. United Artists, which had partly financed another film due to premiere at the same time, *L'Américain*, forced the producer to withdraw the short movie, but the underlying issue remained. Pollard wrote to Abe: "We, too, were shocked by the story in the N.Y. Times reporting that your film was to be used in a motion picture. Our lawyers in Paris were alerted and report that UA has withdrawn the movie. However, we still must find out if there is a bootleg dupe of your film circulating in Europe."

Just a few months later, on December 4, there is the first letter from my father to Dick Pollard. I can't help but think that my grandfather's illness had something to do with this. Maybe Abe needed his son to help him deal with the film at this point. It is cordial but businesslike, referring to a visit they made together to the *LIFE* offices during the summer of 1968 and following up on Abe's inquiry about the *Texas Observer* editorial and the copyright violation of the film. In it, Henry asks for information on the steps that *LIFE* was taking to preserve the integrity of the copyright.

A few days later, Pollard wrote back to Abe, copying Henry. "After your phone call, and the one from the Washington Star, we put our Austin stringer to work on the bootleg film. It was our feeling that the Texas Observer was not the real culprit... However, [Greg Olds] would not tell us the source of the stolen film. Confidentially, we have traced it to District Attorney Garrison's office and to a Ramparts correspondent... As you know, Garrison subpoenaed the film. We can only assume he made a dupe. Your son can attest that this is highly irregular."

Pollard appears not to have known that Abe was ill, and it's possible that Henry's letter seemed like a rebuke, or as if the heavy-hitting DC lawyer was stepping in to handle something that his father could not. But I don't know this for sure. What I do know from the records is that the ongoing problems with the bootlegs (especially those from Greg Olds) and copyright were making general manager Jack Watters a little nervous. He handwrote a note to chief editorial counsel Jack Dowd on one of the early December telegrams with information about the bootlegs: "Here's more on the Zapruder mess. Should we be reacting more emphatically?" But in early January, a note to the file from Dowd reads, "We are in good shape as of now. Will move on them if they violate again."

They didn't. Greg Olds wrote a letter on February 27, 1970, to all those who had requested copies of the film—nearly 150 requests from twenty states and several foreign countries—explaining his decision not to distribute the film after all. Olds graciously conceded defeat, recognizing that it would constitute copyright infringement and that they would likely lose the resulting lawsuit, thus failing to accomplish his goal of distribution of the film to a wide audience. "I appreciate having heard from each of you," he wrote. "The orders for the film confirmed my notion that interest is great in President Kennedy's death and doubt is widespread that we have as yet uncovered the truth as to who was responsible for that tragic loss to mankind." He sent a copy to Pollard with a short cover letter. Pollard's response captures all the exasperation and frustration of being the person who had to handle this unruly, complicated, endlessly controversial historical document. "Thank you very much for sending the letter on the Zapruder film. I suspect it may be the best solution at this time...I look forward to the day when I am no longer responsible for this historic film. I get it from all sides—Zapruder, Time Inc., the networks, etc."

As winter turned to spring 1970, there was one further round of communication between Abe and Dick Pollard. Dick Hitt of the *Dallas Times Herald* published a small item on April 9, 1970, suggesting that *LIFE* magazine was considering selling the Zapruder film, possibly for as much as $250,000. Abe must have called Dick Pollard again. He passed along the article via mail, with a short note: "It was nice talking to you and I was glad to hear that things are well with you. I am enclosing the article of the Dallas Times Herald and, as you see, they don't know everything but it fills part of the column." There is no answer to his letter in the file. It was the last letter Abe Zapruder would write to *LIFE* magazine.

CHAPTER 8

■ ■ ■ ■ ■ ■ ■

LIFE'S DILEMMA

In the summer of 1970, Abe's cancer recurred. This time, there was nothing to be done. He was admitted to Presbyterian Hospital—known as Presby—and Lil went there every day, cooking food for him in the tiny kitchen on the hot plate, trying to find anything that he could tolerate or that would tempt him.

My twin brother and I had been born in the fall of 1969. Both sets of grandparents, along with the rest of the family, came to Washington, DC, for my brother's bris, but I was too small to go home from the hospital. My parents hadn't known my mother was carrying twins until we were born, and I was in an incubator and missed the whole thing. Sometime late in the summer of 1970, we all traveled to Dallas. My aunt remembers that my parents brought us to the hospital to see our grandfather. Michael and I, nine months old, were in our double stroller and Matthew, nearly three, stuck close by. Papa Abe was wheeled down to see us. The moment was surely too short, and no doubt agonizing to all the adults who were present. Still, there is something reassuring to me about the fact that we were even briefly in the same place at the same time. I am glad that he laid eyes on the three of us together, that he looked at our faces and saw for himself the children who would carry his name. He died on August 31, 1970, at the age of sixty-five.

To the world, Abraham Zapruder was the bystander who filmed the assassination of President Kennedy, the ultimate amateur photographer, famous the world over for being in the right place at the right time. Major papers carried obituaries that collapsed his entire life into a few lines about the twenty-six seconds of film that bore his name and came to define him in the public's mind. But none of that had anything to do with who he really was or the real loss that our family felt when he died. Very much like my own father, he was a person who had endless interests, projects, plans, and ideas. He was incapable of being bored. He was happy puttering with the sprinklers in his garden or playing music on his electric organ or tinkering with the wiring in the house. These projects often led to mishaps and hilarity, like the time Abe piped the electric organ to play through the stereo speakers in the den and was happily banging away one morning when Henry—home from college and sleeping off a hangover in the den—was jolted awake and tried in panicked confusion to make the show tunes stop by frantically adjusting the dials on the television and radio.

The funeral was held at Temple Emanu-El in Dallas, the congregation that had welcomed my grandparents in Dallas thirty years before. Rabbi Levi Olan, the revered leader of the community, delivered the eulogy. Afterward, my parents, Aunt Myrna and Uncle Myron, and my grandmother rode in a limousine behind the hearse that carried my grandfather's body in a slow funeral cortege from Temple Emanu-El in Highland Park, through the suburban streets of north Dallas, to the cemetery, which was located about six miles away, toward the downtown area of the city.

As they rode, my family began telling stories about Abe. One after the other, they traded memories of his funniest moments, retold his favorite jokes, and repeated one-liners that always broke up everyone in the room. A favorite one came from the time he and Lil were at a friend's house for brunch and the guests had been waiting a very long time to sit down to eat. As everyone milled around, talking and hoping soon to be invited to eat, the host came over to make an introduction, saying, "Abe, I'd like you to meet a friend of mine." Without missing a beat, and with a wry smile and a mischievous twinkle in his eye, Abe said, "What I'd really like to meet is a bagel and lox." Best of all was his warning against using too many "ta-*ta*-tas," an expression we often repeat in our family to this day. He would say that every automated or mechanical object—cars, refrigerators, toaster ovens—had only so many ta-*ta*-tas, you know, because while they are running, they make noises, going "ta-*ta*-ta, ta-*ta*-ta, ta-*ta*-ta." When Lil would put chicken bones in the waste disposal unit, he would scold her in bemused exasperation, "Lil, don't put the bones in the disposal! You're going to use up the ta-*ta*-tas!"

As the long, black car swung through the deep red wrought-iron gates of the cemetery, my grieving family found themselves laughing uproariously, remembering the inimitable, hilarious, utterly unique man that was Abe Zapruder. I can think of no better legacy for his life than that.

On a fall day in November 2013, I drove east from my home in Chevy Chase to Pasadena, Maryland, to meet Robert Groden, who has—for better and for worse—played a critical role in the history of the Zapruder film. It was a sunny afternoon, the late-changing leaves along the Baltimore–Washington Parkway read as rust and copper with an occasional pop of red. Above me hung a low drape of storm clouds, but in the distance, there were plum-colored wisps in the brightly lit sky. It was the kind of autumn day that feels, even as you are witnessing it, like it is slipping away.

Groden was due to speak that evening about his research on the JFK assassination. Before his talk, we met in the law offices of one of his friends. He is a big man, wearing suspenders that day, with broad features and thick white hair that falls over his ears. He has an amiable manner, a friendly smile, and from the moment we met, he was frank and open-handed with his answers to my questions. It was clear that while I considered him a stranger, he felt deeply connected to our family and our history through the Zapruder film. It was as if all the gratitude he felt for the existence of the film, which he had never been able to express to my grandfather—or my father, for that matter—was finding its way to me. It was endearing and a little uncomfortable; it was impossible not to like him but I wasn't sure I was going to agree with all or even most of what he had to say about the assassination. Then again, I wasn't there to debate the finer points of conspiracy theory with Robert Groden. I was there to hear about how he got hold of a copy of the Zapruder film, hid that fact for six years, labored to make the best possible visual copy he could, and eventually allowed it to be aired, illegally, for the first time to a national audience on *Good Night America* with Geraldo Rivera in 1975.

Groden told me that he had been a big fan of the president and that he had been, like so many others, shocked and devastated when he was assassinated. It happened to be Groden's eighteenth birthday, which made him feel a sort of intense personal connection to the event. "I felt safer as an American with him in the White House," he told me. "And I think...when he was killed it was as if someone had cut an anchor chain and we were adrift in the ocean. It was just a horribly emotional strange thing, and I didn't know what direction my life was taking." He left high school shortly thereafter, while still in eleventh grade, and enlisted in the army, but he soon found that military service was not for him. He returned to his native New York, and after working in the record business for a while, he encountered Moses Weitzman, who was working at EFX Unlimited.

Weitzman had previously made 16mm and 35mm copies of the Zapruder film for *LIFE* magazine when he was working at Manhattan Effects. He had since left that job, but when its parent company, Technical Animations, decided to sell the company, they called him back to help liquidate some of their assets. "And lo and behold," he recalled years later, "in my office, there was my box with that piece of film, that technically imperfect copy...I kept it as a sample of my expertise...drawing a perfect circle, so to speak." He brought that copy with him to his next job, at EFX Unlimited, where he eventually hired Robert Groden, which is how Groden found himself in close proximity to a very good 35mm copy of the Zapruder film.

By this time, Groden was an avid conspiracy theorist. He was convinced that the Warren Commission was nonsense and that the public was being deceived by a massive cover-up. He told me, and has told many others, the story of visiting President Kennedy's grave at Arlington Cemetery in 1965. He thinks he remembers speaking aloud to it but he is not sure. Either way, he introduced himself to the dead president and swore to find out who killed him no matter how long it took and where it took him. In conversation, Groden seems earnest and sincere and, as such, very disarming. It's hard not to believe him. Then again, it's also hard to relate. Perhaps it is only my conventional thinking, but I cannot help but think that such a grandiose life commitment must be psychologically motivated, that it is about something deeper than simply wanting to find out who killed President Kennedy. Perhaps it is a desire to have some purpose, or to escape the confines of an ordinary life in the service of greatness. Or maybe it reflects an unwillingness to face the finality of the president's death, or a reluctance to accept that knowing how he was murdered will do nothing to restore what was shattered. Maybe for some, it is better to dwell in the moments before, to remain in the how because there will never be a satisfying answer to the why.

Or maybe not. Either way, Groden became determined to uncover the truth of the Kennedy assassination. The single most important moment for him occurred in 1969 when he came across that 35mm copy of the Zapruder film. Groden says that Weitzman knew of his interest in the case and showed him a copy of the film. In Groden's words, "Absolutely everything that we had seen—the illicit copies that were made during the Garrison investigation—were visual mud. This was like looking at the original event." Groden says that soon after he saw the film, Weitzman gave him the copy, saying, "You can do more with this than I can." This is not how Weitzman remembers it. In fact, he says that he was not "into the whole underground culture of the Zapruder [film]." To hear Weitzman tell it, the film was not given to anyone. It was taken. "I didn't keep it under lock and key," he said. "Someone made surreptitious copies of it and used it." Either way, when Weitzman was asked in his 1997 testimony before the Assassination Records Review Board how many copies he thought there might be of the Zapruder film, he answered, "Oh, God.

Unfortunately, I probably am the grandfather of many of them...
To the best of my knowledge, that [35 mm] copy is what a great
many copies have been made from."

However it happened, Groden got hold of the 35mm print and
had, in Weitzman's lab, access to equipment that allowed him to work
on it to produce an even better quality version. To this end, he did
several things to the film. First, he "step-framed" it—meaning that
he shot each frame twice so that the whole film runs slightly slower,
allowing the mind a fraction more time to absorb what is happening.
Then, by modifying a technique known as rotoscoping, he reshot the
film frame by frame, zooming in to a particular focal point, such as
the president's head, and keeping that focal point in the center of the
frame for each shot. In this way, the film was both closer up and sta-
bilized, because the image remained in the center of the frame rather
than moving up and down, as it does in the original. Groden repeated
this process several dozen times, creating versions of the film focusing on the reactions of Mrs. Kennedy, the driver, Governor Connally, various Secret Service agents, and parts of the car. The overall
result was multiple versions of the film that were much clearer, more
detailed, and easier to see than previous copies had been.

During the time he was doing this work, Groden describes himself
as deathly afraid, looking through the rearview mirror of his car every
few seconds when he drove anywhere. As he put it in his interview
with the Sixth Floor Museum, "I was very, very paranoid about it. I
had in my hands the Zapruder film, the enhanced Zapruder film—
the proof that at least one shot came from the right front...And I was
really too afraid to deal with this. I didn't know where it would lead.
I didn't know who was involved. And all I knew was here I have this
evidence, and I didn't know what to do with it. So I put it away in a
bank vault because I was too afraid to do anything with it."

*   *   *

While Robert Groden's copies of the Zapruder film sat in a bank vault, waiting to see the light of day, the magazine editors at *LIFE* continued to struggle about what to do with the original and the bootlegs that seemed to pop up continually. In his last letter to Dick Pollard in April 1970, Abe had inquired about a snippet in the *Dallas Times Herald* about a proposal to sell the original film. I suspect he thought it was a rumor. Apparently, it wasn't. That same month, Hollywood cinematographer Haskell Wexler (whose credits at that time included *Who's Afraid of Virginia Woolf?*, *In the Heat of the Night*, and *The Thomas Crown Affair*) wrote to Dick Pollard inquiring about the possibility of purchasing the original Zapruder film. He initially wanted *LIFE* to send the original via courier to its office in LA, but Pollard soon replied, "I've had second thoughts on sending the Zapruder original to the West Coast. It's just too scary to think of losing it—so much so that no one on my staff wants to take the responsibility." They agreed on a compromise and Pollard reported in early June, "If the price is right, we might just go ahead and make a few bucks." The arrangements continued to move ahead for several duplicates of the film to be couriered out to the West Coast in June. Then, nothing.

The matter was taken up again in late January 1971 when Pollard wrote a memo to Time Inc. vice president Rhett Austell explaining that the magazine had decided to sell the film. After updating him on revenue generated by the film and the ongoing problem of bootlegs, Pollard wrote: "I bring this to your attention in case one of your Divisions might have future use for this historic film." In another memo to Dick Clurman, former chief of the Time-Life News Service, he explained that the film had generated little revenue in the past two years and that there were "sizable legal fees" to maintain the copyright.

Around the same time, he showed the film to Austell and Edward "Pat" Lenahan, who was general manager of *LIFE* at the time. Austell and Lenahan had similarly emotional responses to the film, and neither favored selling it. But they had entirely different approaches to dealing with it. "Austell thought the footage too rough to ever use in motion. He advised us to give it to the Library of Congress and take a tax deduction. Lenahan said, 'I don't care if it costs $100,000 a year for the next ten years to protect the copyright, we should not sell or give this film away.' So, the Zapruder film is off the market for one-time use or outright sale." In passing, Pollard mentioned that they had never had a serious offer, so perhaps the Haskell Wexler deal had fizzled over the price. Managing editor Ralph Graves apparently agreed with this decision, though in a handwritten note, he added, "At some point, the Film Division should figure out a way to use it to own credit and profit."

It is clear that, over the years, the fate of the film was largely dependent on the values and tastes of each individual editor who ended up in charge of it. While one editor might be ready to sell it or give it away, another editor was committed to keeping it; while one person thought it should never be seen, another wanted to reserve the right to exploit it for film or TV. Likewise, some editors were attached to the idea of discretion and good taste, while others talked in terms of profit and recouping lost investments. As with most things, the reality was far more complex than the idea of *LIFE* as a monolithic organization in lockstep over using the film for the greatest possible profit and orchestrating a calculated effort to keep the film from the public.

* * *

In the summer of 1973, shortly before the tenth anniversary of the president's death, Bernard Fensterwald, representing an organization called the Committee to Investigate Assassinations (confusingly, the CIA), wrote to *LIFE* to inquire about licensing the Zapruder film for use in a documentary film to be "distributed by the Committee for exhibit on college campuses, before community organizations, and possibly theaters in this country and overseas." The committee claimed no specific agenda regarding the assassination, describing its mission to "seek the truth and inform people of the facts." The board of directors included a significant number of well-known authors of books about the assassination, though none of them endorsed the findings of the Warren Commission. Fensterwald explained that the committee was consulting with Robert Richter, who had previously worked for CBS on the four-part Warren Report series (in which the Zapruder film had not appeared) and who was representing the committee in the negotiations. Jack Beck in *LIFE*'s film division wrote back promptly to say that *LIFE* was investigating the possibility of using the film for the tenth anniversary and was disinclined to discuss the matter until they had reached a decision. They punted it for further review in September.

Sure enough, on September 20, Richter wrote again with an offer: $10,000 for a nonexclusive license for the committee to use the Zapruder film in a documentary he would produce. *LIFE* once again seemed ready to consider a deal. Jack Beck wrote to editorial services director Paul Welch to suggest that they try to work out a deal in which the TV rights would be held back in the hope of eventually profiting from them. "I say this because I share the Committee's view... that some day there is destined to be a break in this story which will tell us more than the Warren Commission was able to find out. When that happens, the Zapruder film will again have heightened historical significance, I imagine. It certainly should remain a house asset." For the moment, the film was apparently back on the market. In the following months, the negotiations continued the way such things do, the complexities of legal jargon obscuring possible hesitations or tensions, and with seemingly endless questions, answers, tweaks, and corrections.

Meanwhile, in November 1973, the committee sponsored a conference at Georgetown University to commemorate the tenth anniversary of the assassination. Notwithstanding their ongoing negotiations with *LIFE* magazine to license the film for documentary use, the committee convinced Robert Groden to premiere his illegal, highly enhanced copy of the Zapruder film at the conference. If anyone at *LIFE* knew about it or objected, their reaction is not captured in the records. As late as mid-December, the two organizations were still trading license agreements and negotiating over details. Perhaps this was because, as Richard Trask and others noted, the film had an enormous impact on the assembled attendees but didn't make a big public splash. The press didn't cover it and it didn't result in Groden's hoped-for popular outcry. Robert Groden told me the same thing: "The hit of the entire conference, if you can call it that, was the fact that 'Here's the film. It exists.'...People were seeing it. We now had confirmation that what we had always suspected the film showed... [it] really did. But nothing happened. There was no press coverage, nothing, it just went away." Is it possible that *LIFE* simply didn't know that their potential partner was premiering an illegal copy of the film in advance of signing a license agreement with them? If Abe had been alive, he would have called that a pretty extraordinary act of *chutzpah*.

By the start of 1974, the committee was out of the negotiations and Richter was representing his own interests with *LIFE* to make a documentary using the film, with the assistance of a financial backer who is not named in the correspondence. Through most of 1974, the back-and-forth continues—enduring a hiccup when Mark Lane screened a bootleg copy of the film and Richter's backer pressed *LIFE* to sue but the magazine refused. As Richter continually expanded his plans for the use of the film—from a short documentary to a long one, from an educational project to a for-profit one, from a nonexclusive license to an exclusive one—*LIFE* was forced to keep changing the terms of the agreement. In late April 1974, Paul Welch wrote to Richter: "We seem to have a whole new launch going with the Zapruder film. I think we have to re-examine back at ground zero and deal with this as purely a commercial flight with none of the educational or public interest overtones of our earlier discussions." Even as they closed in on a deal, the endless game of whack-a-mole with bootleg copies of the Zapruder film would not end. In May, Claude Lelouch, who had been forced to pull a pirated version of the film from *Mort d'un président* in 1969, managed to premiere the movie again under the new title *Toute une vie*—this time including the bootlegged clip from the film—at the Cannes Film Festival in May 1974. Under pressure from *LIFE*, he agreed to take out the illegal clip, but the editors at *LIFE* planned to sue him for infringement anyway.

That same month, the negotiations on Richter's proposed documentary—now called *You Are the Jury*—had gotten far enough along that the prospectus was kicked upstairs to editor in chief Hedley Donovan. When he heard about the offer, managing editor Ralph Graves wrote a memo to his bosses, which, after so much back-and-forth, once again captures the tone of *LIFE* magazine from the old days:

Paul tells me that it is now company policy to entertain responsible offers for use of the Zapruder film. I suppose this constitutes a responsible offer, but I find the treatment questionable at best and highly objectionable at worst...I think the Zapruder film should be seen for its historical importance. But the Richter treatment reveals an intention to exploit the film to the hilt for (a) shock effect and (b) conspiracy controversy. Perhaps any film producer who got his hands on this property would do the same. Paul points out that it would be difficult for us to undertake a censorship role, telling the producer how he can use the film and what he can say about it. I agree. I think we should either say yes or no to the proposition. My own answer is a simple no.

Hedley Donovan circled this last sentence of the memo and scribbled a note at the bottom of the page. "Ralph: I agree. HD."

This decision put a hold on Richter's plans for the film, though he would reappear later in 1975 for one more try. Now, for the umpteenth time, *LIFE* magazine was faced with figuring out what they could or should do with the Zapruder film. Paul Welch sought advice from chief editorial counsel Gabe Perle, who outlined the risks inherent in a company policy that depended on decisions based on editorial content. Although *LIFE* was entitled to make these judgments as the owner of the film, there was also a public interest that remained a competing factor. Sitting in the position of censor was going to end badly, either in the form of another lawsuit or simply the degradation of the copyright through repeated "fair use," which had been allowed by the judgment in the Geis lawsuit. They needed a new approach. There seemed to be two options. One was to make the film available to anyone who asked, based on a standard set of prices, removing themselves from the position of making editorial judgments about whether or not it was an appropriate use. The other was to give it to a public institution and let someone else handle it. Later that same day, Perle wrote a second memo, realizing that this might not be so simple after all. "After re-reading the agreement with Zapruder, I think that we cannot give away title to the film unless we get approval of the gift from whoever is legally responsible for Zapruder's estate."

Welch, clearly frustrated, passed all the documentation along to his colleague Bob Lubar. "Can we get together, possibly with Ralph, to dispose of the Zapruder question once and for all?" Among the considerations he listed, the last one reads: "If we don't go ahead with the Richter deal I think we ought to give the film to the National Archives, Library of Congress, someone, for whatever tax write-off we can claim. Or, at worst, for nothing." It seems that Welch was willing to do nearly anything to be done with the Zapruder film. On a second copy of the memo, Graves handwrote a note at the top: "Lubar, Welch, and I decided on 6/21/74 to give film to National Archives or Library of Congress as historic document belonging to the public."

Excellent. It was done. There was just the little matter of running it by the Zapruder family.

An internal memo documents the beginning of what would be a long conversation on this subject. "Paul talked with Henry Zapruder, who is Abraham's brother [*sic*] and executor of the estate about our suggestion to give the film to the National Archives." Just enough time had passed that no one included in this correspondence had known Abe Zapruder or had any sense of the family. The personal connection between Abe and Dick Stolley and Dick Pollard was a thing of the past. The memo goes on: "Henry wanted to talk first with Abraham's wife (could it be Sarah??) and presumably he has since done so...Please let me know what happens on this. You know we have Richter waiting in the wings and Paul is also holding up on a British film company. The original film is in Lillian Owens' safe."

The conversations continued to heat up as Henry, the executives at *LIFE*, and Bob Richter went back and forth over what to do. *LIFE* clearly didn't want it anymore. Richter did. It's impossible to tell from the memos what Henry really wanted, except that he, like editor in chief Hedley Donovan and managing editor Ralph Graves, did not approve of Richter's prospectus. The question seemed to be what power Henry had to control the outcome of the decision. Welch wrote a memo to the file on January 17, 1975:

> Our legal counsel says that indeed we have an obligation, that Henry does have veto power, that under the terms of the agreement our lawyer feels that the Zapruder estate is entitled to try and make some money on the film before we give it to the National Archives.
>
> I also told Richter that we are in the awkward position of holding on to something too hot to handle and no saucer to put it on. Richter said Zapruder doesn't want us to give the film to the National Archives but that was Henry Zapruder's feeling several months ago when he still thought he could make a buck on it.
>
> I told Richter I was going to call Zapruder and try to reach a decision that would get us off dead center.

LIFE really was in a bind. There seemed to be no way to use the film in a tasteful way, and one memo after the other confirms it was the fundamental conflict of sitting on an incredibly valuable piece of property that could not be used without making too many ethical compromises that led *LIFE* to decide to give it away. A few weeks later, Paul Welch wrote another memo to the file updating the record. He noted that Richter still wanted to use the film but that it seemed unlikely that any proposal would get approval at *LIFE* and that "there was no way of making a film based on the Zapruder footage which would be commercially profitable that would get Time Inc. editorial approval. I said I could continue to pursue with Henry Zapruder the National Archives plan; that I felt very uncomfortable sitting in the middle and wanted to get the film out of Time Inc.'s hands."

While *LIFE* debated whether it could give the film to the National Archives and how to deal with the Zapruders, events were transpiring that would end up having a serious impact on the final outcome. Robert Groden had been approached again, this time by an organization known as the Assassination Information Bureau, a group that was organizing showings of bootleg copies on college campuses around the nation. They asked Groden to present his enhanced version of the film at a conference called "The Politics of Conspiracy," which opened at Boston University on January 31, 1975. The organizers of the conference did not use the event to advocate for one theory or another—in fact, there were some presenters whose ideas offended even Mark Lane—but to challenge once again the official findings of the Warren Commission and to call for a reopening of the JFK investigation. Participants and activists also appealed for a fresh look at the assassinations of Robert F. Kennedy and Martin Luther King Jr.

Groden showed the film at a press conference before the main conference. Unlike the viewing at Georgetown in 1973, this time there was a huge media presence and national reaction. The *New York Times* carried an article about it—albeit with a mistaken description of Mrs. Kennedy's movements—a few days later, on February 3:

> The dramatic high point of the conference was the showing of a "bootleg" copy of what is known as "the Zapruder film." This is an amateur movie made by Abraham Zapruder, a Dallas dressmaker, which is the only known pictorial record of the moment Mr. Kennedy was shot. The film was purchased by Time Inc. and has never been officially released.
>
> In the film, President Kennedy is seen slumping forward in the back seat of the convertible, his hands moving upward toward his neck.
>
> His wife, Jacqueline, is seen moving across Gov. John B. Connally of Texas, who is sitting slightly forward, reaching for the President [*sic*].
>
> Suddenly, the President's head and the upper part of his body are snapped violently backward. Blood gushes about his face.
>
> This moment of the film was marked by groans and gasps from the audience packed into an auditorium at Boston University, the conference site.

That very day, Groden appeared with the film at a press conference in Chicago organized by Dick Gregory, another conspiracy activist. Again, the film was shown, this time to the flabbergasted attention of the media. The snowball was rolling down the hill now, gathering mass and force and speed. There was no way to stop it, particularly because there was no one present at any of these events to offer a dissenting interpretation of what the film showed. Since the images do, in fact, show the president's head snapping backward, there seemed little question that this was, at last, the visual evidence that the fatal shot came from the front, not from the rear, where the Texas School Book Depository was located. Despite the fact that six years earlier, Luis Alvarez and Paul Hoch had carried out exhaustive studies showing that, according to the principles of physics, the backward movement of the president's head was entirely consistent with a shot from the rear, such counter-narratives did not receive widespread attention.

Instead, for the moment, the questions raised seemed to point perfectly toward conspiracy: Why hadn't the public seen the film if there was nothing to hide? Why did the images on the film seem to contradict the explanation given by the Warren Report? How could anyone look at the film and think that all the shots came from behind the president? In the context of an American crisis of faith in the government throughout the late 1960s and '70s, it must have seemed not only absurd but insulting to ask people to take the word of the Warren Report over what they saw with their own eyes.

For his part, Groden was transformed overnight from looking fearfully over his shoulder and hiding the film in a safe into a conspiracy celebrity, showing the film to hundreds of people, among them members of the news media, and even, on February 4, 1975, testifying before the Rockefeller Commission on CIA activities within the United States.

If *LIFE* was aware of the showing of the film at Boston University and the press conference in Chicago, there's no mention of it in the records. While the film was causing an uproar in Boston, Chicago, and Washington, inside the Time & Life Building in New York, the memos flew back and forth about how to give it to the National

Archives and how to convince the Zapruders to allow that. Should there be strings attached? Perhaps there should be restrictions limiting its use to historical or educational purposes only. Could *LIFE* give it away but keep a provision allowing them to use it "editorially or commercially should the occasion arise"? Before reaching a final decision, *LIFE* planned to get the film appraised and, assuming the film's value was more than $20,000, to buy out the Zapruder family for a sum "not to exceed $10,000." All were agreed. The film appraisal came in at $220,000, which is nearly a million dollars in today's money, and matters finally seemed like they were about to be settled. Executives at *LIFE* agreed on a proposal from Henry to share a fifty-fifty tax write-off with the Zapruder heirs when the film was donated to the National Archives.

On March 6, 1975, the inevitable happened. As Groden tells it, while he was testifying at the Rockefeller Commission the month before, a call came in from someone at *Good Night America*, hosted by Geraldo Rivera. Everyone was talking about the conspiracies, about the Zapruder film, about the need to reopen the investigation and reconsider the validity of the Warren Commission findings. Geraldo wanted to broadcast the Zapruder film on his show. Groden, Dick Gregory, and another Warren Commission critic named Ralph Schoenman were invited to the program to air the film and discuss the assassination. (The other guests that evening would include the considerably less controversial Raquel Welch and author Charles Berlitz talking about his best-selling book about the Bermuda Triangle.) There is nothing in the *LIFE* archives about this night, but Groden says that after the program was taped but before it aired, Time Inc. threatened to sue ABC if they ran the film. As Groden tells it, "The executives and attorneys at ABC told Geraldo not to show the film, but he said, 'You're going to run it or you're going to get yourself a new boy.' And he stood up for it and we showed it. And it was the highest ratings he had ever gotten. Ever!"

If we are being very exacting, it would be accurate to point out that the film had actually appeared on television before. One of these showings was on the late-night television program *Underground News* with Chuck Collins, originating on WSNS-TV in Chicago in 1970 and later airing in syndication to Philadelphia, Detroit, Kansas City, and St. Louis. A copy of the film had apparently been given to *Underground News* director Howie Samuelsohn by conspiracy theorist Penn Jones Jr., the editor of the *Midlothian Mirror*. There were probably other broadcasts, as well. But not unlike the showing of the film in the courtroom in New Orleans or the various viewings of bootleg versions, these were essentially limited to local audiences.

Geraldo's program on ABC was another story entirely. This was a national broadcast on a major network, with a viewership of millions. Rivera, with a flowing mane of brown hair and his signature mustache, sits on the set with Dick Gregory and Robert Groden on swivel chairs against the backdrop of a nauseating gold curtain. After interviewing the two men, learning how they became involved in the questions surrounding the assassination, Geraldo introduces the film:

I'm telling you right straight out that if you are at all sensitive, uh, if you're at all queasy, uh, then don't watch this film, just put on the, uh, the late-night movie, uh, because this is, uh, very heavy. It's the film shot by the Dallas dress manufacturer

Abraham, uh, Zapruder, and it's the execution of President Kennedy.

Groden narrates the events, beginning with footage of the president and first lady on Main Street, spliced together with clips from the Marie Muchmore and Orville Nix films. As the Zapruder film begins to roll, Groden continues to narrate, describing how the president is waving to the crowd before disappearing behind the freeway sign. Then the president reappears from behind the Stemmons Freeway sign:

GRODEN: He is shot, then Governor Connally is shot.
GERALDO: He's already been hit.
GRODEN: He's already been hit.
(*There are a few seconds of agonizing silence.*)
GERALDO: And now?
GRODEN: At the bottom of the screen, the head shot.

Behind him, you can hear audible gasps and a sort of moan coming from the audience. Geraldo says, "That's the shot that blew off his head. That's the most horrifying thing I've ever seen in the movies."

After a few minutes discussing the Warren Commission and Groden's view that the Zapruder film definitively refutes its conclusion, they watch an extreme close-up of just President Kennedy's head, one of Groden's carefully reshot versions of the film. For the second time—and this time the image fills the screen—the president is murdered in cold blood. As they go to commercial break, Geraldo addresses the camera again. "Oh, God, that's awful. That's the most upsetting thing I've ever seen. We'll talk about it in a minute."

*   *   *

This moment on national television was a turning point for the film, though in exactly what way really depended on who you were. For Groden and others who felt absolutely committed to make what they saw as the truth of the assassination public, it was a victory over what they saw as years of suppression, lies, and intimidation by the government. Even now, it's impossible when talking to Groden to fail to see his conviction in his views. Then again, on *Good Night America* and elsewhere, there was an absolute conflation of the film itself with a supposedly ironclad view that what we see proves the existence of a second shooter; anything else was heresy. Certainly, Geraldo Rivera didn't present an opposing view on his program. In fact, it was as if there were no opposing view; no one was going on TV and narrating a different story or explaining why the president's head would snap back even if he was shot from the rear. Why? Because *LIFE* controlled the film and *LIFE* would not engage in these debates, nor would it allow others to use the film for this or any other purpose. The unintended result was that even though *LIFE* owned the film, the conspiracists owned its content, defining its meaning with their stolen copies. This polarization did no one any favors. And the conspiracy theorists, while they might have reasonable points to make or questions to ask, defined themselves so completely as against the Establishment that it became impossible to interpret the evidence differently without being accused of being an apologist for the government or part of the cover-up.

It's clear that for Groden and his colleagues, the airing of the film on national television was critical in that it moved the debate forward and opened the possibility of a new investigation, which is of course exactly what eventually happened. For Geraldo, it's hard to say. Did he air the film on television—in flagrant disregard of its copyright, risking a lawsuit or blowback from the executives at ABC—because he was deeply committed to the conspiracists' cause? That seems doubtful. Was it because he felt that—regardless of how one interpreted the evidence—it was a moral imperative to share the film with the public? Or was it just because it was a huge media coup guaranteed to bring huge ratings (which it did) and cement his growing reputation as a fearless young reporter who would stop at nothing to bring the truth, no matter how horrible, to his audiences?

For *LIFE*, the airing of the film on *Good Night America* was the final blow after years of headaches. They had come to the conclusion that there was no way to use it respectfully and tastefully, and that there was therefore nothing to be gained by owning it. Geraldo's program must have confirmed this belief.

Groden says that the following day, Time Inc. issued a one-time agreement with ABC to allow the use of the film, but there is no such record in the *LIFE* archives. In fact, the next item in the records is a letter from Bob Richter with a new prospectus that he hoped *LIFE* would consider. He couldn't, it seems, resist a little dig: "Considering the fact that the footage has been shown so widely in recent months, it seems to me that circumstances have changed regarding its uniqueness and monetary value." In other words, the film was no longer an exclusive; the first-time showing had been blown, and there was no way that *LIFE* was in a position to charge the kinds of fees they had been proposing even a few months before.

I am certain that my father was chagrined about the film airing on *Good Night America*, and I suspect he was glad his own father wasn't alive to see it. But you'd never know it if you didn't know him—especially because on March 13, there is a new development. An unsigned memo states:

> Zapruder now wants to buy the film from Time Inc., and exploit it as he sees fit. Harry Johnston feels this is OK but I have insisted on one major reservation: Zapruder must put up the cash. We cannot accept a percentage as the film generates revenue for Zapruder nor can we accept timed payments spread over a number of years. Either recourse, to my mind, gives Time Inc. a vested interest in the income from the film when said income may be resulting from tasteless forms of use that we would never authorize on our own. Harry decided that we would give Zapruder until next Wednesday evening to put up a $60,000 purchase price. If he has not, we will unilaterally give the film to the National Archives.

This is a puzzling reversal, and a critical one, because it led to our family regaining possession of the film, which in turn led to endless aggravation for my father and the years-long struggle with the government for final ownership of the film. I cannot help but be both amused and slightly annoyed by *LIFE*'s worry that Henry Zapruder would generate income from "tasteless forms of use" of the film that the magazine would never have authorized. For crying out loud, where did they think the original moral imperative regarding the film had come from?

In fact, it's clear from their records that from the beginning of their dealings with Henry, the editors at *LIFE* approached him with a considerable measure of mistrust, supposing that his only reason for wanting to have the film back was that he wanted to "make a buck" off it. It comes up again and again. I don't know if this is just because now they were no longer dealing with Abe Zapruder, the gentle Jewish-immigrant dressmaker, but with his big-shot son, a Harvard-educated tax attorney in a boutique Washington law firm. Maybe they just assumed the worst. It wouldn't be the first or last time someone jumped to conclusions regarding Henry and the Zapruder film. Then again, maybe Henry was tough with them in their negotiations. Although he could be charming, endearing, and engaging, he could also be reserved, keeping his cards close to his chest, especially in an uncomfortable situation. And there was perhaps nothing more uncomfortable for him than dealing with the Zapruder film.

Inside our family and circle of friends, everyone knew that Henry never wanted anything to do with the film. Even those who knew him only tangentially saw his reluctance to deal with it, whether he might make money from it or not. I have to believe that he would have been perfectly glad to cooperate with *LIFE* in giving the film to the National Archives and taking the tax deduction. But as so often happens in families, and in history for that matter, there was an opposing inexorable force that could not easily be ignored or overcome. In this case, it came in the form of my grandmother Lil.

As it turns out, Lil never wanted Abe to sell the film to *LIFE* to begin with. She was, after all, a pragmatist, and as much as she felt deeply the horror of the film, she would be unlikely to let that stand in the way of something that might have a financial benefit for her family. She had grown up in harsh poverty in a tenement in Brooklyn. She knew as well as anyone that money meant security and made important things—education, a home, contingencies for a sickness or a crisis—possible. Abe had a more uncertain view. On one hand, he had been poor, too, even worse off than Lil, and was not insensitive to the peace of mind that financial security could bring. On the other hand, he had experienced the trauma of witnessing the assassination, and he urgently wanted to be rid of the film and responsibility for it. Perhaps the most important factor in their distinct viewpoints was the difference in their personalities and temperaments. He was more sensitive and philosophical in nature, deeply concerned with questions of right and wrong. If Lil's idea of doing the right thing was focused on the outcome for her family, Abe's encompassed a larger set of concerns.

While Abe and Lil might not have seen eye to eye about the financial potential of the film, I wonder if they would have felt similarly ambivalent about *LIFE* giving the film to the National Archives. The original contract provisions to prevent such a third-party transfer existed precisely because Abe feared that one day *LIFE* would want to unburden itself of the film and it might end up with someone who didn't know or care about handling it sensitively. For her part, I suspect that Lil resisted the transfer of the film to the National Archives not only for financial reasons but because she believed it was what Abe would want. She was, after all, his defender and his champion; if he believed that, outside of *LIFE*, the best guardians for it were the members of his own family, she would stop at nothing to fulfill his wishes.

At the same time, as much as she wanted to respect Abe, Lil would have been in a bind if she had been unable to think of anyone in the family who could handle the responsibility of the film. But there was Henry. And Henry was not, in her eyes, merely capable. Like all those she loved, he was the object of her unabashed adoration, faith, and devotion. I keep remembering her 1973 phone interview with Richard Stolley. In that conversation, Lil asked Stolley if he met with Henry and Abe when they came to *LIFE* in the late 1960s. Stolley is momentarily confused and says he doesn't remember. "Oh, if you met Henry, you'd remember," she says breezily. Of course. No one could forget *her* son. I have no doubt that in this critical moment of the film's life, she not only believed that Henry could handle it, but that there was no one in the universe who could do it better.

It was unfortunate for Henry. He didn't want the responsibility and he wasn't interested in the film, which brought back painful memories and unwelcome burdens. But he would not ignore his mother's wishes. As it is remembered among family and friends who were there at the time, Lil did not simply express her views and leave the final decision to my father. She pressed and insisted and pushed until the matter was settled. Her way.

Amid all this back-and-forth, Henry turned to a trusted friend for help navigating the situation with *LIFE*. He and Bob Trien had both lived in Hastings Hall at Harvard Law School and had been fast friends for fifteen years. I had known the Triens all my life. We spent time together in the summers and visited them in New York. Bob and my dad shared a love of music, and I vividly remember them playing the guitar together when we were kids in the seventies, singing Dylan, the Beatles, and all the old folk favorites. They were goofy hippie dads in those days, with their beards and their bell-bottoms and their peace-loving music. Bob played the piano and composed music and awed us kids (and had the adults in hysterical laughter) playing music on an old carpenter's metal saw.

In 2011, I went to New York City to visit Bob and his wife, May, in their apartment. I didn't know until after my father died that Bob had been involved in the dealings with *LIFE*, and I wanted him to tell me what he remembered about that time. It was one of the many times during my work on this book that I found myself triangulating this history—asking those whom my father loved and trusted to tell me the story that he hadn't told me himself—in order to fill in the gaps and correct the one-sided public record. These interviews, conducted in the years after my father's death, were emotional, not only for the people I was interviewing but also for me, as I realized that there were parts of my father scattered around the world and that no matter how much I tried to gather them up, to paint a whole picture of this part of his life, nothing was going to restore him to us. I wasn't even sure it was a part of his life that he would have particularly wanted me to be prying into. But it had to be done. This was the missing information that I needed.

The final twist in the unbelievably torturous saga of *LIFE*'s ownership of the Zapruder film came in April 1975. At the insistence of my grandmother, our family was preparing to purchase the film back from *LIFE* magazine for $60,000. It was not only insiders at *LIFE* (and executives of its parent company, Time Inc., which included *Time*, *Fortune*, and *Sports Illustrated*, among others) who had misgivings about this decision. Then *Sports Illustrated* executive editor Ray Cave wrote a memo to editor in chief Hedley Donovan reporting on a conversation he had had with the Warren Commission attorney David Belin. "Belin makes a fair enough claim of concern that Zapruder intends to exploit the film. I said we were concerned, too, but had no real options and pointed out that the bootlegged version of the film is being thoroughly exploited in the worst possible ways already." It seems that no one thought the Zapruder family could be trusted to handle the Zapruder film.

Then, in the next paragraph, comes a surprising bit. Cave goes on, "The film sale was discussed by the Thursday lunch group at [head of public relations for Time Inc.] Don Wilson's behest; Wilson saying he now felt we should not sell the film to Zapruder. The lawyers and I explained the history and the options, with some success. At [vice chairman of *LIFE*] Mr. Larsen's suggestion, it was finally decided to give the film to Zapruder for $1. That pleased Wilson. It sure should please Zapruder. I still don't agree—I think we should have taken the $60,000."

I never understood why *LIFE* gave the film back to our family for $1. The reversal of the plan is not explained in detail anywhere in the *LIFE* records or news coverage of the time. It wasn't until I spoke with Bob Trien that the missing piece fell into place. He recalled, "There was one newscaster, his name was Tom Snyder, who was a popular newscaster of the era…he was on one of the major stations. And he was pissed. So he gets on the airwaves, on television, and he badmouths Time-Life and the Zapruder family…And he went on at great length. Time-Life was very upset about all of that. So [*LIFE*] called me up and said, 'We want to get this over with. We're going to give it to you for nothing.'"

Sure enough, Tom Snyder's program had aired on Tuesday, April 1. The Thursday lunch group met on April 3, and it was Don Wilson (a man who, in a *New York Times* article about his retirement from the company in 1989, was described as spending twenty years figuring out how to make Time Inc. look good) who proposed returning the film to our family for a dollar. Now it all makes sense. Time Inc., which had taken plenty of beatings over the Zapruder film, hoped at least to get some positive media attention for giving up the film without making any profit. *LIFE* issued a press release on April 8, and articles appeared in the *New York Times* and elsewhere at the same time. The release read:

Time Inc. will return the original Zapruder film of the assassination of President John F. Kennedy and all commercial rights to it to the heirs of Abraham Zapruder for the sum of one dollar, it was announced today. The magazine publisher had been unable to donate the original film and its rights to the National Archives and Records Service in Washington DC because of legal obligations to the Zapruder heirs. It is reported, however, that the Zapruder family is arranging to physically store the film in the National Archives.

In the contract, signed by Lil, Myrna, and Henry, the terms of returning the film to the Zapruders were spelled out. The physical transfer of the original 8mm reel, together with an assortment of copies (one first-day copy, a black-and-white duplicate, and color copies of the film "containing a complete set of all available frames"), was to take place in Room 3201 of the Time & Life Building in Rockefeller Center in New York by the end of the day on April 9. Bob Trien went to represent our family that day. Henry had indeed been in touch with the National Archives and had set up an arrangement whereby the film would be kept in safekeeping there. According to the plan, Bob was supposed to bring it from New York to Washington to deposit it at the Archives. However, at some point that day, he had second thoughts about going anywhere with the one and only original copy of the Zapruder film. "With all of these conspiracy theorists out there and all of this," he told me, "everybody out there looking to the Zapruder film as being the best evidence that anybody had about what happened on that fateful day . . . and there being a lot of people out there with certain agendas, I was frankly afraid to get on a plane with this thing. I was afraid that someone would bop me on the head and take it, you know, just to get it! I did not want to walk out of the building!"

I didn't blame him for being nervous about leaving with the

original film, but I was beginning to wonder where he was going with this. I waited. "So I didn't," Bob says, smiling at me. "There was a bank downstairs. I put it in a bank vault." My mind is racing now, and I already know the answer before I ask: "Did they know that it was the Zapruder film?" No. Bob is still smiling. "So you said, 'I want a...I want a...'" I am literally unable to finish my sentence. Bob helps me. "I want a vault." "Safe deposit box," I say. "Put it in there. Locked it up. And they never knew." Bob is looking at me very seriously now. "Locked it up and that was the end of it."

It never occurred to me not to believe Bob, but it certainly seemed possible that others wouldn't. Then, among our family papers, I found several yellow-orange "Lease and Notice of Rental Due" slips, each dated April 9, from the Manufacturers Hanover Trust Company located at 1275 Avenue of the Americas. Robert Trien is listed as the renter of safe deposit box number 476.

The film remained there for three years.

I sometimes think of the inconspicuous, utterly unremarkable safe deposit box number 476 that housed the little 8mm reel of film, maybe still in a yellow Kodak package, in a wall of identical boxes containing strangers' family papers, jewelry, keys, and legal documents. I think of the employees passing by it, unlocking and pulling out the boxes nearby, the bank customers walking in and out of the bank, conducting their business, chatting or gossiping or laughing or crying, with no idea that the original Zapruder film was sitting quietly just a few feet away. But more than anything else, it is a perfect metaphor for how the film would be compartmentalized within our family, separate and contained but relentlessly present, with obligations not met, questions with no easy answers, and unprecedented problems waiting to spring out and steal my father's time and his peace of mind.

CHAPTER 9

THE ETERNAL FRAME AND THE ENDLESS DEBATES

At the time the Zapruder film came back into our family, my twin brother, Michael, and I were five, and our older brother, Matthew, was seven. It remained part of our family for the next twenty-five years. These were the years in which the film came out of the shadows—and as it became more accessible, the multiplicity of ways in which it could be interpreted, used, read, examined, commented upon, and ultimately parodied and embedded in popular culture only grew. The film, although described as a singular object, in reality had many lives that traveled in parallel, sometimes briefly linking or crossing paths but often existing quite independently. This is how it happened that filmmakers and artists used it as a cultural commentary at the same time as the federal government examined it as evidence and my own father grappled with questions of how to make it available to the public without its being exploited or sensationalized.

CBS was the first network to take advantage of the film's new ownership to request permission to air it on national television. It was to be used in a CBS Reports Inquiry titled "The American Assassins," to air in November 1975. For this purpose, CBS planned to carry out its own exhaustive investigation and contracted with Itek, a Massachusetts photo-optics lab, to study not only the original Zapruder film but also other visual evidence from the assassination. My father gave CBS permission to air the film for a fee, and he must also have allowed Itek to examine the original film, though there is nothing in our family's records about this. It marked the first time that the original film was studied in such depth; even the Warren Commission, which had screened the original, conducted their investigation from high-quality 35mm prints made from it for fear of damaging the original. CBS wanted Itek to seek answers to the most pressing questions being posed by the conspiracy theorists: When was the first shot fired; when was Governor Connally hit; were President Kennedy and Governor Connally hit by the same bullet; and what information could be gathered about the final shot that delivered the mortal blow to the president's head?

In his book *National Nightmare*, Richard Trask explains that "some dozen technical specialists at Itek examined the film in various high quality black-and-white, false-color, and color formats, as well as motion picture copies." He goes on to list a dizzying blur of technical methods they used, including stereophotogrammetry, precision photographic processing, spectral enhancement, coherent spatial filtering, mensuration, and digital plotting. Itek ultimately produced a ninety-four-page report analyzing the Zapruder film and other films from the assassination. Their findings essentially conformed to those of the Warren Report: The president was hit for the first time when he was behind the Stemmons Freeway sign (somewhere between frames 212 and 223) and can be seen reacting to a wound in frame 225, which is also when Governor Connally suddenly reacted to a stimulus (presumably a shot) by raising his arm and flipping his hat. Given how closely their reactions occurred, as well as their positions in the car and the location of their wounds, Itek concluded that they were likely hit by the same bullet. Finally, and probably most important, Itek studied in depth the visual confusion of frame 313, wherein the president appears to be thrown violently backward—and which the conspiracy theorists had emphasized as evidence that the president must have been shot from the front or from the grassy knoll, meaning a second shooter had to have been on the scene.

The Itek report says that the president was moving in a slightly forward direction at the moment of impact and that the brain matter radiated upward and forward in frames 313–314. This suggests, of course, a shot from the rear, or the Texas School Book Depository Building (i.e., Lee Harvey Oswald). This part of the report is consistent with Alvarez's 1969 study, in which he noted that a shot from the rear could cause the explosive forward movement of the president's brain matter which, he argued, could drive the president's head backward. However, the authors of the Itek report presented a different explanation, speculating that Mrs. Kennedy was moving forward at the time of the last shot, leaning in to assist President Kennedy, and that upon the bullet's impact, she recoiled from the "exploding matter from the wound," simultaneously ducking and shoving backward instinctively. The Itek report suggested that her motions at this critical moment "strongly influenced or caused JFK's backward motions." Few found this explanation convincing. In a footnote to the report, there was an attempt to qualify this statement and a nod to Alvarez's jet effect. The authors wrote:

"The statement that Mrs. Kennedy caused the President's backward motion is not intended to mean that she was the sole cause. In fact, calculations made from the theory of jet reaction suggest that this phenomenon could explain some of the movement. Although it is beyond the scope of this report to deal with neurological reaction in a quantitative fashion, it appears plausible that this effect too could have influenced the backward motion. The data presented here does not suggest that she was a strong or the dominant causal factor of the backward motion."

The first part of *The American Assassins* aired in November 1975. Dan Rather hosted the program, in which the film was shown a number of times and the Itek analysis was used heavily to interpret the film. With regard to the fatal shot to the president's head, John Wolf, president of Itek's optical systems division, explained that when the president was hit, his head traveled forward with tremendous speed for a fraction of a second and then took twice as long to return to its original position. In other words, the forward motion of his head was so fast, and the returning rear motion so much slower, that the viewer essentially registers only the backward motion of his head. Rather responded by saying what many people thought: "No matter how many times you look at it, that's not the impression one gets just sitting in a room and looking at the film. The very clear impression is that his head tilts backward faster than it went forward." To which Wolf replies, "That of course is the whole point... It's to get away from the subjective impressions that are developed by looking at a blurred motion picture. My answer to your implied question is: I don't know what I see. I know what I measure."

Needless to say, the Warren Commission critics, assassination researchers, and conspiracy theorists were not impressed. Many disagreed with the conclusions drawn by the report. Others, according to Richard Trask, dismissed CBS News out of hand as being "at the beck and call" of the CIA and complicit with the federal government in covering up the truth. Itek was no less suspect. In the words of one critic, it "still faces the problem of being permanently tied to the CIA, the Pentagon, and the rest of the Invisible Government through a variety of important contracts."

In reading about the Kennedy assassination, I've come to see that there are more nuances among the conspiracy community than might at first appear. The group was not a monolithic block marching in lockstep to a certain set of views. Far from it. Just as individual opinions on the assassination existed along a spectrum, with the Warren Commission at one end and full-scale governmental implication in the murder of the president at the other, the conspiracy community incorporated differing views and levels of fanaticism. For the most fervid critics, the debate was not academic or intellectual, it was deeply political and even personal. Thus, when presented with an interpretation of evidence that contradicted their views (as in the Itek report), they could swiftly shift the conversation away from the material in question to the authenticity and integrity of the person or people doing the examining. As such, the criticisms above do not address what we see on the film or the physical trajectories of the president's head. Instead, they focus on unsubstantiated accusations about Itek and CBS, questioning their motives and their ability to carry out an objective analysis. This is the maddening result of a certain kind of very rigid conspiracy thinking. It's not that people disagree. It's that you cannot disagree. To disagree is to be looped into a meta-view of the whole situation that makes your disagreement one more piece of evidence in the conspiracists' argument. If this divide was extreme in 1975, it grew to rather outlandish proportions by the 1990s, when extreme conspiracy theorists contended that the Zapruder film itself was either altered or, inevitably, a hoax. But all that was still many years away.

If 1975 was a watershed year for the Zapruder film in that its twelve-year embargo was lifted, it also marked another important moment in the establishment of the film as a cultural touchstone. It came about through the collaborative work of two San Francisco–based avant-garde artists' groups. Architects Chip Lord and Doug Michels had created Ant Farm in the late 1960s, its name inspired by the way that ants collectively create elaborate structures under the earth. Doug Hall, Jody Proctor, and Diane Andrews had their own collaborative endeavor, called T.R. Uthco, also based in San Francisco, which staged performances and other creative works on various political and aesthetic themes. These young artists were as different in style and temperament as they could be from the media executives handling the Zapruder film, the conspiracy theorists agitating about it, and my own family. They occupied the fringes of the art world, creating transgressive and sometimes shocking performances designed not only to provoke reactions in audiences but also to grapple with that time period's most pressing questions in a creative way. They were not interested in interpreting the content of the film but in critiquing the pervasive media use of it and the social consequences of its repeated representations in print and on television.

Their film, *The Eternal Frame*, went far beyond Antonioni's *Blow-Up* (1966) or any of the previous cultural references to the film. This was no suggestive nod to the film or the interpretive problems it raised. Instead, the artists went straight for the iconic imagery itself. They saw in the repetitive use of stills from the film and then repeated showings of it on television a media manipulation from which no viewer could escape. Each time, the film begins with handsome Jack and beautiful Jackie in pink waving to the crowd on a sunny day, and each time it ends with the man's gruesome murder and his wife's shocking fall from grace as she crawls on the back of the limousine. As they saw it, each showing reinforced the Kennedys' mythic status and drew the viewer into participating in their hideous, devastating demise.

Doug Hall and Chip Lord were interviewed in 2007 in connection with an installation of *The Eternal Frame* that opened at the J. Paul Getty Museum in Los Angeles in 2008. Hall said, "It was a moment where everyone was kind of locked in step for a short amount of time. There have been other events since that have had similar galvanizing affects, but this was the first of the great televisual spectaculars. The event—the tragic assassination of an American president and the aftermath—became convoluted as it unfolded over time, its original meaning mutating as it was filtered through the media. As the event became popularized, it lost its relationship to its source."

They sought to use artistic collaboration to tackle that fixed, iconic imagery—the Zapruder film itself—that so dominated the public imagination. But as avant-garde artists critiquing accepted norms, they could not operate within traditional structures. They had to do something wildly inappropriate, radical, even taboo. In correspondence with me, Doug Hall explained it this way: "Our need was to break down that wall, to cause fissures to appear in its facade with the belief that these cracks would widen and other hidden 'truths' would reveal themselves. I won't presume that we succeeded but I will stand by our intent."

To that end, they staged an "authentic reenactment" of the Zapruder film in Dealey Plaza in Dallas in August 1975. The cast included Doug Hall as the Artist-President (a mock Kennedy figure with a pronounced Boston accent who appears in other parts of the movie giving speeches and being interviewed), Doug Michels in drag as Jackie in the famous pink Chanel suit, and Stanley Marsh as Governor Connally. Chip Lord was mostly offscreen as the "director," while Skip Blumberg and Bart Friedman were filming. Jody Proctor also played the important role of Secret Service agent Clint Hill, who rode on the rear bumper of the presidential limousine. They planned the event for several months, scrutinizing their own bootlegged 16mm copy of the film to choreograph the movements of the inhabitants of the car, rehearsing, creating full costumes and makeup, and preparing multiple movie and still cameras to shoot in color and black and white from various positions, including from the vantage points of Orville Nix and my grandfather. They bought a Lincoln Continental convertible for $300 and towed it from San Francisco to Amarillo, Texas.

The guerrilla event—the "shooting of the shooting"—took place on August 10, 1975. They got up early, dressed in costume, and went to downtown Dallas, where they got into position and drove through Dealey Plaza. There they reenacted the murder of the president, including his sudden movements after the first shot, the slumping to the side, Jackie leaning in, the jolt of the fatal bullet, and Jackie recoiling and then climbing on the back of the car, only to be pushed back inside by the Secret Service agent as the car disappeared under the triple underpass. Needless to say, they did not have permits, permission, or any sanction to carry out this act, and they fully expected to be able to do it only once or twice before being shut down. "We were nervous," Doug Hall said in the

2007 Getty Museum interview. "We knew we were treading on something that was dangerous; it's an iconic image that we seem to be offhandedly playing around with, and that's why we imagined that we would go there very early in the morning, go through there once, and that would probably be it because everything would close in on us."

If the members of Ant Farm and T.R. Uthco hoped to find hidden truths in the course of their performance, they got their wish, though surely not in the form they expected. What bubbled up among the spectators in Dealey Plaza remains puzzling to this day. Many who saw the reenactment responded not with outrage or anger, nor with a shared sense of irony or any understanding at all of the parody that was taking place. In fact, the intentional bad taste of the performance seemed entirely lost on them. Instead, many believed the event was staged by the city of Dallas or the Department of Commerce for the benefit of tourists who came to visit the site. Some of the artists who were filming the reenactment recorded audio of the spectators and carried out "man on the street" interviews while the motorcade went around and around Dealey Plaza.

At one point, we see the rear of the limousine and hear voices speaking in a foreign tongue; as the car passes by, a man switches to English, saying, with what might be an Asian accent, "Ohh, Mr. President gone," and then, as the actors in the car pantomime the shooting, he says, in what sounds like true dismay, "Oh, they killed the president, ohhh God! They killed...oh, Mr. President!" while behind him we can hear the groans of others with him. Two men, perhaps the speakers, run after the car. The image shifts back to the actors in the car, starting once more at the beginning, ready to go around again, and we hear a lady speaking in the background, saying, "It really is surprising…uh…" What sounds like another voice cuts in: "They probably have it, just more or less so for tourists, like, don't they, for demonstrations or something?"

The scene shifts again to a man filming the proceedings with a movie camera and then pans to a lady with a blond bouffant hairdo and sunglasses, wearing a ruffled sundress and carrying a basket-weave purse, who says, in a flat Midwestern accent, "It does look like her, my God, my—oh, look! Reenacting it." She winces slightly and, realizing what is going to happen, says, "Oh, no." The camera watches her watching until it's over and then she wipes away her tears. "I got it all," a man says in the background, presumably the one with the movie camera. She seems half-embarrassed, laughing, saying, "It feels like the real thing…It's terrible. I cried when I watched it on television. It's terrible." Her companion begins to reminisce about how they heard the news. "How could it happen to somebody so wonderful?" she says, wiping away more tears. "I got all worked up." Then she pulls herself together, saying, "I'm glad we were here. I really am. We just made it in time. To see this. I feel bad and yet I feel good…beautiful reenactment. I wish I'd had our still camera so I would have caught it on—to show it. That was too beautiful."

What could be less beautiful than the assassination of President Kennedy or the Zapruder film? Did she not see that Jackie was a man in drag? What could she possibly mean? Perhaps she meant that it was cathartic. Or that she got what she came for. For the tourists making a pilgrimage to Dealey Plaza, a reenactment of the assassination seemed a natural way to memorialize a place that was famous for only that reason and to provide a meaningful experience for visitors. They even filmed the fake assassination and brought those films home to show their families. There is something especially confusing and troubling about the fact that the specta-tors didn't object to the reenactment on the grounds of bad taste, in part because it means that they didn't recognize it as such and in part because it means that the irony of the exercise totally escaped them. On the other hand, the tourists came to the place in earnest, and so they read the events they witnessed in that same spirit. In a way, their reactions entirely proved the point that the artists were making. The imagery was so entirely intertwined with the event itself that even an exaggerated reenactment gained its own authentic meaning and was worthy of being filmed and preserved.

Whatever they thought or felt, it certainly had nothing to do with what the artists intended. The members of Ant Farm and T.R. Uthco were not trying to teach the bystanders anything or con-vey a fixed message to the rest of the world. They were in search of answers to questions that haunted them in the aftermath of the assassination. Doug Hall wrote: "We approached the subject through a veil of irony. But don't be fooled by this attitude. Look-ing back on it, I think our need was to critique the 'spectaculariza-tion' of the event or at least through our outrageousness to delve deeper into it perhaps as a way to loosen its grip on us. Really, *The Eternal Frame* is a kind of exaggerated appropriation that allowed us to inhabit images that insisted on remaining distant, strangely impersonal, and iconic."

Even in the film itself, the artists acknowledged that they weren't entirely sure what they were after. In my favorite moment of the movie, the Artist-President is sitting at a desk being interviewed by a reporter. Doug Hall explained to me that he had just finished a scene giving a speech as the Artist-President, and Skip Blum-berg caught him off guard in between takes, giving the interview a not-quite-staged quality that perfectly suits the piece.

REPORTER: Do you consider yourself a martyr for art?

ARTIST-PRESIDENT: No, I don't.

REPORTER: How would you characterize this act of yours?

ARTIST-PRESIDENT: It's difficult to characterize. It's crazy, yes. It is crazy. I understand that part of it.

REPORTER: Is this a freedom-of-speech statement?

ARTIST-PRESIDENT: No, it isn't. Ask me what it is, and perhaps we'll together be able to figure it out.

REPORTER: Is it a confrontation with death?

ARTIST-PRESIDENT: No, it isn't. It's close, though. It's . . . But it's not a confrontation with death, no. Ask me another question.

REPORTER: Would you call this art?

ARTIST-PRESIDENT: (Pause) It's not *not* art.

Later in the film, Doug Michels, who played the role of Jackie, is asked on-screen what this project is all about. "What it is is figuring out what it is," he says. Even so, a lot of people didn't buy it. Doug recalled, "We just didn't have any idea what would come out of it. I think we were all very anxious about that. A lot of people in the art world were really upset with us. In the Bay Area, it was: 'Don't talk to those guys, they're just fucked.' And initially, we had difficulty getting anyone to look at it after it was finished."

In January 1976, *National Lampoon* published stills from the reenactment of the film, mimicking the layout of the Zapruder film images and the descriptions that had accompanied them in *LIFE* magazine. Eventually the raw footage was edited into the film, which was called *The Eternal Frame*—a play, of course, on the eternal flame that burns in President Kennedy's memory at Arlington Cemetery—with staged speeches by the Artist-President, interviews with the actors both in character and out, clips from their rehearsals, and the original footage of the Zapruder film. Then, in 1976, *The Eternal Frame* was shown in the Long Beach Museum of Art, as an installation in a re-created, kitschy living room from 1963.

Growing up as I did with reverence for the Kennedy family and a very personal sense of the tragedy of the president's death, my first encounter with *The Eternal Frame* did not go down easy. In fact, I was so uncomfortable with it that for a long time I tried to pretend it didn't exist. But since a central aim of this book is to understand the ways in which the film broke new ground and raised new questions for a changing society, avoidance would not do.

I started by reading about *The Eternal Frame*, but much of the scholarly writing on the subject was rife with academic jargon and impossible to decipher without a PhD in critical theory. So I reached out to Chip Lord and Doug Hall to ask them, as nicely as I could, what the hell this project was all about. As I exchanged e-mails with them and read their interviews, I was struck by the fact that even though the reenactment was irreverent and even vulgar, there is also something sorrowful about it, as if, in their own way, the young artists were seeking to break the stranglehold of this event on their lives. There was no way to undo the president's death, but they chose to smash the idol that had come to represent it. In so doing, they refused to let their experience of the assassination be entirely defined by its images. Certainly, it was very theoretical and it didn't have much to do with how many people felt about it at the time. But the job of the avant-garde is to be ahead of the curve.

To me, what is most interesting is how prescient they turned out to be. As I thought about *The Eternal Frame* and what it has to do with present-day media coverage, I thought back to 1991, when I sat with my family and watched the coverage of the Gulf War on television. I remember the repeated broadcasts of the smart bombs, the reports framed with graphics, theme music, and a logo. Thanks to my brothers and a group of very astute high-school friends who were early adopters of a critical posture toward mainstream media, I knew enough to see in the packaging and presentation of the war something controlled and manipulative. Apparently, even our wars need a logo. Then over the years, there came the many showings of the Rodney King beating, children running out of schools where there had been shootings, and—in the closest analogy to the Kennedy assassination for our time—the planes hitting the Twin Towers and the disbelief that came with watching them fall. If these images become a stand-in for events in which we are to participate collectively, and it is the media that chooses, packages, and presents them to us over and over again, then the Zapruder film was indeed the prototype of its kind. Ant Farm and T.R. Uthco saw it coming. I am not sure how it could be otherwise, what alternative there is for a news media that relies on images to communicate critical national events. But *The Eternal Frame* stands as a reminder that even the images we hold most sacred are just images, and that the emotional truth to be found in the events they depict always requires more than passively sitting, watching, and accepting what is served to us.

At the same time that Ant Farm and T.R. Uthco were carrying out their guerrilla performance art in Dallas, the conspiracy community was nearing success in pushing for a new investigation into the murder of President Kennedy. These researchers occupied, in many ways, the other end of the spectrum from the members of Ant Farm and T.R. Uthco. They not only held the Zapruder film as sacred, but to many it was the Holy Grail, the suppressed evidence that offered definitive proof that the president had been killed by a conspiracy. Still, they did have something in common with Ant Farm and T.R. Uthco in that they were deeply cynical about authority—in their case, governmental more than media—and they were decidedly outside the mainstream, although less and less so as the years went on. They had suffered a serious setback after the debacle of the Shaw trial in 1969, when the district attorney's gross abuse of power and corrupt methods badly damaged their credibility in the eyes of the general public.

Then, in the early 1970s, Carl Oglesby, who had been president of the radical antiwar group Students for a Democratic Society in 1965–66, started the Assassination Information Bureau in Cambridge, Massachusetts. Over the next five years, this group of young critics gave lectures and speeches, circulated petitions, and lobbied members of Congress, relentlessly pushing them to take action and reexamine the evidence surrounding the president's murder. The centerpiece of each presentation was a showing of a bootlegged copy of the Zapruder film. They had acquired copies from the same sources as the earlier bootlegs that *LIFE* had tried to track down—Jim Garrison, Mark Lane, Penn Jones Jr., and others who had obtained copies of the film and sold them as widely as they could. Although the copies were generally of very poor quality, many times removed from the original, they showed the only thing that the conspiracy activists needed people to see: the backward head snap of the president. David Wrone describes these showings in his book *The Zapruder Film*:

Although public showings of the bootleg Zapruder film could take place in such diverse places as the living rooms of the wealthy, the back rooms of taverns, or the meetings of small social clubs, the most typical one was in colleges across the nation. A typical showing of the film in a college lecture hall would occur before an audience of two or three hundred students, a scattering of local people (conservatives and liberals) and representatives of the press... A student sponsor typically would introduce the subject with a few words on its importance and then present a second student, who was in charge of the meeting. She or he would then explain the credentials of the speaker and how important the subject was to America, often criticizing both the right wing and liberals for permitting a cover-up... The featured presenter would then launch into a speech. In animated terms, he would hammer at the evidence and the cover-up, describe fallacies, frauds, and corruption, and then ask for the lights to be dimmed. The Zapruder film typically would be shown several times, at first without explanation, then with comments by the speaker to bring attention to main points.

The film would be the highlight of the evening, the central point in the speaker's argument, and at the end the audience would usually be silent, sensing the profound seriousness of the problem. The lights would go on, and questions would be taken, often for as long as the speaker's formal presentation. After the speech, various books on the subject of the assassination and copies of the film and slides were often sold.

It's impossible to disentangle these efforts from the changing cultural and political climate of America in the early 1970s. By 1975, the country had witnessed the assassinations of Malcolm X, Martin Luther King, and Robert Kennedy. Following the death of Dr. King, grief and outrage in the black community led to race riots in major cities around the country. The long, divisive, bloody Vietnam War came to an end in April, but the disillusionment and mistrust that it had engendered would remain. Perhaps most significant for this story, the Watergate scandal had revealed an actual conspiracy carried out at the highest levels of government. This was no mere paranoid fantasy; the public had seen evidence that government agencies—the president, his aides, the CIA, the FBI, and the IRS—were capable of working in concert against the interests of the American people and democracy itself. This fact lent legitimacy and momentum to the conspiracy community.

It was against the backdrop of rising mistrust, and in the wake of relentless agitating by the Assassination Information Bureau and other individuals and organizations that likewise sought to reopen the investigation, that Robert Groden had aired his copy of the Zapruder film on Geraldo Rivera's program *Good Night America* in April 1975. Suddenly, it seemed that the whole nation could see what the small counterculture had been trying to say for so long. Public trust in the findings of the Warren Commission, which had been shaky for some time, plummeted. In September 1976, the conspiracy proponents succeeded in their efforts when the US House of Representatives authorized the House Select Committee on Assassinations (HSCA) to take on a new investigation of the murders of President Kennedy and Martin Luther King Jr.

Rep. Thomas Downing, the first chairman of the committee, retired from Congress in January 1977, and his position was taken over by Texas representative Henry Gonzalez. Considerable conflict between Gonzalez and chief counsel Richard Sprague led to the resignation of both from the committee. By March 1977, when the committee began in earnest, Louis Stokes of Ohio was chairman, with Richardson Preyer of North Carolina in charge of the Kennedy investigation task force. By the summer, G. Robert Blakey was named chief counsel. They had until the end of the Ninety-Fifth Congress, which concluded on January 3, 1979, to complete their work.

The work of the select committee has been amply described elsewhere, notably in Richard Trask's book *National Nightmare*, in which the author meticulously details its changing leadership, the time and budgetary pressures, and its methods of inquiry into the ballistic, forensic, acoustic, and visual evidence. In his book, Trask focuses especially on their analysis of the Zapruder film, describing the new photographic methods that attempted to deblur certain frames and to pinpoint the exact moments of the president's and Governor Connally's reactions to external stimuli—namely, bullet wounds or the sound of gunfire. This work was undertaken by the Los Alamos Scientific Laboratory of the University of California, and it focused especially on examining the frames that seemed to raise the most questions. The photographic evidence panel, composed of twenty-some consultants and experts, reviewed multiple versions of the film in moving and still frames on one hundred different occasions. In the end, their findings differed from those of the Warren Commission and Itek in the details but not in the essentials.

According to their review, Governor Connally reacted to something—a sound, perhaps—by suddenly turning his head to the right and shifting his body in the same direction considerably earlier than others had observed. They saw this in frames 168–170, well before the limousine passed behind the freeway sign. His sudden movements coincided with those of Rosemary Willis, who was a little girl at the time and can be seen on the grass behind the car. She was running toward the limousine and suddenly stopped and turned her head in the direction of the Texas School Book Depository. As Trask points out, she later said that she had stopped running because she heard a gunshot, though at this point, no one in the car had been hit.

The panel then looked at the president's movement to see when he first reacted to any kind of stimulus. In previous investigations of the film, it was generally agreed that he showed signs of having been wounded after coming out from behind the Stemmons Freeway sign at frames 224–225. This panel saw a reaction as early as 1.5 seconds earlier, at frame 200, when, they said, he suddenly stopped waving and seemed to freeze momentarily. Further, they saw evidence of a severe reaction by frame 207, when he went behind the sign.

They also found that his position and that of Governor Connally were aligned, and their reactions synced in such a way as to confirm that a single bullet could have hit them both. The panel believed that by the time they reappear from behind the street sign at frame 224, they had clearly both been shot. Five seconds later, the president was fatally shot in the head, at frames 312–313. Based on the photographic evidence and the corresponding forensics, they believed that Lee Harvey Oswald fired three shots from the Texas School Book Depository Building, that one of them missed (though when it was fired is not clear), one hit both the president and Connally (albeit a bit earlier than other investigations had found), and another had fatally wounded the president. They did not find visual evidence that supported a second shooter firing from the grassy knoll. In essence, their findings as they prepared to wrap up their work in December 1978 conformed with the Warren Report.

I have to wonder if some readers will glaze over at this point. Others will ask, as I have, what difference it could possibly make. What are we trying to pinpoint here? And how it is possible that each successive examination of the film shows something slightly different but not so different as to make a real difference or tell us anything that we didn't already know? Bear with me. There are times when understanding the Zapruder film requires zooming out—to see it as a whole, to look at it in its cultural context and think about the questions and meanings that it offered to different people at different times. For example, Antonioni's film *Blow-Up* from 1966 seems positively prescient in light of the events of 1979. After all, the thousands of hours, financial resources, photographic techniques and methods, imagination, energy, and eye strain spent on the Zapruder film did not lead to consensus or clarity any more than Thomas's enlargement of the suspected dead body proves that it was actually there.

There are other times, however, when understanding the Zapruder film requires zooming in, scrutinizing each frame and following the arguments of each successive investigation—whether by an individual, a private group, or a governmental organization—if only to try to understand the collective effort of a great many people who tried to find answers to the confounding questions of what happened to the president. And while the Zapruder film is not the only piece of evidence—though many have suggested, probably rightly, that it has been privileged as evidence in ways that have not always been helpful—the minute examination of it reveals the lengths to which people went to create a narrative of events in hopes of getting closer to knowledge and understanding. There were many who felt that it was simply unacceptable to let the matter lie and accept not knowing. For some of them, abandoning the quest was tantamount to abandoning their responsibility to a president they loved. These are not my questions, but I understand that they were vitally important and remain so to this day for some people. And it is impossible to understand the meaning and significance of the Zapruder film without them.

At the eleventh hour, new evidence was introduced that dramatically changed the course of the committee's investigation. This was the Dictabelt recording from a microphone stuck in the "on" position that was said to belong to a police officer who had been stationed in Dealey Plaza at the time of the shooting. A flurry of acoustical analysis followed, a highly detailed and careful account of which can be found in Richard Trask's book and elsewhere, though I will not analyze it at length here. The panel concluded on the basis of two studies of the acoustics that four shots were fired at the president, three from the TSBD and one from, you guessed it, the grassy knoll. In the words of the final report, "Scientific acoustical evidence establishes a high probability that two gunmen fired at President John F. Kennedy; other scientific evidence does not preclude the possibility of two gunmen firing at the president." In other words, although the Zapruder film did not alone prove that the president was hit by a second gunman, as the conspiracy community believed, it also did not prove that he *wasn't* hit by a second gunman. As the Artist-President had said in *The Eternal Frame*, "It's not *not* art."

In the end, the select committee concluded "on the basis of the evidence available to it, that President John F. Kennedy was probably assassinated as a result of a conspiracy. The committee is unable to identify the other gunman or the extent of the conspiracy." They went on to say that they did not believe that either the Soviet Union or Cuba were involved, and that they did not believe that it was the work of anti-Castro groups or the Mafia, though they could not say that individuals from these groups had not been involved. The committee wrapped up its work in January 1979.

As it happened, the victory for the conspiracy community was neither sweet nor long lasting. Many felt that the committee did not go nearly far enough and were disappointed by its findings, since it conformed with the Warren Report in many ways. Even the "probable" second shooter was unsatisfying, since the report didn't provide any conclusions as to who the shooter might have been, whom they represented, or what larger significance a second shooter might have had. Not only that, but this mysterious second shooter hadn't even hit anybody, which made his role considerably less relevant. One year later, the acoustic evidence itself was called into question when assassination researcher Steve Barber determined by careful examination that the recording had actually taken place a full minute after the shooting had occurred. In the fall of 1980, at the behest of the Justice Department, the National Research Council established the Committee on Ballistics Acoustics to reexamine the evidence. Chaired by Norman F. Ramsey, the committee published its study in 1982, concluding after exhaustive analysis of the methodologies used in the previous studies and its own original examination of the evidence that the sounds on the Dictabelt did not record a gunshot from the grassy knoll. The HSCA conclusion of a "probable conspiracy" in the murder of the president had to be discounted.

This was, of course, not the end of the matter. There would be no end to it. The debates about the validity of the acoustic evidence, in addition to the visual, ballistic, and forensic evidence and the eyewitness testimony continued—and continue to this day.

CHAPTER 10

∎∎∎∎∎∎∎

THE FLOODGATES OPEN

Beginning in 1975, my father found himself the guardian of the original Zapruder film and the rights to it, responsible for deciding who could use it and under what circumstances, how to provide copies, and when to license it for fees or provide it for free. He was a young tax attorney at the time, in private practice at a firm called Cohen and Uretz, having worked first at the Justice Department and then at Treasury. In August 1970, a young redheaded woman named Anita Lawless turned up at the firm, having applied for a job as a secretary. She would work with my father for thirty-five years and, not unlike Lillian Rogers, she would become a loved and trusted member of our family. Although her job was to support him in his tax practice, which was very busy and often intense, she also took on another critical role, working with my father as he sorted out how to handle the film and the many demands that came with it.

In 2011, I interviewed Anita about her years working with my father and especially how they handled the Zapruder film. I began by asking her to describe her first impressions of my dad and what it was like when she came to work for him before the film was returned to our family. She told me that she had been interviewed by one of the other partners, and then my dad was supposed to meet her but was late, which, if you knew him, would not come as a surprise. Suddenly, the door swung open, she said, "and this very tall man comes in, sits down on this tiny chair that's by the wall, and just looks at me. And he says, 'Okay. Yeah, I just have a couple of questions.' And I said, 'Okay.' And he says, 'Now, really this is my only question,' he says. 'If I have a draft of something and I dictate it and you type it in draft, and then if I write on it and give it back to you, and then you correct it, and then I write on it again and give it back to you and you correct it again . . .' he said. 'Now, if I do this, like, seventeen times, is that going to bother you?' "

She started her new job in early September 1970 while my parents were in Dallas for my grandfather's funeral. After my father returned to Washington, it took a few weeks for them to click. Anita remembers that in the beginning he would never talk to her but would appear suddenly from around the corner, scaring her to death, throwing dictation tapes at her and then disappearing into his office. She typed as fast as she could, and no sooner did she finish something than he would reappear and hand her another draft, or more dictation tapes, and then vanish again. Weeks went by like this, during which time she occasionally tried to ask a question but found that he would not answer the door when she knocked. She would go home at night and cry.

Finally, she decided she needed to either quit or talk to him. She went into his office and explained her problem: "'Well, you know, I'm here to do whatever you want me to do, you know, but you come out there frantic and you throw things at me and then you run back in your office and slam the door.' And he's like, 'Oh. Well, I don't mean to do that,' he says. 'I don't know why I do that.' Then he thought for a minute, and he said, 'Yes, I do know why I do that. When I was at Treasury, you know, I didn't have a secretary. It was a typing pool. To get the secretaries to do anything, you had to run out there and scream at them and throw the stuff and run away so they couldn't find you. Because if they found you, they'd bring you the tape back and say, "I can't do this." So that's why I don't answer the door.'" Anita laughed when she told me this story. She told me that she said to him, "I'll do anything you want, but just don't throw things and don't run away." "I can do that," he said. "That's good. That would be much better." From then on, she said, "it was just peachy. Everything got so much better. He still would bring the tapes in and he'd throw them and then smile. A great, big smile."

The copyright to the film had been registered with our family on April 11, 1975, and shortly thereafter, Henry established a company to handle the finances and taxes related to the film. It was incorporated as the LMH Company (the initials of Lillian, Myrna, and Henry, the immediate heirs of Abraham Zapruder). In 1978, Henry and his mother brought the original film to the National Archives to put it in safekeeping there. I suppose he must have gone up to New York to get it from the safe deposit box and bring it back to Washington but I don't know anything specific about that. The agreement with the National Archives was clear and specific. The film was being entrusted to them for safekeeping; it was not a donation or gift. It would still belong to our family and could be removed by us or our representatives at any time. The goal was to ensure that it was safely preserved in the proper archival conditions, that it was physically secure, and that no harm would come to it.

As soon as *LIFE* returned the film and copyright to our family, Henry began getting requests for its use. Since it had essentially been under embargo for the twelve years that it was owned by *LIFE*, the executives there had never hashed out a policy regarding public access and use of the film. There was no road map for Henry to follow, and no experience to draw upon. He was going to have to make it up as he went along. For the next twenty-five years, Henry handled licensing and all other aspects of the film's legal status on behalf of our family under the auspices of LMH.

To my surprise, I found a few letters in my father's files from April 1975 that Dick Pollard, by then retired from *LIFE*, had sent to my father. They seemed to be in response to a request for advice about what to do with the film. Pollard wrote that there was the possibility that a "Hollywood group would buy the film outright," giving my grandmother a set sum of money as an option and "so much per year thereafter, as a guaranteed sum or a piece of the action." He also mentioned that there was a wealthy distributor of foreign films, "a gentleman you can trust completely" who was "not motivated by money" and who might help arrange a sale, and there was the possibility that the BBC might handle a US sale. Finally, Pollard suggested a picture agency run by two brothers, who he said were honorable and could be trusted to handle it.

The problem, as Pollard outlined very clearly to Henry, was that the film continued to be pirated and shown illegally, not only privately but also on television. Dick wrote: "Mort Sahl ran your film on Channel 13 Friday night. Poor quality to be sure but a frightening erosion of copyright. I'm not an expert on preservation of copyright but from my experiences with the Zapruder film I came to the conclusion that if Time Inc. did not consistently prosecute every invasion of copyright the pirating would proliferate and eventually, a judge might say that the film was public domain." He went on to advise Henry to have a lawyer stop Sahl, by lawsuit if necessary, and to let it be known that the film was now owned by "your mother, a widow, and not a cold corporate entity like Time Inc."

Henry responded to this letter with a warm one of his own, thanking Dick for his expertise and help. He had two proposals for use of the film in documentaries to consider at the time, and none of the other possibilities could work until those were resolved. In the end, he rejected both of the offers, and his correspondence with Dick Pollard on the subject ends there. He had clearly decided not to sell the film and not to turn his decision-making responsibilities over to an agent. Perhaps he hoped that he could manage it himself without it being too burdensome. And although the film became a very considerable responsibility, and there were plenty of problems along the way, he and Anita did essentially manage it themselves for the next thirteen years. Henry's friend Bob Trien, who had handled the negotiations with *LIFE* over the return of the film, also remained involved in managing the film, fielding requests, advising my father, corresponding with organizations and individuals on his behalf, and generally helping to lessen the growing load of requests wherever possible.

It took me many days of concentrated effort to pore over the request letters, responses, licenses, and other correspondence related to the film from 1975 until 1991, when circumstances regarding the film changed again. Requests came from news programs and personalities on every network, including the *Today* show, *Nightline*, *Entertainment Tonight*, Geraldo Rivera, Phil Donahue, and

Oprah Winfrey, to name just a few, in addition to public television stations. Film requests ranged from the obvious—producers making movies about the death of Kennedy—to the far-fetched, such as one from a director making a movie about the prophecies of Nostradamus. Hollywood came calling quite a few times. Requests came from Japan, Canada, Australia, Germany, Belgium, Italy, and France. (International licensing of the film was ultimately handled by a company called Colorfic!)

People wrote to request the use of stills in books about the assassination—among them well-known assassination researchers like Harold Weisberg, David Lifton, and John K. Lattimer. There were also writers, artists, theater directors, independent documentary filmmakers, scientists, medical doctors, and law enforcement agencies. Other requests came from writers of books on copyright law, history readers, or archivists and librarians who wanted a copy for their collections.

Requests came in from editors of newspapers, magazines, and journals ranging from the *Dallas Morning News* to the *Atom* (a periodical from Los Alamos Scientific Laboratory). There were requests for use of the film's images in exhibitions about Kennedy in Dallas and about the history of newspapers at the Museum of Science and Industry in Chicago, for projection on the side of a building, for use by an Italian playwright in his latest work; and there were appeals from private collectors who wanted the film for their own personal reasons. For commercial use (that is, where the organization would profit from use of the images), Henry and Anita set fees. Rates for stills were fairly modest, in the range of a few hundred dollars, but for the moving footage by the networks or major film producers, fees could range from several thousand dollars to as much as $20,000–$30,000 in later years, depending on how often the work would be aired, how it would be distributed, and the like.

The majority of requests came from individuals, primarily from researchers, teachers, or students. A teacher writing from a small farming community twenty miles west of Champagne, Illinois, wrote: "I would like very much to have a copy of the Zapruder film and not, I repeat not, because of the graphic depiction of Kennedy's wounds but because the Zapruder film may very well be the most important piece of historical film taken in the last 20 years." There is a marked contrast between these letters and the requests for commercial use. Many individuals wrote heartfelt personal letters to my father, expressing sensitivity about the burden that the film represented and explaining their own reasons for wanting to see it. A young man from Montreal, Canada, wrote: "I have recently attempted to reach you by telephone to speak with you regarding the historical films recorded by your father. Unfortunately, I was not able to talk to you...I can understand your position as I imagine you have been pestered frequently on the subject and are quite weary about the whole thing." A researcher from Flint, Michigan, requested a copy of the film, with the following caveat: "I wish to state that the film is strictly for my own personal use, and no misuse of the film is intended. I am willing to sign a statement to that effect and pay whatever fees are involved...I am aware that there are many bootleg copies of the film currently on the market, but hope that my coming to you will give you an indication of my honorable intentions." Another researcher explained his wanting the film by saying, "The young people don't remember President Kennedy or the controversy over his murder, and with the aid of showing this film, maybe one of them will be the researcher possible [sic] for bringing his killer to justice."

There are a few letters that stand out, capturing the personal feeling that so many strangers had when writing to our family. One interested student of the assassination wrote from Iowa in April 1977: "I wish to express my sincere gratitude to you and the Zapruder family for permitting me the right to secure a copy of your father's film. The act of kindness will not be forgotten or misused." When, two years later, this same individual wrote again because his copy of the film had been damaged and he wanted another copy, he was deeply apologetic. "Is it possible for me to secure your permission just one more time? I promise that I will never ask this favor of you ever again. I give you my word on that...I am sure sorry to trouble you again concerning the film. If this film didn't mean so much to me I wouldn't think of troubling you." Henry wrote a note to Anita in his barely legible scrawl: "OK. Tell him promise is unnecessary."

A favorite of mine is a letter addressed to Abe Zapruder, written many years after his death, from a gentleman in Casper, Wyoming. "Some years ago my father purchased a 16mm print of the movie you took of the assassination," he wrote, explaining that this (presumably bootlegged) copy of the film was beginning to show signs of wear. He wanted to have it transferred to video, but the lab refused to do it unless he obtained a release form. "I have never personally requested anything of this nature from anyone and I do not have any idea as to what the cost would be for obtaining a release form from your family," he wrote. His best guess was twenty dollars, so he enclosed a twenty-dollar bill with the word "LOVE" written on it—and a postage stamp.

To these kinds of personal appeals, Henry usually responded with reserved politeness and agreement. He did not charge fees for nonprofit, research, teaching, or study uses. The only cost to the requester after 1978 was the administrative fee from the National Archives, which Henry instructed the company, LMH, to pay when the person couldn't afford it.

There must be hundreds of letters written by students from grade school all the way to university. A young boy wrote from Milwaukee to ask for a copy of the film, explaining, "I need pictures to make [my] report good." Another boy from North Carolina wanted it for an oral presentation to go with an essay he was assigned to write. A girl wrote from Oklahoma to use the film in her science fair project. A student of criminal justice at Temple University, "staunch critic of the Warren Commission," and member of the Philadelphia police force, made a request; so did a senior at Bishop Ward High School, a Catholic school in Kansas City, who wrote: "I had an interest in this film since the sixth grade, when I had to do a report on President Kennedy, and my mother pulled out an old *LIFE* magazine which the film was printed in. So I've always had an interest in the film, not for research but for something to have for a keepsake of a president who was shot and killed in Dallas and a president that I deeply admire."

To the youngest writers, Henry often wrote short personal letters, wishing them luck with their work and offering a few words of encouragement. He frequently explained that the National Archives charged a small fee and suggested that the students request an exemption. He also required that their parents cosign the permissions letters. In the mideighties, he got a letter from a young girl who handwrote on stationery printed with a sad-looking hound wearing a sailor's cap and a T-shirt that said "Guard Dog" and holding a dripping, relieved-looking puppy in one paw. She had been reading historical biographies in school. "I have become interested in the Kennedys," she wrote in her loopy, adolescent handwriting, "and I have been trying to get all the stuff on them that I can... Would you please be so kind as to give the Archives your permission so I can get a copy of the film? I would really appreciate it." A few months later, she wrote again to remind him of her request, this time on Garfield stationery with scalloped edges. His answer is one of the few in the thousands he wrote that give a hint of his feelings about the film. "You certainly may have my permission to obtain a copy of the film," he wrote. "I hope, however, that your interest in John Kennedy focuses on the constructive aspects of his life (which you may find in his own writings and the writings of those who knew him or have studied the period), rather than on the tragic circumstances recorded on this unhappy film." Reading the letter now, I realize that I was thirteen at the time it was written, probably about the same age as this young girl. This is just the kind of thing he would have said to me.

Amid the voluminous correspondence, there were, of course, a fair number of bizarre requests. For instance, one group wanted to use the film in conjunction with a political campaign and—stranger still—another group wanted it for an issues campaign about child abuse. Sometimes, the requests were in dubious taste, like a company that wanted to use an image from the film on history trading cards. Others were just downright appalling, like the proposal from a famous camera company to make an advertisement using "one of Abraham Zapruder's grandchildren" on Dealey Plaza with a camcorder, with a voice-over telling the viewer how much clearer and better the images of the killing would have been if only he had been able to use their camera. To petitions like these, Henry often didn't respond at all. There were other refusals made along very specific lines. For many years, there was to be no use of the film in home video productions, and he consistently declined to permit the film to be used by the *National Enquirer* or *Star*. "The *National Enquirer* would call," Anita remembered, "and I would very gently try to say no, but they knew other people were getting it so I would end up finally telling the truth. I would say, 'I'm not trying to be critical, but you are a rather sensational magazine.' I would just tell them that Henry's father asked that it wasn't used for sensationalism. So I really had to say no…And that's why we were so busy. There would be weeks when I probably got one hundred calls."

It could be hard to keep up with the demand for access to the film, which ebbed and flowed depending on the year and the season. There were often hiccups in the process of getting copies of the film, and the files are filled with letters from people who wrote more than once to follow up on a stalled request. Delays happened in part because Henry was an extraordinarily busy tax attorney, Anita was his constantly harassed secretary, and the film could not be their top priority. They also occurred because Anita sometimes had trouble getting Henry to attend to requests. "Sometimes, I would get very frustrated," she remembered, "because Henry didn't really want to think about it much. I think it made him sad. Because he would think of his dad." More and more, Anita would handle the routine requests and set the fees, seeking Henry's advice only if there was something unusual or complicated. Sometimes, researchers grew annoyed after several attempts to get copies of the film, but their angry letters rarely resulted in an apology. As Anita put it in a letter to one history professor, "I am in receipt of all three of your letters to Mr. Zapruder. Mr. Zapruder is an attorney and his first responsibility is to his clients. We receive many requests each month for the Zapruder film and/or the slides. We answer each request as quickly as possible…Mr. Zapruder has to consider each request and respond accordingly."

Another hindrance was the cumbersome process by which someone obtained a copy of the film, which reflected the technical limitations of working from 8mm film before the digital age. First, a requester had to write or call Henry's office to make a request. Then Anita would send a license agreement letter with two copies. The requester had to sign and return both of them, after which Anita would send one copy to the National Archives. The requester then had to contact James Moore, director of the Audio-Visual Division at the National Archives, who handled these requests. He would provide the requester with a copy of the film, possession of which was granted on a temporary basis. It had to be returned after a certain period of time. The process got increasingly complicated if the person wanted to keep the film, reproduce it, or the like. There were plenty of ways for a person navigating this system to hit a snag or find his or her request delayed.

In the end, the overwhelming impression in reviewing these records is that managing the film was every bit as much of a pain in the ass as *LIFE* magazine had anticipated it would be. It was time-consuming and tiresome, requiring decisions, correspondence, and differing kinds of license agreements and arrangements. As Anita put it, "It was a major thing and they [the law firm] didn't want me to work on it during the office hours. So I would do it [at other times]...and it was interesting. Sometimes, it was difficult because people would call and this was their life. They had conspiracy theories and they would want to talk to me about it. And it was hard to interrupt them, but you know, I'm thinking, 'You don't know how much work we have and I really need to get back to work.'" Against the backdrop of the usual steady stream of requests, on major anniversaries of the assassination they would be besieged by requests from all the major networks, all urgently wanting the film.

Under these circumstances, I can see how someone might ask why my father didn't turn the management of the film over to a professional better equipped to handle it. He was well aware that the permissions weren't always managed smoothly and that outsourcing the work would be easier for him, easier for Anita, and better for the many hundreds of people who wanted the film for legitimate and reasonable uses. But, in the end, he always pulled back from this course of action, in part—I'm sure—because he could not escape the sense of personal responsibility for the film. For while it was becoming a more and more important historical record, it also remained a home movie, and he believed that our guardianship of the film should take into consideration his father's wishes as well as our family's values and our respect for the Kennedys. These were not abstract, distant concepts; they lived inside my father's head and heart, and it would not have been easy—even with a policy in place—for him to entrust the film to anyone else to make the decisions that he could instinctively make himself.

As a possible alternative solution, my father periodically tried to find someone in the family who could take on the responsibility for managing the film. In February of 1988, he wrote a letter to my uncle Ernie, my aunt Myrna's second husband, asking him if he might be willing to handle it, especially in view of the upcoming twenty-fifth anniversary of the assassination, at which time he and Anita would surely be deluged with requests. In the letter, he explained the policy regarding the film: to grant free access for nonprofit use by researchers, teachers, and students and to charge for commercial use under limited licenses. At this time, the broadest and most flexible use—with no geographic, media, or time limitations—could cost as much as $30,000. "When one begins slicing off uses or areas, the price declines," he wrote. "It is all a matter of judgment and we attempt to be somewhat consistent with past practices and to be fair." He acknowledged that it might help everyone if someone else could deal with the film. "The requests we receive invariably are assigned low priority in light of the other demands upon Anita and me. More responsive treatment of the inquiries together with more care and attention to the needs of the potential licensees will probably benefit all."

He continued his letter with what is probably the most direct acknowledgment of the problems the film caused:

> I am reluctant to conclude a discussion of the commercial aspects of the film without a reference to what I am sure has already occurred to you—a somewhat public responsibility with respect to this private property. I want to assure you that I have always had a free hand in exercising the judgments necessary to avoid foreclosing anyone who has a legitimate interest in the assassination from examining or borrowing copies of the film or frames. Our policy reflects that decision by charging only where licensees intend themselves to benefit economically from exploitation. Sometimes judgments are required to further the interest of easy access by legitimate researchers...I am sure you would want to do the same and want to reassure you that I am in favor of that approach.

I do not have a response in the file from Ernie, so I'm not sure if my father decided against sending this letter or if he did and they discussed it by phone. In any case, Ernie didn't take on the work at that time. Just over a year later, he would die of a sudden heart attack, leaving my aunt Myrna heartbroken and widowed for a second time (her husband Myron had died of cancer at just forty-six, when their four boys were still quite young). It was a shocking and terrible loss for his children, my cousins, and the whole family, who had quickly come to love and appreciate him as much as my father clearly did.

Just months after Henry wrote the letter to Ernie, he and Anita found themselves in the middle of a flap with two very angry and frustrated researchers. In April 1985, nearly three and a half years before, they had received a request from Gerard "Chip" Selby, a master's candidate in the Department of Communication Arts and Theatre at the University of Maryland, who wanted to use the film in a documentary for his master's thesis. He assured Henry that its use was for educational purposes only, and that if he decided later to show the film in public or for profit, he would secure a separate permission. In September, he wrote again, having changed his address, urgently asking for an answer. He apparently did not get a reply. In March 1988, he finished his documentary, wherein he used the film without permission, having failed to get authorization from LMH. When he began to receive interest from various networks interested in airing the documentary, he inquired again, this time about fees and permissions for commercial release. According to Selby, he had enormous difficulty reaching Henry and Anita, and when he did, they quoted $30,000—the top of the range as described to Ernie—which was not feasible for him. Henry apparently assured him that he did not want to "close down his project" and that they would "work something out."

At the same time, Harold Weisberg, the early critic of the Warren Commission, was also trying to get access to the film, particularly to make copies from the original that showed the "inter-sprocket material"—that is, the bit of film between the sprocket holes that was not reproduced in many of the copies. He also was having trouble getting an answer from Henry. Selby and Weisberg decided to join forces to try to move their grievances with LMH forward.

There is no question that by the summer of 1988, Selby in particular was very frustrated. Anita wrote a memo at the time describing an angry call from him in which, she reported, he was verbally abusive. Selby recalls the call differently, relating how he laid a verbal trap for her, getting her to say that LMH had sued people for copyright infringement when he knew they hadn't. He describes Anita as insensitive and uncaring. Whatever exactly transpired, the conversation did not go well. Meanwhile, in periodic letters, Harold Weisberg was continuing to express his aggravation with the delays in the process. On one of Weisberg's letters in the file, to which they had not yet responded, Henry wrote a note to Anita: "Write: sorry. Truly busy. Will try to attend to this when I return." Whereas Anita had a fiery personality, Henry was even-tempered and usually quick to apologize, even if he was not entirely in the wrong.

However, Selby and Weisberg would not be appeased by mea culpas. They quickly turned their logistical problem of getting access to the film into a much larger attack on LMH's ownership of it. Selby spoke with journalist Jerry Urban from the *Houston Chronicle*, who wrote a splashy article about the "price tag" for using the Zapruder film.

The family of the man who made the most famous home movie in history is selling the Zapruder film for as much as $30,000 per use nearly 25 years after it captured the assassination of John F Kennedy.

While the footage is under copyright protection, some believe profiteering from the historical film made by Abraham

Zapruder Nov. 22, 1963, is wrong and that the home movie should be in the public domain.

Henry would be the first to agree that "profiteering" from the film would be wrong, but it does not follow that the film should be in the public domain and that there were no grounds for managing its use. In the article, Urban interviewed David Wrone, author of *The Zapruder Film* (2003), in which he would devote an entire chapter to this unfortunate episode and casually slander my father in the process. In the interview with Urban, Wrone declared: "You shouldn't be able to copyright something like that. It should be in the public domain, just like the crucifixion of Jesus. It's immoral, socially speaking."

There are so many troubling things about this quote that it's difficult to know where to start. But let's begin with this: The crucifixion of Jesus is an event, like the murder of Julius Caesar or the signing of the Declaration of Independence or the moon landing. No one was copyrighting the Kennedy assassination. It could be written about, represented, and portrayed in any number of ways. And although they are deeply conflated in the public mind, the Zapruder film is not actually the same thing as the Kennedy assassination. One is the thing that happened and the other is a single representation of that thing from a very specific vantage point made by an individual person with a certain kind of camera, a certain kind of film, and so on. Which is exactly why there is a copyright to it.

It was a problem that plagued the film. For many, "something like that," to use Wrone's words, seemed to exist outside legal norms. But what are those "somethings" exactly? Important things? Things that people care about? Things that people want? Should the mere fact that the images are historically important, or in demand, or subject to much debate, or even that people have a strong emotional or intellectual attachment to them be enough of a reason to dismantle the protections that our society guarantees for private property? It is interesting to think for a moment about what else would be summarily moved into the public domain under that argument. Besides, the question is not as black and white as Wrone would make it seem. Our society has protected the public interest by creating the "fair use" doctrine, which allows for a certain portion of copyrighted works to be used without permission. The Bernard Geis case many years before had asserted Josiah Thompson's right to use frames of the film exactly for that reason.

Jerry Urban interviewed plenty of others who were happy to pile on. A network executive who declined to be named shared a helpful rumor: "What I hear is that there is a kind of rate card... They (network negotiators) are saying, 'Well, they're trying to stick us as high as they can go. They have a different rate if you are local public broadcasting, or if you're a local Houston station—a different rate for this and that.'" And Robert Groden, who is described as finding Henry's handling of the film "questionable," chimed in with what seems to me to be a rather tired theme at this point: "The worst part of the whole thing has been the suppression of the film. Not so much that one person is making a lot of money, but if somebody really wants to do something really good with it, they're restricted. It's like their hands are tied." To describe the film as being suppressed in 1988 is just silly. Henry wasn't restricting Selby because he didn't want him to make his documentary, or prohibiting Harold Weisberg access to the film because he didn't want him to see what was between the sprocket holes. He had made the film available to thousands of people, institutions, network programs, and others by that time. He was a busy tax attorney with a demanding practice, a big social life, a lot of professional and community responsibilities, a mother whose health was failing, and in-laws who weren't doing too much better, not to mention a wife and three children. He was overworked and overwhelmed. He was human. He was doing the best he could. So sue him.

Which is exactly what they did. Weisberg and Selby engaged attorney James Lesar and filed suit against Henry and the LMH Company, seeking "injunctive relief and declaratory judgment" in the matter, and also used the opportunity—nominally at least—to try to dismantle the copyright protection in the film. They did this by focusing on a narrow aspect of the law, arguing that LMH's failure to prosecute similar violations over the years was tantamount to abandonment of copyright. To clarify, LMH was, in their argument, guilty of aggressively controlling the copyright—by allowing certain uses and charging for the film—but also guilty of not pursuing aggressively enough those who failed to gain legal permission to use it. Their attorney, James Lesar, added this to their complaint: "At issue in this case is whether one man acting for the alleged copyright owner of perhaps the most vital piece of documentary evidence in the history of the United States is to be allowed to use the Copyright Act to dictate what ideas and information the public may receive concerning the President's assassination and what evidence scholars and researchers may study."

In an instant, Henry Zapruder went from being the harassed, busy lawyer trying his best and occasionally failing to effectively manage public access to the Zapruder film to the Joseph Stalin of the Kennedy assassination, sitting in the lofty heights of his corner office on K Street, dictating who could and could not study the material evidence (as if the Zapruder film incorporated the sum total of it all) and thus the very "ideas and information the public may receive" on the subject. I can understand my father's disbelief when presented with the suit. First of all, he had spent countless hours in the previous thirteen years making the film available to the vast majority of people and institutions that asked. Second, he barely thought about who killed President Kennedy: The topic was among the least interesting to him in a life defined by intense curiosity about nearly everything he encountered. For him, the death of the president had been a devastating personal and national blow, but the damage was done and the wounds sustained. Who, how, exactly when, in what way, from which direction, under what circumstances, even how many—these were simply not questions he felt the need to ask. If anything, he was somewhat baffled by people's interest in the film and the details of the assassination. But he had no vested interest in thwarting it, much less in trying to influence public dialogue on the subject through control of the film.

Still, the suit had been filed and it needed to be dealt with. This is when Jamie Silverberg, an intellectual property lawyer, came into the picture. He would go on to represent our family and the film for nearly a decade. Within weeks, the case was settled out of court. Why? Because it was never Henry's intention to prevent either Selby or Weisberg from getting access to the film. Selby and Weisberg, on the other hand, had not merely sued for permission to use the film but, under the mantle of a principled objection to individual ownership of the film, had tried to challenge the copyright itself. The instant they got the permissions they wanted, however, they abandoned their claim. The terms of the settlement remained confidential and the public language ran as follows: "The matter has been amicably resolved. It has been resolved in a manner that respects the copyright in the Zapruder film. The license granted is consistent with the Licensor's policies for commercial and noncommercial use."

In thinking about this controversy and later ones that erupted over our family's handling of the film, I keep coming back to my father's letter to Ernie. He had explained the policy, but he had also said something else. Managing the film required judgment. And herein lies both the strength of the arrangement and also the source of many objections to it.

The film had been made by our grandfather, sold to *LIFE*, and returned to our family. Like it or not, there was a copyright in the film and LMH was responsible for it. It is certainly easy to criticize my father's actions, but it's also worthwhile to consider the universe of possible ways in which a copyright holder could act. There was, after all, no precedent; there were no rules or limitations externally imposed on him. At the Extremely Controlling end of the spectrum, he could have been far more restrictive: He could have refused to allow any uses at all, or he could have acted as a censor, making decisions about who could use it strictly on the basis of what he believed had actually happened, or some other completely arbitrary rule. He could have been inconsistent or capricious, deciding each case on an ad hoc basis or ignoring his own precedents when considering new requests. On the Totally Irresponsible end, he could have abdicated any sense of personal obligation for the film's content and turned it over to a profit-based agency that would market it, sell it, and make as much money as possible. Or he could have made it available for free to everyone who asked, no matter what they wanted to do with it, allowing images of the Zapruder film to proliferate and multiply.

Instead, he did his best to develop a policy that reflected respect for both the public interest and his father's wishes. He sought to treat the film in a way that reflected our family's values but also served the public by making it available and seeing to the safe stewardship of the original. So when he felt that the request reflected the public good, he granted access and did not charge for its use. Those were the easy decisions. But when it came to commercial use, it was far more difficult. Here, it was clear that prohibiting its use altogether would not be fair to the public. On the other hand, to let anyone and everyone have permission would have meant, as he once said to me, that there would be hats and T-shirts with images of the Zapruder film for sale down by the National Mall. There were many hundreds of decisions that fell somewhere between those two poles, and someone had to make them. My father was uniquely suited to the task—much as he disliked it—because he intuitively understood better than anyone what his father would have wanted, but he also lived in the modern world in a way that allowed him to understand that those wishes could not be absolute. They needed to be adapted and changed over time. This required judgment.

Any human mechanism is imperfect. A well-known violinist repeatedly requested permission to use the film in a performance piece, sending letters, articles, information about her work, and a list of distinguished venues where she had performed. She used video and photo images as a backdrop on huge screens to accompany her music and wanted to include a clip of the film. Henry said no. Why? Maybe he didn't fully understand or feel comfortable with the appearance of the film in this kind of venue. Maybe he felt that it cut too close to an unnecessary or gratuitous screening of it, or that its use in the context of entertainment or even art felt wrong. Someone else almost surely would have made a different decision. I can certainly see why the artist would have been frustrated or unhappy about this, and I am sympathetic to her feelings. After all, as the film became more and more embedded in America's cultural heritage, more and more people felt a sense of entitlement to it. Slowly but surely, it was becoming not just ours but also America's.

By contrast, in June 1989, Henry granted permission to a Los Angeles–based filmmaker to use the film, though there are no specific details about his project in the files. In October, Anita wrote a furious note to Henry, having learned that he had acquiesced to the use of the film in a movie that was going to be distributed on home video. This was a medium that they had strictly and repeatedly prohibited prior to that time. "I told [him] NO VIDEO RIGHTS! Why did you say Okay? I told him I would tell yes or no by tomorrow! I told him I thought NO—I told him I have had several other requests for video rights and all NOs! So it is not really fair to say yes to him. Also, impossible to control!" On her note, he circled the word "Okay" and wrote this: "Why not? I don't think we should stop video now—too much pressure." In this case, he was very much aware of the difficulty in holding on to restrictions that made sense in the seventies and early eighties but that had to change given advances in technology and the increase in the use of home video nationwide. Policy regarding the film was not a static set of rules that could be established once and then routinely applied to every situation. To the contrary, they existed against the backdrop of changing times, which meant that decisions had to be revisited in light of shifting cultural and social mores, technological advances, public pressure, and a host of other factors.

I seriously doubt that the Selby/Weisberg matter raised these issues in any explicit way in my father's mind. He barely had time to deal with Selby and Weisberg, let alone to agonize over what their lawsuit was really about. What it did illustrate for him was that it was increasingly difficult for Anita and him to handle licensing and permissions for the film by themselves. Things were falling through the cracks, and LMH did not always effectively manage the film and serve the public. To Anita's immense relief, and my father's as well, Jamie Silverberg agreed to take over management of the film. And just in time, too, because in 1991, things were going to change again.

CHAPTER 11

■■■■■■■

JFK: THE MOVIE AND THE ASSASSINATION RECORDS ACT

There is no telling what might have happened to the Zapruder film if it hadn't been for Oliver Stone. In fact, it was the release of his 1991 movie *JFK* that triggered a series of events that dramatically changed the course of the film's life and our family's relationship to it for the last time.

There was nothing about the first inquiry, written on innocuous-looking letterhead from Camelot Productions, to distinguish it from the hundreds of requests like it that LMH had received over the previous fifteen years. Certainly, there was no hint that the letter represented Oliver Stone, a famous and controversial Hollywood director, or that the film would be featured in a multi-million-dollar movie about a conspiracy to kill JFK. Instead, a researcher wrote to Anita requesting information and explaining that she wasn't sure how the film would be used in their project but that the production company was interested in finding out the terms of licensing. She must have subsequently spoken on the phone with Anita, because another letter followed a few weeks later. The film, she wrote, was a biographical one about John F. Kennedy, and the producers were hoping to use "actual news footage" of the president and the assassination if possible. "To ease any concerns about exploitation or misrepresentation, I can assure you that the film, although fiction, is based on fact, not conjecture." It took a few rounds of correspondence to sort out the details of the license agreement. The fee was eventually set at $50,000 (not the $80,000 that was later and repeatedly quoted in the media and elsewhere).

In fact, the final film was not a biography of JFK at all; if it was anyone's story, it was that of New Orleans district attorney Jim Garrison and his crusade to convict Clay Shaw for conspiracy to murder the president. Stone had optioned Garrison's memoir, *On the Trail of the Assassins*, in 1988, and another book on the subject, titled *Crossfire*, by Jim Marrs a year later. The screenplay, cowritten by Stone and Zachary Sklar, used Garrison's story as a frame to open up bigger questions about the dark forces at work behind the seemingly benign facade of the early sixties and to create, as Stone later described it, a counter-myth to the Warren Commission. This took the form of an alternative story line in which the president was ambushed by three teams of assassins who fired six shots at his motorcade as he passed through Dealey Plaza.

In Stone's telling, the assassination was anything but the work of a single lunatic; to the contrary, he employed district attorney Jim Garrison, portrayed by Kevin Costner, to argue that officials at the highest level of the US government—namely, the FBI, the CIA, the military, and possibly Lyndon Johnson—in concert with Cuban exiles and the Mafia collaborated in a conspiracy to carry out and then cover up the murder of President Kennedy. According to this scenario, killing Kennedy was necessary to prevent his gaining a second term and being able to pull out of Vietnam, which would in turn have hurt profits for the military-industrial complex in the United States.

Given the premise of the movie, it's not surprising that the producers took a low-key approach when they wrote to LMH. No doubt they did not want to call attention to their famous director, their high-budget film, and their controversial plotline. It was probably a smart move, since Henry almost certainly would have balked at letting them use the film if he'd had any idea of the troubling implications of the movie. In fact, Jamie says that Anita was tricked into granting the license. Either way, Camelot Productions' request—which came in while Anita was still handling some of the licensing and Jamie was gradually taking over—definitely flew under the radar.

The movie was released in December 1991 to a mixture of critical acclaim and fierce criticism, none of which had anything to do with the use of the Zapruder film. Those who saw the movie as a creative endeavor, who watched it for the experience of being told a story in film, praised it for its compelling story line, the technical complexity of flashbacks within flashbacks, the pacing, the editing, and the way the various story lines layer upon each other and come together in the end. Many of them considered it wildly creative, incredibly daring and provocative. It won Academy Awards for cinematography and editing, and Oliver Stone won a Golden Globe for Best Director. On the other hand, many of those who saw it through the lens of historical experience or study—journalists, scholars, certain assassination researchers, and especially those who were alive at the time but who had children who were not—reacted with anger and disgust. Stone said, and surely believed, that these reactions stemmed from the fact that he had touched "a raw nerve" and that he had dared to tamper with the official history.

In fact, there had been plenty of movies and best-selling books on conspiracy theories by 1991, and the Warren Commission was anything but sacred. The controversy was about something else. For one thing, many resented Stone's revisionist portrayal of Jim Garrison as a lone hero when, in fact, he was widely considered to be a corrupt egocentric who at best was wildly misguided in his attempt to prosecute Clay Shaw and at worst used an innocent man as a vehicle to attack the Warren Commission findings and challenge the federal government's conclusions on the assassination. Others felt that the jumble of unsubstantiated assertions, accusations, and speculations was historically dishonest. But what really drove the critics mad was Stone's combination of real and invented facts and events, not to mention actual and re-created still photographs, newsreels, and film footage (including the Zapruder film) that were nearly indistinguishable from one another to create a seamless story that, if you believed it, had devastating emotional consequences and political implications.

I was not much interested in the movie when it came out, though of course I was aware of the controversy swirling around it. I recall that my parents saw it in the theater and that my mother, in particular, agreed with those who criticized the mixture of real and re-created visual and documentary evidence. The original footage of the Zapruder film appears periodically throughout the film, and when it does, it is often juxtaposed with re-created footage that looks like the original, a distinction that the average viewer certainly could not make amid the jump cuts, flashbacks, and fast-paced scene changes. In addition, there are two courtroom scenes in which the Zapruder film is prominently featured. The first one is when Costner, as Garrison, shows the film for the first time in public (only partly re-creating the actual events of that day, which included Abe's testimony) and then analyzes the trajectory of the so-called magic bullet. His voice dripping with sarcasm, Costner, as DA Jim Garrison, describes the bullet's path and the seven wounds it inflicted as follows:

> The magic bullet enters the president's back, headed downward at an angle of seventeen degrees. It then moves upwards in order to leave Kennedy's body from the front of his neck—wound number two—where it waits 1.6 seconds, presumably in midair, where it turns right, then left, right, then left, and continues into Connally's body at the rear of his right armpit—wound number three. The bullet then heads downward at an angle of twenty-seven degrees, shattering Connally's fifth rib and exiting from the right side of his chest—wound number four. The bullet then turns right and reenters Connally's body at his right wrist—wound number five. Shattering the radius bone, the bullet then exits Connally's wrist—wound number six—makes a dramatic U-turn and buries itself into Connally's left thigh—wound number seven—from which it later falls out and is found in almost pristine condition on a stretcher in a corridor of Parkland Hospital.
>
> That's some bullet.

Needless to say, the more dramatic elements of this description do not match the theory put forth by the Warren Commission, since no person in their right mind would theorize that a bullet could behave in such a way. But Stone chose not just to voice an alternative theory from the one proposed by the Warren Commission but to ridicule its supporters by exaggerating their theory past the point of recognition. Because of this, even some sympathetic viewers became suspicious of Stone's premise: If he could invent the content of this scene for effect, what else in the film's exposition might be skewed, or inflated, or flat-out untrue?

The second major use of the Zapruder film in *JFK* came in the climactic scene in which Garrison delivers his summation of the case. Stone uses the footage showing the fatal shot to the president's head as the damning, incontrovertible evidence that there had to be a second shooter because the president so clearly appears to have been shot from the front. Again, there is nothing new here—it is the same argument made during countless showings of pirated copies of the film over the decades and, by this time, plenty of legal viewings, as well. Unlike those muddy versions, Stone's movie presents the footage repeatedly, in full zoom and slow motion, to horrific, graphic effect. It is impossible that the president was shot from the back, Garrison explains, because his head goes *back and to the left*. The few seconds of the president's death flash on the screen over and over again. *Back and to the left. Back and to the left.* I am sure my father winced more than a few times when he sat through that.

As an adult, I have seen the movie many times and read much of the newspaper and magazine coverage from the time, as well as the critical literature about the film written in retrospect. The film raised provocative questions about the role of cinema, the use of documentary elements in a feature film, and the mixture of fact and invention in the search for truth. It presented a radical alternative scenario and planted seeds of doubt as to whether we think diabolically enough when we wonder what our government is doing behind our backs. But ultimately, the most concrete result of the movie was not to change the hearts and minds of the American public about what happened to President Kennedy. It was to mobilize the public to demand the release of previously closed records about the president's assassination in order to learn, once and for all, what did happen—if such a thing were possible. At the end of the movie, against a black screen, the viewer reads that government files related to the Kennedy assassination that were part of the House Select Committee on Assassinations investigation had been sequestered in 1979 for fifty years—until 2029. In interviews and written pieces, Oliver Stone demanded to know why this stricture was in place. He urged people to write to their elected members of Congress to demand the release of the files. And that is exactly what they did.

As the public conversation about *JFK* rippled through newspapers, magazines, editorials, and television programming, *Seinfeld*, then in its third season, aired a two-part episode called "The Boyfriend." The larger story concerned Jerry's man-crush on former New York Mets first baseman Keith Hernandez and the awkwardness of two grown men forming a new friendship. When Kramer (Michael Richards) and Newman (Wayne Knight) become aware of this budding relationship, they are horrified. They *hate* Keith Hernandez. Why? Because, they explain, on June 14, 1987, he ruined their day by making a "crucial error" in a game against the Phillies, causing the Mets to lose. As Kramer recounts what happened next, the scene cuts to a sequence that runs over his narration. It is a Zapruder-film version of their encounter with Hernandez, complete with the faded, nostalgic color of an old home movie, the shaky handheld camera technique, the quiet clicking sound of a movie projector in the background, and their own renditions of the most iconic moments of the film. "We're coming down the ramp," Kramer says, as a man in the foreground opens an umbrella (a nod to the mysterious "umbrella man" in the Zapruder film around whom there has been so much speculation and who figures prominently in *JFK*). "Newman was in front of me. Hernandez was coming toward us. As he passes us, Newman turns and sneers, 'Nice game, pretty boy.'" We see Newman's exaggerated, slow-motion mouthing of the words, the turn of his head and motion of his body perfectly mimicking the Zapruder film's footage of the limousine riding down Elm Street. "A second later," Newman goes on, "something happened that changed us in a very deep and profound way from that day forward."

"What was it?" Elaine (Julia Louis-Dreyfus) asks, breathless.

Kramer answers, "He spit on us." We see Kramer in the film, flailing backward, snapping his head sideways, imitating the movement of the president's head after the fatal shot. There is a brief flash of a man standing on a ledge holding a film camera. "And I screamed out, 'I'm hit!'" Newman goes on: "Then I turned"—the scene cuts back to the film, showing Newman falling forward as the spit bounces off Kramer and strikes him in the back—"and the spit ricocheted off him and it hit me."

Jerry, meanwhile, has been scowling through the whole story. Determined to defend his new friend Hernandez against this accusation, he steps in, formally re-creating the scene in order to show how Kramer and Newman's account of the events could never have happened. In a long, perfectly delivered speech—one that Jerry Seinfeld described as among his favorite moments in the entire series—he parodies Kevin Costner as Jim Garrison contemptuously describing the implausibility of the magic bullet.

Unfortunately, the immutable laws of physics contradict the whole premise of your account. Allow me to reconstruct this, if I may, for Miss Benes, as I've heard this story a number of times.

…According to your story, Hernandez passes you and starts walking up the ramp. Then—you say—you were struck on the right temple. The spit then proceeds to ricochet off the temple, striking Newman between the third and the fourth rib. The spit then came off the rib, made a right turn, hitting Newman in the right wrist, causing him to drop his baseball cap. The spit then splashed off the wrist, pauses—in midair, mind you—makes a left turn, and lands on Newman's left thigh.

That is one magic loogie.

"Well, that's the way it happened," Newman says defensively. Then Jerry asks Kramer what happened when his head was hit.

KRAMER: Well, uh, my head went back and to the left.
JERRY: Say that again.
KRAMER: Back and to the left.
JERRY: *Back and to the left. Back and to the left.*

Based on the movement of Kramer's head, Jerry argues triumphantly, there *had* to have been "a second spitter behind the bushes on the gravelly road." It could not have been Hernandez (who was behind Kramer) because had the spit come from the rear, Kramer's head would have pitched forward and not back. When Elaine muses that the spit must therefore have come from the front and to the right, Jerry says dismissively, "But that's not what *they* would have you believe."

The *Seinfeld* episode was one of the few times that I saw my father really laugh about anything related to the Zapruder film. In fact, we all watched *Seinfeld* and loved its unsentimental approach to comedy, embodied by Larry David's mantra: "No hugging, no learning." It's hard to imagine who but the writers and producers of *Seinfeld* could have pulled this scene off. Jerry Seinfeld remembered his "magic loogie" speech getting one of the longest and most sustained laughs in the history of the series. Everyone, it seemed, got the joke—not only *Seinfeld*'s satire of Stone's exaggerated deconstruction of the single-bullet theory in *JFK* but also the way it reflected decades of endless analysis, scrutiny, argument, and ultimately unresolved questions about the Zapruder film and the assassination.

A lot of people thought *Seinfeld*'s *JFK* parody was funny, but there were many who thought Oliver Stone had a very strong point. The movie brought about a public outcry that caused members of Congress to take up the question of public access to the JFK assassination records in January 1992. Over the following months, these efforts gained traction as more and more powerful voices joined the chorus of those clamoring for the release of the files. Even former presidents Richard Nixon and Gerald Ford, the latter of whom had sat on the Warren Commission, lent their support. In the eyes of those who favored the release of the files, the reason was, of course, to prove that there had been no government conspiracy, no collusion, and no cover-up. In March 1992, Rep. Louis Stokes, who had chaired the House Select Committee on Assassinations in 1979, introduced legislation to open the government's assassination records, and Sen. David Boren did the same in the Senate. Hearings were held through the summer and, in spite of minor disagreements over the substance of the law, both houses passed the Senate version of the President John F. Kennedy Assassination Records Collection Act of 1992. It was signed into law by George H. W. Bush on October 26, 1992.

The passage of the JFK Act, as it was called, was a bold and important step for government transparency and for public access to much classified material from one of the most controversial periods in American history. A five-member Assassination Records Review Board (ARRB), to be appointed by newly inaugurated President Bill Clinton, would be charged with defining what constituted an "assassination record" and then carrying out the monumental task of identifying, gathering, and making available millions of them from dozens of agencies.

Needless to say, I didn't know about the JFK Act when it was passed, and at the time I had no idea it would have any effect on my life or my family's future. Nor, apparently, did my father at first—or even Jamie Silverberg, who was still handling license requests for the film. Jamie found out about the Act from another lawyer, Mark Zaid, who called and casually asked Jamie what he thought about it. Jamie didn't really know what he was talking about. Then Zaid dropped a bombshell. "I'm thinking the Zapruder film might be included in the legislation." It didn't take Jamie long to get up to speed. He recalled, "I'm reading the legislation and in sum and substance, it indicates that whatever had been in the possession or was in the possession of the federal government pertaining to the assassination would be included in the JFK records for the government... And I read that and I'm thinking, well, the Zapruder film is in the possession of the government because it's on loan with the National Archives and maybe this is an assassination record."

In 2013, Jamie and I had a conversation about this period at a deserted Chinese restaurant outside Baltimore in the middle of the day. His office had previously provided me with all the correspondence, license agreements, legal records, and other documents related to the history of the Zapruder film from 1975 to 2000.

He had also invited me to his home, under construction at the time, where he served me brunch and handed over several sets of very high-quality first-generation prints of the Zapruder film, the responsibility for which had been keeping him up at night. Like many of the people who knew and worked with Henry, Jamie is shamelessly partisan and loyal to his memory. It may not be typical of the lawyer-client relationship, but Jamie admired and loved him. In fact, at the end of our interview, after I had probed his memory and raised with him many moral and ethical questions about the film that I never asked my father, I asked Jamie if there was anything else he wanted to add. "Just... I miss your dad," he said, his eyes filling with tears. "It's great seeing you. I look in your eyes and I see his eyes."

It was not immediately clear whether the JFK Act automatically made the film part of the holdings of the federal government or whether a decision was required to make it so. For one thing, the ARRB had not yet been formed and there was only a preliminary definition of an "assassination record." But more than that, as Jamie explained it to me, the uncertainty stemmed from the fact that those who had written the law had not considered the Zapruder film in their legislation. They had been focused on making government records—especially previously classified ones—available to the public. If it turned out that the legislation constituted a "taking" of the film, it was inadvertent and unexpected not just for our family but for everyone. Jamie described to me a phone call he had with one of the drafters of the legislation: "I called and talked to the person who actually wrote the legislation. I said, 'My name is Jamie Silverberg and I represent the Zapruder family and... I'm just wondering, can you tell me what were you thinking when you wrote this? It appears that you possibly have taken the Zapruder film.'" Jamie laughed a little when he told me this story. He said the man on the other end was quiet for a minute, and then he said, "Oh, shit. We did that?!"

Jamie can laugh about it now, but he remembers that, at the time, he was immensely concerned about what the JFK Act meant for the film, especially if the government had unceremoniously taken possession of it. He was an intellectual property lawyer and had worked in the "collectibles" industry around antique paper and philatelic items, so he knew firsthand how otherwise unremarkable objects like postage stamps could be very valuable. "And the Zapruder film was no postage stamp," he told me. "And so, plagued by this question, I called your father." Henry, on the other hand, was anything but alarmed. When Jamie said that the government might have taken the film, he asked, "Why do we care about that?" Jamie explained that it might have substantial financial value as a historical object. "Your dad had a great sense of humor and a great laugh," Jamie told me, "and he gave me one of his Henry Zapruder guffaws, like, 'Come on. You've got to be kidding.'"

It strikes me now that this could seem disingenuous. After all, Henry was a sophisticated and experienced attorney, and he was used to big business deals and large sums of money. Certainly, he was aware of the licensing potential of the film and he knew that the print and moving-footage rights had financial value. But the original film was another story. It undoubtedly had historical value and emotional meaning for many people, but who would pay money to own it? And why? It was too fragile to be run through a projector. There were a great many copies of it by then. But more than that, it was already in the possession of the only entity my father would ever consider for its safekeeping—the federal government. In fact, Jamie recalled that one of my dad's first questions upon realizing that the government might have taken the film was, "Why would they take a film they already have?" Another way to ask the question is: Why would the government pay huge sums to own something that LMH and the Zapruder family had already entrusted to them? This question would turn into the basis for Henry's dealings with the government for the next five years.

Before Henry could get off the phone, Jamie tried to persuade him to get the film appraised, to try to establish a sense of its value. Henry brushed him off. Jamie pushed, knowing that his reluctance stemmed at least in part from the fact that he didn't want to know. They ended the conversation there, and Henry must have decided to think about it for a few days. During that time, he discussed it with Anita and his longtime law partner and trusted friend Roger Pies. "He said, fine, he didn't care. He was going to let them take [the film]," Anita remembered. "I was just thinking to myself, you know, 'This is yours. I don't care what this new [law] said.' There was an agreement with the Archives that they were the caretaker. They didn't own this…And I thought, 'That's wrong. They can't do that.' Then I talked to Roger. And he's like, 'That's wrong.' And I said, 'We've got to convince him that that's wrong.'" Roger said the same thing Jamie did: He had to get it appraised. But Henry didn't want to do that. Not yet.

Henry spoke to Jamie a few days later and asked him if it was clear whether or not the government had even taken the film. It wasn't. But Jamie had a plan. He said, "The loan agreement says we can go into the National Archives to view the film any time we want, and I'm going to call them up and tell them that we want to view the film. And I'm going to go in and view it and then I'm going to tell them that I'm going to leave with it." Jamie laughed as he recalled the conversation. "Your father almost had a heart attack. He said, 'You're going to get arrested!' I said, 'Well, you can't get arrested for stealing your own property.' He was laughing and he said, 'Well, let me know if we need to post bail.'"

Jamie had some legwork to do before he was ready to go to the National Archives. He contacted Kodak and learned that he could identify the original Zapruder film by checking the edge markings on the film. He was fairly confident that he could get in to see it. But everything after that point was up in the air. He spoke again with Henry to sort out the thinking behind testing the law in this way. As Henry put it to Jamie, "We just want to know if they've 'taken' it or not. We don't want it back. So if you walk out of the door, then we know they haven't taken it; and if they don't let you walk out of the door and they have marshals with guns, you know, pointing at you, then don't take it." Of course, there was the problem of what to do if Jamie successfully left with the film. Then what? Walk it around the block for some fresh air and return it? No one knew.

On March 15, 1993 (five months after the passage of the law), Jamie turned up at the National Archives having made his formal request to examine the film. "I went in and I looked at the edge markings on the film and I was able to determine that it was the original Zapruder film...And so I put it back in the canister and I walked out with it in my hand and I said—I had a notarized copy of the loan agreement with the National Archives that said we could remove it at any time, and I said, 'I'm removing the film.'"

Jamie recalled that he was asked to wait for what seemed like a very long time. And then he was put on the phone with someone— he thinks perhaps from the Justice Department. The conversation went something like this:

Person on the phone: What do you think you're doing?
Jamie: I'm taking the film.

Person on the phone: What do you mean you are taking the film?

Jamie: Well, I have the loan agreement and the loan agreement says that the family can remove the film at any time and so, you know, I'm removing the film.

Person on the phone: I don't think that's a very good idea.

Jamie: Well, are *you* taking the film? I mean, are you saying that you're seizing ownership of the film?

Person on the phone: I'm not saying we're taking the film. And I'm not saying we're *not* taking the film. I'm just saying that *you're* not taking the film.

With that, Jamie had no choice but to leave the film in the custody of the National Archives and Records Administration (NARA) and return to his office to call Henry. "He answered the phone, laughing with a lilt in his voice, 'Are you calling me from jail?'" After Jamie reported what had happened, Henry asked him, "Well, do they own it or not?" And Jamie told him, "I don't know." Little did either of them know how long it would take for that question to be fully resolved.

People are often shocked when I casually mention that the government "took" the film from our family. Out of context, it can sound a bit totalitarian, so now might be a good time to pause briefly to discuss eminent domain and the Takings Clause of the Fifth Amendment of the US Constitution. The principle of eminent domain says that the government has the authority to take private property for public use, but that it must pay just compensation to the owners of the property. Most commonly, the government invokes the power of eminent domain to take an individual's home or land for the building of something that is deemed to be for the public good (like a highway, for instance). Just compensation is established by the fair market value of the property—for example, by finding out how much has been paid for similar houses in the same or a similar neighborhood. The principle of just compensation is to leave the individual whose property is taken in exactly the same financial position they would have been in if their property had not been taken.

For the vast majority of the records that were affected by the JFK Act, there was no issue of ownership. After all, the purpose of the law was not to seize property but to make government documents available. Congress stated that records relating to the assassination would, in the words of the Assassination Records Review Board report, "carry a presumption of immediate disclosure." Since most assassination records were more than thirty years old, Congress stipulated that "only in the rarest of cases is there any legitimate need for continued protection of such records." Whereas in the past, government agencies would make material available on a case-by-case basis, often determined by Freedom of Information Act requests, the JFK Act flipped the burden of responsibility from individual researchers to the federal government. Thus, unless an agency could make a specific case to keep something classified and this request was approved by the ARRB or the president, all documents related to the assassination were to be transferred immediately to the JFK Collection at the National Archives. In order to achieve this, the authors of the report wrote, "The JFK Act required all government agencies to search for the records in their possession concerning the assassination and place them in the National Archives."

If the Zapruder film had still been in a safe deposit box in New York City, or in a private storage facility or in my mother's closet, the question of taking the film would almost surely have been different. It's a little hard to imagine federal agents storming my parents' house and compelling them to turn over the film. But it was literally sitting in the National Archives, in the physical custody of the federal government (though not owned by it) and, therefore, "in the possession" of a government agency. Furthermore, the government agency that had possession of the film was also the agency to which it was supposed to be transferred—the National Archives. Which brings us back to Henry's original question: Why would the government take something it already had?

The Zapruder film wasn't the only object in the holdings of the government for which there was an issue of ownership. But it was certainly in a category of its own, in part because of the visual information contained on the film and in part because of its fame, cultural status, and emotional and symbolic value. The situation with the Zapruder film was also considerably more complicated than the highway-through-the-house model of eminent domain. If the government decided to exercise its constitutional right to take the film—that is, taking ownership of it, not just physical custody—it would be necessary to determine just compensation. But "just compensation" was determined by fair market value, which usually depended on the value of comparable items. What, exactly, was "comparable" to the Zapruder film?

While I'm sure it didn't take my father long to see where this situation might be headed, he was not, by nature, a reactive or hysterical person. He was even-tempered and had a long fuse (though on the rare occasions when he got angry, it was best to scatter), and he tended to project an air of calm, deliberative patience. While

Jamie worried, and Anita fumed, and Roger furrowed his brow and shook his head at the wrongness of it all, I can see my father sitting on a couch in his office, his long legs crossed in front of him, resting his chin in his hand, thinking.

One month after Jamie's visit to the National Archives, the chief archivist wrote to LMH, deferring the decision on the disposition of the in-camera original of the Zapruder film to the Assassination Records Review Board. The problem was that there was still no ARRB. Its five members had not yet been appointed, nor were there staff in place, and the critical early work of the board—namely, refining Congress's very general definition of an assassination record into a more specific one—had not been done. It's therefore not surprising that no one at the National Archives knew whether or not the film had in fact been taken. No one knew because someone would have to decide—and that someone would be the ARRB.

On a December day in 1993, my phone rang. It was my father. I knew from the sound of his voice that he was calling with bad news. I asked him what was wrong and I remember that he laughed ruefully at his transparency. Nana from Texas, the brazen, big-hearted, generous, wildly biased matriarch of our family, had died. She had been slowly fading away for at least five or six years, her memory gradually erased by Alzheimer's disease, and though caring for her was difficult, she retained her cheerful good nature even after she had to leave her second husband, Martin, and move into Golden Acres, the Jewish nursing home in Dallas.

I visited her there the summer before she died. She was up and dressed when I arrived, and she knew exactly who I was. She was lucid and able to have simple conversations, and even if it was difficult for her to remember the details of her days, she was as abundantly affectionate as she had always been. Since this was her great ability in life, it was a relief to all of us that Alzheimer's could not touch that indomitable core of her persona. I remember sitting with her by a window and showing her that I was wearing the exquisite art deco rose-gold watch that my grandfather had given to her on the occasion of their tenth wedding anniversary in 1943. On the inside it was engraved with Lillian's and Abe's initials and the date of their anniversary. She touched it lightly and said, in a wondering tone, "I remember that watch. Was that mine?" I told her it was and asked her if I could keep it. "Of course!" she said, in the emphatic, almost indignant way she always had whenever she was asked for anything by her family. "What do I need it for? You should have it! You wear it. You enjoy it!" We sat for a while, our heads bent together, and I was again, for one last time, Lil Zapruder's adored only granddaughter, trying on her jewelry and basking in her beauty, generosity, and boundless love.

CHAPTER 12

TO TAKE OR NOT TO TAKE THE FILM

In September 1993, President Bill Clinton appointed the five members of the Assassination Records Review Board. It was headed by Judge John R. Tunheim, the chairman, and included Henry F. Graff, Kermit L. Hall, William L. Joyce, and Anna K. Nelson. Their work began in earnest in April 1994. Two months later, Jamie wrote to the chairman to ask for clarification on whether the JFK Act constituted a taking of the Zapruder film. In the letter, Jamie argued that the government should not take the film, articulating for the first time Henry's position on the issue. First of all, he wrote, according to the JFK Act the " 'Collection' is to 'consist of record copies' of government records so that information can be preserved, essentially for public examination and study.'" According to this language, a high-quality copy of the Zapruder film, made available to researchers, would fulfill the terms of the law.

Nowhere was it stated in the JFK Act that the government had to collect *original* documents.

In his letter, Jamie also made a related point, which was that the law did not provide for the gathering of material via eminent domain, nor did Congress provide for the "fixing of just compensation" for the seizure of private property. In other words, there was no money set aside by Congress to compensate individuals whose property was taken by the terms of the JFK Act. Jamie argued this was because Congress never intended to use the law for this purpose. Its purpose was to collect and gather "record copies" and make those available to the public. NARA already had not only multiple reproductions of the film that had been used for researchers but also some of the material that had been at *LIFE*. In fact, just to thoroughly complicate matters, there was an argument to be made that the terms of the JFK Act could *not* be fulfilled by taking the original film, since the original was far too fragile to be run through a projector and would not, under any circumstances, be made available to researchers.

It might seem counterintuitive that my father would not want the government to take the film. After all, our family's best chance of making money on the original would be if the government took it and then had to pay us for it. But this presupposes that it was our intention to make money from the original film. It wasn't, and the best evidence of that is that the film had been sitting in the National Archives, undisturbed, for sixteen years. If our family had, at any point, wanted to capitalize on the film as a financial asset, we could have pulled it out of the Archives and put it on the auction block at Sotheby's or Christie's.

The reality was that my father, more than any of us, understood the long-term implications of the government taking the film under eminent domain. This action would require the fixing of just compensation, and the American taxpayers were going to have to pay that amount of money. There was no telling what the figure would be, and from his point of view, it just didn't make sense. Why pay for something whose ownership was largely academic, as long as we didn't remove it or try to sell it, which we had no intention of doing? There had to be another way to resolve the problem.

In the late summer of 1994, David Marwell was hired as the executive director of the ARRB. He would remain there until September 1997, leaving shortly after the question of the ownership of the film was resolved once and for all. He was, metaphorically and sometimes literally, on the other side of the table from my father, representing the government's interests with respect to the film. When he left the Review Board in 1997, he took a senior position at the United States Holocaust Memorial Museum, where I was working in 1996 after getting my master's degree in Education. We crossed paths briefly, but it wasn't until the 2000s, after I published my first book, *Salvaged Pages*, that David and I became friends. He was then the director of the Museum of Jewish Heritage, where I spoke just weeks before *Salvaged Pages* was published and then visited with some regularity to work with teachers and to speak at the museum's distinguished programs.

Early in my thinking about this book, I wrote to David to ask him if he'd let me interview him about his work for the ARRB. I recall feeling a little like I was falling off a cliff. I had not yet spoken to anyone outside our trusted circle of family and friends about the book, much less dared to talk to anyone who was in a somewhat oppositional role. What if he had a negative view of my father or our family? What if he said something that made me defensive? It was possible that he knew something I didn't, that he had some information that would cause me to doubt my faith in my own perspective. I might find that it was too difficult to discuss this topic with equanimity, or that I was unable to tolerate new perspectives in the way I knew this book would require. David wrote back immediately to say he'd be glad to meet and talk.

In time, I would become comfortable making cold calls, sending e-mails, and conducting interviews with Washington power brokers and lawyers, leaders in government, novelists, filmmakers, journalists, artists, scholars, and assassination researchers. Eventually, I learned that most people didn't have an ax to grind with our family, and the bunker mentality we had adopted—the sense that it was best to avoid any conversation about the film for fear of what might be said—was not really necessary. In fact, nearly everyone I wanted to talk to was not only willing to talk with me but also remarkably kind, generous, and encouraging. For those who had reason to be critical of our family, I gradually learned the difference between hearing their views and being threatened by them.

Still, this first interview required an internal shift, a readiness to open a part of my life that had always been closed in order to encounter a genuinely different point of view, hoping that I would begin to get to the deeper currents of the story that I was just beginning to explore. It helped that I knew and trusted David. It also helped that David has always reminded me a little of my father. But most of all, it helped that David is who he is. He is immensely generous, likable, and kind, with an understated but irreverent sense of humor. He has a big smile and a hearty laugh. He is exceedingly smart but never condescending. He is soft-spoken and unassuming, with a gentle manner that is most unusual for someone who has had such a distinguished career.

We met in his office at the Museum of Jewish Heritage in Battery Park City in May 2011. From his window, we had a breathtaking, sweeping view of New York Harbor and the Statue of Liberty. As we sat down to talk about the Zapruder film, I briefly thought of my grandfather as a fifteen-year-old boy, jammed in steerage on the SS *Rotterdam*, steaming into that very harbor ninety-one years earlier. Origins and legacies, choices and twists of fate, and accidents and consequences—there was so much to untangle and to try to understand.

We began by talking about the JFK Act and the purpose of the law, about his own memories of the assassination when he was eleven years old, and about what had drawn him to this politically complicated job. Eventually, we got around to the film. David remembered that by the time the ARRB was established, it was clear that there was going to be a problem with the Zapruder film. There had been several years of correspondence between LMH and the National Archives on the matter of the film's ownership by this point, and no one was sure whether the government had or hadn't taken the film. "I think we all realized that this was the prime, archetypal assassination record," David said. "I think it was in our minds all along, that this was an issue we had to address."

Although it felt like an obvious question to ask, I wanted to know why the board felt it was necessary to have the original film rather than a record copy. Part of David's answer had to do with questions around the authenticity of the film, a point of contention that had gained considerable currency at the time (and that would continue to occupy some researchers' attention long after the matter was settled to most reasonable scholars' satisfaction). As David explained it, "If in fact it was altered in some way, then the original was the best evidence. So it wasn't just the information on it...There was forensic evidence to be derived from the examination of the film itself."

At the same time, David acknowledged that the analysis could have been done on the film without taking it. It was clear from our conversation that although members of the board could list the practical, concrete reasons why it was important for the federal government to take possession of the original film, and someone like my father could argue point for point all the ways in which taking the original was not necessary to satisfy their requirements, there was an imperative that went beyond specific, practical reasons. David described it as a "philosophical certainty" in the film's importance not only as evidence but as a symbol, the quintessential assassination record. "It was not a debatable point for the board," David told me.

When I later pored through the correspondence between LMH, the National Archives, the ARRB, and the Justice Department between 1994 and 1997, it struck me that, from our family's point of view, the government seemed utterly undecided about what to do with the film. Of course, I believe David when he says that it was a "philosophical certainty" for the board, but their actions telegraphed paralysis rather than certainty. Every time Jamie wrote a letter, he received one back saying that the decision about what to do with the film would have to be further deferred. First, NARA could not make a decision until the ARRB was in place, which happened in the spring of 1994. Then, in January 1995, the ARRB designated NARA as the "lead agency" on the matter and announced that they would be "handling correspondence and inquiries" on the issue. In July 1995, NARA wrote to Jamie to say that they could not resolve the issue of the film until it was determined whether the government had, in fact, taken it. This decision would be made by the ARRB.

Jamie wrote back in frustration at the confusing bureaucratic structure that stymied efforts to resolve the issue. He also rearticulated the offer that LMH had repeatedly made by this point: In order to satisfy the requirements of the JFK Act while avoiding a taking, Henry had proposed that the Zapruder family make, at its own expense, the highest possible quality reproduction of the film. This print could be used as the "record copy" for the government, which would have a royalty-free license in perpetuity. The original would stay exactly where it was, and the government would have the right of first refusal in the unlikely event that the family ever decided to sell it. As Jamie put it in his letter of August 2, 1995, "It seems senseless for the government to take the Film rather than to simply use a CD or the other record copies which we have repeatedly offered to develop for free...It is my client's principal objective to assure that the government does not make wasteful expenditures relative to the 'takings' claim." Jamie, acting on behalf of LMH, would continue to make this offer right up until the last possible moment, five weeks before the ARRB reached its final decision.

Since it seems clear from David's recollection that the ARRB wanted the original film all along, why did they entertain all these alternative offers, and why did it take so long to resolve the matter? One answer is that while the Zapruder film was the most public and famous assassination record—and as such drew an enormous amount of press attention—it was only one of a great many issues that the ARRB was trying to resolve in a very short period of time. The process of deciding this matter should be seen not in isolation but in the context of the whole effort of the ARRB to coordinate a great many agencies and other organizations that were being asked to sort, categorize, and deliver material to NARA.

There were other reasons why the government hesitated, however. These touch on the monumental nature of the decision and its unpredictable consequences. The ARRB might have known that it wanted to have the film for the JFK Collection, but deciding to exercise the government's constitutional right to take it by eminent domain was no small matter, especially as the agency was being asked to make this decision without congressional or executive approval. They had no budget to purchase the film, and exercising a taking meant committing American taxpayers to paying an uncertain sum of money. Then again, letting the film slip through the ARRB's fingers and remain in the custody of our family seemed like a failure to secure one of the most important records of the assassination for the American people. Either way, this was a monumental decision with the potential to attract criticism—for getting the film and spending too much on it or for not getting it at all.

Henry's position was not particularly enviable, either. He earnestly wished that the government would accept the offer of a record copy rather than the original, because he did not want to appraise its value. Dealing with the financial value of the film always meant grappling with a moral problem. If the film's value were assessed by an appraiser to be very high and then the government took it, he was going to face a higher-stakes, more public, and costlier version of his father's dilemma from thirty years before. He would have to weigh the interests of his own family against the public interest regarding the film. He would have to explicitly address its financial value while adhering to his own moral imperative not to exploit it. Like his father, he had not asked for this problem. He had been minding his own business, with the film responsibly stored at the National Archives, when the passage of the JFK Act raised an issue of ownership to which he had no choice but to react.

As so often happens with the Zapruder film, there were now genuine differing interests that simply could not coexist without conflict. The ARRB felt that having the film was nonnegotiable, though they could hold out hope that our family would donate it to the federal government, thus freeing them of the responsibility of committing to just compensation. Henry felt that allowing the film to be taken without just compensation was nonnegotiable (though he repeatedly made it clear that he was willing to accept far less than "fair market value" for the film), and he could hold out hope that the government would accept his offer of compromise, thus freeing him of the responsibility of fighting for compensation. But, as the years went by, the ARRB could see that our family was not going to give the film to the government, and Henry could see the ARRB was not going to give the film back to our family. And so, nothing happened.

When I sat with David, he recalled how he felt about the situation and his very few memories of my father. "I have an image in my mind of sitting across the table from him, but I don't remember what the subject of the meeting was. I had, before I met you, some sympathy for him, in a way, because he seemed uncomfortable in that role." He recalled that there were members of the staff and the board who interpreted Henry's position in the worst possible light. Later, when I corresponded with Judge Tunheim about this, he agreed, explaining that some members of the board were "militant" and that they didn't even want to meet with the family. As David put it, "Some…thought this was just greed talking here. And I didn't feel that way…I would say to them, 'You can't expect someone to give up something that is of such great value. Would you do that?' And everyone had this cavalier attitude. Quite frankly, after I met your father, I became sympathetic to his quandary in all this."

The situation between the ARRB and our family inched forward incrementally over the course of 1995 to 1997. During this time, both sides worked with appraisers to value the film and proposed settlement offers that failed to satisfy the other side. Finally, in March 1997, the board announced that it would hold a public hearing on the subject of the Zapruder film, inviting comment and debate on the subject of whether the board should initiate a taking of the film or accept a negotiated settlement with the Zapruder family. It was scheduled for April 2, 1997.

At the same time, and not by coincidence, a company called McCrone Associates was preparing to produce a highly specialized color reproduction of the original Zapruder film at the National Archives. Jamie had originally proposed the creation of a reliable record copy with two related thoughts in mind. First, it was an integral part of LMH's offer to provide the government with the best possible duplicate of the film—one that would be clearer and more readily useful to researchers than the original—in hopes of avoiding the taking. Second, there was the possibility that the government would take the original film but not the copyright, in which case LMH might well have to continue managing license requests. In this case, a high-quality version of the film would allow LMH to better meet researchers' needs and streamline the process for access.

Jamie had learned about McCrone Associates, recognized for decades as industry leaders in microscopy and materials analysis, through his own personal interest in philately. Long before the company was actually hired, Jamie contacted Joseph Barabe, McCrone's director of scientific imaging, on behalf of LMH to discuss the delicate and complex project of duplicating the film from the original.

In order to better understand the technical aspects of this process, I called Barabe, who is retired from the company but who recalled with a scientist's precision every detail of McCrone's dealings with LMH and the particulars of the work. He told me that after his first conversation with Jamie, he wrote a proposal and submitted it, but then he heard nothing. Some months passed before LMH contacted McCrone again, this time requesting a more detailed proposal as soon as possible. Barabe and Don Brooks, the head of the company at the time, stayed up late into the night to complete and submit it. Again, months went by and they heard nothing. Then Jamie called. LMH was prepared to hire McCrone to do the reproduction but there was a catch: They had to begin the work in five days. Barabe negotiated for a sixth day for the preparations and then began what he described to me as "the most frenetic experience" of his professional life.

Well into the writing of this book, I had never thought very much about the process by which the original film was reproduced by McCrone. It was not until I spoke with Barabe that I had any idea just how intensely complex, involved, and ambitious it was and how much it demanded of him and the large team of experts who worked to complete it. In the most basic terms, the goal of the reproduction was to create an unquestionable, absolutely faithful record of every frame of the film. That doesn't sound so hard, right? But each frame is about the size of a fingernail, and the original film is old and brittle, so it had to be handled with the utmost care.

To ensure accuracy and safety, Barabe and his team had to make a series of critical decisions concerning, for example, the type of film, equipment, and light sources they would use, and the method itself. The color balance and exposure had to be perfectly calibrated in each frame and consistent across all of them. They had to carefully choose the proper f-stop for the camera to get the highest possible resolution without compromising the depth of field in each image. They had to test everything, ship all the materials to the National Archives in advance, and work with the staff of the Motion Picture, Sound, and Video Branch, in particular with Assistant Branch Chief Alan Lewis, to carry out the effort. It was daunting just hearing about it.

Barabe explained to me that he and his team chose to use slide duplicating film rather than a digital format, in part because digital technology was still fairly new and McCrone did not have the appropriate instrumentation to reproduce the film that way, but more importantly because film, unlike digital images, cannot easily be altered or manipulated. Clearly, this met a primary objective of the project. They opted to make 4 x 5-inch color transparencies of each image because these are easily readable—unlike negatives, which, Barabe said, require some "mental gymnastics" to decipher—and they could be used to create prints or to assemble an exceptionally clear version of the moving footage.

They made three copies of each transparency in order to have backups. Each image included a millimeter rule and a neutral-density color reference, so that if the original were to fade or shrink over time, this information about it would be preserved. Each transparency showed the tail half of the preceding frame and the lead half of the following frame, and it was assigned a number, to avoid any confusion about the sequence of the images.

After his hectic six days designing and testing every element of the method they would use to reproduce the film, Barabe and his team arrived at the National Archives. They set up their equipment and got to work, using a method called photomacrography, by which they used a single objective lens microscope to magnify the images on the film and then shot each image in sequence. On the first morning, they photographed a test frame, rushing it to a nearby photo lab run by Alan King so he could ensure the correct exposure and color balance. Amazingly, after one small adjustment, the settings were perfect. By noon on the first day, Barabe told me, they were under way.

As if this meticulous preparation were not astonishing enough, Barabe's description of the work itself nearly knocked me off my seat. There were twelve to fifteen people in the room working on the project, each with a specific job to do. Barabe would shoot an individual frame, then an assistant ran it to the lab, where Alan King developed and checked it to make sure it was correct. If there were problems—as there occasionally were—Barabe would reshoot the image. He had two assistants whose tasks included loading the film into the 4 x 5-inch transparency holders, moving the film, and brushing off any dust. He gave specific instructions to one of them, photographer Dean Alexander, which he repeated to me with a laugh. "I told him his main job was to keep me from screwing up." In the end, it was like a well-oiled machine. Nevertheless, it took a dozen or so people a full week of eleven-hour days—except for Sunday—to complete the work.

I couldn't help but wonder what this experience was like for the man peering through the magnifying lens and shooting the frames day after day. When I asked him, he said that he was doing his job, focusing on the technical aspects of the work and ensuring that everything was running smoothly. But then he paused, remembering one difficult moment. I could hear the thickening of his voice as he said, "I'm tearing up now just thinking about it." It was when he was photographing frame 313, the infamous image of the fatal shot to the president's head. "I was looking at Jackie," he said, "and I lost it a bit there." Through the microscope, Barabe had the clearest possible view of Jackie's anguished face, her mouth open in an agonized scream. It was the very same sight that Abe had seen in real time and that had haunted his dreams for the rest of his life.

Upon completion of the duplication of the film but before the public hearing, Jamie wrote a letter to Jeremy Gunn, general counsel at the ARRB, on March 19, 1997. On behalf of LMH, he offered to donate a full set of the 4 x 5-inch color transparencies to the National Archives. The transparencies were also about to be digitized, which would allow the images to be assembled into motion picture format, effectively creating the most visually clear version of the film to date—one that would not suffer from damage, shrinkage, or other quality problems. Our family offered to donate the digital copies to NARA, as well, and gave the agency free rein to make archival or digital copies from either the donated transparencies or the original film. Jamie reiterated what our family had said many times, which was that we had no intention of removing the film from the National Archives, where it had been stored for nearly twenty years, and that if that should ever change, LMH would cooperate fully with the board to ensure that it had whatever information it needed from the original film. In previous letters, in addition to repeatedly offering the right of first refusal should LMH ever decide to sell the film, LMH offered to give the Archives six months' notice before removing the film so that there would be ample time for the government to move to acquire it if it wanted to do so. Whatever the government ultimately decided to do, it could not be said that the information on the original film was being withheld in any way from the government, the National Archives, the ARRB, or the American public. Jamie concluded his letter by writing, "If you would please bring these points to the attention of the Board Members who will be deliberating at the Board's next public meeting, it would be greatly appreciated. In this regard, we would also ask that you make this correspondence a part of the public record."

On April 2, 1997, the ARRB convened a "Hearing on the Status and Disposition of the 'Zapruder Film'" and a public meeting in the Archivist's Reception Room at the National Archives in Washington, DC. In attendance were the five members of the board, staff members David Marwell and Jeremy Gunn, and several witnesses who were experts in various aspects of the film's history, significance as an assassination record, cultural importance, photographic value, and the like. No one representing the Zapruder family was present, and no one testified on our behalf. Perhaps we were not asked, or perhaps my father or Jamie declined. I had come across bits and pieces of the testimony during the early years of working on this book, but like many records from the history of the film, its significance was not clear until I was able to see the testimony in the full context of the long period between the 1992 passage of the JFK Act and the eventual 1997 resolution of the disposition of the film.

I finally sat down to read the transcript of the hearing as I was nearing the completion of this book. I was staying in my parents' house on the western shore of the Chesapeake, and it was early morning, when the mist collects in the small cove that sits at the end of the dock. I was drinking strong coffee, and the sun was just rising from behind the barren trees on the far side of the cove, casting a blinding light over the water. I knew from having read parts of the transcript before that many who testified had harshly criticized our family, and I knew from experience that it was emotionally trying to face their judgments and opinions. At the same time, I knew that this was one of many times when I had to curtail my natural defensiveness on behalf of my father and my family, to read the transcript for what it actually revealed about this moment in time and this turning point in the life of the film.

I read the introduction by Judge Tunheim and then Jeremy Gunn's more detailed explanation of the purpose and scope of the meeting. In his remarks, he explained that the core decision to be debated was whether the ARRB should effect an eminent domain "taking" of the original film or whether it should seek a negotiated settlement with LMH that would provide copies for researchers and satisfy other provisions of the JFK Act. Gunn went on to explain that if the government took the film, "one likely scenario is that LMH Company would then sue the Federal Government... and demand just compensation for having been deprived of its property." Immediately, I feel myself tensing up. The Fifth Amendment of the Constitution clearly says that the government shall not take private property for public use without just compensation. No demands should be necessary.

Then Gunn went on to lay out the alternative scenario. In the event of a negotiated settlement, he said, "LMH would agree to make the best available copy of the Zapruder film using the best available technology... The high-quality copy would include images that are between the sprocket holes on the original film. A digitized version of this film or of the original film could then be made. Second, LMH would agree to make this high-quality copy available to researchers for their individual use... Congress would be given an option to purchase the film."

I had to read this part of the transcript several times. Hadn't LMH already made these offers repeatedly over the previous five years? Why didn't Jeremy Gunn make it clear that the terms of this "negotiated settlement" were our family's proposed no-cost solution to the problems posed by the JFK Act and that we would, in fact, keep the film exactly where it was, put protections in place for the government should we ever decide to sell it, and fulfill the terms of the JFK Act by making excellent record copies available to the government with a royalty-free license for noncommercial use? Not only that, but LMH had already made the very high quality copies that Gunn was describing and had, two weeks before, offered to give them to the government for the benefit of the American people. Jamie had specifically asked Gunn to present this information to the board and enter it into the public record. And yet, there is no mention of it. I couldn't help but feel that Gunn's introduction to the hearing subtly but clearly set up the terms of the discussion—it was the government, representing the public good, against LMH, representing the greed of the Zapruder family.

The hearing began with a statement by and questioning of Robert Brauneis, a law expert who spoke at length about eminent domain and the legal issues around a taking of personal property under the Fifth Amendment. Then the board queried several experts about the wisdom of acquiring the original either to secure it as a benchmark against which all future versions of the film could be compared or, conversely, as a potential "wasting asset" that would eventually deteriorate to the point of having no use or value at all.

Moses Weitzman, who had produced the first 35mm version of the film for *LIFE*, reflected on what might be possible in the future. "Technology is advancing exponentially," he pointed out. "In the future we will have better capability of duplicating and analyzing the images both photochemically and digitally...Because of...digital scanning, which would enable someone to accurately record but also unfortunately to manipulate the image, it would be important to keep the original as a benchmark of accuracy to guard against irresponsible manipulations of the image."

Richard Trask, whose book *Pictures of the Pain* was the first to collect and analyze all the photographic evidence of the assassination, spoke to the centrality of the Zapruder film in the canon of visual records from the assassination. He stressed the importance of the original not only as an artifact but also as the best possible copy of the visual images of the president's murder that would ever exist, and he unequivocally pressed the ARRB to take possession of the original.

Many others, among them three experts from the assassination researcher community—Jim Lesar, Josiah Thompson, and Debra Conway—also spoke of the film to great effect and advocated strongly for the government to take possession of it for permanent inclusion in the National Archives. Clearly, this is what the board needed and wanted to hear. To justify a taking and the possible complications that would come with it, they needed recognized experts to publicly state that such a step was essential for the common good.

The board did not stop there, however. They also asked many of the experts how much the government should pay for the Zapruder film, and whether there was a ceiling, an amount of money that was simply too much to ask the taxpayers to bear. Predictably, this is where things got unpleasant. In fact, it's difficult for me to understand why the board asked these questions, considering that just compensation is clearly measured by fair market value. No one there was an expert in establishing fair market value for films or photographs, original artifacts, or unique historical objects. But that did not stop the majority from having their say—not to answer the question posed by the board about the film's value, but to express righteous indignation about the seemingly vast sums of money that the Zapruders had been raking in over the decades.

The board made no attempt to redirect their questions, curtail baseless speculations, correct the record, or keep personal attacks on our family out of the discussion.

Jim Lesar was first, saying, "More as a personal reaction than as a legal matter, I would think that the fair market value should be offset by the very large sums of monies that have been paid out in the past... I would hope that there would be some recognition that the copyright holder has already garnered an enormous windfall profit from this film." Kermit Hall then asked Lesar to speculate on how much LMH might have earned on the film. "It probably would approach a million dollars is my guess," Lesar answered. Josiah Thompson was up next. After describing his own history with the film, he was asked by Judge Tunheim if he felt there was a limit to how much taxpayers should pay for the film. Dispensing handily with the Fifth Amendment to the Constitution, Thompson declared: "I don't think the taxpayers should pay a penny for the film." Then, musing on licensing rights, he said, "I have no idea whether Jim Lesar's estimate of under a million dollars is accurate. In my opinion, it could run as far as three to five million at this point." Richard Trask, while agreeing that the film should be in the government's hands, expressed hesitation at a taking by the government. He would have preferred—as did some on the ARRB—that LMH donate the film to the National Archives. Board Member Kermit Hall played devil's advocate, asking why LMH shouldn't be able to profit from the film. To which Trask responded, "Well, I think they have. I think it is quite evident that money has been made off of it from day one."

Finally, there was Debra Conway, president of JFK Lancer, a website that serves the assassination research community, who went further than any of her colleagues in arguing for the public's right to own the original film and the legitimacy of the government's seizing individual property without compensation. Once again, a member of the board, Anna Nelson, asked Ms. Conway whether she thought there should be a ceiling on the amount that the taxpayers were asked to pay for the film. "It is priceless to me as a researcher," she said. "However, as a citizen, I don't feel that we should be held ransom by the Zapruder family...I agree with the speakers before me who said the family should donate the film. I think they have made enough money." She went on, "Do research on what they have been paid. Once you make that public, maybe they should be shamed into donating it. Maybe you need to use the president and the public to help you with that." Finally, she concluded with this: "I don't think the American people or the citizens of the world should be held hostage by this family's right to something that may already belong to us and should belong to us. Be bold."

I thought long and hard about these statements. Do they sting because they contain a grain of truth, or because there is some part of me that feels that our family was wrong to resist a government taking of the film, or because I wonder if we should have donated the film to the National Archives? Or do they sting because it is painful to read unchallenged misrepresentations about my family? Josiah Thompson's estimate that LMH made $3–5 million on licensing the film is preposterous. Debra Conway twice stated that the Zapruders were holding the American people hostage for the use of the film, when in reality, since 1975, individuals could request a copy of the film for research or study purposes and get it at cost. The experts and the board also ignored the full licensing history of the film, in which many hundreds of researchers were given free access to the film over the decades. Most of all, the board knew and yet didn't say that our family had already made many offers and gone to considerable expense to provide exactly the kind of access that they wanted going forward.

All of this was unpleasant and frustrating. But it was something Kermit Hall said that really stayed with me. When Richard Trask proposed that our family donate the film to the government, Kermit Hall said rhetorically, "This is America. Why don't they have a right to make something off their good fortune?" And herein lies the real crux of the matter. Throughout the entire hearing, when the experts or members of the board imagined the film from our point of view, they could see it only as a financial asset. But this is not what the Zapruder film was to the Zapruder family. From our point of view, the film represented a trauma for our grandfather. It was a source of pain for the Kennedys. It was a reminder of crushing disappointment and abandoned plans for my parents' generation. It was a burden. It was an intrusion. It was a serious and complicated responsibility. It was a moral dilemma. It brought public censure and personal attacks on our family. It appropriated our name and changed the course of our lives. In the end, it was a legacy we never asked for. No one in our family ever talked or thought about the film in the terms that members of the board or the so-called experts used in this hearing. Not once. Never about using it for power or to withhold information or to influence public debate or to benefit financially at the expense of others. That anyone could refer to the Zapruder film as our family's "good fortune" shows a profound misunderstanding not only of what the film represented to us, but of who we are.

There was one expert who was different from all the others. This was Art Simon, then an assistant professor in the English Department at Montclair State University. In 1996, he published a book titled *Dangerous Knowledge: The JFK Assassination in Art and Film*. In his book, he looked for the deeper meanings about American culture that might lie in our reading of the Zapruder film and the ways in which its controversies mirrored a crisis of faith in the visual record and perhaps in the idea of truth itself. His comments were, to me, the most provocative and interesting of anyone's—not because he didn't criticize our family but because he moved beyond the literal analysis of the film that limited the contributions of all the others. In his prepared statement, he said:

> I understand that one of the arguments for preserving the original print holds on to the possibility that some future optical technology might be employed that allows the original to yield new information...I think this may well be an enabling fiction, a fantasy, a fantasy that motivates further study and fuels a faith that someday historical ambiguities will ultimately be made clear.
>
> The film has become a fetishized object, invested with the potential to cover up our lack of reliable answers to many questions. In fact, this faith in future enhancements of the film has been a recurring trope over the last thirty years. And of course, a variety of such processes have been applied to the film. The Zapruder footage has repeatedly been cast in the role of ultimate witness, and investigators on both sides of the debate have insisted that with the proper scrutiny its images can render a legible view of the event.
>
> Now, while three decades of analysis has produced a significant challenge to initial readings of the film offered by both the government and the mainstream press, it has also produced a multiplicity of interpretations, a crisis of knowledge,

a serious critique of film's capacity to offer a unified vision and discernible truth. In other words, the application of new technologies has not and probably would not guarantee a unanimity of interpretation.

In Simon's view, the government did not need the original film because it still held the secret to the Kennedy assassination; to the contrary, it had yielded what it could and, more than thirty years after the fact, it was time to understand its value and meaning in totally different ways. He went on to speak eloquently about that meaning. It is, he said, "a secular relic," and as a culture that values origins and "first things," such original objects matter to us, maybe for reasons we don't fully understand. "Perhaps preserving such objects functions symbolically as the government's way of saying historical consciousness is important," he said, "and that although the past cannot be preserved, some index of it can be located in tangible artifacts which have been kept or rediscovered."

Although the board members engaged Simon on his ideas, one member in particular seemed thrown by the way the terms of the discussion had changed. William Joyce remarked, "You have quite a turn of phrase, 'enabling fiction' and 'fetishized objects' and 'secularized relic' among them, all of which speak to a certain kind of, in my view, marginalization of the film in the sense of the film as a record." Simon responded, in what well might be my favorite moment of the hearing, "I am not sure that fetishes are marginal." He went on to clarify that, of course, he believed the film had tremendous value in that regard but that it probably didn't have much new value left, since it seemed unlikely that any technology could come along that would allow a universal interpretation of the film and, finally, a consensus on what happened to Kennedy.

Art Simon was the only one who looked past the literal, practical reasons the government needed to have the original Zapruder film to the emotional and symbolic reasons that lay beneath. He didn't dismiss those reasons; to the contrary, he articulated and even validated them. It is a keeper of memory—the film that caught a moment in time of profound loss, a national disgrace, a dream destroyed from which America would never fully recover. It is a maddening puzzle—we see what happened but we don't know what happened—that raised new questions about our faith in visual representation itself. And it is contested evidence—the object around which there developed such deep mistrust toward government.

I would go even further. I agree that the original film didn't need to belong to the government because it contains hidden information that will change the way we think of the assassination; there is almost certainly no mystery contained within, waiting to be decoded by future technology. But maybe it needed to be preserved in the National Archives because it represents the *hope* of such a thing, the eternal optimism that everything is solvable and that, in time, our most vexing questions will be answered. Likewise, the original film did not need to be owned by the government because our family could not be trusted with it—as if every minute it remained in our possession it was at risk of being cut up, sold to the highest bidder, or scattered across the four corners of the earth. But maybe it needed to be owned by the government because there was *fear* of such a thing. Debra Conway said it herself in the hearing: "We should be very fearful of what a collector would offer the Zapruder family for this film." For her, and others, fear of our greed was a shill for a deeper anxiety about the corrupting power of money or the uncertainty of how the American propensity to value wealth might end up affecting the fate of one of its most important historical artifacts.

Seen in this light, it is true that there were many ways in which the government's needs could not be satisfied by a record copy of the film, no matter how excellent that copy might be. This was what rendered all of our family's offers inadequate, no matter how neatly they matched up with the language of the JFK Act. Ultimately, our family's private attachment to the film had to give way under the weight of a competing reality, which was that as the twentieth century drew to a close, the American public had become attached to it, too.

At the end of March 2016, very late in the writing of this book, I called David Marwell. The undercurrent of hostility toward our family that had run through the ARRB hearing bothered and puzzled me. I could understand that our offers of compromise did not satisfy the board. But how did that turn us into enemies of the common good? Why did they see us as oppositional forces, when our father had tried so hard to compromise? In his own words, "We entered into discussions with the Review Board on a completely cooperative and open basis, appreciating the difficulty facing the Board. We did not challenge the Archives' refusal to honor its agreement to return the film but instead permitted the Board to extend its deliberations over five years." In terms of the family's offers to the government, my father wrote, "We [proposed options] with the express understanding that we were not advocating any course of action for the Board but were simply providing it with alternatives to consider in its deliberation." There was a disconnect somewhere.

For answers to these and other questions, I had a date to interview Judge John Tunheim, chief judge of the United States District Court for the District of Minnesota and former chairman of the ARRB. But before I raised these issues with him, I wanted to float my questions by David. He was circumspect, as usual. He said that there was, indeed, some negativity toward our family on the part of some of the board members and the staff. He said that some felt we should have donated the film, and that it was difficult to resolve the board's fundamental, elemental conviction that the government should have the film with our resistance to the taking. In other words, I wasn't wrong. He also said that Jack Tunheim was thoughtful, reasonable, and a very decent guy. "Just ask him," he said.

So I did. We met for breakfast at the Mayflower Hotel in downtown DC early in the morning on March 31. Judge Tunheim has a boyish face that belies his twenty-one years on the federal bench. He was cordial and easygoing, making small talk as we navigated our way to a table and got some coffee. Then he handed me a thick file of papers. "This is my entire file, by the way," he said. "It's not censored." I was, of course, immediately disarmed.

Judge Tunheim was unequivocal and clear about his point of view regarding the inclusion of the original film in the JFK Collection. He had, from the outset, wanted our family to donate the camera-original film to the government. His focus was entirely on fulfilling his obligation to create a comprehensive public record of the assassination that would be preserved for future generations. When it came to the Zapruder film, the preeminent assassination record, the board wanted to end any ambiguity about its ownership and legal status. That is why all of our offers utterly failed to impress them. He explained that when a researcher approached the board to raise a question about a possible conspiracy theory, even if it were far-fetched, they would move to declassify records related to that subject so that they would become publicly available. The point was to hold nothing back. If the board was committed to this level of transparency about marginal records, how could it ignore the original Zapruder film sitting in NARA? Time and again, he emphasized the fact that he was taking the long view, looking ahead a hundred years or more, and that he felt a deep sense of responsibility to ensure that the film would be permanently secured. Given the goals of the JFK Act, he and the board wanted the reassurance that the film would always be safely lodged inside the government.

As we talked, another thread began to surface. Judge Tunheim recalled that from the time he became head of the board in the spring of 1994 (two years after the passage of the JFK Act), there was a nearly constant stream of letters from LMH, many of them threatening legal action regarding the film. It was a "tense legal relationship," Tunheim said. I had been through the letters and, although I hadn't read them that way, I could certainly see how he would. It was clear to me that Judge Tunheim didn't come to our meeting with this as a focused point he wanted to make. As I pressed to understand, I could see him scrolling back in his memory, trying to describe his experience of dealing with LMH in those years.

Toward the end of our meeting, he showed me some of the papers in the file. He explained that the first letter from Jamie on behalf of LMH demanding the return of the film arrived on his desk before the board had a budget, office space, or a staff. David hadn't been hired as chief of staff, and they didn't have a legal counsel yet. This was, he explained, the context in which the board was operating. "Before we had a staff, we had [LMH] breathing down our necks for what was probably the first issue we had to deal with. The frame of reference was: threaten litigation, threaten to go to Congress to get an act to take power away from us to make any decisions about the film, the National Archives saying 'What should we do?' the Justice Department saying 'We don't know, let this board decide,' It was caught up in legal mechanics right from the start."

While I could understand his point of view, I also knew that by the time the board assembled, there had already been two years of back-and-forth about the film. It was, in Tunheim's words, "abundantly unclear" whether the government had taken the film, a fact that caused significant frustration for Jamie and our family. Jamie was, after all, trying his utmost to protect our interests, both because that's what good lawyers do and because he cared about us. The more I thought about it later, the more I thought about the relationship between trust and strategy when it comes to resolving contentious issues. Our family had entrusted the film to NARA. We had an agreement. The government violated that trust when, after the passage of the JFK Act, they refused to return the film. For two years, Jamie, on behalf of our family, tried to get clarity on the status of the film and offer a compromise. For two years, nothing happened. Inevitably, by the time the board assembled, there was frustration and even anxiety about the possible outcome. Three more years went by, during which time the issue remained unresolved. I'm sure it's true that the ARRB felt the threats from our family's side; on the other hand, it's threatening when the government seizes something that belongs to you and that you had entrusted to it for safekeeping in the first place. Meanwhile, the legal strategies designed to bring about a resolution just further alienated each side and caused them to dig their heels in deeper.

Ultimately, Judge Tunheim said that he did not like having to exercise the taking of the film. He hoped until the end that we would donate it, though he understood that it was a reasonable, rational decision on my father's part not to do so. Still, the board was running out of time, and he and the other members felt there was no other good option left.

Two weeks after the hearing, on April 24, 1997, the ARRB announced its "Statement of Policy and Intent with Regard to the Zapruder Film." It began with the recognition that the Zapruder film was an "assassination record" within the meaning of the President John F. Kennedy Assassination Records Collection Act of 1992. The statement went on to outline the implications of this decision, especially as it concerned ensuring public access to the film and establishing its authenticity. The statement ended with this: "*Resolved*, that the Review Board intends to exercise its authority, as formulated in its enabling legislation, to direct that the film be transferred, on August 1, 1998, to the John F. Kennedy Assassination Records Collection at NARA and that the Review Board will work with Congress to resolve this issue."

It had taken five years and countless hours of discussion, debate, analysis, study, strategy, meetings, letters, proposals, and efforts. The federal government and the American people were soon to be the proud owners of the original Zapruder film.

CHAPTER 13

■■■■■■■

A FINAL FIRESTORM

In the course of deciding whether to take the film, the ARRB launched a comprehensive examination of the original film and took inventory of various other materials related to the film in NARA's possession. Specifically, they sought to authenticate the original and to understand how certain visual anomalies on the film might be explained. This was partly a response to a claim made in the early 1990s by a group of assassination researchers—namely, Harrison Livingstone, James Fetzer, and David Mantik—that the original Zapruder film, along with other evidence, had been altered over the weekend of the assassination. Inside the ARRB, Douglas Horne, who had been hired as a senior analyst and ultimately served as chief analyst for military records, pressed for an independent review of the film in an August 1996 memo to David Marwell.

Roland Zavada, a retired Kodak standards director for imaging technologies, was hired to carry out the analysis, which Kodak agreed to donate to the ARRB in pro bono services. Zavada's analysis, which focused largely on the Zapruder film but also included other assassination films, provides a thorough technical study of the original film, the camera, the developing process, and the film's provenance. He reviewed and clarified the edge markings on the film, which indicate when and where it was processed, as well as the various dimensions and developing details of 8mm film, focusing especially on the inter-sprocket material. He also carried out studies to examine the irregularities that appeared on the film and that had caused alarm among certain researchers. In the words of the report, the objective of these film tests, using the identical type of camera that Abe had used, was to "determine whether the recognized anomalies in the Zapruder film theoretically attributed to claw flare, claw shadow, development turbidity, first frame inertial effect, and the design of the photo-electric cell are borne out by actual tests with film." Zavada's study provides not only a highly detailed report on every aspect of the Zapruder film and Abe's camera but also proves the film's authenticity beyond any doubt.

It should come as no surprise that this was not the end of the story as far as suspicions of alteration went. James Fetzer was the champion of the argument, joined by David Lifton, among others. Douglas Horne, too, remained skeptical about the validity of Zavada's tests, continuing to speculate that the film had been altered and that the original film in the National Archives is not, in fact, the original Zapruder film—though his case was based largely on the impressions and memories of several former CIA agents who were interviewed nearly thirty years after the fact. There are so many different theories and variations on these theories, each of which slices and dices the evidence in a different way, that trying to address them is like playing a diabolical game of whack-a-mole.

Not to be outdone, there is a still fringier lunatic element who believe that the film was fabricated by cutting and pasting frames, and that it is a hoax and a fraud.

There are many who have vociferously and thoroughly argued against these claims. The captain of the authenticity team is none other than Josiah Thompson, who used the film back in 1966 to make his case for a conspiracy. This is a perfect indicator of the way that the community of assassination researchers has splintered over the years into ever-narrower categories of belief and thought. Just because a researcher believes in conspiracy does not mean he believes in alteration, though certainly the alteration theories, by definition, involve a conspiracy. Thompson is joined in his defense of the film's authenticity by both conspiracy theorists and advocates of the single-shooter theory, who may vehemently disagree on what happened to the president but who all grant that there is no evidence to suggest that the original film was altered.

So why bother with the alterationists? After all, tangling with this kind of assassination conspiracy usually means getting lured into a sticky web of largely irrelevant but distracting assertions that never seem to end and from which it is nearly impossible to escape. Eventually, despair sets in, usually followed by resignation and the desire to take a nap. On the other hand, the alterationists' ideas have been defended in conferences and symposia, in articles and, amazingly, in entire books. Now their ideas proliferate all over the Internet. Unfortunately, when writing about the Zapruder film, they cannot be ignored. Not only that, but when the alterationists begin theorizing, they nearly always attack my grandfather's integrity in the process. For twenty years, they have done so with impunity.

Douglas Horne's theory, while far from the only one, provides a case in point. Horne posits that the original film and the three first-day copies were developed in Dallas on November 22, exactly as the record has always shown. But, for reasons that are not entirely clear, he says that Abe lied about having the affidavits signed by the lab technicians on that day. In an interview with Dick Russell, author of *On the Trail of the JFK Assassins*, he says: "I think the affidavits recording these events were probably really executed on Monday, November 25, and backdated to the twenty-second. (No one I am aware of saw Abraham Zapruder running around Dallas on November 22 with a manual typewriter under his arm.)" When *LIFE* returned to purchase the film rights a few days later, Horne says, "I believe he then had to prove the provenance of the film so he created the appropriate paper trail in the form of the backdated affidavits."

There is not a single shred of proof for these statements, but there is the formulation of a narrative that suits the theory and the adjustment of facts to prop up the narrative. For my part, I believe it is more likely that there was a typewriter at Kodak and at Jamieson that Abe could have used to type up the documents on Friday than that he would have needed to carry one around with him in Dallas on the day of the assassination in order to have the affidavits signed. I also don't believe that he concocted a plan to traipse around town tracking down all the technicians from the two labs and a notary public and convinced them to collude in a deception by signing the backdated affidavits on Monday. In other words, I don't believe that my grandfather was a liar.

The next part of Horne's theory is so elaborate and based on such incredibly thin "evidence" that it is painful to bother with it. I will not give it excessive airtime, and if readers are curious, they can have the experience of trying to sift through the mass of unsubstantiated facts for themselves. Just by way of reminder, the non-conspiracy version of this story holds that the Secret Service worked with the CIA and NPIC analysts to produce enlargements from their copy of the film (Copy 3) over the weekend of the assassination. This information did not come to light until decades after the fact, when the ARRB interviewed Ben Hunter and Homer McMahon, who had been employees of NPIC and had carried out the top-secret work. Their accounts reflect varying degrees of reliability due to age, the passage of time, and other factors. It is thought, based on CIA Document 450, which surfaced in the 1970s, that these enlargements were used to create briefing boards in December 1963 in order to better understand the timing and effects of the shots fired at the president and Governor Connally.

Horne does not accept this simple version of the story. Instead, he argues that the original film—purchased by *LIFE* magazine on Saturday, November 23—was not sent by *LIFE* to Chicago that day. Instead, he says it was sent to Washington, where it was delivered to the NPIC. In this theory, it was photo analyst Dino Brugioni (whom Horne interviewed at length long after the work of the ARRB was concluded) who worked on the original at the NPIC and prepared briefing boards with enlargements of the film. Horne's entire theory rests on Brugioni's memory and interpretation of these events. For example, in an interview, Horne asked Brugioni why he believes the film he was working with was the original and not a copy. "Because two reasons," he replied. "One, the fact that the Secret Service was bringing it in, and the second thing is when I looked at it, it was not processed in a typical commercial fashion, in a little box or anything like that. It was very well controlled all the time; that film was controlled by the Secret Service all the time it was there." The Secret Service was bringing it in? It wasn't in a little box? If he had a visual record from that day of the original edge markings from the film, or he had made prints that included the inter-sprocket material (which existed only on the original), it might be harder to discount this interview. But with all due respect to Mr. Brugioni, these details do not prove anything.

If Horne acknowledged that the original film went to *LIFE* (which it did), then the government had already lost control of the images and no alteration would have been possible. But instead, the theory gets still more convoluted. He says that it was the next night, Sunday, November 24, when McMahon and Hunter were called in to the NPIC to work on what *they* were told was the original film. As in the case of Brugioni, Horne's case hinges on a particular detail that McMahon provided in his interview with the ARRB. He stated that he had received the film from a Secret Service agent named Bill Smith (of whom there is no record) who brought it not directly from Dallas but from Dallas to Washington via Rochester, where it had been developed at the Kodak plant. Ben Hunter does not recall it this way, and there is no physical evidence on the copy of the film in question to support this assertion. Horne seizes on this detail to claim that McMahon and Hunter were deceived into thinking that they were working from the original film, when it was instead a doctored version that had been produced in Rochester in a secret lab with the code name Hawkeye Works. And—wait for it—this is the one passing itself off as the original in NARA today.

As if this were not absurd enough on the face of it, McMahon cheerfully decimated his own reliability in an interview with Jeremy Gunn on July 14, 1997. Horne was present at the time. Asked by Gunn if he was sure he worked on the Zapruder film, McMahon replied: "I have senile dementia...I can't remember really anything...I am a recovering drug addict and alcoholic. Do you know what a wet brain is? Well, you're looking at one.

I damn near died. And I'm not a competent witness because I don't have accurate recall." Gunn pressed on. "With regards to the other events that you talked about, what is your sense of how accurate your memory is of that?" McMahon answered, "I just told you, I don't have a full deck...So whether you are talking to a reliable witness or not, that's up to you to decide."

Apparently, Horne decided he was. There are countless additional threads to this story, facts and suppositions that could be presented, refuted, and argued. But then we'd be down the rabbit hole, and that's far beyond either the scope or intention of this book. However, there is one matter that must be put to rest. In this version of the alteration theory, Abraham Zapruder remains a loose end that must be tied up. He had seen the original film repeatedly over the weekend and would—the alterationists suppose—have noticed the discrepancies between his film and the reworked one brought to the NPIC on Sunday night and passed off as the original. Never mind that several Secret Service agents, technicians at Kodak and Jamieson, a great many members of print and broadcast media, and Abe's own family and office staff had also seen the film that weekend. Horne ignores them. But he does posit a handy solution for why Abe never protested this inconsistency:

> Perhaps a "film switch" is even why Zapruder was allowed to renegotiate his contract with *LIFE* magazine, perhaps that additional $150,000 [*sic*] (which was pro-rated over a six-year period) bought his silence and future cooperation. After all, he did see the true original in the Kodak lab the day of the assassination, and did screen it for others (such as Dan Rather) on Saturday, November 23 [*sic*]. (Perhaps this is why Dan Rather's contemporaneous account of what he saw in

the film that weekend, broadcast on the radio, differs from what we see in the film in the archives today!) It would have been imperative to reliably obtain Zapruder's silence over the weekend.

There are many reasons why I shouldn't care about the alterationists and their preposterous school of thought. But at the heart of every alterationist theory there lies the implicit or outright declared belief that Abe Zapruder was complicit in the conspiracy. Douglas Horne adds to this the familiar trope of greed—to him, the obvious solution to the problems his own theory raises is that Abe allowed his silence to be purchased for $150,000. I do care about that. I have elsewhere in this book acknowledged the ways in which Abe handled the ethical dilemmas posed by the film. He was not perfect, nor did he need to be. But, unlike the alterationists— theorizing, interpreting, and speculating thirty years after the fact—Abe was the one who saw the president murdered in real time; he was the one who was responsible for the film; and he was the one who did his best to handle an unprecedented situation with dignity and moral balance. I am more than willing to leave it to Josiah Thompson and others more versed in the facts to take down the alterationists' theories. But for our family, it is unforgivable to allow the casual defamation of my grandfather's character with absolutely no proof or evidence of any kind. In this, the alterationists and their ideas are an affront to Abraham Zapruder's reputation and to his memory.

When it comes to the Zapruder film—and I am not the first to say this—the committed alterationists represent the final, inevitable outcome of decades of scrutiny and excessive faith in the power of the Zapruder film to tell us what happened to President Kennedy.

They want every anomaly explained, every inconsistency resolved, every doubt tied up in a seamless narrative. But life isn't like that. When the film failed to deliver a clear and consistent story, and when even the most advanced technological methods failed to provide consensus on the maddening question of what happened to our president, there was nothing left to do but question the evidence itself. Thus, alteration became the de facto solution. For this school of thought, there is no simple human error, or failure of memory, or unanticipated outcomes of decisions made in haste. Instead, the answers to their questions can only be found by following the traces of a bigger, darker history that they alone can see.

In October 1997, acclaimed author Don DeLillo published *Underworld*. Across two short scenes in the novel, his characters Klara and Miles visit an art installation in 1974 in which bootleg copies of the Zapruder film are playing in continuous loops at different speeds on hundreds of TV screens in a New York City apartment. These pages remain as provocative and haunting as anything I've read about the film. Unlike the alterationists, who were busy bogging down an understanding of the Zapruder film (Fetzer's *Assassination Science* came out in 1997), DeLillo conjured up a scene that suggests the film's meaning not only in the context of 1974 but also in the enduring present.

When I wrote to Don DeLillo's publicist, Kate Lloyd, to find out if he would talk to me about the Zapruder film (he has said that it "could probably fuel college courses in a dozen subjects from history to physics"), the last thing I expected was to end up having lunch with him in a quiet French restaurant on a fall afternoon in Manhattan. He is famously reticent and had, according to Kate, granted only two interviews in the five years she had been working with him. At first, he seems shy, quiet, and reserved. It is hard to square his gentle presence with the dangerous, sometimes frightening worlds he has created in his fiction. Then again, he has a quick laugh and a distinct twinkle in his hazel-brown eyes. When we sat down, I asked if I could record our conversation and then pushed the small machine to the side, assuring him that we would forget about it once we started talking. Our lunch was less an interview than a conversation, as I found myself not only asking the questions but also answering them.

The Kennedy assassination has figured largely in DeLillo's work, and the film has been an object of fascination for him for decades. He explored the idea of conspiracy and its unexpected, pervasive influences in his novel of the JFK assassination, *Libra*. He told me that it was while he was working on an article for *Rolling Stone* about the assassination that he was able to get a bootleg copy of the film from a dealer in Quebec. In fact, in the mideighties he probably could have gotten it from my father. The fact that he didn't know he could and had to procure it from a dealer who was "beyond US law" speaks to the ongoing sense that the film was suppressed or difficult to obtain in America.

In an interview in the *Paris Review* in 1993, Adam Begley asked DeLillo to speak about what the film meant to him. Among many other things, he said, "There's something inevitable about the Zapruder film. It had to happen this way. The moment belongs to the twentieth century, which means it had to be captured on film." I didn't entirely understand what he meant until we talked. He described the twentieth century as the age of film, just as today is the age of the Internet—by the 1960s, cameras had become commonplace and everyone was filming everything. He is right; after all, there were twenty-one other photographers on Dealey Plaza that day alone. But I understand that he was talking about something more than just the odds that someone would record the murder. There is a kind of poetic logic, if such a phrase exists, in capturing such a defining moment of the twentieth century on film, which remains the technology most associated with that time. In this, film is distinctly different from videotape or, most relevant for today, digital media with its clarity, permanence, perfection, ability to be manipulated and replicated ad infinitum. In contrast, 8mm film is tangible and fragile, its images grainy and saturated, paradoxically preserving memory and degrading over time. Everything about it offers tantalizing, nostalgic glimpses of a time that has slipped away.

In *Underworld*, Klara and Miles enter the apartment in which they will see the Zapruder film, finding it filled with every kind of TV set from "the smallest imported eyeball to the great proscenium face of the household god," including a whole wall of TV sets from floor to ceiling. People are smoking pot, sitting on the floor, and waiting. I asked DeLillo to tell me how the idea came to him. "I'd seen something like that in a museum or gallery," he said, where the artist had "stacked TV sets on top of each other, and I don't remember whether he had a pattern that each screen related to each other screen [or] whether they were old television sets but it struck me as an interesting thing to do in the apartment of some sort of avant-garde individual. And so there we are."

As the scene begins, everyone is slightly edgy, anticipating what they will see.

The footage started rolling in one room but not the others and it was filled with slurs and jostles, it was totally jostled footage, a home movie shot with a Super 8, and the limousine came down the street, muddied by sunglint, and the head dipped out of the frame and reappeared and then the force of the shot that killed him, unexpectedly, the headshot, and people in the room went ohh, and then the next ohh, and five seconds later, the room at the back went ohh, the same release of breath every time, like blurts of disbelief, and a woman seated on the floor spun away and covered her face because it was completely new, you see, suppressed all these years, this was the famous headshot and they had to contend with the impact—aside from the fact that this was the President being shot, past the outer limits of this fact they had to contend with the impact that any high-velocity bullet of a certain lethal engineering will make on any human head, and the sheering of tissue and braincase was a terrible revelation.

In our conversation, DeLillo elaborated on how he thought about that scene when he was writing it. "Of course, the key to the whole thing is that I think the people went to look at it expecting to see some sort of art that they hadn't seen before," he said, "and then to see this terrible drama of violence was terrifically shocking, even for highly sophisticated people." For me, there is also the prominence of the home movie, the "jostled footage," the car dipping out of the frame. DeLillo captures so perfectly what others so often forget in discussing the film—the man standing and holding the camera, taking a home movie, the imperfections that lend the film its terrible sense of intimacy.

There is a break in the narrative, and then we are back in the studio with Klara and Miles, people are more stoned, a couple is making out in a closet, and the loop of the film continues to play. While it is still (always) 1974 for Klara and Miles—that last moment before the film exploded into the public realm on national television—it is not the case for us reading *Underworld* in 1997 and after. As DeLillo repeats in varying forms the description of the footage rolling on the television sets, I began to see a narrative in the piece itself—not a perfectly sequential one, of course, but the echoing ways in which the film jolted Americans into new and upsetting confrontations. There is the shock of seeing a head encountering a bullet for the first time ("the sheering of tissue and braincase was a terrible revelation") and then the shock of realizing that it will always be a shock ("the head dipped out of the frame and reappeared and the shot was unexpected"). The footage rolls again, and each time, it seems, there is the possibility for a new revelation, like the idea that the murder could have been the product of a darker political reality than anyone had previously conceived. "Here comes the car, here comes the shot," he writes, "and it was amazing that there were forces in the culture that could out-imagine them, make their druggiest terrors seem futile and cheap."

As the scene continues to build, the images on the screen become more and more abstracted, more out of control. "Different phases of the sequence showed on different screens and the spectator's eye could jump from Zapruder 239 back to 185, and down to the headshot, and over to the opening frames, and on the TV wall the sets and frames were geared to patterns. The TV wall was a kind of game board of diagonals and verticals and so on, interlocking tarots of elemental fate, or synchronous footage running in an X pattern, and whatever the mathematics of the wall there were a hundred images running at once, here comes the car, here comes the shot." The film, which has the clearest imaginable narrative, is abstracted in this scene—it's playing on different TV sets, in various rooms, at varying speeds. It shatters the narrative and makes literal the deeper truth beneath, which is that in spite of its very clear story, it is incomprehensible. When I asked him about this, DeLillo nodded and added, "It's as though the fragmentation will ease the shock of impact. But I don't think it does."

By the time we reach the climactic end of the scene, the film has played endlessly, looped constantly, in slow motion, close-up, at different speeds, to the people coming and going, running inside the different frames of hundreds of televisions sets. Finally, Klara sees the story of the film and its meaning transcending any particular time and place, understanding instead how it preys on our deepest fears of death and enacts our nightmares.

The progress of the car down Elm Street, the movement of the film through the camera body, some sharable darkness—this was a death that seemed to rise from the steamy debris of the deep mind, it came from some night of the mind, there was some trick of film emulsion that showed the ghost of consciousness. Or so [Klara] thought to wonder. She thought to wonder if this home movie was some crude living likeness of the mind's own technology, the sort of death plot that runs in the mind, because it seemed so familiar, the footage did—it seemed a thing we might see, not see but know, a model of the nights when we are intimate with our own dying.

As we sat and talked at lunch, we eventually drifted off the topic of the Zapruder film. We talked about our families, and writing, and where he grew up and how I planned to finish the book in time for my deadline. Finally, as we were getting ready to say goodbye, he looked at me quietly, and with a mischievous smile, he said,

"Would you like to turn off the eavesdropping device?" He had not forgotten that it was there.

I have no idea if my father was aware of Don DeLillo's extraordinary description of the film in *Underworld*. He more than had his hands full with far more prosaic matters, such as negotiations with the government over the film. The ARRB finished its work in 1997 and handed the matter off to the Justice Department, which continued negotiations with LMH on just compensation for the film. In fact, the financial conflict stretched even farther back than that. During the eternal season of the "negotiated settlement," before the ARRB decided to take the film, both LMH and the government had commissioned appraisals. Philip Moore at J. & W. Seligman had appraised it for LMH, and C. Cameron Macauley and Ernest D. Rose had done the same for the government. They had adopted radically different approaches to assessing the value of the film, which resulted in a vast gulf between their appraisals. Even the government's highest offer and LMH's lowest were millions apart, a fact that had made a settlement all but impossible.

The efforts to reach an agreement continued to sputter through 1997. Since the last thing my father wanted was to enter into litigation with the government, he took steps to avert this eventuality during the fall of 1997. At that time, my mother's cousin Dana Freyer and her husband, Bruce, visited my parents. Our families have always been close, and my mother and Dana—in spite of having traveled very different paths in life—are kindred spirits. While they were together, Henry confided in Dana about the state of affairs with the government. He tended to lean on close family and friends, especially when it came to the Zapruder film, and Dana was no exception. Dana was the head of the arbitration and alternative dispute resolution practice at Skadden Arps in New York and had many years of experience in this area. She is a seasoned attorney, but she also balances her brilliant analytical mind with a generous heart and a deeply thoughtful manner. Henry and Dana could speak the same language when it came to the law, but she also implicitly understood and shared the deeper values that drove so much of his thinking. "Henry was explaining to me that the negotiations were really not proceeding satisfactorily," she said, recalling their first conversation about the situation. "And he asked if I could get involved in having Skadden represent the family, in negotiating with the government."

I was having this conversation with Dana on a mild summer day in late June 2011 while I was visiting her at her home in Scarsdale, New York. We were sitting outside on a tranquil patio, periodically being interrupted by her toddler grandson Henry—named in memory of my father—who was busily coming and going. Dana explained to me that after this conversation, she spoke with Robert Bennett, a partner in Skadden's DC office at the time who was a well-known and highly respected litigation attorney, famous for having defended President Bill Clinton in the Paula Jones lawsuit, among many other high-profile cases. They took on the case, bringing in attorneys Richard Brusca and Harold Reeves. Jamie remained an integral part of the process, and our first cousin Adam Hauser—Myrna's second son, who was very close to my father and practiced law in Texas—remained closely involved, as well.

At this point, LMH still had the option of challenging the taking of the film in court. Both sides show in their internal records that this was a viable legal question and believed that such a challenge could potentially result in the reversal of the taking. In addition to interviewing Dana, I visited Bob Bennett at his office at Hogan Lovells, and Rich Brusca at his home on the Eastern Shore. Both of them provided invaluable insight into the process of working through this problem. Brusca explained: "We thought that a very good case could be made that the government just was wrong in taking the film and could be challenged [in court]." Although the letters from the LMH attorneys to the government repeatedly put this forward as part of the legal strategy to keep the pressure on the Justice Department, these same lawyers—Bob, Dana, and Rich—each independently stressed that Henry did not want to sue the government for the return of the film. According to Brusca, "Your dad told us…'Well…it probably is important for the government to have it. So I really don't want to challenge that. Let's just figure out how much we can ask for and let's just get it over with.'" Dana explained it further: "As lawyers, we were leaving no stone unturned, so to speak, and we did ask him, 'Do you want to resist the taking?' And he was clear that he did not want to resist the taking. He wanted [the film] to be with the government. He felt that it was proper [that it] should be publicly accessible as an American historical document."

The problem was that if LMH didn't resist the taking in court, that still left the matter of determining just compensation. If the two sides could not reach a negotiated settlement, the matter would have to be resolved by some higher authority. The normal course of action would be to settle the issue in the US Court of Federal Claims. Brusca explained to me that LMH didn't want to go this route, partly because the Court of Federal Claims is known for being "more pro-government than most courts" and also because, if the Justice Department didn't like the outcome, they could appeal the decision. Thus, the dispute could go on indefinitely. That was the last thing our family wanted.

But there was another possibility, which was to convince the government to go to arbitration. Unlike the open-ended and contentious nature of litigation, such an arrangement would mean that an independent panel of arbitrators would render a decision on the matter, with no possibility of appeal, and both parties would abide by it. Which brings us back to Dana. She told me that Henry asked her if she might be able to help "in structuring an arbitration proceeding in which the film's fair market value would be determined by a panel of impartial arbitrators. This was fairly novel, as I recall. Because the government traditionally had not…I don't know if never but, as I recall, had not in the past agreed to binding arbitration." So while Jamie and Henry continued to try to reach an agreement with the Justice Department, Dana and Bob Bennett began working on a proposal for an arbitration proceeding to submit to the government.

In mid-June 1998, Washingtonians opened the *Washington Post* to find an article about the Zapruder film taking up half of the front page above the fold. The headline read "Haggling over History; Zapruders, U.S. Far Apart on Price of Kennedy Film," with a black-and-white frame from the film of Jacqueline Kennedy climbing on to the back of the limousine. Major newspapers and magazines, including the *New York Times*, the *Dallas Morning News*, and *Newsweek*, ran similar articles with similar headlines. It was a mere six weeks until the government would officially take possession of the film and, as the article explained it, the two parties were far from reaching an agreement on just compensation. "They are millions of dollars apart. The Zapruders have asked for $18.5 million for the film and the copyright, informed sources said, and have hired Washington power lawyer Robert S. Bennett to press their claim. The Justice

Department contends that price is much too high and has offered $750,000 while suggesting it might go as high as $3 million."

As the paper said, LMH proposed $18.5 million, based on the Seligman appraisal, although additional appraisals conducted by other experts had come in as high as $25 million or even $41 million. LMH had done a separate valuation of the "intangible rights" in the film—i.e., the copyright—which came in at $10 million. Taking it all into account, the original film and its copyright appeared to have a staggeringly high potential value. And while $18.5 million was a hell of a lot of money, it was many times less than what the film would sell for on the open market. The government's appraisal of the in-camera original film by Macauley and Rose had put the film's value at $750,000. Ultimately, the government went up to $3 million for the original film, and at a certain point, LMH indicated that it might settle at $9 million or $10 million. Meanwhile, the Justice Department decided to exclude the copyright to the film from the taking, on the grounds that without it, the value of the artifact itself would be considerably less. It was a move that outraged assassination critics, who felt that allowing LMH to retain the copyright left our family in control of the use of the film in exactly the way they had resented for so long. Attorney Mark Zaid even filed a lawsuit to challenge the government on this matter. As the months passed, the negotiations again broke down. If the government did not accept the proposal for arbitration, the matter would be headed for litigation.

At the end of June 1998, my father wrote a letter to the family. Such direct words from him about the film were extremely rare. "We have made one final proposal to the Justice Department," he wrote. "You can be both proud and assured that we have followed through on the standard set by your grandfather in his original dealing with the film. We have done everything reasonable to contribute to the United States ownership by offering to waive any challenge to the legal authority to take the film and by proposing to accept an amount substantially below estimates of fair market value. Regardless of the outcome, I think we have acted properly."

The last salvo to the government was no longer an offer to try to reach a financial settlement. It was the proposal for arbitration, the outcome of his initial conversations with Dana Freyer from the previous fall. What my father didn't write in his letter, and what I didn't fully realize until I spoke with Jamie much later, was that all of this was taking place against the backdrop of an uncertain but potentially serious deadline. Jamie explained to me that there is a six-year statute of limitations on filing suit for just compensation (or for filing a suit contesting a taking) in the Court of Federal Claims. It was true that the ARRB had declared it was taking the film on April 24, 1997, but the JFK Act had been passed on October 26, 1992. The government could conceivably claim that it was the passage of the Act that made the Zapruder film the property of the US government and that the statute of limitations ran out six years after that date. That was a mere four months away from the date of my father's letter. Regardless of how likely it was the government would act on this strategy or that it would work if they did, this was not a chance that Jamie, or any attorney, was going to take. LMH and its legal team had to either secure an arbitration agreement or file a lawsuit before October 26, 1998.

Bob Bennett wrote in a letter to assistant attorney general Frank Hunger, "In a final effort to resolve this matter without litigation, LMH is prepared to . . . submit the question of value to independent arbitration…We understand that the US requires that an upper limit be placed on the results of the arbitration. LMH is prepared to accept a maximum of $30 million on the results of binding arbitration for the value of the Film and all intangible rights (copyright, etc.). No agreement on any minimum outcome is necessary." In other words, if the government and LMH could sort out all the issues—primarily the number of arbitrators and a mutually agreeable method of selecting them—the upper limit, or ceiling, would be $30 million. There would be no floor.

I spoke at length with my father's law partner and longtime friend Roger Pies about this. Roger is a quiet man, rather shy, and he tends not to seek the spotlight. Even though they were very different in personality, he and my father were perfectly matched in wit, brilliance, and knowledge of the law. My father relied greatly on him over the years for advice and counsel in many areas, not just the Zapruder film. I interviewed Roger at my home in the early days of thinking about this book. He brought me stacks of papers about the film, and he spoke with me for nearly two hours, reflecting on every aspect of the government taking, its approach to valuing the film, my father's thinking, the ups and downs of the process, and the stresses that were involved.

At one point, Roger told me that he encouraged Henry to accept the arbitration agreement without a floor, or a minimum value, that the arbitrators would have to assign the film. "It was a leap of faith. Big, pretty big leap of faith." A big part of the risk was that in binding arbitration, there is no possibility of an appeal. If the arbitrators decided that the film had a value of one dollar, nothing could be done about it. But Roger understood Henry, encouraging him to have faith in the process. He reminded him, "You know you're going to present it properly, you're going to have good representation. You're going to do the very best you can and you're going to have reasonable people involved."

From my point of view, the terms of the arbitration agreement reflect my father's final act of good faith in trying to resolve the issue with the government. But I recognize that there is another point of view. I can see how a person could ask why, if he was such an altruist, he fought for any value at all, let alone for a higher value than the government was offering. If he was so committed to the film remaining in the government's possession, and he wasn't trying to exploit the film for money, why not donate it? Here, I think, my father's background and character are of critical importance. For one thing, I believe he saw a difference between trying to persuade the government not to take the film and letting them off the hook for just compensation once they had taken it. He believed in and even revered the law, regarding it as the best chance of ensuring fairness and justice in a random and unpredictable world. For him, when the government took the film, they implicitly committed to compensating our family for that taking. It would not have been in his character to disregard the consequences of the law even if it meant doing something that was personally uncomfortable for him.

At the same time, it would be dishonest to ignore the truth of the money. I asked my father about this at some point during these years. Not knowing everything that had already happened, I wondered aloud if we were right, morally speaking, to be fighting for even a partial value of the film. He didn't school me on all the efforts he had made to work things out with the government. But I remember he fixed his large light-blue eyes seriously on me and said simply, "I don't feel that our family is in a position to make an $18 million donation to the federal government." In the easy way that privileged, well-educated children can think they know everything, I remember thinking that this was a clever way to answer my question. But now that I am an adult, and I have children of my own, I hear his answer very differently.

He was in a tough spot. He wanted the government to have the film—every person who worked with him said this, and in everything he wrote, said, and did, he reaffirmed this basic conviction. He had done everything he could to behave ethically and responsibly in this regard and to avoid exploiting the film for its full value. Still, his moral obligations extended beyond the American people and the government. They extended to his own family, his wife and children, the grandchildren that he hoped he would see, not to mention his sister, her four sons—whom he loved like his own—and their wives and children. At the end of the day, he wanted to protect us, too.

When it comes to money, there is a fine line between altruism and foolishness, realism and greed. Each one of us has to walk that line for ourselves. Our grandfather did it when he made the deal with *LIFE*. Our father did it by neither donating the film to the government nor fighting to get it back and selling it to the highest bidder. And although those nuances did not get picked up in the public discourse around the film, they guided our father's actions in everything he did. I don't believe he ever wavered in his absolute conviction to deliver what he felt we owed to the American people and also to protect his own family. But accomplishing this was no easy task.

Before any decision was reached about an arbitration agreement, a new development once again raised some of the film's most long-standing and contentious issues. That summer, a company called MPI Home Video, founded in 1976 and headed by brothers Waleed and Malik Ali, was putting the finishing touches on a video about the Zapruder film, *Image of an Assassination: A New Look at the Zapruder Film*, for distribution to the public. Years before, MPI—video distributors for ABC's *Nightline* and leaders in non-fiction video distribution nationwide, as well as managers for the North American rights in the British Pathé newsreel collection—had approached Jamie with the idea of doing a documentary about the Zapruder film. Henry had flat-out refused.

When LMH hired McCrone Associates to create the record copy of the film in the National Archives, Jamie again proposed that MPI create a documentary film. This time, the project had several functions. First, the main feature of the documentary would be McCrone's reproduction of the Zapruder film, digitized and assembled into moving footage, at last making an extremely high-quality reproduction widely available at low cost and resolving researchers' frustrations about accessing it. Further, MPI filmed the duplication process and would incorporate it into the documentary, confirming the accuracy of the visual images and the efforts undertaken to safeguard the original. Finally, there was the hope that the distribution and sale of the documentary might help subsidize the very high cost of having had McCrone Associates produce the record copy in the first place.

Seen in this light and given the history of the film, it was not the craziest idea. VHS was in its heyday in 1998, and although DVDs had recently been invented, it would be another ten years before they fully replaced the videotape format. At that time, well before the quantum leap into the digital age of the 2000s—with its ubiquitous access to the Internet, smartphones, and social media—there was no cheap, easy, and free way to distribute visual information such as the film. In time, the existence of YouTube in particular would entirely solve the problem of access to the Zapruder film, but that invention was years away.

On the other side, the risks were pretty clear. Would making the film available to a mass market fly in the face of our long-standing policy to avoid exploitation of the film? Would it be disrespectful to the Kennedy family? Would we be criticized for seeking to profit from the film? "Your father didn't like it," Jamie remembers. Henry's internal barometer about what was and wasn't appropriate tallied more or less with that of mainstream society, which could not have foreseen how soon we would be just a few clicks away from the most violent, graphic, sexually explicit, vulgar, and tasteless material the world has to offer. While he could see why people wanted access to the film for research purposes, he never wanted to normalize it by making it available for casual viewing or, worse yet, for entertainment. Conversely, it was clear that the public had a claim on the film that could not be ignored. Perhaps it was time to just let the world see it. Perhaps it was time to put the question of access to rest once and for all.

When the video was finished, it did include not only several versions of the film running at different speeds and with different degrees of close-up but also a history of the film, interviews with a variety of people connected to it, and documentation about the digital reproduction of the film that had taken place at NARA. In his letter to our family about the effort to reach an agreement with the government, my father mentioned the upcoming film. "A video containing the film, in a digitized format and with inter-sprocket material, will be released during July or August. We agreed to this release on two bases—we have for years provided videos on an individual request basis for study, research, and personal use. This method is cumbersome both for the requester and for us. When we made the copies of the film as part of an offer we made to provide a free copy to the Assassination Review Board, we incurred very substantial costs and the license helped finance some of those costs."

The content was certainly controversial and undoubtedly would have been met with some criticism under any set of circumstances. The fact that it was home video was problematic; it seemed a big step from previous showings of the film, even in commercial settings such as television or movies. Unfortunately, its packaging—and the marketing and promotion that went with it—did not help. A large-scale brochure, with a close-up image of Mrs. Kennedy leaning in toward the president an instant before the fatal shot, includes this introductory text: "One of the most important documents of the 20th century is now available to the public for the very first time! Witness the assassination of President John F. Kennedy in the first-ever digitally enlarged version of the Zapruder film." At the bottom of the page, after a bulleted list of the video's features, we read that it is "A collector's item for all Americans!" Similar language and imagery appeared on the cover design for the VHS copies. I don't know if Henry was just not aware of the marketing plan or he missed a step somewhere along the way. Maybe he was distracted and preoccupied by negotiating the value of the film and working with Skadden on trying to persuade the government to enter arbitration. Maybe he didn't focus on it carefully enough. Maybe he deferred to others when he should have been more involved. I'm sure he cringed—as I do—when he saw the promotional materials. I have to believe that he also braced for impact.

When the film was released in early July, several weeks in advance of the scheduled August 1998 date, it was greeted nearly immediately by an onslaught of press attention. This wasn't the usual handful of articles in the *New York Times*, the *Washington Post*, and the *Dallas Morning News*. It was nearly five hundred printed articles, editorials, comments, cartoons, and other items from large and small newspapers from one end of the country to the other. By the third week in August, there had been as many as 1,300 calls from reporters and members of the press requesting interviews or comment for inclusion in print, radio, and broadcast pieces. While a number of articles were neutral, simply describing the release of the film, the vast majority of them landed on one side or the other of an impassioned and vitriolic debate about whether, how, and under what circumstances the Zapruder film should be made widely available to the public.

The main criticism was, of course, that the video showed the violent assassination of the president and that it should not be distributed for that reason. There were countless editorials and headlines decrying the video's degradation of American culture, the disrespect to the president, his memory, and his family, the damage to future generations, and the harm that would come to those who would see it now. A common theme was the concern that kids or even adults would go down to their local video store on a Friday night, grab some beers and popcorn, and sit around watching the president getting murdered. Some felt the video "cheapened history"; others found it "nauseating" or called it "true pornography." It was repeatedly called a "snuff film," and the *Storm Lake Pilot-Tribune* called it "The Granddaddy of all Money-Grubbing Videos."

A number of editorials (though not as many) defended the video, arguing that it was the public's right to see it, that the horror of it was part of history, and that it was long overdue. In the *Muskegon Chronicle*, an article is titled "Public Needs to Have Zapruder Film." The Long Beach *Press-Telegram* reported "Zapruder Film is More than Just Voyeurism," and the *Rockford Register Star* printed "Zapruder Film is Must Viewing for Americans."

In a perfect example of the kind of back-and-forth that went on during this hype, there is a letter to the editor from Kathryne Kirkpatrick in the *Tennessean* that reads: "What kind of demented person would pay $20 for six separate showings of Kennedy's head exploding? This isn't a Hollywood movie, folks. There are no special effects. It is real blood." In response, Robert T. Grammer wrote: "I will probably buy a copy of [the video] but I am not a 'demented person' as she so aptly put it. One has to have reverence when watching such an event on film. I think Ms. Kirkpatrick underestimates the American public's values and morals in regard to such things. Everyone who thinks that the video should not be released also underestimates [them]."

I didn't realize until I did the research for this book the absolutely massive coverage that this event garnered and the personally hateful criticism we received. We were accused of shameless greed, disrespect for the Kennedy family, insensitivity to history and the public, a lack of morality, and on and on. Many writers linked the video's release to the government taking of the film, the status of the film's copyright, and the efforts to negotiate just compensation. In a safely anonymous editorial from Jena, Louisiana, the *Jena Times* chastised us for the damaging effect of the video on the youth of America, writing: "The government offered the family $3 million, but the family wants $18 million. The country would be better off if the government paid the bloodsuckers what they want to keep it out of the sight of children." As always, Henry endured the criticism without defending himself and only admitted in private that although he felt that the decision was grossly misunderstood, he regretted that the film was released in that particular way.

I have one vivid memory from this time. The subject of the MPI video was debated on *The NewsHour with Jim Lehrer*, with Doris

Kearns Goodwin, Michael Beschloss, and Haynes Johnson on one side and Waleed Ali on the other. The broad outlines of the debate went predictably, with the guests lamenting the bad taste, lack of dignity, and the sad selling of tragedy that the video represented. Waleed defended the film, explaining the reasoning behind it and pointing out that while many people were criticizing the content of the film, he felt that it was really the home video format that most offended people. After all, the film had been shown publicly many times, and it had been used in Oliver Stone's movie—repeatedly and in close-up—but no one had objected to that.

What I remember most is Doris Kearns Goodwin's comments, because I had read *No Ordinary Time* in my early twenties and I had long seen her as the kind of writer I wanted to be. Like her, I wanted to write deeply researched, provocative, beautiful prose on big subjects, and like her, I wanted to be part of a public conversation about ideas and history. So her criticism of our family felt like a personal slap in the face. I can still feel the burn on my cheeks when I remember that public censure.

Now, reading the transcript and focusing on her remarks, I realize that her comments—far from elucidating a clear point—capture all the ambivalence that is inherent in the life of the film. She began by saying:

> Well, there's no question that the film itself is a piece of history and that the enhanced version of it may contribute to history, but I don't see any historical value in its mass marketing to the public as a whole. In fact, I find it really troubling that for the collective mind of so many people who may see this enhanced version it will wipe out—it is so powerful—the other images that we tend to hold of the Kennedys. I think

most of us—though we obviously knew he died—we had that blurry image, which was crowded out before by images of him smiling, talking at Berlin to tens of thousands of people, holding that buttercup in front of Little John, next to Caroline on the pony...I don't want the American people to have this so powerful image in their head that it wipes out the rest of what we remembered about the Kennedys.

I am so struck by this statement. It reminds me of what my father wrote to the young girl who had requested a copy of the film from him so many years before—that he hoped she would learn about President Kennedy's accomplishments and not just focus on the terrible fact of his death. The difference was that my father was talking about Kennedy's actual accomplishments, not a rosy, romantic image of Camelot; not only that, but he was writing to a teenage girl. This was Doris Kearns Goodwin, who was arguing on television that making the Zapruder film available thirty-five years after the assassination would somehow blot out the idyllic image of the Kennedys, an image that was as carefully constructed as the image of the assassination is horrifyingly real. I can't help but think, too, of *The Eternal Frame* and Doug Hall and Chip Lord's guerrilla efforts to break exactly this kind of stranglehold, reenacting the film in order to escape not only its singular perspective on the killing but also the image of the Kennedy mystique created and constructed by the media.

Nevertheless, I understand her feelings, especially when I think of her as a participant in that history, as someone who had her own memories to protect. It wasn't unlike how my parents felt. The problem came in trying to extend this highly personal feeling to the public, because with all due respect, who is Doris Kearns Goodwin, or anyone else, to "want" the American collective mind to have one image of the Kennedys over another? This is exactly the kind of paternalistic impulse that led C. D. Jackson to purchase the film to keep it away from the public. Then again, that was in 1963, days after the president was assassinated. Times had changed since then, as Henry had reluctantly acknowledged when he first permitted the film to appear in home video back in 1998.

Jim Lehrer responded by asking Kearns Goodwin what she would have done with it, and like most who criticized our family, she didn't really know. She said again and again that she recognized the film's importance, and when pressed (perhaps remembering that it was 1998 and not 1963) conceded that it wasn't right to keep it from the public. Still, the fact of its distribution bothered her. "I'm not saying that it shouldn't be out there, that we can't do it. All I'm expressing is my sadness that it's there. I wish it had been done in a different way. I wish they had put it in the National Archives, as it's been for these last twenty years, that somehow it had been made more available to scholars who wanted to see it, more available to anyone who wanted to go there." Of course, it *was* in the National Archives. Making it more available to scholars wasn't the point at all. And what might that "different way" be, that perfectly calibrated approach that would somehow magically take the Zapruder out of the Zapruder film? Her vagueness speaks to the very real problems that the film poses.

Waleed immediately accused her of elitism, asking why it should be available only to scholars and researchers. "Nobody is saying that you cannot make it," she said. "All we're expressing—at least I am— is sadness that our standards are such now that such violence might become something popular and this might become mass marketed. I'm not saying you can't do it. I'm just expressing sadness that it's happening…There will be people who will want to see somebody at the moment of a death. It's the mystery that we're all confronting with ourselves. I'm not denying it. It may be out there, but it doesn't mean you can't have some standard and feel bad about it."

This moment is absolutely classic in the annals of public debate about the Zapruder film. The tone is totally different from some of the accusatory editorials that flooded through the public discourse but the essence is the same. The Zapruder film makes people uncomfortable. It makes them sad, or angry, or disgusted, or horrified. It feels degrading, tasteless, insensitive, grotesque. It is offensive, appalling, nauseating, and repulsive. All of that is true. But how to reconcile those truths about the film with the fact that it also records a watershed moment in American history, a public event that belongs not just to the Zapruder family, or to the scholars who study it, but to everyone? How to reconcile them with the fact that time, tastes, standards of appropriateness, and technologies change? How to reconcile them with the fact that people want to know what happened to their president, or they want to try to untangle its confusions, or they even—as Doris Kearns Goodwin suggests—just want to see someone die?

One way is to assume that those who have made it available are lacking sensitivity, public concern, or care for the Kennedys, and to imagine that the only reason to make such a film available is money. That is the easy narrative so many adopted in the absence of any effort to see it from all sides. Another way is to conflate the content of the film with the responsibility for managing it, and to render those who handle it responsible for the feelings it evokes. I think we can agree that the Zapruder film makes us sad. It's sad that the president was killed, and it's sad that he was killed in a horrible, graphic way, and it's sad that it was caught on film. But someone still has to figure out what to do with it.

What is interesting to me is that between 1963 and 1998, the intrinsic questions about the film never really changed; only the context did. Some would always feel that making the film public—whether in the form of stills in *LIFE* magazine or a bootleg on Geraldo's *Good Night America* or a video for purchase at a local store—was tasteless, exploitative, and crass. They would say there was no virtue in it, that it offered nothing new, and that sharing it simply hastened the demise of decent society. Others would always feel that it was the public's right to see it, to examine and study it, to confront history, no matter how bloody and horrific it was. They would argue that it was not democratic for a small elite to have access to it when it was everyone's history, and that a media company, a family, or the government shouldn't decide what the American people should or shouldn't be able to see about their history. The hard truth is that they are all right.

In October 1998, LMH and the federal government entered into an agreement for binding arbitration to determine just compensation for the in-camera original of the Zapruder film. The copyright was excluded and remained, for the time being, owned by LMH. Each side would pick an arbitrator and, together, the two parties would pick a third. Each side would prepare a pre-hearing brief and provide affidavits from witnesses who would speak to the value of the film. The witnesses would have the opportunity to read the material written by the other side and write rebuttal affidavits in response. There would be a two-day hearing in May 1999 in which the government and LMH would present their cases to the arbitration panel. Post-hearing briefs were allowed shortly after. The arbitrators would render a decision that would be binding.

The end was very nearly in sight.

CHAPTER 14

■■■■■■■

ARBITRATION AND RESOLUTION

The arbitration hearing for the Zapruder film took place on May 25–26, 1999, in the Howard T. Markey National Courts Building. The court is located in the very heart of presidential Washington, overlooking the expansive Lafayette Square and with a view of the White House. Across the park sit historic Blair House and Decatur House. The court is kitty-corner to the end of Sixteenth Street, from where one can easily see the elegant Hay-Adams Hotel and the pale yellow and white St. John's Episcopal Church, with its gleaming gold bell tower, where every sitting president since James Madison has gone to pray. It seemed both strange and fitting that this final public question about the Zapruder film would be debated here. Abraham Zapruder's home movie had traveled a very long way indeed.

I remember watching Bob Bennett, Dana Freyer, Rich Brusca, and Harold Reeves file in, loaded down with binders, notebooks, and materials. They looked serious. My parents, Aunt Myrna, and my cousin Adam were there for both days of the hearing. Myrna's eldest son, Jeffrey, was there for one day, as were my brother Matthew and I. The government lawyers were Leslie Batchelor and Kirk Manhardt. The arbitrators, an esteemed group by any measure, sat at the front of the room. LMH had asked well-known attorney and mediator Kenneth Feinberg to be our arbitrator. The government had chosen Walter Dellinger, former solicitor general of the United States. Together, Feinberg and Dellinger had asked retired federal judge Arlin Adams, who had been chief judge of the Third Circuit Court of Appeals in Philadelphia. The matter before them was clear but exceedingly difficult to resolve: What is the fair market value of the camera original of the Zapruder film?

Each side faced its own particular challenges. In terms of argument, the government had the bigger uphill climb. It was their attorneys' job to make a case for the lowest possible value for the film, which was difficult to do not only on the basis of pure common sense but also because there was an element of hypocrisy in it. As Bob Bennett repeatedly argued during the hearing, when the government wanted to take the film, they argued that it was an icon, a relic, a unique, essential artifact that had to be in the National Archives in perpetuity. But when it came time to pay for it, they focused on all the ways in which its value was diminished or limited either by its intrinsic characteristics or market forces. Meanwhile, LMH had an easier case to make since there was little question that extremely wealthy (and perhaps slightly unhinged) collectors of various stripes would be willing to spend excessive amounts of money to own the original Zapruder film. Still, if the intellectual argument was more evident, in this last moment the film exacted its final emotional toll from my father in irony. The price for being free of the film was having had to focus on it for the better part of a decade. Likewise, the price for receiving just compensation was to argue for its highest financial value, which was the very thing he had always despised.

In the seven months between the signing of the arbitration agreement and the hearing, both sides had hired experts to appraise the camera-original film and build their cases as to its value. While we were aiming for a high value and the government was aiming for a low one, both sides faced a foundational problem. Just compensation is generally established by determining fair market value—that is, what a willing buyer would pay a willing seller if neither party was under any compulsion to buy or sell. The most reliable way to find fair market value is to look at items comparable to the one in question. But, as Bob Bennett put it, "The more unique something is, the more difficult it is to find comparables from which a logical conclusion as to value can be reached. There simply were no comparable films of the assassination of presidents."

In fact, the larger question was whether there was any object at all that was truly comparable to the Zapruder film. If not, could one establish a comparable market—films and photos, rare manuscripts, collectibles, artwork, Kennedy memorabilia, etc.—in order to approximate a value? Or should an appraiser abandon comparables altogether and try a different method instead? Disagree on these basic questions and you will disagree on value. Bob Bennett rightly assessed the arbitration hearing as a "battle of experts." While it's true that each side used politics and strategy, the very real disagreements in approach not only resulted in hugely disparate estimates but also presented a tough knot of problems for the arbitrators to untangle.

*   *   *

LMH hired four experts—Beth Gates Warren, Jerry Patterson, Steve Johnson, and Sylvia Leonard Wolf—each of whom submitted detailed appraisals of the camera-original Zapruder film. LMH also had affidavits from Joseph Barabe of McCrone Associates, who had carried out the macrographic reproduction of the original film, to testify as to the film's quality and condition, and from Professor William Landes, an economist from the University of Chicago. The four appraisal experts had extensive experience valuing, marketing, and selling a wide variety of materials at auction, including historical objects, presidential memorabilia, photographs, and audiovisual media. The government hired C. Cameron Macauley, under the name CCM Associates, and John Staszyn to develop appraisals and testify as their experts.

Unlike the government appraisers, two of the LMH experts had held senior positions inside prestigious auction houses, such as Sotheby's and Christie's. While each LMH expert had prepared an independent appraisal, all shared the view that the film was an icon or a relic and that the closest possible comparables would be found by identifying the key attributes of the film and then finding other items that shared them. The experts emphasized that this is exactly the process they would have employed—and that they routinely did employ with other objects—if the Zapruder film had come up for auction. In Beth Gates Warren's words, "It's a process that you would have to go through…When something is rare and so unique and there's nothing comparable to it that's come on the market, then the best and the only fair thing to do is to look to other objects that are sold and what the real prices are that have been paid for them." All of the experts argued that the camera-original Zapruder film should be evaluated within the context of the market for highly desirable, valuable, unique items that collectors would pay high prices to own.

In their affidavits, provided to the arbitration panel before the hearing, the appraisers identified the key characteristics of the Zapruder film that would justify the high valuations they assigned to it. While their categories were not identical, there was significant overlap. They all agreed that it was a completely unique historical document that could never be replicated, which is exactly what collectors seek and value. It was a relic of President Kennedy, described by Jerry Patterson as "inextricably associated with the final tragic moment of a beloved US president who was revered at home and abroad." It was an "icon" of a generation's lost innocence. It was famous, not only because of its association with President Kennedy but also because of the well-known and controversial history of the film itself. Beth Gates Warren, in particular, assessed the intrinsic value of the images as part of the film's value, arguing that they had "artistic qualities" such as vibrant color and excellent composition and framing, as well as "powerful content" that elicits a strong response in viewers. In addition, the film's condition was excellent and it had the best possible provenance (meaning that it was accounted for from the time of its creation until the time of the arbitration and there was no gap in the chain of possession). The appraisers repeatedly made the very important point that a collector would not be put off by the fact that the copyright was not included in the sale. Furthermore, it could be displayed in a powerful and effective manner, even though it could not be run through a projector. They also argued that collectors are accustomed to, and take seriously, their role as stewards of precious objects, and that the type of collector who would pay for the Zapruder film would not be deterred by the fact that it needed to be carefully preserved and exhibited. Finally, several of the appraisers focused on "breadth of appeal" as an important factor, describing the kind of individuals, institutions, or consortia that might wish to bid on the Zapruder film.

The first day of the arbitration hearing was devoted to two of the LMH witnesses, Beth Gates Warren and Jerry Patterson. Warren spoke to the process of appraising the film if it were to be put up at auction, and Patterson was called primarily to critique the government's approach. At the hearing, Rich Brusca set the tone by playing the Zapruder film for the panel, reminding them of its emotional power and iconic status. He then called Beth Gates Warren as the first expert. After she gave her qualifications and outlined her experience, Brusca asked her to explain in depth her method for valuing the film. She focused on five qualities that were of paramount importance in assessing its value: historical significance, iconographic importance, fame, breadth of appeal, and uniqueness. She then identified objects that had recently sold at auction that shared these characteristics, including unique or rare furniture such as the so-called Badminton Cabinet and a Nicholas Brown desk and bookcase; paintings by Van Gogh and Renoir; and manuscripts such as *The Gospels of Henry the Lion* and Leonardo da Vinci's manuscript known as the *Codex Leicester*.

In a series of questions that must have driven the government attorneys around the bend, she then compared these objects to the Zapruder film. She unflinchingly gave the Zapruder film a "10" in every category, while Leonardo, Van Gogh, and Renoir got mostly 8s and 9s, with the occasional 7 and even a 4. I dearly wish I had caught my father's eye at that moment in the hearing; I can perfectly imagine the grimace he would have given me. While Warren's argument was well reasoned and based on decades of experience, her conclusions did seem startling, especially in light of the extraordinary objects she was citing as comparables. After all, Leonardo da Vinci was a creative, intellectual, and visionary genius, among the greatest masters of art and science the world has ever known. His codex includes his thoughts on astronomy, fossils, erosion, the properties of water, and the moon, some of which correctly predicted the scientific findings of later centuries. Van Gogh was an exceptionally gifted painter whose radical, pioneering work changed the course of the visual arts in the twentieth century and beyond. These works reflect the pinnacle of human achievement. Meanwhile, the Zapruder film is a home movie that accidentally captured the horrific murder of a young, beloved president. It reflects existential frailty and the depth of human depravity. But here it's useful to remember that the purpose of the valuation was not to render subjective judgment on the film's content but to see it through the eyes of a collector, whose decisions about what to purchase may or may not have anything to do with conventional notions of beauty, genius, or achievement.

Warren then established the market range by looking at the real prices paid for these other objects. They had sold in the range of $26–80 million. Being conservative, Warren placed the value of the film at $25 million—meaning that this was the starting price from which the bidding would begin. Given the intensity of interest that would likely be generated by the sale of the original film, the massive publicity that would surround it, and the wildly unpredictable nature of auctions themselves, Warren explained that the final price could easily end up at twice or even three times that number.

Warren also described the marketing tools that would typically accompany a private auction of this kind, including a "lavishly produced auction catalog" with high production values, essays by experts, images of the film, and the like. She estimated the net profits from such a catalog to be $5 million. Additionally, there was the possibility of selling limited-edition prints from the film, so-called Iris prints, made from the 4 x 5-inch transparencies McCrone Associates had created from the original film. She estimated that these could bring in an additional $10 million. All told, including the starting value of the film, the catalog, and the Iris prints, she felt that the camera-original Zapruder film had a minimum value of $40 million but that it was quite possibly worth many times more than that. In this light, LMH argued for the highest possible award allowed by the previously agreed-upon cap on the arbitration, which was $30 million.

The arbitration hearing was anything but simple. This was not just because the two parties' approaches were different but because each attorney was making his or her case and attacking the other side at the same time, while the arbitrators were trying to ask questions of the witnesses and attorneys, all the while untangling the actual issue. But as I read through the pre-hearing briefs and the transcript, focusing especially on the second day, when the government witnesses testified, I eventually came to see the fundamentally different lens through which the government viewed the entire question of the film's value. The government attorneys adhered to the idea that fair market value for the Zapruder film could be established only by comparing it to like objects—in this case, camera-original films. They utterly rejected the LMH approach of comparing the Zapruder film to collectibles such as works of art, furniture, or manuscripts, because—essentially—it was not made of the same material. By finding other camera-original films, and seeing how or whether they had sold, they would determine whether there was a market and what value might be established. If there was no proven market for camera-original films, they would propose alternative methods to arrive at a fair market valuation.

In the government's pre-hearing brief, the writers began with a description of the film's characteristics, to show how its value would be reduced by its detriments. It is, we are told, "small"—each frame being only one-eighth of an inch long and the whole film being only six feet—and has a running time of just twenty-six seconds. They pointed out that the film is spliced in two places and several frames are missing, and that the film has slightly shrunk over time. The implication was that the original film was, first of all, not much to look at and, second, not in pristine condition.

They turned next to the iconic status of the film, arguing that its fame was, in fact, attributable only to the copyright and not the actual camera-original film itself. After all, they write, "Our familiarity with the Zapruder film derives from our viewing of copies of the film, not the camera original." Their argument hinged on the idea that since people's familiarity with the images on the film does not come from looking at the original spool of film in the Archives (the camera original) but from the images disseminated on copies of it, it is not the camera original but the right to reproduce the image (the copyright) that has the value.

Finally, the government appraisers assessed the content of the film's images. Unlike Beth Gates Warren, who acknowledged the film's power to move viewers by its images, they described the film's images as follows: "First, they are horrifying. Any attempt to deny this fact by describing the images as 'strangely beautiful and hauntingly compelling' simply casts doubt upon the utterer's judgment and credibility. No appraiser in this case has disputed that tragedy and ugliness depress value." They conclude by arguing that the film's value is further lowered by the fact that it does not conclusively solve the murder of the president. "Far from being a source of mystery that enhances value, this inability to provide answers is an inherent limiting characteristic."

All of these points were taken on and argued point for point by Jerry Patterson in his rebuttal affidavit and in direct examination by Dana Freyer on the afternoon of the first day of the hearing. In the end, the government concluded, "the camera original is a very small tragic historic film that, despite its limitations, is a collectible object."

So in what market might this small, depressing, inconclusive, limited spool of celluloid be sold? Government attorney Kirk Manhardt called on Macauley to discuss this matter on the morning of the second day of the hearings. Rejecting the idea that the collectibles market was the appropriate place to situate it, he argued instead that the only true comparables are camera-original films, which have the same physical attributes as the Zapruder film. To me, this is where the government's argument just breaks down under the weight of common sense. It's true that the film is like camera-original films. But it's also true that it's like valuable collectible objects. Can't it exist in more than one market? Which is the most sensible? Isn't it possible that just because of all the inexplicable, complicated, coincidental aspects of the Zapruder film that its "collectibleness" is more pronounced than its "camera-filmness"? No, not according to Macauley, or John Staszyn, or the government attorneys.

Macauley sought high and low for camera-original films and the equivalent of original prints to try to establish a market in which the Zapruder film could be situated. The crown jewel of comparables was the 1934 filmed assassination of King Alexander of Yugoslavia. After all, it's a film, he was a head of state, and it was an assassination. So it's exactly like the Zapruder film. But no one wanted to buy that one. He cited other murders on film of prominent figures and national leaders, and mentioned historically significant events captured on film, such as the bombing of Pearl Harbor and the explosion of the *Hindenburg*, as well as iconic images from the sixties. No one was interested in buying those, either. As the attorneys explained in their brief, "Many of these are no less a witness to the events they capture than the Zapruder film. The events captured on these images are no less jarring to the public consciousness. Yet there is no record of sale."

It's an interesting point. There was, it seemed, no proven market for camera-original films. And that would make it hard to value the Zapruder film if that was, in fact, the only way you could look at it. But the more I thought about it, the more it seemed that the government was just making LMH's case. The fact that there was no market for camera-original films and the Zapruder film is a camera-original film does not mean there is no market for the Zapruder film. Because there obviously *was* a market for the Zapruder film. So there must be some other way to value it aside from merely characterizing it as a spool of film on a plastic reel. Most films and photos derive their value from the images themselves, a point that the government repeatedly made. This is absolutely true. But, for some reason, that was not the case here. The question is, Why is the Zapruder film different from these others? I'm not sure anyone really knows. And that is, ultimately, kind of the point.

In what they believed was the absence of a market for camera-original films, the government appraisers provided two different approaches to assessing the value of the Zapruder film. And here things really go off the rails. Macauley argued that since there was no market that could be used to establish just compensation, the next best approach was to use the sales history of the object to establish value. To do so, he began with the $150,000 purchase price that *LIFE* had paid for the film in 1963 and then applied the Consumer Price Index to determine its present-day value at around $780,000 as of the time of the taking in August 1998.

Asked by Manhardt to elaborate, Macauley did so: "The Consumer Price Index is often referred to as a market basket, and that's a misnomer. It includes very many things. I think forty percent of it is housing. It includes cars. It includes education. It includes entertainment. It's a bundle of all the things that most families spend their money on. Consequently, it's pretty well validated. There are people who quarrel with it, of course, but it seems to be the most sensible way of updating a thing of this kind or of any kind." Leaving aside the obvious criticism that the original Zapruder film is not "the kind of thing that most people spend their money on," it's hard to see how any serious person could use the same inflation rate for common household items and for the original Zapruder film, which is—I believe we've established—the exact opposite of a common household item. Or, to point out another inconsistency, the government claimed the film couldn't be compared to collectible items at auction because it's not made of the same material, but it could be compared to butter, TV sets, theater tickets, and cars.

The government's second expert was called in the afternoon. John Staszyn used a different approach, one that, among other things, left the government open to attack on cross-examination by Bob Bennett. Finding no market for camera-original films, he surveyed the market for items that had sold at auction and had elements in common with the film. This was in direct contradiction to Macauley's stated approach that only camera-original films were appropriate comparables; it also contradicted the government's attack on the LMH experts for comparing the film to furniture, manuscripts, and artwork. For example, he compared it to other manuscripts, such as Abraham Lincoln's handwritten notes for the "House Divided" speech (admittedly, an extraordinary document to own), which sold for $1.5 million at auction, and a printed broadside of the Declaration of Independence that sold for $2.4 million at auction. He compared the camera-original film to original historic photos, such as the first known daguerreotype of the Capitol Building from 1846, which had sold for $189,500. Finally, he made some comparisons with Kennedy memorabilia, pointing out that the top of the market was the $1.4 million desk on which Kennedy signed the Nuclear Test Ban Treaty. But rather than breaking down the specific characteristics that these objects did or didn't share with the Zapruder film, as the LMH appraisers had, he simply used the range of prices paid at auction for these items as a range for the market for the Zapruder film. And then he provided a number that was not grounded in any actual comparable, a symbolic figure that seems vague and disconnected from reality. He concluded, "It is this appraiser's expert conclusion based upon extensive research, that the fair market value of the original Zapruder film spool is no higher than one million dollars. Indeed, it can be argued that the film is worth as little as four hundred thousand dollars."

Both of the government witnesses were cross-examined by Bob Bennett, unfortunately for them. In his book *In the Ring: The Trials of a Washington Lawyer*, he wrote: "Remember, a good cross-examiner is like a guerrilla fighter. You go in quickly, make your hits, and get out." He started by hitting Macauley on his approach. He showed Macauley a brand-new baseball and asked him to explain how Mark McGwire's historic seventieth home run baseball could sell for $3 million at auction when a baseball in far better condition could be bought for ten dollars.

MACAULEY: Well, we're comparing apples and oranges here.

BENNETT: No. We're comparing two baseballs. That baseball and the three-million-dollar baseball. How do you explain that?

MACAULEY: Of course, it's the aura of his having hit it.

BENNETT: It is associated with him?

MACAULEY: Yes.

BENNETT: It is associated with an important event, the breaking of a baseball record. Is that right?

MACAULEY: Yes.

BENNETT: And yet you are testifying today before this panel that the Zapruder film—which you have said in your report and which you have repeated before this panel here again today is probably one of the most valuable films ever—you are saying that film is worth a third or a quarter of Mark McGwire's baseball?

Bob Bennett is very good at cross-examination. It's impossible to read the transcripts without admiring his style, humor, and obvious pleasure in the work, while simultaneously feeling sorry for the witnesses he cross-examines and hoping that you are never one of them. In this case, he did not need to resort to the kind of tricks for which trial lawyers are famous. Instead, he had plenty of material just by focusing on the flaws in the government's case and the inconsistencies in their experts' approaches.

One of the most damning moments came when Bennett made Macauley admit on the stand that he had, just ten days before, hired one of LMH's experts, Steve Johnson, to appraise a vintage film about a rare bird. The government's expert had hired the LMH expert to do his appraisal. When Bennett asked Macauley if he thought Steve Johnson was qualified, he said, "Oh yes. Yes. I think he would do a good job."

Likewise, in his cross-examination of the government's second witness, John Staszyn, Bennett questioned him about his approach to establishing value, and in so doing, caused him to discredit the previous government expert's method. Bennett made sure the arbitrators noticed that the government was presenting two different approaches instead of consolidating their efforts around one completely airtight one.

Throughout the hearing, the arbitrators rigorously questioned all the experts. At the end of the hearing, they each had the opportunity to lay out their concerns and lingering questions to the attorneys. All of this was critical fine-tuning as they challenged each side's assumptions and pressed them to justify the assessments their experts had made. There was one moment in the hearing that I think reflected the "battle of experts" that Bob Bennett described and the challenge that the arbitrators faced in judging which approach was the right one. It came when Ken Feinberg questioned the government's expert John Staszyn. He had just finished explaining why the Zapruder film was less valuable than the "House Divided" speech and the Declaration of Independence broadside. Feinberg asked why he had not factored the codex into his calculation. Staszyn stumbled a little, saying that it was because da Vinci was known as the Renaissance Man, the manuscript was over five hundred years old, there were a lot of drawings in it, and it was the last one that was ever going to be available. Feinberg was not convinced: "All I'm raising is, there is Mr. Patterson sitting there and Ms. Warren. I mean if you read their testimony there is no comparable. Just like you, there is nothing comparable. The closest is the codex... You're saying no, it isn't the codex." Staszyn responded, "I think it's in the wrong market, though. I think it's in the wrong market." Feinberg responded in exasperation, "I am just telling you we are getting this testimony arguing it was the codex, not the codex, baseballs, not baseballs, documents, not documents."

In the end, that's exactly right. The sheer range of possible comparables that flooded through the courtroom over the two days of hearings was dizzying. There were Jack Kennedy's golf woods and his cigar humidor, the desk on which the Nuclear Test Ban Treaty was signed and the Badminton Cabinet, the film of King Alexander of Yugoslavia's assassination and an original daguerreotype from 1846, iconic photos from the 1960s and films showing the bombing of Pearl Harbor, a printed broadside of the Declaration of Independence and the manuscript of the "House Divided" speech, Van Gogh's *Irises*, Mark McGwire's baseball, and Leonardo's codex. Much as the experts tried to apply logic, to break down the characteristics, to figure out where the Zapruder film best belonged, it was subjective. In the end, the Zapruder film was worth what someone would pay for it. The arbitrators were not going to find a real comparable. They had to listen to both sides, read all the material, lean toward the experts they felt were most convincing, and then somehow pick a number.

In my meeting with Judge Tunheim about his experience heading the ARRB, he had surprised me by expressing his dismay that the government had gotten "hoodwinked" into agreeing to arbitration. At first, I didn't understand. I thought that arbitration represented the best option for both sides, because it avoided litigation and the protracted appeals that usually follow. He felt, however, that the case should have been tried in the Court of Federal Claims, where such disputes would normally be resolved. In a later e-mail exchange, he elaborated: "Of course, I am a federal judge and I believe courts are typically better suited to determine such important questions rather than paid private arbitrators, but that is my obvious bias." He had more confidence in the courts in part because, in his words, large companies have used arbitration to take rights away from the "little guy." In this case, the "little guy" was America, whose public money was going to be spent on the film.

As Judge Tunheim explained it in his e-mail to me, "A court that was accustomed to setting values for many kinds of claims made against the government (and with the possibility of an appeal to the Federal Circuit) would likely be more receptive to the public interest argument and the Review Board's statutory mandate of acting in the public interest, than would a private arbitration panel more interested in establishing value." In his view, it was utterly inappropriate to get caught up in comparing the Zapruder film to Jack Kennedy's golf woods, not because one was a film and the other was sports equipment, but because it didn't matter to history and society who owned JFK's golf clubs but it mattered very much who owned the Zapruder film. That's why the ARRB took the film to begin with.

So why did the government agree to arbitration when doing so put them at a disadvantage compared to arguing the case in court? When I visited Rich Brusca, he told me he thought the Justice Department feared it was on "shaky ground" with the taking (though Judge Tunheim later told me he felt confident that the ARRB was on solid legal footing with the taking and that the public hearing had established that the nation would be best served by the permanent inclusion of the original film in the National Archives). Right up to the last minute, LMH held the option of suing the government for the return of the film. Henry, of course, wanted to avoid such action at all costs, but the Justice Department didn't know that. Meanwhile, pressure was mounting on our family's side to do something before October 28, 1998, which may or may not have been the expiration date on the six-year statute of limitations for the taking of the film. LMH had made it clear that its offer of arbitration (which was not a bad offer, considering that there was a $30-million ceiling and no floor) would be the last one before it would file suit to challenge the taking. It seems that, in the end, the government and LMH both had the same reasons for agreeing to binding arbitration: to get the whole thing over with.

Nearly everyone I interviewed—our attorneys, my dad's partners, and even some on the side of the government—was deeply perplexed by the government's handling of the arbitration hearing. There were so many inconsistencies and so many places where the logic fell apart. No one could quite understand how something so important, with so much money at stake, was handled this way. Some said they thought the attorneys' hearts weren't in it; others said they were young and inexperienced; still others said they simply didn't have a case. But as I thought about what Judge Tunheim and Rich Brusca had said, and the forum in which the matter had been argued, I started to see the government's approach in a different light. It seemed to me that, ultimately, the government didn't really argue the fair market value of the Zapruder film so much as what they felt would be fair to the American people. After all, $750,000 clearly wasn't the absolute value of the film (Judge Tunheim himself acknowledged this when I asked him), but perhaps it was the number they felt was the justifiable one if they took the public interest and all the other factors into account. This was the number they had offered in negotiations back in 1996 and it was the number they stuck to all along. Maybe it was also the number they wanted the American people to know they had fought for, even if fighting for it meant presenting some pretty tortured arguments. In the mother of all ironies, it was the arbitration itself that gave them the political cover to make their case, flawed as it was. They could start with the figure and work backward (rather than the other way around), surely knowing that, in the end, the arbitration panel was likely to award more than they felt was fair. The question really was just how *much* more. But whatever it turned out to be, the Justice Department would not be the ones to take the heat.

On Saturday morning, July 17, I was at home in my apartment in DC and my parents were away for the weekend. The following Monday, July 19, the three arbitrators were due to hand down their decision in the matter of the Zapruder film. I was very much aware that the decision was soon going to be made public, but as always with things related to the film, we hadn't discussed it much; if my father was worried about it, he hadn't said. I was listening to the radio when I heard that JFK Jr.'s small plane had been reported missing with his wife and her sister on board off the coast of Martha's Vineyard. I remember sitting down, overcome by a feeling of dread. I was absolutely sure that he was dead. I was sure that my father didn't know. I was sure that I didn't want to tell him. And I was sure that I needed to call him immediately.

When I told him, my father said little. He tended to be very reserved in moments like that. The awfulness of the situation was perfectly obvious. I don't know who called whom, but everyone had the same thought. The decision was postponed for several weeks.

The previous Wednesday, July 14, the *Dallas Morning News* had published an editorial in the paper titled "Zapruder Film: Attempt to Profit from Tragedy Is Sad and Disturbing." In it, the editorial board wrote that they did not envy the task before the arbitration panel to decide on the value of the Zapruder film, especially as it was a "decision that no one should have had to make." In the opinion of the *Dallas Morning News*, our family had more than recouped the cost of our grandfather having made the film—a reel of film, bus ticket, or tank of gas—and we should simply donate it to the National Archives. They went on to explain that the film is a record of a national tragedy, and that it is not "sports memorabilia" or the "cocktail napkin scribblings" of a famous artist. In the end, we were publicly rebuked for our lack of moral character. "The film's historic significance makes it priceless. Yet common decency dictates that people shouldn't try to profit from tragedy...If the family will not donate it, the arbitration panel should set a price at the low end of the suggested range—perhaps $1 million. It will be blood money."

It was the one and only time that our father ever responded publicly to criticism. He wrote and the paper printed a response, which was very restrained but in which he outlined, with absolute consistency, the principles that had guided him for so many decades.

The Zapruder family has always sought to balance the public's interest in access to the Film with the respect that our family has for President Kennedy and his family...There are, no doubt, many who would have chosen to auction the Film to the highest bidder years ago. We chose not to because we believed that it was best that the Film remain in the United States under our guardianship. Our family was not, however, in a position to turn over the entire value of the Film to the government...

The government decided, for its own reasons, that it had to have the original Film itself. The government agrees that we are entitled under the Constitution to just compensation for this "taking" and we have, by amicable agreement, placed the matter entirely in the hands of an impeccable panel of arbitrators. In light of how we have balanced the interests in the Film, we find your assertion that we have violated principles of "common decency" as baseless as it is offensive.

On August 3, 1999, the arbitrators reached a decision. In a two-to-one decision, the panel awarded our family $16 million for the camera-original Zapruder film. Ken Feinberg and Judge Arlin Adams wrote the arbitration decision and Walter Dellinger, the government-appointed arbitrator, wrote a dissent. In the decision, Feinberg and Adams first summarized the history of the film and the case made by both sides. Then they outlined the reasons they believed that "the record makes clear that a substantial valuation is warranted in this case." First, they relied on the "uncontroverted testimony" of our appraisers, whom they described as "world-class experts" with years of experience auctioning famous historical items. The government, they said, failed to offer witnesses with similar expertise who could contradict them. Second, they argued that the very fact of the "taking" of the film proved its value. "In what appears to be a most unusual act," they wrote, "the Government 'took' the film from its private owners, concluding that its historical importance was so significant that it should be secured under Government protection." Next, they pointed to the rise in the auction market in general, and the fact that the evidence showed that individuals were purchasing items for far more than they were predicted to be worth, and that this trend would likely apply to the Zapruder film were it put up for auction. Finally, they acknowledged that there was a special place in the American mind and heart for the Kennedys, a fact that caused many items belonging to the family to sell for high prices at auction. "In terms of its emotional and historical significance, the film would undoubtedly surpass previous Kennedy memorabilia."

Walter Dellinger wrote a dissent because he believed "that the award of $16 million is simply too large an amount in light of the evidence in the record." He began his opinion by acknowledging the importance of the film, writing: "The vivid images captured by the Zapruder film are eminently recognizable, perhaps more so than any film footage ever captured, and so much so that anyone who reflects on President Kennedy's assassination quite likely does so instinctively from Abraham Zapruder's vantage point. Indeed, when a copy of the Zapruder film was shown to the panel at the outset of our two days of hearings, I found the dramatic images far more riveting than I had recalled or imagined." Still, Dellinger took pains to separate the images on the film, which were by then widely available, from the original reel of film. "Thus, the sole issue here is the value of the out-of-camera original film itself as an artifact." He emphasized the government's point that there was no proven market for camera-original films, writing that they have "little independent value." For this reason, he was convinced that the alternative method provided by Cameron Macauley of taking the 1963 purchase price of the film and applying the Consumer Price Index to determine the value in 1998 dollars was more reliable. At the end of that calculation, he was closer to $1 million than $16 million. He took issue with several points made by his arbitrator colleagues, especially challenging the comparables provided by the LMH experts on the grounds that the "status of their artist or creator, their artistic appeal, and their sales and ownership history" had little to do with the Zapruder film. Finally, Dellinger did agree with Feinberg and Adams that the Kennedy factor was a real one and that it would increase the value of the film "at most threefold, fourfold, or even fivefold, to between $3–5 million." It would be ample recognition, he felt, for "the value as a historical object of this strip of film."

Feinberg and Adams responded in their opinion to Dellinger's points, arguing that it was "a creative argument to justify a much lower figure but that creative argument is not found in the record." They answered several of his points, but there was one element that is, I think, the most important one. The government and their experts repeatedly stressed that the lack of a market for camera-original films was the critical factor. In his dissent, Dellinger wrote that it "speaks volumes." To this, Feinberg and Adams wrote:

> Whatever the reason for the absence of a competitive market for historical films, we emphasize that, when it comes to the Zapruder film, it is the Government's seizure of the film that "speaks volumes." We know of no other situation...when the Government decided that it was in the public interest to assume control over an original historical film (or any other privately owned historical memorabilia). The participants in the arbitration, including all of the witnesses called by both sides, commented repeatedly on the unique quality of the Zapruder film, and on the fact that it was different from any other historical item previously evaluated. To attempt to reduce the value of this item by referencing the absence of a market in other film which has neither the notoriety nor

indelible imprint of history on it is to advance an argument not supported by the record. Simply stated, the Zapruder film is one of a kind.

I went to speak with Walter Dellinger toward the end of writing this book. I was curious about his thinking regarding the film's value and what, if anything, I might learn from hearing his point of view. Dellinger is an enormously respected attorney, having served as solicitor general of the United States in the Justice Department under President Bill Clinton, and is now a senior partner at O'Melveny & Myers. He has a calm, amiable demeanor, a relaxed Southern drawl, and piercing blue eyes that don't miss a thing. If he had been convinced by the government's arguments, then I definitely wanted to know more.

He recalled in our interview that he had been approached by assistant attorney general Frank Hunger, who was head of the Civil Division, about serving as their arbitrator. When I asked him why he thought they approached him specifically, he said, "I was well known to them from more than four years at the Justice Department in the Clinton administration. I had worked with the attorney general and senior officials so they knew how I handled issues and that there would not be acrimony if I was involved. They wanted to handle it in a respectful way." Dellinger willingly agreed.

He explained that the first and most important task that he and Ken Feinberg had to accomplish was to choose a third arbitrator. This person would, together with Feinberg and Dellinger, assess the experts' credibility and consider the merits of the various arguments. But he would also bring his background and life experience to the question. In this regard, he said, "Ken and I both understood that it mattered whether the third arbitrator was someone who thought, say, five million dollars was a lot of money or not much money." Dellinger remembered, with a laugh, that Ken's first suggestion was Jack Welch, the CEO of General Electric, who, in his words, "made hundreds of millions of dollars a year and who would have thought of thirty million dollars as, like, what you leave for a tip." Dellinger's first suggestion, on the other hand, was his Duke colleague John Hope Franklin, whom he described as "the greatest African-American historian of the century." He was a man who not only had a tremendous sense of history but who had always lived very modestly on the salary of an academic. Each rejected the other.

Next, Dellinger tried to persuade Feinberg to agree to bring on Dixon Phillips, federal Court of Appeals judge from North Carolina. Dellinger, chuckling, said that Phillips "still drove his twenty-five-year-old Plymouth and had not bought a new suit in many years; he would have thought several thousand was a lavish award." Needless to say, it was no dice. Ultimately, however, the two men agreed on Judge Arlin Adams, who not only had the intellectual qualities and discernment they needed but had also sat on the federal bench from 1969 to 1987 before going into private practice in Philadelphia. He was quiet, thoughtful, and could see both perspectives and would serve as a fair and impartial third arbitrator.

Dellinger told me he had been very impressed by our attorneys' description of what Abe Zapruder accomplished in taking the film. Before then, Dellinger said, he had assumed that Abe was there purely as a matter of accident or coincidence, and that nothing he had done reflected his skill or judgment. He walked away from the hearing with a very different sense of that part of the story, aware not only of the considerable care that Abe had taken to find the right spot and to use his camera skills to record the motorcade but, most of all, of what he had accomplished once the shots started to ring out. "Everybody else is screaming and running," Dellinger explained, "and [Abe] follows that car and the motorcade; he knows to keep his focus on where the president is...The steadiness and the resolve with which he pulled it off was really extraordinary." In Dellinger's mind, there was a sort of athleticism to the way he kept his balance on the ledge, his focus on the president, and his nerve when pandemonium broke out around him.

Nevertheless, as much as he admired Abe for what he did that day, it did not change his basic view of the valuation of his film. He agreed with the government experts who said that there was no market for camera-original films and that it was the images that had been disseminated from it—not the individual, original reel of film—that had the real value. "No one came up with any other strip of film," he said, firmly tapping his finger on the desk for emphasis, "that had ever been sold. To me, that was the single most important point." Remarking on other historic films, such as the footage of the *Hindenburg* explosion, he went on: "If they really had great intrinsic value, I think some of them would have been captured, would have been sold; some museum would have them and be displaying them. But no one's ever *cared* about that; you care about being able to witness the *Hindenburg* explosion, not about the strip of film."

I couldn't disagree with him, though, of course, I believe that one can view the argument in exactly the inverse way: The fact that there is no market for camera-original films, and that experts from Sotheby's could nevertheless be so sure that the Zapruder film would sell for millions at auction, just proves its exceptional status. When I raised this point with Dellinger, he agreed that the argument had a certain logic, and, like everyone else, he struggled during the course of our conversation to identify what exactly it was about the film that made it defy all the models. Even so, he simply did not believe it would sell for the kind of money that our experts suggested. "I honestly think," he said, "and this is just so utterly speculative, I can't defend this, [but] I don't believe the strip would have gone for more than three million dollars if it were sold." "Really?" I said. "Even with all those experts?" "I was totally unpersuaded," he told me.

Beyond the question of whether there was a market for camera-original films, Dellinger's real objection to the value that Feinberg and Adams proposed came down to the stripping away of the right to own, reproduce, and distribute its images, i.e., the copyright in the film. In fact, toward the end of our conversation, he surprised me in an entirely different way: He said that although he felt the value of the camera-original film was wildly inflated, he also felt that the rights in it were similarly underestimated. "I guess it shows the balance of the universe," he said, half laughing. "I think the rights to the film—not the strip but the rights to the image—were greatly undervalued. Hugely undervalued. So, in fact, I think that the total compensation for the 'package' is way under, in my view." If they had been asked to value both the original film and the copyright, he would have been inclined to award a much higher figure than $16 million. Of course, this is exactly why the government left the copyright out of the taking to begin with.

To hear Ken Feinberg's perspective on the arbitration, I had an appointment to meet him in his office at the Willard Office Building in Washington, DC, on what turned out to be a slushy, messy winter morning. In the fifteen years since the Zapruder film hearing, Ken had become a household name, having served as special master of the federal September 11th Victim Compensation Fund and administrator of both the Hokie Spirit Memorial Fund after the Virginia Tech massacre in 2007 and the Gulf Coast Claims Facility following the 2010 *Deepwater Horizon* oil spill. While

Dellinger has an unhurried style, Feinberg is brisk and energetic; he talks quickly, with a classic Massachusetts accent that instantly endeared him to me. His office wall is covered with framed articles about his high-profile cases, letters from famous people, and photos of himself with presidents and heads of state. In spite of this, he is warm, friendly, and very down-to-earth. As soon as I walked in the door, he showed me a framed *New York Times* opinion piece about the Zapruder film arbitration decision hanging on his wall. It had been published on August 5, 1999, the day after the decision was made public. "Have you seen this?" he asked me. "It's good. It's very good. You should read it. You've read it? OK, good. That's good."

When we sat down to talk, I asked him how he felt about arbitrating this matter and how he had approached the hearing. "I had been chief of staff to Ted Kennedy," he said. "I had grown up in Massachusetts when his brother was president, a son of Massachusetts, and to be part of this, I felt, was an honor... Before I accepted Bob Bennett, I went and asked Senator Kennedy, and I said, 'Senator, they've asked me to arbitrate this and it's part of the law and I'm not going to do it if you have any qualms about it,' and he thought it over and he said, 'You know, I'm glad you're doing it. I'm glad somebody who I know very well and who I trust... It's history. You should do it.' He was very supportive, actually." He told me that Senator Kennedy had even sent him to talk to the rare-books and manuscripts collector on Seventy-Ninth and Madison who had sold a lot of Kennedy memorabilia. Feinberg told me, "So I went to see him. On my own! I said, 'I'm doing this arbitration,' and he said, 'Boy, it's one thing to value what a Kennedy letter is worth or a president's autograph... This?' Wasn't helpful. Wasn't helpful."

Unlike Dellinger, who agreed with the government experts that the camera original did not have intrinsic value, especially without the copyright, Feinberg was convinced by the LMH experts who argued that the film had tremendous financial worth—regardless of the existence of a market for camera-original films and quite apart from the copyright. For Feinberg, the biggest flaw in the government's case was that their experts failed to provide testimony that undermined or contradicted the LMH appraisers on the question of the film's value on the open market. "It was uncontroverted testimony!" he said. "I remember saying to Adams, 'Judge... one can agree or disagree, I guess, with Sotheby's but they haven't!' They didn't call anybody to say, 'I'm an auctioneer and it's only worth two million dollars.' They didn't call anybody! Why was it that... they never did it?" Feinberg's question is a very good one. Maybe it was because there was no appraiser inside an auction house who would say such a thing.

I asked both Feinberg and Dellinger to talk about how they arrived at the final number. Dellinger remembered that the three men had talked together during the hearing, carrying on a lively, cordial discussion over the various issues at hand. Based on Adams's questions and the substance of their conversations, Dellinger was pretty sure that Adams was leaning toward a lower figure. It came as a shock to Dellinger to find out that he was the outlier. "I was really surprised," he said, "when Judge Adams said, basically, well, 'I agree with Ken.'" Although Feinberg and Adams came up with an award of $22 million, they strongly hoped to reach a consensus. Feinberg said, "I remember saying to Dellinger, 'Walter, there's so much divisiveness and emotion and conspiracy theories about all of this, doesn't history require a unanimous decision?'"

In my interview with him, Dellinger remembered that it was in that spirit that they dropped the number from $22 million to $16 million. "They came down hoping that I would come up," he said, "but I wasn't going above [my number]. We just had a different view for the reasons stated in the dissent." In the end, Adams and Feinberg kept the award at $16 million and Dellinger dissented. I had heard a version of this story from my father's partner Roger Pies. When he told it to me, he said, "Just like that. Six million dollars. Poof!"

In fact, it does point to the arbitrary nature of the whole thing. Ken Feinberg agreed. "One reason I think the government was so quick to say 'Let's just move on and get this done' [is that] there was no legal, principled way to come up with a valuation that could withstand legal scrutiny." Instead, the question was subjective, emotional, philosophical, and even existential. In Ken Feinberg's words:

> If you lived through that day, the film was priceless. If you didn't live [through] that day, if you're just a student of history, it can't possibly have the same emotional impact. See, it's a moment; it stands for a moment where there is no competition. We all knew this was historical. We all knew that this was a singular event. The whole hearing was very existential. Because, you see, what is this tiny piece of celluloid worth? It's not a painting, it's not something that we're going to value because it can be reproduced in color and shown as a documentary. None of that is…it's all irrelevant! What's it worth as a piece of history? That's an existential thing! That's like historical impact! That, that thing you're looking at. And it was a philosophical problem valuing that.

Following the public announcement of the arbitration decision, I remember an extremely uncomfortable media frenzy, including segments on the evening news and articles in newspapers across the country. The phone rang off the hook with well-meaning friends calling to congratulate us, unwittingly adding to our embarrassment. Inside our family, the decision was acknowledged but not celebrated. Long after my father died, his dear friend Bill Truettner told me that, on the day of the decision, my father and several friends met for lunch, as they did every month. Bill said that Henry sat down, smacked both of his hands on the table, exhaled hard, and said, "It's over."

The media coverage was mixed. There were anticipated headlines, like the *San Francisco Chronicle*'s "Taxpayers Gouged on Zapruder Film," and predictable quotes, like the one from Gerald Posner, author of *Case Closed* (a best seller arguing that Oswald was the sole assassin in the murder of JFK), who opined: "I understand it's the American way to get as much as you can for something, but there is something unseemly about it." Judge Tunheim and Anna Nelson from the ARRB called the award "excessive," and Jim Lesar and Harold Weisberg—still spitting mad about the copyright—called it "outrageous." G. Robert Blakey, chief counsel for the House Select Committee on Assassinations in the late 1970s, did them one better, calling it "obscene," pointing out that "this was just the raw film. Its value was purely symbolic."

Such flat and simplistic statements never contribute anything to the cultural conversation about the Zapruder film. Anyone who has really grappled with it knows that, on every level, it defies snap judgments and easy generalities. It is only by having the patience to sit with its maddening, shifting ambiguities, its internal contradictions and ironies, that any real understanding may be found. David Marwell wrote something about this to me that I thought perfectly encapsulated these contradictions. I had written to ask him if he thought the final award was a fair one. He wrote this back to me: "You pose a difficult question... How do you place a value on something that is without equal or analog? The simple answer is that you really can't—its value is what someone is willing to pay, and that calculus is a product of the times and the context. Do I think $16 million was excessive? Yes, but it was the right price."

In some ways, the last, best word on the arbitration appeared in the *New York Times* opinion piece that Ken Feinberg had framed and hanging on his wall. It was neither favorable nor unfavorable. The author wrote that, if the "only standard of the film's value is what the market will bear," it was clear how the panel could award the sum of $16 million, given the high prices commanded by Kennedy memorabilia and the rise in the auction market in general. At the same time, the author also pointed out that what the government had purchased was an "expensive paradox," a film too fragile to have any practical use and yet so deeply familiar that its images are burned into the American consciousness. It was unique, of course, and accidental; and even its uniqueness was accidental—a consequence of a time before cameras were ever-present (and little could the editors have imagined how much more prevalent they would become over the next decades).

It was, the writer reflected, the gap between accident and intent that made $16 million seem like a lot of money to pay for the original Zapruder film. Usually, collectors pay for works of art made with "sober artistic intent." The fact that the price paid for the film was, at the time, the highest amount ever paid for an American historical artifact just added to the vague sense of unease. In the end, its value lay in what the film meant to a generation and to an era. "There is no question that what Abraham Zapruder filmed that day is of surpassing historical interest. But it is hard to escape the feeling that what has raised the price of this film so high is its generational interest, the sense that this is history that defined our lifetime, history caught in a medium that has defined our age."

PUBLIC AND PRIVATE LEGACY

In late January 2000, about six months after the arbitration decision was reached, our family donated the copyright in the Zapruder film to the Sixth Floor Museum at Dealey Plaza, the Dallas museum that educates the public about President Kennedy's assassination and memorializes him on the site where he was killed. At the same time, we also donated a 1,900-item collection that included documents, copies of the film in the form of slides, transparencies, and stills, and the third first-day copy of the film. Though the film is and will always remain linked to us through history and our singular name, that gesture marked the end of our family's long guardianship over one of the most controversial and contested objects of the twentieth century.

For a long time, I thought that the end of our family's relationship with the film was also the end of the story. What more was there to say? There was no more contention, no more argument, no more controversy. Moreover, in the years that followed, the technological changes brought about by the Internet made moot the question of access to the Zapruder film that had dominated the decades before. Hundreds of versions of the Zapruder film are instantly available in every format—enhanced, slowed down, sped up, zoomed in, narrated—and accompanied by discussion threads in which writers continue to argue the same points that have dogged the film for decades. Although the Sixth Floor Museum still licenses the images for publication, the Zapruder film will never be under embargo again.

But as I came to the end of writing this book, I could see that the end of the story for our family was not the end of the film's story at all. Since 2000, interest in the film has not dimmed. Scholarship—and in some cases, speculation—on what actually happened on Dealey Plaza continues, and the Zapruder film is still at the center of the debate.

Back in 2003, James Fetzer published a collection of essays on the alteration of the film, clownishly titled *The Great Zapruder Film Hoax*; also in 2003, David Wrone—who will remain forever in my mind as the professor who tried to make a moral argument against copyright protection for the Zapruder film by comparing it to the crucifixion of Jesus—published *The Zapruder Film*, in which he makes his case for conspiracy.

On the other end of the spectrum, in 2015 I met Max Holland, who had published an op-ed in the *New York Times* in 2007 putting forth the compelling and quite radical idea that the Zapruder film does not show all three shots fired at the president, which has long been an article of faith among researchers and the public. Instead, he makes the case that Oswald fired the first shot from the Book Depository (and missed) during the brief interval when Abe had turned off his camera after having filmed the lead motorcycles and before he turned it back on when he saw the president's limousine. While this does not fundamentally alter the Warren Commission conclusion that Lee Harvey Oswald acted alone (since it still means a single bullet struck President Kennedy and Governor Connally, and the third bullet hit the president in the head from the rear), it does drastically lengthen the time clock of the assassination and leaves ample time for Oswald to have gotten off three shots. Holland has challenged the long-standing thought conventions around the Zapruder film and gathered extensive additional evidence in support of his theory. He published a lengthy article in *Newsweek* on the subject in 2014, and his political and cultural history of the Kennedy assassination, titled *A Need to Know*, is forthcoming.

The film's life as evidence has always coexisted with its life as a cultural object. In the decades after the assassination, the film inspired some of the most influential artists and filmmakers of the latter half of the twentieth century; now, in the twenty-first, scholars and academics are tracing those reverberating connections, trying to make sense of how the film changed the artistic and cultural landscape of its time. The questions have been taken up by film and cultural historians like Art Simon who published a new edition of his 1996 book *Dangerous Knowledge: The JFK Assassination in Art and Film* in 2013; art historians like David Lubin in *Shooting Kennedy* (2003); and scholars in media studies such as Norwegian academic Øyvind Vågnes in *Zaprudered* (2013).

There are nearly too many articles to count about the Zapruder film, though each takes its own particular angle on the film's place in American culture, including "Livin' and Dyin' in Zapruderville," "Zapruder, Warhol and the Accident of Images," and "Climbing the Zapruder Curve," to name just a few. The film's life as a contested object and a commodity remains of interest, and I found articles and scholarly volumes that analyzed the question of the Zapruder film's valuation and the methods used in the appraisals for the arbitration hearing. Artists such as Christopher Brown have painted frames from the film in haunting abstractions, and in 2009, Jamey Hecht published *Limousine: Midnight Blue*, a series of fifty poems, each inspired by a different frame of the film. In 2008, *The Eternal Frame* was installed anew at the Getty Museum in Los Angeles.

Perhaps it was inevitable that our name would earn its place as—and simultaneously be reduced to—an item of trivia, the answer to questions in Trivial Pursuit, *Jeopardy!*, and the *New York Times* crossword. Likewise, the film's name has become a catchphrase, turning up in TV shows like *The X-Files* and *The Simpsons* and movies like *Independence Day*, parodied on *Mad TV* and in the *Onion*. When it crops up, it is a sort of stand-in for the idea of "conspiracy" or "tongue-in-cheek conspiracy" or "coincidence" or "paranoia" or "unimpeachable truth" or "unreliable evidence" or "accidental bystander" or, as it turns out, whatever the writer wants it to mean.

Likewise, our name has been appropriated in any number of ways, used as the title of an Italian magazine and in the names of several bands—the French band Zapruder, the Zapruders (now defunct, apparently), and Zapruder Point. And it would be nearly impossible to catalog the number of times the term "Zapruder," including the more recent use of our name as a verb, has appeared on Twitter or in social media in connection with a snippet about an event that, whether controversial, unusual, or accidental, has been captured on tape, replayed endlessly, and scrutinized for information or insight. As in, "Check out the Zapruder film of

Janet Jackson's wardrobe malfunction," or "They've Zaprudered that play a hundred times to see if the ball was in bounds," or my favorite: "You don't get to Zapruder her truth away!"

Each November 22, people still grapple with what the Zapruder film means and why it matters. In fact, it was on the fortieth anniversary of the assassination, in 2003, that arts critic Richard B. Woodward wrote an article for the *New York Times* that is surely among the most intelligent and thoughtful ones about the film ever published. Perhaps the vantage point of four decades partly accounts for it, but he was able to capture many of the film's firsts, including its status for its generation, the way its images have become "fused" with the assassination itself, *LIFE*'s purchase of it as an early example of "checkbook journalism," the film's challenge to the idea of the camera as witness, and how it dovetailed with the "crumbling of censorship rules" that had kept violence at the margins of society. "Above all," he wrote, "the Zapruder film is a home movie, its images suffused with nostalgia for an unredeemable past."

Ten years later, on the occasion of the fiftieth anniversary of the assassination, there was a spate of renewed interest about the "man behind the camera" and the enduring meaning of the film. *Parkland*, written and directed by Peter Landesman and produced by Playtone (the production company owned by Gary Goetzman and Tom Hanks) dramatized Abe Zapruder's story in feature film for the first time, with Paul Giamatti playing the role of our grandfather. The filmmaker Errol Morris made a short film about the "Umbrella Man," whose appearance in the film has given rise to its own conspiracy theories. In the film, Josiah Thompson reflects on the fact that fifty years after the event, there is still no conclusive answer as to what happened to President Kennedy on Dealey Plaza.

George Packer wrote a beautiful short piece about the Zapruder film for the *New Yorker*. And the great Don DeLillo joined journalist and writer Mark Danner and Errol Morris on a panel at the Telluride Film Festival to screen the Zapruder film and talk at length about its meaning in American life and in his novels.

As I came close to finishing this book, I found myself revisiting some of my early questions about the place of the film in my personal life. Why *didn't* we ever talk about the film when I was growing up? Was there something that I needed to understand in order to make sense of the film's place in our family's life? Was there a personal legacy of the Zapruder film and, if so, what was it?

My grandfather had once described the assassination as "a wound"—one that leaves residual pain even after it heals. It wasn't until I wrote this book that I saw how well his words reflected the experience of the rest of the family who were alive at the time and how perfectly they summed up our family's relationship to the film. For my grandparents, my aunt and uncle, and for my parents, this wound was composed of many parts: the crushing of the Kennedy dream; the association with the grotesque visual record of his murder; the moral dilemmas that the film raised; the unease that came with financial gain and the public criticism that followed. At its core, however, was the unavoidable reminder of that other family, the Kennedys, whose shattering tragedy our family's home movie records.

What I did not fully grasp until writing this book was that the ongoing life and intrusions of the film made it a living wound inside our family that could never fully heal. Over time, most of the American public moved on, deciding when and where—or even if—they wanted to revisit the JFK assassination. This was not so for my grandfather first of all, and then for my father, who hardly experienced a week over the course of twenty-five years during which he did not have to deal with something related to the film. Seen from this vantage point, I can understand why the Zapruder film didn't come up at our family dinner table. More to the point, I can see why there was no family story that we inherited the way we absorbed the memories of our grandfather. For our parents' generation—permanently, irrevocably tethered to the JFK assassination by virtue of the Zapruder film—there was never enough time or distance to see the story and its implications clearly enough to even fully realize that there was a legacy to pass on, let alone to shape and tell it.

As in all families, time passes, new generations appear, and we take what we have inherited and form our own stories. Even if what we have inherited is ambivalence, confusion, or silence. As much as I feel the pathos of that time, Kennedy's death was not my personal loss and the Zapruder film was not my wound. I wrote this book for myself and for the historical record, to document the film's history as fully, honestly, and forthrightly as I could. But I also wrote it for our family, especially for the next generation of Zapruders and Hausers, to whom I wanted to bequeath something more than silence, questions, and doubts about this part of our history. For me, the messy, complicated, tangled story of the Zapruder film *is* our family's legacy. Now, all that remains is for us to claim it.

If that is the last word, for the moment, on the private dimension of the Zapruder film, there is still a bigger and more important question. What is its public legacy? What is the compelling lure that makes the assassination researchers, the film, art, and cultural historians, the writers and journalists, the academics and students and hobbyists and Kennedy buffs return to it as a touchstone time and again? I have come to think it is because the

Zapruder film is in every way a conundrum. It contains its own irreconcilable contradictions: It is visual evidence that refuses to solve the mystery of who murdered the president, why, and how. It is a single strip of film in which we all see different things. It shows the entire course of history changing under the influence of a single bullet. It is quite possibly the most important historical film ever made and yet it is an amateur home movie. It is six feet of 8mm film on a plastic reel that turned out to be worth sixteen million dollars. It is the most private and the most public of records. It is gruesome and terrible but we cannot stop looking at it.

But more than that, the deepest, most compelling conundrum of the film is an existential one. It lies in the arc of the film itself, the fall from grace, the unforgiving inevitability of it. It is a sunny day, a handsome husband and his beautiful wife are riding down the street, smiling and waving, with their lives stretched out before them, and within less than half a minute, his head explodes and he is dead and she is covered in his brains and blood, trying to recover his skull from the trunk of the limousine. He is alive and then he is dead. She is a wife and then she is a widow. She is grace itself and then she is sprawled across the back of the car. How can it be that our protections and illusions can be stripped from us so quickly?

Most of us are able to live our days exactly because we are not confronted with this vulnerability, the inexplicable capriciousness of fate, the permanence of death. And yet, there is the Zapruder film. It exists and we cannot turn away even though we fear it and we avert our eyes and we wish desperately that it would end differently every time. Maybe it is the same impulse that causes us to watch the *Challenger* explode in the bright blue Florida sky or the Twin Towers crash down into Lower Manhattan on a crisp fall morning. It is because we resist the knowledge that hope sometimes turns to despair in an instant, and that tragedy comes out of nowhere on a beautiful day. And, paradoxically, because sometimes we need to confront that very truth, simply to see the thing that we feel cannot happen in order to touch for a moment the very limits of what we know about life and to remind ourselves of the fragility of it all.

In the end, we are perhaps like Don DeLillo's characters in *Underworld*, who eventually drifted away from the all-too-real confrontations of the Zapruder film playing on hundreds of TV sets in an apartment in Manhattan and "got something to eat and went to the loft, where they played cards for a couple of hours and did not talk about Zapruder." The Zapruder film is not a reality that we can live with every minute of every day. But it holds in its terrible twenty-six seconds a painful, fundamental human truth that will never grow old and that every generation must grapple with for itself.

ACKNOWLEDGMENTS

I am profoundly grateful to many people who supported and encouraged me throughout the many years it took to complete this book.

My friends and colleagues at the Sixth Floor Museum at Dealey Plaza were unfailingly helpful with research and guidance. I wish to thank Nicola Longford, Megan Bryant, Stephen Fagin, and especially the late Gary Mack, who not only answered innumerable questions and provided me with invaluable information, but was also one of my earliest and most enthusiastic cheerleaders.

The staff of Time Inc. opened the *LIFE* magazine archives and gave me unfettered access to the Zapruder film records, an act of trust that enabled me to fill in a previously unknown period in the film's history. I wish to thank Ali Zelenko, Steve Koepp, and Bob Sullivan for welcoming me in and Time Inc. Chief Archivist Bill Hooper for opening up the files, answering a million questions, and accommodating every request with patience and care. Roy Rowan spoke with me by phone about his memories and clarified important details in the manuscript.

I wish especially to acknowledge Dick Stolley, whose friendship is one of the great gifts to have come from this work. He provided me with facts and insights about his dealings with my grandfather, reviewed my account for accuracy, and helped me in whatever way he could whenever I asked. Put simply, and in words my grandfather would surely have used, Dick is a mensch.

I so appreciate the help provided by Alexis Ferguson at the Dallas Jewish Historical Society in sharing an interview with my grandmother Lillian Zapruder, conducted by Miriam Creemer in 1991. I also wish to thank Stefana Breitwieser and Stacey Chandler of the John F. Kennedy Presidential Library, who located and provided me with the letter my father wrote to John F. Kennedy in 1962. They also made available a copy of his 1960 letter (which Gary Mack had previously found). I am grateful to have these letters for the book and for our family. Freddie Rios at Skadden Arps provided all the Zapruder film arbitration documents I needed and gave me an office in which to review them. She cheerfully answered questions, provided contacts, and helped in whatever way I needed, and I'm very grateful.

I wish to acknowledge the excellent work of Gloria Thiede, who meticulously and with much-appreciated speed transcribed a great many interviews for me. I also thank Jean Dotts from Bop and Awe on Etsy, who rescued several Jennifer Juniors dresses from my grandfather's era and sold them to me for a song. I loved seeing these garments for myself and adding them to our family treasures.

My thanks go to Jamie Henderson, the grandson of Harry McCormick, who generously provided me with a letter from his grandfather written shortly after the assassination and other helpful materials.

I especially thank my grandmother's longest-time friend Alice Feld, and my grandparents' dear friend Ada Lynn, for allowing me to interview them about my grandparents. Some of those memories, stories, and anecdotes made their way into this book but, more than that, they remain precious contributions to our family's personal history.

One of the best parts of writing this book was meeting film and cultural historians, journalists, writers, filmmakers, and others who have thought and written about the Zapruder film. I have enjoyed and benefited from these lengthy, wide-ranging, and provocative conversations, whether they took place in person, on the phone, or in written correspondence. My thanks go to Tom Doherty, Chip Lord, David Lubin, Bill Minutaglio, Errol Morris, George Packer, and Richard Woodward. I especially appreciated and enjoyed my ongoing e-mail dialogue with Doug Hall about *The Eternal Frame* and many other subjects. Art Simon immediately proved himself to be a kindred spirit and, even beyond his book (which was an essential source for me), his encouragement and insights have been a sustaining influence.

I hardly know how to thank Don DeLillo and his publicist, Kate Lloyd, for their kindness and generosity. In particular, I wish to thank Don for sharing his time and reflections about the film and its place in his work, and for his compassion and understanding about what it means to be a Zapruder. He also took me to lunch. It is not a day I will soon forget.

I wish to express my gratitude to ChaeRan Freeze, who generously provided me with historical insights about Jewish life in Imperial Russia. She translated texts, directed my reading, read and corrected my manuscript pages, and answered all my questions in writing. Her vast knowledge deepened my understanding of my grandfather's childhood in Russia and its effect on his later life.

I am so thankful to the small group of our family's intimates who played key roles in the life of the film and allowed me to interview them, provided materials, and patted me on the back when my spirits flagged. It is with gratitude and love that I thank Anita

Dove, Dana Freyer, Adam Hauser, Roger Pies, Jamie Silverberg, and Bob Trien for their constancy and contributions.

I remain especially grateful to my father Henry's close friends who showed me so much love and support through the writing of this book. They took me to lunch to talk about their memories of my dad and the film, discussed the project with me, engaged on various ethical and historical questions, and sometimes simply stood in as surrogates when I was missing my own father. My love and thanks go to Bill Truettner, David Mathiasen, Bob Adler, Paul Isenman, David Fischer, and Rabbi Daniel Zemel.

I wish to express my particular gratitude to David Marwell for his unflagging guidance in helping me understand the ARRB and the taking of the Zapruder film. He answered every question forthrightly, made helpful suggestions to the manuscript, and engaged with me in some of the most difficult questions I faced. Beyond that, he is a true friend, for which I feel exceptionally lucky.

My heartfelt thanks go to a number of very busy, often high-profile people who spoke with me about the ARRB, the taking of the film, and the Zapruder film arbitration. They did not hesitate to share their thoughts and opinions, asking nothing in return, and gave me free rein to use the material as I wished. In some cases, they read my pages and offered corrections. In all cases, they made this a much better book. My thanks go to Bob Bennett, Rich Brusca, Walter Dellinger, Ken Feinberg, Judge John Tunheim, and Beth Gates Warren.

There are many people in various professions who have worked directly with the Zapruder film or studied it, gathering materials and writing books that were foundational to my understanding of its public life. I wish to acknowledge and thank those who helped me personally, including Joseph Barabe, Robert Groden, Clayton Ogilvie, Richard Trask, Howard Willens, and Roland Zavada. My special thanks go to Paul Hoch, who carefully read the parts of my manuscript dealing with the assassination and the subsequent investigations, and scrupulously corrected it, providing me with sources to consider and cite and saving me from many embarrassing mistakes. He did so with kindness and generosity and I will always remember that.

There is a special place in my heart for Max Holland, who is one of the most thorough, careful, and thoughtful thinkers I've ever met. He was exceptionally generous with his time and his impressive collection of research materials about the assassination. He clarified my thinking on many important issues, gently challenging me on my assumptions, and supported the writing of this book in every possible way.

I wrote this book at the Writers Room in DC, and I thank Charles and Alex Karelis for creating this place in which creative and intellectual work can flourish and a fellowship of writers can support each other.

I am so fortunate to have a community of writers who offer solidarity, advice, empathy, and sometimes just a willing ear for my complaints. At the Writers Room, my days were sustained by Liz Flock, Caitriona Palmer, Carolyn Parkhurst, Kimberly Stephens, and Judy Warner. Other writer-friends bolstered my spirits and pushed me on in big and small ways, including Matt Bai, Jim Baker, Michelle Brafman, Margaret Hutton-Griffin, Molly McCloskey, Donna Oetzel, Jennifer Oko, and Mary Kay Zuravleff. I wish especially to thank Elizabeth Shreve, who has given me so much encouragement and advice, not only on substance but on tricky questions of publishing and media, and who has been a true friend since the moment I met her. Finally, I have especially treasured my little writers group, which includes Hanna Rosin, Margaret Talbot, and Florence Williams; they saw me through this work from the first to the last written word.

Susan Shreve gets her own paragraph. She was among the first to encourage the idea of writing this book and she did a great deal on its behalf, introducing me to people, spending hours discussing all aspects of it, and pushing me to face the personal element of this story even when I resisted it. She read the first draft of the book and offered deeply thoughtful comments and important improvements. Her brilliant mind and generous heart are all over these pages.

And then there's Michael Downing. He started listening to me talk about this book before anyone else and, if the world were fair, he would be credited as its coauthor. He shaped and challenged my ideas, waited patiently while I stumbled over my own thoughts, untangled my confusions, rescued me when I was stuck, and read my pages and offered superb insights. Most of all, he made me laugh when I wanted to cry and remains the dearest and most steadfast of friends. Having Michael in my life is one of the very best things that has ever happened to me.

I am eternally grateful to my literary agent, Gail Hochman, who immediately grasped the potential of this book, threw her considerable passion behind it, and, most important, found it the best possible home. I also wish to thank Marianne Merola and Jody Kahn from Brandt and Hochman, who have supported and doubtless will continue to support this book well after its initial publication.

The team at Twelve has been nothing less than extraordinary. I wish to thank Twelve's publisher Jamie Raab for her enthusiasm and support of this book every step of the way. Jarrod Taylor designed it, including the cover, endpapers, and photo inserts with sensitivity, creativity, and care. Crack publicists Paul Samuelson and Brian McLendon showed unflagging excitement, even as they waited far too long to get to read it. They put their full effort toward making sure it would reach the largest possible audience, and I am deeply grateful. The production team was heroic: My great thanks go to Carolyn Kurek, Bob Castillo, and Giraud Lorber for their extraordinary patience and meticulous care in seeing the book through from its first incarnations to its final form. I wish also to thank Susan Gutentag and Mark Steven Long for proofreading it and Stephen Callahan for indexing it. My dear childhood friend Dierdre Baule, who works in finance at Hachette Book Group, could not have been a more enthusiastic, encouraging cheerleader. Finally, there should be a special place in Paradise for copyeditor Rick Ball, whose abilities stretch from correcting misplaced commas to catching major inconsistencies, faults of logic, incorrect quotations, and bad writing. He saved me from looking like an ass at least a dozen times over and I will never forget it.

Elizabeth Kulhanek helped in innumerable ways, serving as my liaison with the production team at Twelve, shepherding the manuscript through the process, answering my questions, and resolving every issue with patience, kindness, and good cheer.

I am most of all indebted to the great Deb Futter, who saw the potential of this book when it was still a half-formed proposal, snatched it up, and never looked back. She has shown nothing less than unbounded enthusiasm and excitement for the book, which is what every writer most wants and needs. Her editorial read of the manuscript was, of course, invaluable. But it is her faith in my work as a writer and in the meaning and value of this book in particular that made all the difference.

I wish to thank my friend Linda Fittante, who took extraordinary pains to capture my best side in my author photograph. She spent far more time and energy, and charged me far less, on this than any photographer of her caliber should. But that's part of what makes her such a dear friend.

To my everlasting good fortune, my cousin Micah Hauser took on the role of researcher for me in the early stages of this work. He tracked down books and articles, created master lists of sources, compiled ideas for interviews, and spent hours talking with me about the substance of the work itself. He assembled my file cabinets when they arrived in boxes at my house and then filled them with the records he had gathered. He brightened my days with his huge smile, his wonderful energy, and his stellar insights. It was pure joy to work with him on this project.

I am immensely lucky to have a wide circle of friends in Washington and elsewhere who are smart, funny, warm, generous, and who always have my back. I could not possibly mention every one but I trust they know who they are. I do, however, want to thank a small handful of close friends who were with me on a nearly daily basis over the years it took to write this book and whose enduring support went above and beyond. They include Ilana Drimmer, Dini Karasik, Carin Zelenko, and Lynne Englert.

Our au pair Anna Gebauer turned up, like Mary Poppins, when we needed her most. Just as I started dropping things, she caught and handled them, not only taking care of our children in every way, but walking and playing with our dog, cleaning the kitchen, learning to make meals, and putting up with the ups and downs that exist in every family. All of us love and appreciate Anna for everything she has brought to our lives, and to this I would add that I'm overwhelmed with gratitude to her for making it possible for me to finish this book.

Words begin to fail as I try to find a way to thank my family. I will just say that the love and trust we share is the single most important, sustaining element of my life. I want to mention my sister-in-law Shelley Stone, my cousins Alicia Seiger, Joanne Harpel, and Fran

Sterling, and my aunt Randee Seiger, all of whom cheered me on in every way. I also want to thank my first cousins and their children who share this story with me for their support: Jeffrey and Nancy Hauser and their children Meir, Aviva, and Leah, who is married to Avrohom Eliezer; Adam and Rhonda Hauser and their children, Micah and Alana; David and Kim Hauser and their children, Melani and Reed; and my cousin Aaron, a writer in his own right, who has always expressed a deep understanding and faith in this book.

This book would never have happened if it weren't for my aunt Myrna Ries. She quite simply gave me everything I needed from the first minute to the last, including family papers and photos, answers to questions, her time, empathy, and a totally biased and often unrealistic faith in my abilities. In this respect, my Nana from Texas and my father, Henry, live on in her, and I heard their love and encouragement ringing through in her words and actions.

My older brother, Matthew, and my twin brother, Michael, listened, questioned, helped, supported, encouraged, and bolstered my work on this book in every way. They each brought their own exceptional creative, intellective, and artistic abilities to our conversations, and their contributions shaped the book in deeply meaningful ways. Above all, in this book, as in life, they have never failed me. I wish also to thank my sisters-in-law Jessica Michaelson Zapruder and Sarah Karlinsky, who are always loving and kind, and who have been rock solid in their conviction that I could and should do this work.

I have special gratitude for my mother, Marjorie Zapruder. She had her own burdens to bear that sometimes made it difficult for her to understand and accept the necessity of my writing this book. In the end, however, love prevailed. This is a testament not only to her values but to her devotion to her children, for which I remain eternally thankful.

My last and deepest thanks are reserved for my immediate family. My husband, Craig, has always given me the freedom and space to have a creative life, and that is a rare and precious gift. In spite of his own busy professional life, he picked up the slack for me more times than I can count and supported my work by quietly making it possible for me to do it without guilt or recrimination. I have counted on his patience and understanding and he has always lived up to it.

Finally, there are my children, Hannah and Toby, who may have made more keenly felt sacrifices during the writing of this book than anyone else, myself included. They forgave my absences, my travels, my distracted attention, and my disorganized approach to managing their lives. Not only that, they cheered me on, offering me words of encouragement, praise, hugs and kisses, and boundless, unfathomable love every single day. In this and a thousand other ways, they never fail to inspire me and I hope that I will always do the same for them.

NOTES

In addition to relying on the sources listed below, this book was vetted and corrected by a number of experts in different areas, as well as by some whose involvement with the film is reflected in my account. I am extremely grateful to them for their help. They include Joseph Barabe, ChaeRan Freeze, Dana Freyer, Doug Hall, Adam Hauser, Paul Hoch, Bill Hooper, Chip Lord, David Marwell, Jamie Silverberg, Dick Stolley, Judge John Tunheim, and Beth Gates Warren.

Introduction

Description of Abraham Zapruder's experiences on the day of the assassination from William Manchester, *The Death of a President: November 1963* (New York: Harper & Row, 1967).

Quote from José Saramago, *The Cave* (New York: Harcourt, 2002).

Prologue: Home Movie

The description of the events that took place in the Zapruder home on the evening of November 22, 1963, comes from Myrna (Zapruder Hauser) Ries interview conducted by the author on February 24 and 25, 2011.

Quotes and descriptions of JFK's assassination from Abraham Zapruder's perspective came from a variety of sources, including family accounts; a televised interview with Jay Watson on WFAA-TV on November 22, 1963; his testimony in *Hearings Before the President's Commission on the Assassination of President Kennedy*, vol. 7 (Washington, DC: US Government Printing Office, 1964), pp. 569–571; William Manchester's interview notes for *The Death of a President* (from the William Manchester Papers, Special Collections and Archives, Wesleyan University, Middletown, CT); "Marvin Scott Interviews Abraham Zapruder, 1966" (Marvin Scott Collection, Sixth Floor Museum at Dealey Plaza); and Abraham Zapruder's testimony in State of Louisiana v. Clay L. Shaw, on February 13, 1969, in New Orleans.

Other sources include Kodak technician Phil Chamberlain's recollections about developing the film, as included in Roland J. Zavada, *Analysis of Selected Motion Picture Photographic Evidence: Kodak Technical Report* (Rochester, NY: Eastman Kodak, 1998); Abraham Zapruder's home movies from 1934 to 1970; Marilyn Sitzman interview conducted by Marjorie Zapruder and Myrna Ries on June 10, 1993; and Henry Zapruder, Rebuttal Affidavit prepared for the Zapruder film arbitration hearing, February 11, 1999.

Chapter 1: Assassination

Quotes and descriptions of the Zapruder family's experiences before, during, and immediately after President Kennedy's assassination come from previously cited written accounts and interviews with Myrna Ries, Henry Zapruder, and Marilyn Sitzman. Additional information comes from Marjorie Zapruder interview conducted by the author on October 17, 2013, and interviews with Marilyn Sitzman (conducted by Wes Wise with Bob Porter on June 29, 1993) and Erwin Schwartz (conducted by Bob Porter on December 30, 1997), both courtesy of the Oral History Collection, Sixth Floor Museum at Dealey Plaza.

General information about President Kennedy's visit to Dallas and the events of the assassination came from relevant sections in Richard B. Trask, *National Nightmare on Six Feet of Film: Mr. Zapruder's Home Movie and the Murder of President Kennedy* (Danvers, MA: Yeoman Press, 2005); Vincent Bugliosi, *Four Days in November: The Assassination of President John F. Kennedy* (New York: W. W. Norton, 2008); William Manchester, *The Death of a President: November 1963* (New York: Harper & Row, 1967); Robert A. Caro, *The Passage of Power: The Years of Lyndon Johnson* (New York: Knopf, 2012);

and articles in the *Dallas Morning News* and the *Dallas Times Herald* in November 1963.

Information about the reactionary climate in Dallas came primarily from Bill Minutaglio and Steven L. Davis, *Dallas 1963* (New York: Twelve, 2013).

Details about Abraham Zapruder filming the assassination of President Kennedy and quotes come from previously cited interviews and testimonies.

List of other photographers and their locations on and around Dealey Plaza comes from Richard B. Trask, *Pictures of the Pain: Photography and the Assassination of President Kennedy* (Danvers, MA: Yeoman Press, 1994), and Josiah Thompson, *Six Seconds in Dallas* (New York: Bernard Geis Associates, 1967).

Information and quotes from Harry McCormick's encounter with Abraham Zapruder come from his account in *Memoirs of Dallas Morning News Reporters and Photographers Covering the JFK Assassination* (The *Dallas Morning News* Collection, Belo Records, DeGolyer Library, Southern Methodist University), and from an unpublished letter McCormick wrote to his family on December 8, 1963, provided to the author by McCormick's grandson, Jamie Henderson.

Details and quotes about Darwin Payne's encounter with Abraham Zapruder come from Darwin Payne interview conducted by Bob Porter on January 19, 1995 (Oral History Collection, Sixth Floor Museum at Dealey Plaza), and from two sets of handwritten notes he took that day (Darwin Payne Collection, Sixth Floor Museum at Dealey Plaza).

Information and quotes from Forrest Sorrels come from his testimony in *Hearings*, vol. 7, p. 352, and from a memorandum on file at NARA that Sorrels wrote to Inspector Thomas J. Kelley on January 22, 1964.

Abraham Zapruder interview with Jay Watson, WFAA-TV, November 22, 1963.

Information and quotes from Bert Shipp come from an interview conducted by Wes Wise with Bob Porter on November 17, 1992 (Oral History Collection, Sixth Floor Museum at Dealey Plaza).

Information and quotes from Phil Chamberlain come from an interview conducted by Bob Porter with Gary Mack on September 21, 1994 (Oral History Collection, Sixth Floor Museum at Dealey Plaza).

Chapter 2: Exposure

Information and quotes regarding the processing of the original film at the Kodak Lab in Dallas come primarily from interviews with John Harrison (conducted by Bob Porter with Gary Mack on August 30, 1994) and Bert Shipp (conducted by Wes Wise with Bob Porter on November 17, 1992), both courtesy of the Oral History Collection, Sixth Floor Museum at Dealey Plaza, as well as previously cited Phil Chamberlain interview and his written recollection in Zavada, *Analysis of Selected*. Additional information and quotes drawn from previously cited interview with Erwin Schwartz and written accounts by Harry McCormick.

Information about the Bell and Howell Director Series camera comes from close observation and examination of Abraham Zapruder's replica camera; *Instructional Booklet: Bell and Howell Director Series, 8mm Movie Camera, Model 414-414P*; and from previously cited Zavada, *Analysis of Selected*. Quote from *Modern Photography* taken from Trask, *National Nightmare*, pp. 24–25.

Facts and quotes about duplicating the film at Jamieson Film Company came from Bruce Jamieson interview conducted by Bob Porter on February 23, 2000 (Oral History Collection, Sixth Floor Museum at Dealey Plaza), and previously cited interviews with Kodak technicians and Erwin Schwartz.

Affidavits certifying the processing of the original film at Kodak, the duplication of three copies at Jamieson Film Company, and the processing of those three duplicates at Kodak exist in the Time Inc. Archives. Copies of the affidavits were reprinted in the appendices in David R. Wrone, *The Zapruder Film: Reframing JFK's Assassination* (Lawrence, KS: University Press of Kansas, 2003), pp. 281–283.

Additional general information about processing the in-camera original film at Kodak, duplicating it at Jamieson, and developing the three first-day copies at Kodak, and technical details regarding the edge print markings come primarily from relevant sections of Trask, *National Nightmare*, and Zavada, *Analysis of Selected*.

Details about bringing the duplicate copies of the film to the Secret Service come from previously cited interview with Erwin Schwartz. Confirmation of the transmittal of first-day copies of the film to the Secret Service come from previously cited memo by Forrest Sorrels to Inspector Thomas J. Kelley on January 22, 1964 (with a mistaken recollection by Agent Sorrels that he picked up the film from Zapruder's office), and from a memo written by Chief of Secret Service James Rowley to Henry Suydam, *LIFE* Washington bureau chief, on January 27, 1964, both on file at NARA. This account is commonly accepted as the accurate chain of possession for the two first-day copies and is repeated in Trask, Zavada, and multiple other sources.

Additional confirmation of the processing of the original film and the duplication of it comes from a letter written by Abraham Zapruder to C. D. Jackson, publisher of *LIFE* magazine, on November 25, 1975. This letter served as a statement of authenticity for the film, and accompanied the signed contract with *LIFE* and the affidavits from Kodak and Jamieson.

Zapruder family background comes from interviews with Myrna Ries and Marjorie Zapruder conducted by the author; with Lillian Rogers and Marilyn Sitzman conducted by Marjorie Zapruder and Myrna Ries; with Marilyn Sitzman and Erwin Schwartz from the Oral History Collection, Sixth Floor Museum at Dealey Plaza; and with Lillian Zapruder conducted by Miriam Creemer on April 1, 1981, from the collections of the Dallas Jewish Historical Society. Additional background and anecdotes came from interviews conducted by the author with Alice Feld on May 7, 2011, and Ada Lynn in November 2013.

Birth, marriage, and death records for the Zapruder family; immigration and census documents, voter registration, draft registration, and naturalization certificate for Israel Zapruder; and emergency passport application for Chana Zapruder came from JewishGen.org. Ship manifests showing Israel Zapruder (1909) and Chana Zapruder with children (1920) came from the Ellis Island website, LibertyEllisFoundation.org.

Background on Jewish life in Imperial Russia came from correspondence with ChaeRan Freeze, associate professor of Jewish Studies in the Department of Near Eastern and Judaic Studies at Brandeis University, and from relevant portions of her published work, including *Jewish Marriage and Divorce in Imperial Russia* (Waltham, MA: Brandeis University Press, 2001) and *Everyday Jewish Life in Imperial Russia: Select Documents, 1772–1914* (Waltham, MA: Brandeis University Press, 2013).

Information about Kovel came from a translation of *Kowel; sefer edut ve-zikaron le-kehilatenu she-ala aleha ha-koret* (*Kowel; Testimony and Memorial Book of Our Destroyed Community*), edited by Eliezer Leoni-Zopperfin (Tel Aviv: 1957) on JewishGen.org, and from correspondence with ChaeRan Freeze (including a translation of the Kovel entry in *Evreiskaia entsiklopediia*, vol. 19, pp. 577–579).

General information about Jewish life in Dallas came from Rose G. Biderman, *They Came to Stay: The Story of the Jews of Dallas, 1870–1997* (Fort

Worth, TX: Eakin Press, 2002); Gerry Cristol, *A Light in the Prairie: Temple Emanu-El of Dallas, 1872–1997* (Fort Worth, TX: Texas Christian University, 1998); and David Ritz, "The Jews Who Built Dallas," *D Magazine*, November 2008.

Some information about Ben Gold and Nardis came from Paula Bosse, "Nardis of Dallas: The Fashion Connection Between 'The Dick Van Dyke Show' and the Kennedy Assassination" on flashbackdallas.com.

Information about the Chalet union dispute can be found in "Decision and Order in Chalet, Inc. and International Ladies' Garment Workers' Union, AFL, Cutters Local no. 387. (Case No. 16-ca-596. November 19, 1953.)"

Letters from Henry Zapruder to John F. Kennedy (September 1, 1960, and February 3, 1962) from the John F. Kennedy Presidential Library and Museum in Boston, MA.

Chapter 3: First Glimpses

Myrna Ries's story and quotes come from her previously cited interview with the author.

Richard Stolley's background, experiences during the Kennedy assassination, and interactions with Abraham Zapruder come from a variety of published and unpublished sources. Most important was an interview conducted by the author on March 5, 2013, in New York, NY, and follow-up conversations and e-mail correspondence. Further information came from interviews with Richard Stolley on November 22, 1996; November 21, 2003; October 15, 2008; and November 19, 2011 (Oral History Collection, Sixth Floor Museum at Dealey Plaza). Published accounts written by Richard Stolley include "LIFE Is on the Story," in *The Day Kennedy Died: Fifty Years Later* LIFE *Remembers the Man and the Moment* (New York: LIFE Books, 2013), pp. 72–79; "Zapruder Rewound," *LIFE*, September 1998; "Shots Seen Round the World," *Entertainment Weekly*, January 17, 1992; "Four Days in Dallas: 25 Years Later," *Columbia, the Magazine of Columbia University*, October 1988, p. 57; and "What Happened Next…" *Esquire*, November 1973.

Patsy Swank interview conducted by Bob Porter on June 11, 1996 (Oral History Collection, Sixth Floor Museum at Dealey Plaza).

General history of *LIFE* magazine comes from Loudon Wainwright, *The Great American Magazine: An Inside History of* LIFE (New York: Knopf, 1986).

Description of the events of Saturday morning, November 23, 1963, and quotes come from previously cited interviews with Lillian Rogers and Erwin Schwartz, and interviews and written accounts by Richard Stolley.

Information about the chain of possession of the original Zapruder film (edge print marked 0183) and the first-day copy that Abe Zapruder retained (edge print marked 0186) over the weekend of the assassination is well documented in Trask, *National Nightmare*; Zavada, *Analysis of Selected*; on the website of the Sixth Floor Museum at Dealey Plaza, jfk.org; and verified by Abraham Zapruder testimonies and documents in Time Inc. Archives, and by Secret Service documents, as previously cited.

Information about the review and chain of possession of first-day Copy 1 (edge print number 0185) by the Secret Service and the FBI comes from documents on file in the JFK Assassination Records Collection at NARA, including two memos from C. D. DeLoach to Mr. Mohr on November 23, 1963; transmittal documents and letters from the Dallas FBI field office to Washington HQ; and a short interview with Abraham Zapruder and other FBI correspondence regarding the handling of the film. Confirmation of these facts and additional details come from previously cited Zavada, *Analysis of Selected*, and Trask, *National Nightmare*.

Information about the reporting and coverage of the JFK assassination at *LIFE* comes from previously cited Wainwright, *The Great American Magazine*, and from "The Man Who Shot JFK Being Shot," in Roy Rowan, *Powerful People: From Mao to Now* (New York: Carroll and Graf, 1996).

Max Holland, "The Truth Behind JFK's Assassination," *Newsweek*, November 20, 2014.

For a comparison of the Zapruder film, the *Challenger* explosion, and the Rodney King beating, see chapter 1 of Marita Sturken, *Tangled Memories: The Vietnam War, the AIDS Epidemic, and the Politics of Remembering* (Berkeley and Los Angeles: University of California Press, 1997).

Quotes from Forrest Sorrels come from previously cited memorandum to Inspector Thomas J. Kelley, January 22, 1964, in JFK Assassination Records Collection at NARA.

Abraham Zapruder quote from previously cited William Manchester interview.

The description of Henry and Marjorie Zapruder's experiences the weekend of the assassination comes from previously cited Marjorie Zapruder interview with the author.

Information about President Kennedy's funeral and burial comes from previously cited published sources about the Kennedy assassination, newspaper coverage, and previously cited *The Day Kennedy Died*.

Chapter 4: All Rights to *LIFE*

Myrna Ries and Richard Stolley recollections come from previously cited sources.

Information and quotes from Sam Passman regarding the sale of the moving picture rights to the film come from Sam Passman interview conducted by Marjorie and Henry Zapruder on November 5, 1994, and legal records from the offices of Passman & Jones, provided by Robert Trien and James L. Silverberg.

Information and quotes from Dan Rather's experiences during the weekend of the Kennedy assassination and his involvement with the Zapruder film come from Dan Rather with Mickey Herskowitz, *The Camera Never Blinks: Adventures of a TV Journalist* (New York: William Morrow, 1977), and from an interview conducted by the John F. Kennedy Presidential Library on February 11, 2003 (transcript available online at archive1.jfklibrary.org). A third account, consistent with his written and recorded interviews, comes from "Dan Rather Discusses the Zapruder Film" on EmmyTVLegends.org, www.YouTube.com/watch?v=PIBNuxzN15M. Multiple versions of Dan Rather's television broadcast on CBS on November 25, 1963, can be found on YouTube.

Additional information came from relevant sections in Trask, *National Nightmare*. In fact, the timeline and events of that day are difficult to pinpoint. Trask points out that it is not clear how many times Rather delivered his spoken recollections of the film on the air, but that he believes he first spoke on CBS radio, interviewed by Hughes Rudd and Richard C. Hottelet, and then, that afternoon, went on CBS News with Walter Cronkite to describe it again. Rather's own account does not mention the radio and says simply that he went on the air immediately. In addition to defending his misreporting of the direction of the president's head at the moment of the bullet's impact, he explained how he described Jackie Kennedy's movements in the film and his bosses' urging to do another take with a more dignified account of the first lady's actions.

Don Hewitt quote is from Don Hewitt, *Tell Me a Story: Fifty Years and 60 Minutes in Television* (New York: Public Affairs, 2001).

Details about *LIFE*'s acquisition of all rights to the Zapruder film are from previously cited interviews and written accounts by Richard Stolley.

The contract terms between Abraham Zapruder and *LIFE* magazine come from the *LIFE* contract and accompanying documents in the *LIFE* magazine archives.

Information about the donation to Mrs. Tippit comes primarily from previously cited interview with Sam Passman and legal files from Passman & Jones.

"Man Who Got $25,000 for Assassination Film Gives It to Widow of Patrolman," Associated Press, November 27, 1963.

Information and quotes from the letters, telegrams, and postcards addressed to Abraham Zapruder and additional newspaper clippings in US and foreign newspapers regarding his donation to Mrs. Tippit come from Zapruder family papers.

Abraham Zapruder's statement regarding his donation to the Tippit family came from the legal files of Passman & Jones. Quote is from previously cited AP article.

Articles about the donation come from Zapruder family papers and include "Film's $25,000 Given to Tippits," *Denver Post*, November 27, 1963; "Tippitt's [*sic*] Widow Gets $25,000 Paid for Assassination Movies," *New York Times*, November 28, 1963, from November 27 AP report; "JFK Death Film Proceeds Given to Officer's Family," *Rocky Mountain News*, November 28, 1963; "As Camera Recorded the Assassination," *Kansas City Star*, November 29, 1963; "The President's Assassination," *New York Daily News*, November 30, 1963; "Abraham Zapruder's Fine Gesture," Baton Rouge *Morning Advocate*, December 1, 1963.

Associated Press, "Contributor of $25,000 to Tippets Won't Talk," *Reading Eagle*, November 30, 1963.

"Generosity Forces Gentle Abe Into Hiding," *Houston Chronicle*, undated clipping in Zapruder family papers.

"He's Sorry He Filmed Assassination," *Miami Herald*, December 21, 1963.

Lillian Zapruder quote is from previously cited *Houston Chronicle* article.

Chapter 5: Images in Print

The history of the film at *LIFE*, including direct quotations from memos, letters, internal documents, and other correspondence comes from the Zapruder film files in the Time Inc. Archives. Materials from Time Inc. and *LIFE* are used with permission.

Descriptions from "President John F. Kennedy 1917–1963," *LIFE*, November 29, 1963, and "John F. Kennedy Memorial Edition," *LIFE*, December 14, 1963.

Information about the Warren Commission and its use of the Zapruder film comes primarily from previously cited *Hearings*; *Report of the President's Commission on the Assassination of President Kennedy* (Washington, DC: US Government Printing Office, 1964); Trask, *National Nightmare*; Bugliosi, *Four Days in November*; and Howard P. Willens, *History Will Prove Us Right* (New York: Overlook Press, 2013).

Additional information came from an interview with Warren Commission Associate Counsel Howard P. Willens conducted by the author on November 10, 2015.

Paul Mandel, "End to Nagging Rumors," *LIFE*, December 6, 1963.

Secret Service chief James Rowley memo to *LIFE* Washington bureau chief Henry Suydam comes from the Zapruder film files in Time Inc. Archives.

Information about Secret Service efforts in conjunction with the CIA and NPIC to enlarge and print frames from the film and the apparently subsequent analysis of it several weeks later was pieced together from a number of sources, including previously cited Trask, *National Nightmare*; CIA Document 450 and related records on file in the JFK Assassination Records Collection at NARA; and a brief mention of the NPIC analysis in David Robarge, *John McCone as Director of Central Intelligence 1961–1965* (Washington, DC: Center for the Study of Intelligence, CIA, 2005). For this section, I am indebted to Max Holland and Paul Hoch, who provided me with documentation and a careful, prudent review of my text.

Secret Service chief James Rowley's letter to *LIFE*'s Washington bureau chief Henry Suydam came from the Time Inc. Archives.

Information about the analysis of the Zapruder film by the Warren Commission comes primarily from Lyndal Shaneyfelt's testimony in *Hearings*, vol. 5, pp. 138–142, and from Trask, *National Nightmare*.

Receipt for the loan of the original Bell and Howell camera to Robert Barrett of the FBI comes from Zapruder family papers.

Details and excerpts of Abraham Zapruder's testimony comes from previously cited *Hearings*, vol. 7, pp. 569–571.

Correspondence and memos regarding the sale of the film to *LIFE* magazine come from legal files at Passman & Jones.

Letters to and from William Manchester and from the office of Jacqueline Kennedy come from Zapruder family papers. Notes from William Manchester's interview with Abraham Zapruder come from previously cited William Manchester Papers at Wesleyan University.

Quotes come from Richard Stolley telephone interview with Lillian Zapruder, July 1973 (Richard B. Stolley Collection, Sixth Floor Museum at Dealey Plaza).

Chapter 6: Mounting Pressure

As previously cited, the history of the film at *LIFE*, including direct quotations from memos, letters, internal documents, and other correspondence comes from the Zapruder film files in the Time Inc. Archives. Materials from Time Inc. and *LIFE* are used with permission.

Information about the three versions of the Zapruder film images comes from versions of "The Warren Report: How the Commission Pieced Together the Evidence," *LIFE*, October 2, 1964; and Vincent J. Salandria, "A Philadelphia Lawyer Analyzes the Shots, Trajectories, and Wounds," *Liberation*, January 1965, pp. 13–19.

Letters to *LIFE* are from Time Inc. Archives. Material is used with permission of Time Inc.

Richard Trask, *National Nightmare*, pp. 13, 178.

Harold Weisberg, *Whitewash: The Report on the Warren Report* (New York: Dell, 1965).

Art Simon provides an exceptionally clear and helpful overview of what he calls the "assassination debates" in the introduction to *Dangerous Knowledge: The JFK Assassination in Art and Film* (Philadelphia: Temple University Press, 2013) and a detailed and insightful chapter on the Zapruder film.

The account of Mark Lane's interview with Abraham Zapruder came from the previously cited interview with Lillian Rogers.

For critical analysis of *Blow-Up*, I consulted relevant sections in Art Simon, *Dangerous Knowledge*; David M. Lubin, *Shooting Kennedy: JFK and the Culture of Images* (Berkeley and Los Angeles: University of California Press, 2003); and Øyvind Vågnes, *Zaprudered: The Kennedy Assassination Film in Visual Culture* (Austin, TX: University of Texas Press, 2013).

Loudon Wainwright, "Editorial," *LIFE*, October 7, 1967.

Calvin Trillin, "The Buffs," *New Yorker*, June 10, 1967.

"A Matter of Reasonable Doubt," *LIFE*, November 25, 1966.

Information and quotations from Josiah Thompson about his work on "A Matter of Reasonable Doubt" and his copying of the Zapruder film came from Trask, *National Nightmare*, especially from the notes, which include a lengthy chronology written by Thompson himself; Josiah Thompson interview conducted by Bob Porter on November 21, 1998 (Oral History Collection, Sixth Floor Museum at Dealey Plaza); and his testimony before the ARRB on April 2, 1997.

"Marvin Scott Interviews Abraham Zapruder, 1966" (Marvin Scott Collection, Sixth Floor Museum at Dealey Plaza); and Marvin Scott, "Zapruder Film Frame by Frame: Listen to Him Narrate the Kennedy Assassination," *PIX11*, WPIX New York, pix11.com/2013/11/18, posted November 18, 2013.

Details about CBS and *LIFE* negotiations about the use of the Zapruder film come from internal records in the Zapruder film file in the Time Inc. Archives.

Unpublished statement from Wesley Liebeler about the Zapruder film comes from the Zapruder film file in the Time Inc. Archives. Useful additional information comes from Richard Levine, "Film of Kennedy Torn, Life says," *Baltimore Sun*, December 22, 1966.

Information and quotes come from Thompson, *Six Seconds in Dallas*; Josiah Thompson, "The Crossfire that Killed President Kennedy," *Saturday Evening Post*, December 2, 1967; and "A New Assassination Theory," *Newsweek*, November 27, 1967. Background information about the interaction between Thompson and *LIFE* executives came primarily from records from Time Inc. v. Bernard Geis Associates, 293 F. Supp. 130 (S.D.N.Y. 1968), and from "Life Sues to Halt Book on Kennedy; Magazine Charges Misuse of Its Assassination Film Drawings Based on Film Called Public," *New York Times*, December 9, 1967.

A CBS News Inquiry: The Warren Report, CBS, June 27–30, 1967. (The broadcast can be seen at http://jfk-archives.blogspot.com/2011/05/cbs-news-inquiry -warren-report.html.)

Chapter 7: Court Cases and Bootlegs

As previously cited, the history of the film at *LIFE*, including direct quotations from memos, letters, internal documents, and other correspondence comes from the Zapruder film files in the Time Inc. Archives. Materials from Time Inc. and *LIFE* are used with permission.

Quotations are from Bernard Geis's preface in previously cited Thompson, *Six Seconds in Dallas*.

Background information and quotations come from previously cited Josiah Thompson interview in the Oral History Collection, Sixth Floor Museum at Dealey Plaza, and testimony before the ARRB. Additional quotes are from a transcript of Thompson's interview on *The Mike Douglas Show* (December 14, 1967).

Background on Moses Weitzman's history with the Zapruder film and quotations come from Weitzman's testimony before the ARRB, April 2, 1997.

Information about the judgment in Time Inc. v. Bernard Geis Associates comes from previously cited court case, and from "Time Inc. Loses Suit on 'Dallas' Photos," *New York Times*, October 1, 1968.

Information about Jim Garrison and the Clay Shaw trial came from James Kirkwood, *American Grotesque: An Account of the Clay Shaw–Jim Garrison Affair in the City of New Orleans* (New York: Simon and Schuster, 1970); internal documents from Time Inc. Archives; contemporaneous newspaper accounts, including "Garrison Subpoenas Film of Kennedy Assassination," *New York Times*, February 5, 1969; and the extensive online records from the trial, including testimonies from the Grand Jury hearings and the trial itself, which can be found online.

Mark Lane, "Editorial: The Story of Two Subpoenas," *Midlothian Mirror*, April 25, 1968.

Mark Lane, *Rush to Judgment* (London: Bodley Head, 1966).

Information about Luis Alvarez and his research into the assassination came from Trask, *National Nightmare*, and from correspondence with Paul Hoch, who added a great deal to my understanding of Alvarez's experiments. Additional sources include Luis W. Alvarez, "A Physicist Examines the Kennedy Assassination Film," *American Journal of Physics*, vol. 44, no. 9 (September 1976), pp. 813–827.

Letter and summons for Abraham Zapruder to appear at the Clay Shaw trial comes from Zapruder family papers. Information about the trial comes primarily from previously cited *American Grotesque* and from contemporaneous accounts, including "Zapruder Put on Stand, New Trial Phase Begins," *New Orleans States-Item*, February 13, 1969; "Shaw Trial Sees the Death of

JFK," *New York Post*, February 14, 1969; "Shaw Trial Jury Shown Film of Kennedy Murder," *Times-Picayune*, February 14, 1969; and Martin Waldron, "Zapruder Film of Kennedy Shown at Shaw Trial," *New York Times*, February 14, 1969.

Abraham Zapruder's testimony in The State of Louisiana v. Clay Shaw can be found online.

Greg Olds, "Editorial: The Zapruder Film," *Texas Observer*, December 19, 1969. Two contemporaneous accounts of Greg Olds's bootleg copies of the Zapruder film in circulation include "Texan Pushes Cause: Bootleg Film of JFK Slaying Offered," *Washington Evening Star*, November 29, 1969, and "Bootleg Film of Kennedy Killing Turns Up in Texas," *Dallas Times Herald*, December 19, 1969.

Extensive records in the Time Inc. Archives include correspondence with Greg Olds, Abraham Zapruder, and others about this issue and detailed efforts to trace the source of the bootleg copies. They include a second article by Greg Olds on the subject, titled "A Report," *Texas Observer*, December 19, 1969, and a letter he wrote to those who requested copies of the film after his decision not to continue distributing it.

Information and quotations about Abraham Zapruder's illness came from previously cited interviews with Marjorie Zapruder and Myrna Ries.

"A Kennedy Film Canceled in Paris; Director Says United Artists Blocked Sept. 17 Premiere," *New York Times*, September 6, 1969.

Dick Hitt, "Historic Film on the Market?" *Dallas Times Herald*, April 9, 1970.

Chapter 8: *LIFE*'s Dilemma

Recollections about Abraham Zapruder and his funeral came from the author's father and from previously cited Marjorie Zapruder, Myrna Ries, and Lillian Rogers interviews.

"Abraham Zapruder Dies; Filmed Kennedy Death: Footage of Tragedy in Dallas Had Role in Shaw Trial and Warren Commission Report," *New York Times*, August 31, 1970; "A. Zapruder Dies," *Dallas Morning News*, August 31, 1970.

Interview with Robert Groden conducted by the author on November 1 and 2, 2013. Additional information came from Trask, *National Nightmare*; F. Peter Model and Robert J. Groden, *JFK: The Case for Conspiracy* (New York: Manor Books, 1976); Robert Groden interview conducted by Bob Porter on June 20,

1994 (Oral History Collection, Sixth Floor Museum at Dealey Plaza); and his deposition before the ARRB on July 2, 1996, which can be found online.

Moses Weitzman quotes come from his testimony before the ARRB, April 2, 1997.

Information about the potential sale of the original Zapruder film and subsequent debate about disposition of it comes from the Zapruder film files in the Time Inc. Archives.

Correspondence with the Committee to Investigate Assassinations and communication with Robert Richter regarding possible documentary film comes from the Zapruder film files in the Time Inc. Archives.

Negotiations with Zapruder family over disposition of the film comes from the Zapruder film files in the Time Inc. Archives, and from Bob Trien interview conducted by the author on May 8, 2011.

John Kifner, "Critics of Warren Report Meet to Ask New Study," *New York Times*, February 3, 1975.

The screening of the Zapruder film on *Good Night America* is available on YouTube. Contemporaneous articles about it include John J. O'Connor, "TV: Two Programs Exploit Subjects; Hope Diamond Study Remains Tall Tale, Dallas Assassination Viewed by Rivera," *New York Times*, March 27, 1975; and Earl Golz, "Assassination Film to Air," *Dallas Morning News*, March 5, 1975.

Details regarding the return of the Zapruder film to the Zapruder family from *LIFE* and subsequent storage at the Manufacturers Hanover Trust Company come from Zapruder family papers and Bob Trien interview with the author.

Chapter 9: *The Eternal Frame* and the Endless Debates

Information about CBS's first authorized use of the film, the Itek analysis, and Luis Alvarez's theory come from Itek Corporation, *John F. Kennedy Assassination Film Analysis, Conducted by Itek Corporation, May 2, 1976*; Trask, *National Nightmare*, pp. 224–232; and from articles and information provided to the author by Paul Hoch.

"The American Assassins," CBS Reports Inquiry, November 26, 1975.

"Film Analysis Backs Warren Report," *New York Times*, November 26, 1975.

To learn about *The Eternal Frame*, I watched the film (provided to me by Doug Hall and Chip Lord) and I read the relevant portions of previously cited Art Simon, *Dangerous Knowledge*; David Lubin, *Shooting Kennedy*; and Øyvind

Vågnes, *Zaprudered*. Other materials include "The Eternal Frame," *National Lampoon*, January 1976; "Glenn Phillips Interviews Doug Hall and Chip Lord About *The Eternal Frame*," in *California Video: Artists and Histories*, exhibition catalog, J. Paul Getty Museum, Los Angeles, 2007; and e-mail correspondence with Chip Lord and Doug Hall. There is also a wealth of materials on Doug Hall's website (http://www.doughallstudio.com), including essays, articles, and images from *The Eternal Frame*.

Information about the Assassination Information Bureau and the showings of the film around the country come primarily from David R. Wrone, *The Zapruder Film: Reframing JFK's Assassination* (Lawrence, KS: University Press of Kansas, 2003).

Details about the House Select Committee came from relevant sections of Trask, *National Nightmare*; from *Report of the Select Committee on Assassinations of the U.S. House of Representatives* (Washington, DC: US Government Printing Office, 1979); and from the National Academy of Sciences, *Report of the Committee on Ballistic Acoustics* (Washington, DC: National Academy Press, 1982).

Chapter 10: The Floodgates Open

Recollections about Henry Zapruder and the early years of managing the Zapruder film came from Anita Dove interview conducted by the author on May 17, 2011.

Information and quotes from letters, legal records, and license agreements concerning the Zapruder film come from LMH legal files.

Information regarding Chip Selby and Harold Weisberg's lawsuit comes primarily from "Gerard A. Selby and Harold Weisberg (Plaintiffs) v. Henry G. Zapruder and the LMH Company (Defendants), Complaint for Preliminary and Permanent Injunctive Relief and for Declaratory Judgment," United States District Court for the District of Columbia, October 20, 1988. Other sources include relevant section in Wrone, *The Zapruder Film*, and "2 Sue over Film Rights on Kennedy Slaying," *New York Times*, October 26, 1988.

Jerry Urban, "Price Tag on JFK Death Film: Up to $30,000 a Client," *Houston Chronicle*, September 4, 1988.

Additional information about the resolution of the Selby and Weisberg lawsuit came from Jamie Silverberg interview conducted by the author on April 16, 2013.

Chapter 11: *JFK*: The Movie and the Assassination Records Act

As previously cited, information and quotes from letters, legal records, and license agreements concerning the Zapruder film come from LMH legal files.

Information about Oliver Stone's film *JFK* comes from a wide variety of sources, including relevant sections in Trask, *National Nightmare*; Simon, *Dangerous Knowledge*; and Vågnes, *Zaprudered*; and from Oliver Stone and Zachary Sklar, *JFK: The Book of the Film* (Montclair, NJ: Applause Theatre & Cinema Books, 1992).

Material also came from voluminous contemporaneous news articles and reviews, including George Lardner Jr., "On the Set: Dallas in Wonderland—How Oliver Stone's Version of the Kennedy Assassination Exploits the Edge of Paranoia," *Washington Post*, May 19, 1991; Oliver Stone, "Stone's 'JFK' a Higher Truth? The Post, George Lardner and My Version of the JFK Assassination," *Washington Post*, June 2, 1991; "Who Is Rewriting History?" *New York Times*, December 20, 1991; Phil McCombs, "Oliver Stone, Returning the Fire: In Defending His 'JFK' Conspiracy Film, the Director Reveals His Rage and Reasoning," *Washington Post*, December 21, 1991; and "What Does Oliver Stone Owe History?" *Newsweek*, December 23, 1991.

I also read the transcript of a panel discussion with Oliver Stone, Norman Mailer, Edward J. Epstein, and Nora Ephron titled *Hollywood and History: The Debate over* JFK, sponsored by the Nation Institute and the Center for American Culture Studies at Columbia University, March 3, 1992. The transcript and audio can be accessed online at http://www.pbs.org/wgbh/pages/frontline/shows/oswald/conspiracy/jfkpanel1.html.

"The Boyfriend," *Seinfeld*, February 12, 1992.

Jerry Seinfeld's comment about his speech and additional information about the episode came from the extras section for the episode in the *Seinfeld* Season 3 DVD.

Background information from relevant section of Vågnes, *Zaprudered*.

General information about the JFK Assassination Records Collection Act came from David Marwell interview conducted by the author on May 6, 2011; Judge John Tunheim interview conducted by the author on March 31, 2016; and the extensive records about the JFK Act online. Additional information came from ARRB, *Final Report of the Assassination Records Review Board* (Washington, DC: September 1998), and from Trask, *National Nightmare*.

Information about the consequences of the JFK Act for the taking of the Zapruder film came from previously cited interviews conducted by the author with Jamie Silverberg and Anita Dove, and from an interview with Roger Pies conducted by the author in 2011.

My understanding of the Takings Clause of the Fifth Amendment to the Constitution comes from "The Takings Clause," entry in the online version of *The Heritage Guide to the Constitution* at Heritage.org, and from previously cited interviews with Jamie Silverberg, Roger Pies, David Marwell, and Judge John Tunheim.

Information and quotations come from extensive correspondence between Jamie Silverberg on behalf of LMH and the Justice Department and NARA in LMH legal files. Copies of these letters are on file in the JFK Assassination Records Collection at NARA.

Chapter 12: To Take or Not to Take the Film

Information about the ARRB comes from previously cited ARRB *Report*; from correspondence between LMH and the ARRB, Justice Department, and NARA, on file in the JFK Assassination Records Collection at NARA; from internal memos and other documents in LMH legal files; and from previously cited interviews with Jamie Silverberg, David Marwell, and Judge John Tunheim.

Details about appraisals of the Zapruder film come from LMH legal files.

Understanding of the McCrone reproduction of the film came from LMH correspondence with McCrone Associates in LMH legal files, and from a phone interview with Joseph Barabe conducted by the author on June 21, 2011.

The April 2, 1997, transcript of the "Hearing on the Status and Disposition of the 'Zapruder Film'" is readily available online and on file in the JFK Assassination Records Collection at NARA. In the ARRB records, there is also a lengthy e-mail from David Lifton on the subject.

Additional information and insights came from Art Simon interview conducted by the author on September 19, 2015.

Phone conversation with David Marwell conducted by the author on March 30, 2016, and previously cited interview with Judge John Tunheim and subsequent e-mail correspondence. Copies of records from Tunheim's file on the Zapruder film can be found in the JFK Assassination Records Collection at NARA.

ARRB, "Statement of Policy and Intent with Regard to the Zapruder film," April 24, 1997.

George Lardner Jr., "Zapruder Film of JFK Assassination Is Public Record, Review Board Decides," *Washington Post*, April 25, 1997.

Chapter 13: A Final Firestorm

For obvious reasons, there are not indisputably reliable records when it comes to arguing for or against the alterationist theory of the Zapruder film. I did not attempt to engage in a full debate on this question as it was far outside the scope of my work or my personal interest. My main intent was to introduce readers to the broad outlines of the alterationist theory and to point out where the theory calls into question Abraham Zapruder's credibility. I considered a great many sources in order to untangle this; they include, most importantly, previously cited Zavada, *Analysis of Selected*, which can be found online (http://www.jfk-info.com/zreport.htm) and which provides an exceptionally thorough and clear review of all documentation relating to the film's authenticity, interviews to establish the chain of possession, and a careful physical examination of the original and first-day copies.

My main source for information on Douglas Horne's presentation of the alterationist theory is his article "The Two NPIC Zapruder Film Events: Signposts Pointing to the Film's Alteration," which can easily be found online; and a lengthy video titled *The Zapruder Film Mystery: Doug Horne interviews legendary NPIC photo interpreter Dino Brugioni*, which can be found on YouTube. Dino Brugioni quotes come from the above video on YouTube. Horne's quote questioning the authenticity of Abraham Zapruder's affidavits came from an interview conducted by Dick Russell in *On the Trail of the JFK Assassins: A Groundbreaking Look at America's Most Infamous Conspiracy* (New York: Skyhorse Publishing, 2008) and online at http://www.whokilledjfk.net/doug_horne.htm.

Homer McMahon's quote about having "wet brain" came from his interview with the ARRB on July 14, 1997. The interview is not available online at NARA, but a transcript of it was produced by Horne and is available online. However, Horne includes his opinions and interpretations as facts throughout in "Transcriber's Notes," which compromises its usefulness as an objective source. I've used the quote from a transcript produced and posted by William Kelly, which differs slightly from Horne's (http://educationforum.ipbhost.com/index.php?showtopic=15387).

In addition, I consulted the literature supporting the film's authenticity, most of which can be accessed online. This includes a presentation Josiah Thompson gave in Dallas on November 20, 1998, titled "Why the Zapruder Film is Authentic" (http://www.jfklancer.com/thompZ.html); Josiah Thompson, "Proof that the Zapruder Film Is Authentic" (http://home.earthlink.net/~joejd/jfk/zaphoax/thompson-proof.html); Josiah Thompson, "Bedrock Evidence in the Kennedy Assassination" (https://www.maryferrell.org/pages/Essay_-_Bedrock_Evidence_in_the_Kennedy_Assassination.html); and Thompson's letter "Goodbye to Fetzer and All That" (http://www.kenrahn.com/Marsh/Jfk-conspiracy/Thompson.txt). I also read Clint Bradford, "Fetzer's New Book...His Third Miserable Attempt at Scholarly Work" (http://www.jfk-info.com/fetzerfails3.htm), and Martin Shackelford, "A Brief Overview of the Zapruder Film Alteration Argument," December 1998 (http://www.jfk-info.com/martin2.htm).

Horne's quote about Abraham Zapruder having been paid off in exchange for his silence comes from previously cited Russell, *On the Trail of the JFK Assassins.*

Passages cited from Don DeLillo, *Underworld* (New York: Scribner, 1997), pp. 487–489 and 494–496.

Additional information came from *Conversations with Don DeLillo,* edited by Thomas DePietro (Jackson, MS: University Press of Mississippi, 2005), and relevant sections of Vågnes, *Zaprudered.*

Adam Begley, "Don DeLillo, The Art of Fiction No. 135," *Paris Review,* fall 1993.

Quotations come from Don DeLillo interview conducted by the author on September 18, 2015.

Valuations for the Zapruder film by Philip Moore at J. & W. Seligman and C. Cameron Macauley and Ernest D. Rose came from LMH legal files.

Information about proposals and negotiations with the Justice Department, the structure of the arbitration hearing and the final agreement, and the approach to resolving the issues came from extensive Zapruder film legal records kept by the law firm of Skadden, Arps, Slate, Meagher, & Flom (hereafter Skadden Arps), and from additional documents provided by Jamie Silverberg.

Further facts and details came from Dana Freyer interview conducted by the author on June 26, 2011; Bob Bennett interview conducted by the author on

February 11, 2016; and Rich Brusca interview conducted by the author on February 17, 2016. Additional information came from the relevant section of Robert S. Bennett, *In the Ring: Trials of a Washington Lawyer* (New York: Crown, 2008).

George Lardner Jr., "Haggling over History; Zapruders, U.S. Far Apart on Price of Kennedy Film," *Washington Post*, June 13, 1998.

Other articles not cited include "Opinion: The Zapruder Film," *New York Times*, June 23, 1998, and Frank Rich, "Journal; From Here to Zapruder," *New York Times*, July 4, 1998.

Information about Mark Zaid's lawsuit regarding the copyright to the Zapruder film can be found at www.jfk-info.com/zaid-1.htm.

Henry Zapruder's letter to the Zapruder family came from Zapruder family papers.

Information about the statute of limitations on seeking just compensation for the Zapruder film taking came from phone conversations and e-mail correspondence with Jamie Silverberg.

Information about considerations for the structure of the arbitration hearing came from previously cited Roger Pies interview conducted by the author.

Image of an Assassination: A New Look at the Zapruder Film, directed by H. D. Motyl (Orlando Park, IL: MPI Video, 1998).

Background information about MPI and the making of *Image of an Assassination* came from LMH legal records and from previously cited interview with Jamie Silverberg, in addition to follow-up e-mails and phone conversations.

The hundreds of newspaper articles and reviews of the film were gathered and preserved in the Zapruder film legal files at Skadden Arps.

Kathryne Kirkpatrick, "Viewing JKF [*sic*] Killing Would Be Revolting," Letter to the Editor, *Tennessean*, July 16, 1998; and Robert T. Grammer, "Video Is Interesting for History Buffs," Letter to the Editor, *Tennessean*, July 17, 1998.

"Film of Kennedy Not Entertaining," *Jena Times*, July 22, 1998.

Information and quotes from transcript of *The NewsHour with Jim Lehrer*, July 14, 1998.

Chapter 14: Arbitration and Resolution

Information and quotes from the Zapruder film arbitration hearing come from pre-hearing briefs provided by LMH and the Justice Department; response briefs; affidavits from LMH witnesses Beth Gates Warren, Jerry Patterson,

Steve Johnson, Sylvia Leonard Wolf, Joseph Barabe, and Professor William Landes, and from Justice Department witnesses John Staszyn and C. Cameron Macauley; rebuttal affidavits; the transcript of the arbitration hearing; and the post-hearing briefs provided by LMH and by the government. All of these documents were made available to me through the Zapruder film legal records at Skadden Arps.

Further information comes from previously cited interviews with Dana Freyer, Rich Brusca, Bob Bennett, and Judge John Tunheim, and from Bennett, *In the Ring*. Additional help understanding the experts' approach to valuing the Zapruder film came from e-mail correspondence with Beth Gates Warren.

"Zapruder Film: Attempt to Profit from Tragedy Is Sad and Disturbing," *Dallas Morning News*, July 14, 1999.

Henry Zapruder, "Letter to the Editor," *Dallas Morning News*, July 20, 1999.

Kenneth Feinberg, Arlin Adams, and Walter Dellinger, *In the Matter of the Zapruder Film* (Washington, DC: Department of Justice, 1999).

Information and quotes come from Ken Feinberg interview conducted by the author on February 16, 2016, and Walter Dellinger interview conducted by the author on May 11, 2016.

Information about media response comes from numerous articles about the arbitration decision, including the following: James Vicini, "US to Pay $16 Million for Kennedy Shooting Film," Reuters, August 3, 1999; Rita Delfiner, "Zapruder Heirs to Reel In $16M for JFK-Slay Film," *New York Post*, August 4, 1999; Deb Riechmann, "$16 Million for Film of JFK's Death: Arbitrators Set Price for Zapruder Footage," *San Francisco Chronicle*, August 4, 1999; David Jackson, "Zapruders to Be Paid $16 Million for Film," *Dallas Morning News*, August 4, 1999; David Johnston, "Zapruder Heirs Get $16 Million For Dallas Film," *New York Times*, August 4, 1999; Will Woodward and George Lardner Jr., "Zapruder Film Nets $16 Million," *Washington Post*, August 4, 1999; Eric Lichtblau, "Film of JFK Assassination Brings Family $16 Million," *Los Angeles Times*, August 4, 1999; Ellen Joan Pollock, "Film of JFK's Assassination Gets Price Tag of $16 Million," *Wall Street Journal*, August 4, 1999; James Rosen, "$16 Million for Zapruder Film," *Sacramento Bee*, August 4, 1999; "Zapruder Film Ruling," *Sacramento Bee*, August 4, 1999; Tom Squitieri, "Zapruders Get $16M for JFK film," *USA Today*, August 4, 1999; and Mary Panzer, "What Price History?" *Art in America*, October 1999, pp. 67–71.

"Opinion: Pricing the Past," *New York Times*, August 5, 1999.

Epilogue: Public and Private Legacy

Mark Wrolstad, "Zapruders Donate JFK Film, Rights," *Dallas Morning News*, January 26, 2000.

Max Holland and Johann Rush, "J.F.K.'s Death, Re-Framed," *New York Times*, November 22, 2007; and Max Holland, "The Truth Behind JFK's Assassination," *Newsweek*, November 20, 2014.

Tom Mullin, "Livin' and Dyin' in Zapruderville: A Code of Representation, Reality and Its Exhaustion," *Cineaction*, no. 38, 1995, pp. 12–15.

John Beck, "Zapruder, Warhol, and the Accident of Images," in *American Visual Cultures*, edited by David Holloway and John Beck (London: Continuum, 2005), pp. 183–189.

Tom Sutcliff, "Climbing the Zapruder Curve," *Dox: Documentary Film Quarterly*, no. 1, spring 1994.

Richard B. Woodward, "ART; The 40th Anniversary of a 26-Second Reel," *New York Times*, November 16, 2003.

Another article worth mentioning but not cited in Epilogue is J. G. Ballard, "The Film of Kennedy's Assassination Is the Sistine Chapel of Our Era," interview by William Feaver on March 24, 1999, *Art Newspaper*, July–August 1999, pp. 24–25, online at www.jgballard.ca/media/1999_art_newspaper.html.

Karen F. Gracy, "Film as Art, Film as Evidence: Mediating the Value of the Zapruder Film," unpublished manuscript provided by author; Sam Kula, *Appraising Moving Images: Assessing the Archival and Monetary Value of Film and Video Records* (Lanham, MD: Scarecrow, 2002).

Errol Morris's film *The Umbrella Man* (November 22, 2011) is available on YouTube at https://www.youtube.com/watch?v=iuoZWb9gqv0. In addition, I conducted a phone interview with Errol Morris on April 13, 2011, in which he shared insightful and thoughtful observations about the Zapruder film.

Audio of the session about the Zapruder film at the 2013 Telluride Film Festival with Mark Danner, Don DeLillo, and Errol Morris can be found on Mark Danner's website at http://www.markdanner.com/orations/telluride-film-festival-2013-danner-delillo-and-morris-on-the-kennedy-assassination.

Articles about the Zapruder film on the occasion of the fiftieth anniversary of the JFK assassination include: Ron Rosenbaum, "What Does the Zapruder Film Really Tell Us? Documentary Filmmaker Errol Morris Deconstructs the Most Famous 26 Seconds in Film History," *Smithsonian*, October 2013; George Packer, "Leaving Dealey Plaza," *New Yorker*, October 14, 2013;

Steve Rose, "Abraham Zapruder: The Man behind History's Most Infamous Home Movie," *Guardian*, November 14, 2013; A. O. Scott, "Footage of Death Plays On in Memory: Abraham Zapruder and the Evolution of Film," *New York Times*, November 15, 2013; Owen Gleiberman, "JFK: What the Zapruder Film Really Means," *Entertainment Weekly*, EW.com, November 22, 2013; and Alex Pasternack, "The Other Shooter: The Saddest and Most Expensive 26 Seconds of Amateur Film Ever Made," *Motherboard*, November 23, 2012.

Don DeLillo, *Underworld*, p. 496.

READING GROUP GUIDE

Discussion Questions

1. How is this book on the JFK assassination and the Zapruder film different from others on the same subjects?

2. Did you know that the Zapruder film was a home movie and not the work of a professional news reporter? Did the fact that it was taken by an amateur private citizen affect how you thought about it?

3. "Your grandfather should have been famous for who he was, for being a good person and a funny, wonderful man, and not for the film." What do you think the author's mother means by this comment? Can you think of other individuals who have been thrust into the public eye who might have felt a disconnect between their "real" selves and the public perception of them?

4. Before his father ever filmed the JFK assassination, Henry Zapruder wrote to President Kennedy asking what he could do to be of service: "I deeply sense the crises confronting this Nation; I want to devote my energy and talent toward meeting these crises." What does the tone of this letter suggest about

the political climate of the early 1960s? How does it compare to the present day? How do you think the Zapruder family's affection and political support for the Kennedys shaped their later responsibility for the film?

5. How did Abraham Zapruder's status as an immigrant affect his experience of the JFK assassination and how he handled the film?

6. After learning how Abraham Zapruder struggled to reconcile the moral dilemma of selling the film, how do you think you might have behaved under those same circumstances? Are the considerations that Abraham weighed when making his decision a product of the time he lived in, or do they pertain to basic human values?

7. How did the private ownership of the film by *LIFE* magazine from 1963–75 affect the public perception of the JFK assassination and the conspiracy theories in particular?

8. "It is true that Abe Zapruder's intersection with history is laced with coincidence and chance." Can you think of any other momentous historical events that were brought about largely through coincidence or chance?

9. The author recalled that her father said of seeking just compensation for the eminent-domain taking of the Zapruder film: "I don't feel that our family is in a position to make an $18 million donation to the federal government." Did this quote make you see the Zapruder family's situation in a new light?

10. The Zapruder film is often considered the first instance of "citizen journalism." Can you think of other visual images or events captured on film by amateurs that became part of American memory and culture? If so, are they like the Zapruder film or different from it? How?

11. How did the controversies and dilemmas of the Zapruder film shape the way we handle and think about similar images? How have changes in culture, technology, and social norms influenced these debates?

12. Much of the early debate surrounding the film pertained to the graphic violence of the images—whether the public should be shielded from seeing a death caught on film, and whether showing the footage was respectful to the Kennedy family. Do you think *LIFE* magazine was right to withhold the images the way they did? How did that attitude reflect the times? Certainly, our approach to violence has changed. Have we gone too far? What is to be gained by witnessing extreme violence and does it help or hurt our society?

13. The Zapruder film—captured with state-of-the-art 1960s technology—was a central piece of evidence in the murder of President Kennedy that also raised questions about the reliability of visual images, privacy, and ownership of information. More and more, we rely on visual records from a variety of sources—from bystanders with smartphones to drones—to capture and record information. How might the controversies raised by the Zapruder film serve as a precedent for thinking about similar issues in our own time?

14. Throughout the book, the author fuses her personal family story with the public historical record of her grandfather's film. How did having this dual perspective affect your understanding of the history and significance of the Zapruder film?

15. As the author writes: "What is the compelling lure that makes the assassination researchers, the film, art, and cultural historians, the writers and journalists, the academics and students

and hobbyists and Kennedy buffs return to it as a touchstone time and again?"

16. The author writes that part of the Zapruder film's public legacy is that "it is the most private and the most public of records... It lies in the arc of the film itself, the fall from grace, the unforgiving inevitability of it... He is alive and then he is dead... it holds in its terrible twenty-six seconds a painful, fundamental human truth." Do you agree?

A Conversation with Alexandra Zapruder

Twenty-Six Seconds is quite different from your previous book, *Salvaged Pages*, which was a collection of young writers' diaries from the Holocaust. How was your researching and writing experience different? Despite their different subject matter, did you find any common threads running through them?

This is a big question and there are many parts to the answer. The research for *Salvaged Pages* was largely informed by the fact that it was the 1990s, before the creation of Google, which meant that the work of gathering the diaries from survivors and archives was time-consuming, laborious, and difficult. I was working with documents in multiple languages, in a subject matter that is vast and complex, and that can be emotionally overwhelming. Not only that but I was very young. It was a project that stretched my abilities in every way and ended up being a defining experience for me as a writer and a person. Among many other things, I learned that the long, confusing, even muddled period of absorbing new information and struggling to formulate original ideas is not necessarily a reflection of fatal flaws in the project (or the writer) but is an integral part of the creative and intellectual process.

The research for *Twenty-Six Seconds* was very different. Although the JFK assassination is an enormous topic, like the Holocaust, and it was certainly daunting to get my bearings in it, I was older and approached the work with more experience and confidence. Most research now is conducted online, which makes things faster and easier but also more dangerous, as it's all too easy to be led astray into unreliable sources without realizing it—a fact that is equally true of research into the JFK assassination and the Holocaust.

But the biggest difference—beyond the fact that *Salvaged Pages* is composed of other people's writings whereas *Twenty-Six Seconds* is entirely my own—is one of role and voice. For *Salvaged Pages*, I wanted to provide a framework that would allow the reader to experience the extraordinary value and meaning of the diaries without my getting in the way. In the case of *Twenty-Six Seconds*, there was no way to tell the story of the Zapruder film without putting myself and my family in the middle of it. I fought this for some time, wanting to take the emotionally safer path of writing a work of narrative nonfiction about the Zapruder film—something closer to the tone and style of *Salvaged Pages*. But eventually it became clear that this would not work. I had to delve into my own family's past, and my own memories, in order to tell the story in a voice that was not only truthful and authentic but also uniquely my own. This was a difficult shift and required dealing with my family's history of reticence and even silence around the Zapruder film. But in the end, of course, I think the book is better for it.

I do think there is one important similarity between the two books. In the introduction to *Salvaged Pages*, I wrote about Anne Frank's iconic *Diary of a Young Girl* and how it was more often viewed as a symbol of lost lives than mined as a serious primary source of the Holocaust. I challenged this idea and reframed the diaries in my book as historical and literary records, unpacking them for what they could contribute to an understanding of everything from the nuances of daily life during the Holocaust to the deepest existential questions of human suffering. Likewise, the Zapruder film is an iconic representation of the Kennedy assassination. As such, its poignant history and inherent contradictions can be lost in the endless replaying of it, which reduces it to a symbolic, even clichéd set of images. As in the case of Anne Frank's *Diary*, what is required is to slow down, to look again at what we think we know, to reconsider the touchstones of our history. I think when we look skeptically at our symbols, we find that there is nearly always a story, or a richer, more provocative set of ideas, beneath the surface. That is the story I wanted to tell in *Twenty-Six Seconds*.

You say, "As much as I feel the pathos of that time, Kennedy's death was not my personal loss and the Zapruder film was not my wound." Can you discuss this quote further?

When I see the Zapruder film or any of the images and footage from that time, or read the accounts of the period, I feel acutely how heartbreaking the moment must have been. I feel deeply for Jack Kennedy's widow and children, for those who loved him, and for the many millions around the nation—including my own family—who mourned him so personally. But I was not alive at the time. I did not live in that moment, and John Kennedy was never my president. So, I suppose I just mean that it is somewhat removed from my own personal experience. Likewise, the film—which was such a painful reminder of that loss and those disappointed hopes for my grandfather, my father, and my family—never had that direct resonance for me. It was more abstract.

A much more direct analogy for me would be images of watching the Twin Towers fall on 9/11. I was at home in my apartment in Washington, DC, when that event occurred, and I experienced it unfolding in real time together with the rest of the nation. Like everyone else who was alive at the time, when I see that footage again now, I remember where I was, what it felt like, and the fears and implications of the moment. This is not the case for me with the Zapruder film—despite its personal connection to my family—though it is for those who experienced the assassination, the film, and the aftermath firsthand: my mother and my aunt, and my father, my uncle, and my grandparents.

How did you balance the telling of an intimate family story with recounting a public historical account? Was it a difficult line to walk?

For me, writing about historical events is much easier than telling a private or intimate family story. There is something uniquely risky about writing about one's family—as a writer, you are speaking for yourself but also imposing your own narrative and interpretation on those you love who may or may not agree. You have to be honest and authentic, but doing so might potentially harm the memory or feelings of those who mean the most to you.

In this case, I felt that the personal element of the story was justified because it was integral to a full understanding of the public story of the life of the Zapruder film. Our family's life and that of the film were intertwined in such complex ways that it was essentially impossible to understand the film without having that window into who my grandfather was, the decisions he made and the deal he struck with *LIFE* magazine, the reverberating consequences of the agreement, the questions my father faced when the film was returned to our family in 1975, and the legal issues around ownership of the film in the 1990s. I suppose it was less about balance than it was about putting two stories that had been kept apart for many decades together in order to create a complete and coherent narrative for the first time.

In one way, it was difficult because it involved deconstructing established ideas and then reconstructing them. As a Zapruder, it was not difficult for me to see things from the perspective of our family or to understand why my grandfather or father did the things they did. Certainly, it was not as hard for me as it probably would have been for someone else. What was difficult was overcoming the instinct to defend my family or to leave out anything that might be even slightly unflattering or to skew the story to protect their images. But since, in the end, I believed that the worst that could be said of them was that they were human, I didn't need to whitewash the story to protect them. So that made things much easier for me from both an ethical and a storytelling perspective.

Is history by definition objective, or can it also be personal as well?

I don't think history is strictly objective. I mean, events occurred in the past the way they occurred, but our only access to the past—to history—is through the telling of it in various forms. And we don't do it once; we continue to tell and retell, and new documents and materials surface, and times change, and we revisit the eras in question and reconstruct our understanding of them. In this sense, history is very personal because the person who is writing or teaching it is, by definition, shaping a narrative, or imposing a set of views or interpretations upon the information. Having said that, I think that different subjective or personal historical accounts can be true or have overlapping truths. Or, to put it another way, there is not one single absolute historical truth that we should imagine that we are in search of, and if we find it, we will be finished. I don't see historical inquiry that way.

In fact, you could use the Zapruder film as an analogy. In

one sense, the film itself is what it is. It is literally an unchanging record—it shows exactly the same thing every single time it is run. It never changes. And yet, different people over different eras have seen vastly different things in it. It's not that the film changes—although perhaps time and technology have permitted it to become somewhat clearer and to therefore reveal more of its details. But really, what changes over time are the people looking at it, their interests, beliefs, and social constructs, and the time and context from which they are looking. They interpret it differently over time, and in very personal ways. This is an evolving process. And while the truth might be out there, it's hard to imagine that there will ever be a simple consensus on what it is because everything continues to change.

The generations for whom the Kennedy assassination was a personal, visceral experience are aging. What will happen to our understanding of the events—and seminal records like the Zapruder film—when that generation is no longer the keeper of its memory?

It's interesting because this is really the same question as what will happen when there are no more Holocaust survivors. I think that artifacts—or "secular relics" as scholar Art Simon has called them—like the Zapruder film and the Holocaust diaries of young writers become increasingly important, in a way, as time passes. They are historical remnants that were actually there, that witnessed the events in question, and that will remain to testify after the people who lived through that history are gone.

At the same time, future generations are not likely to have an intuitive understanding of these documents, nor may they necessarily have an emotional connection to them. It's possible that people won't care much about the Zapruder film in one hundred years when no one is alive who remembers John F. Kennedy. Or that few will be particularly interested in the diaries of teenagers in the Holocaust when that event is a distant memory from a previous century. I think that's why I write the books that I do. Because I believe that these sources not only tell us important things about the historical moments they reflect but that their stories tell us a great deal about what it means to be human in any time and place. I like the idea of preserving that meaning—or at least my understanding of it—in books for generations long after the ones who lived this history themselves.

INDEX

ABC, 192, 194, 371
  Abe's WFAA TV interview, 43–45
  Good Night America, 226–27,
    241–46, 270
Adams, Arlin, 382, 401–10
Adolphus Hotel, 32, 77, 79
Air Force One, 47, 133–34
Alcock, James, 204, 207
Alexander, Dean, 331
Alford, William, 204
Alger, Bruce, 32, 118
Ali, Waleed and Malik, 370–75, 376
Alterationist theory, 111, 349–56, 451*n*
Altgens, James, 35, 36
Alvarez, Luis, 201–4, 240, 256–57
American Assassins, The (TV report),
    255, 257–59
American Grotesque (Kirkwood),
    205–6
Anderson, John Kenneth, 49
Andres, Ruth, 75, 76–77
Andrews, Diane, 259
Ant Farm, 259–67
Anti-Semitism, 60–61, 114, 153–54
Antonioni, Michelangelo, 166–68,
    259, 273

Assassination Information Bureau
    (AIB), 238–39, 268–69, 270
Assassination Records Collection Act
    of 1992, 308–17, 319–28
Assassination Records Review Board
    (ARRB), 321–28, 337–49
  Conway testimony, 336, 337–38,
    342–43
  establishment of, 309, 310, 315, 317
  "Hearing on the Status and
    Disposition of the 'Zapruder
    Film,'" 333–47, 348–49
  Marwell and, 321–27, 333–35,
    343–44, 348–49
  members, 319
  resolution of hearing, 347, 362–63
  Simon testimony, 339–42
  Weitzman testimony, 228–29,
    335–36
  Zavada study, 348–50
Assassination Science (Fetzer), 356
Austell, Rhett, 230, 231
Aynesworth, Hugh, 218

Barabe, Joseph, 328–33, 384
Barber, Steve, 275

Barker, Eddie, 106, 107
Barnard, Bill, 105, 116
Barrett, Robert, 92, 146
Batchelor, Leslie, 382
Beck, Jack, 232–33
Begley, Adam, 357–58
Belin, David, 250
Bell and Howell movie camera,
    50–53, 121–22, 146
Bennett, Robert S., 363–68,
    381–83, 393–95, 408
Berlitz, Charles, 241
Bernard Geis Associates, 169–70,
    171–72, 190–93, 195–98,
    235, 293
Beschloss, Michael, 376
Billings, Richard, 173
Blair, Richard "Dick," 48–49, 55
Blakey, G. Robert, 271, 411
Blow-Up (film), 166–68, 259, 273
Blumberg, Skip, 261, 264
Bookhout, James, 92
Boren, David, 308
Brauneis, Robert, 335
Brooklyn, 62–67
Brown, Christopher, 416
Brugioni, Dino, 142, 352–53
Brusca, Richard, 363, 364–65,
    381–82, 386, 397, 398
"Buffs, The" (Trillin), 169
Bush, George H. W., 308

Camelot Productions, 299–301
Camera Never Blinks, The (Rather),
    105, 106–7, 110–11
Carlo, Jay, 204
Case Closed (Posner), 411
Cave, Ray, 250–51
Cave, The (Saramago), 12–13
CBS
    The American Assassins, 255,
        257–59

    clashes with *LIFE* over film,
        105–13, 177–82, 186–88, 218
    News Inquiry: The Warren Report,
        187–88
Chamberlain, Philip, 46–47, 48,
    53–55
Chambers, James, 40
CIA (Central Intelligence Agency), 258
    analysis of film, 141–43, 352–54
    Document 450, 142–44, 352, 442*n*
    Rockefeller Commission and,
        240–41
Clinton, Bill, 309, 319, 363, 404
Clurman, Dick, 230–31
Cohen and Uretz, 276–77
Collins, Chuck, 242
Colorfic!, 281
Committee on Ballistics Acoustics, 275
Committee to Investigate
    Assassinations, 232–33
Communism, 32, 33, 63–64
Confidentiality agreements, 110–11
Connally, Idanell "Nellie," 27, 138, 148
Connally, John, 27, 36, 93, 138, 140,
    141, 146, 147, 158, 255, 256,
    271–72, 415
Connick, Harry, 200
Conspiracy theories, 258–59, 267–75
    Alvarez and, 201–4, 256–57
    Garrison and Shaw, 198–201, 205,
        206, 207
    Groden and, 227–28, 238–40,
        241–45
    in *JFK* (film), 8, 299–308
    missing frames, 95, 163–65, 173,
        176, 182–83
    second shooter, 199, 244, 256,
        272, 275, 304
    Warren Commission and, 140–41,
        143, 159, 163–64, 170, 171, 258
Consumer Price Index, 392, 402
Conway, Debra, 336, 337–38, 342

Copyright, of Zapruder film
  donation to Sixth Floor
    Museum, 413
  LIFE and Time Inc., 115, 179,
    181, 185, 189–92, 194–98,
    216–17, 220–21
  Thompson and Geis case, 190–93,
    195–98
  Wrone and, 292–93, 414
  Zapruder family and LMH, 278–80,
    291–96, 337, 366, 380, 413
Copyright Act of 1976, 294
Copies of film. *See* Zapruder film,
  duplicates of
Copy 1, 56, 57, 90, 92, 93–94
Copy 3, 56, 57, 141–42, 352
Cortázar, Julio, 166
Costner, Kevin, 300–301, 303, 306–7
Court of Federal Claims, U.S.,
  364–65, 367, 396–97
Criswell, W. A., 32
Cronkite, Walter, 187–88, 440*n*
Crossfire (Marrs), 300
Cuba, 274, 300–301
Curry, Jesse, 96–97
Czyzyk, Herschel, 61

Dallas County Jail, 96–97
Dallas Morning News, 32, 33, 37, 41,
  42–43, 55, 105, 230, 281, 365,
  399–401
  interest in purchasing film, 37,
    41–43, 46, 49
Dallas Police Department, 39–42,
  49–50, 55–57, 96, 100–101
Dallas Policemen's and Firemen's Welfare
  Fund, 116–18, 123–24, 152–53
Dallas Times Herald, 39–40, 105, 222
Dallas Trade Mart, 27, 37, 106
Dangerous Knowledge (Simon), 340, 415
Danner, Mark, 418
David, Larry, 308

Davis, Bobby, 49
Dealey, Ted, 32
Death of a President, The
  (Manchester), 1–2, 7, 156
Declaration of Independence, 393,
  395, 396
Deepwater Horizon oil spill, 407–8
DeLillo, Don, 356–62, 418, 421
Dellinger, Walter, 382, 401–10
DeLoach, Cartha, 91–94, 99–101
Dictabelt recording, 274, 275
Donahue, Phil, 280
Donovan, Hedley, 234–35, 237
Dowd, Jack, 221
Downing, Thomas, 270–71
Dymond, Irvin, 204, 206, 209, 214

Eastman Kodak Laboratory, 46–49,
  53–57, 90, 351
EFX Unlimited, 227
Eminent domain, 314–15, 319–28
Esquire (magazine), 205
Eternal Frame, The (film), 259–67, 416

Fair market value, 315, 316, 327,
  336–37, 338, 365, 367, 382,
  383, 388–89, 393, 398–99
Fair use doctrine, 197–98, 293
FBI (Federal Bureau of Investigation),
  90–94, 96, 99–101, 140,
  143–47, 179
Feinberg, Kenneth, 382, 395–96,
  401–10, 412
Feld, Alice, 62–64
Feld, Sarah Ida, 59, 61, 62, 65, 67
Fensterwald, Bernard, 232
Ferrie, David, 199, 207
Fetzer, James, 348, 349–50, 356, 414
First Amendment, 197
Ford, Gerald, 159, 308
Francis, John, 199–200
Franklin, John Hope, 405

Freedom of Information Act, 142, 203, 315

Freyer, Bruce, 362

Freyer, Dana, 362–65, 367, 381–82, 390

Friedman, Bart, 261

Garner, John Nance, 106

Garrison, Jim, 268
  Abe's trial testimony, 204–13
  JFK (film), 300–301, 302–4
  Seinfeld's JFK parody, 306–7
  Shaw trial, 198–201, 204–15, 218–19

Geis, Bernard, 169–70, 171–72, 190–93, 195–98, 235, 293

Getty Museum, 260, 261–62, 416

Goetzman, Gary, 417

Gold, Irving, 67–68, 70

Gonzalez, Henry, 270

Good Night America (TV show), 226–27, 241–46, 270

Goodwin, Doris Kearns, 8, 321

Graff, Henry F., 319

Graves, Ralph, 231, 234–37

Great American Magazine, The (Wainwright), 81–82

Great Zapruder Film Hoax, The (Fetzer), 414

Gregory, Dick, 239–42

Groden, Robert, 225–29, 233, 238–40, 241–45, 250, 270, 293

Gunn, Jeremy, 332, 333–35, 353–54

Gurvich, William, 219

Haggerty, Edward A., 204–5, 207–8, 211–14

Hall, Doug, 259–67

Hall, Kermit, 337, 339

Hall, Kermit L., 319

Hamilton, Don, 112

Hamilton, Douglas, 185

Hanks, Tom, 417

Harpel, Joanne, 129

Harrison, Jack, 47, 48, 54

Harvard Law School, 72, 249

Hauser, Aaron, 6–7

Hauser, Adam, 6–7, 10–11, 363, 382

Hauser, David, 6–7

Hauser, Jeffrey, 6–7, 382

Hauser, Myrna. *See* Ries, Myrna

Hauser, Myron, 6, 32, 105, 151, 202
  day of assassination, 74, 75–76, 78
  death of, 289–90
  death of Abe, 224–25
  screening of film, 20–21, 24, 77

Hawkeye Works, 353

Hecht, Jamey, 416

Hemmings, David, 166–67

Hernandez, Keith, 305–8

Hester, Beatrice, 22, 34, 37, 39

Hester, Charles, 22, 34, 37, 39

Hewitt, Don, 108–9

Hill, Clint, 36, 210

Hitt, Dick, 222

Hoch, Paul, 142–44, 202–4, 240

Holland, Max, 97, 147, 414–15

Hooper, Bill, 130, 131, 132

Hoover, J. Edgar, 91

Horne, Douglas, 348, 349, 350–56

Hottelet, Richard C., 440*n*

House Select Committee on Assassinations (HSCA), 270–75, 305, 308, 411

Houston Chronicle, 124, 291–92

Hunger, Frank, 367–68, 404

Hunt, George, 78, 133, 137, 139, 178–79, 183, 193

Hunt, H. L., 32

Hunter, Ben, 142–43, 352–53

Image of an Assassination (film), 371–79

International Ladies' Garment Workers' Union, 70

In the Ring: The Trials of a Washington Lawyer (Bennett), 393
Itek Corporation, 255–57, 258

Jackson, C. D., 97–99, 135, 178, 194
Jackson, Janet, 417
Jamieson, Bruce, 54–56, 351
Jamieson Film Company, 54–56, 57, 85, 89–90, 351
Jenkisson, John, 143–44
Jennifer Juniors, 21–22, 27–28, 33–34, 37, 40–41, 55, 70–71, 82, 100
Jet-effect hypothesis, 203–4, 256–57
JFK (film), 8, 299–308
JFK Act of 1992, 309–17, 319–28, 332–47
JFK Lancer, 337–38
"Jiggle theory," 202–3
Johnson, Claudia "Lady Bird," 32–34
Johnson, Haynes, 376
Johnson, Lyndon, 32–34, 47, 134
Johnson, Steve, 384–85, 394
Johnston, Harry, 246
Jones, Paula, 363
Jones, Penn, Jr., 242, 268
Joyce, William L., 319, 341
Justice Department, U.S., 38, 74, 155–56, 275, 324, 346, 362, 364–67, 397–99, 404

Kearns Goodwin, Doris, 8, 375–79
Kelley, Thomas, 92
Kennedy, Edward M. "Ted," 408
Kennedy, Jacqueline "Jackie," 71
    assassination of JFK, 36, 75–76, 133–34
Kennedy, John F.
    funeral of, 102–3
    gravesite of, 227–28
    Henry's admiration of, 72–74

political tensions in Dallas and, 32–33, 77, 106
    presidential election of 1960, 71–72
Kennedy, John F., assassination of, 35–37
    basic narrative of Warren Commission, 140–41
    CBS Reports Inquiry, 255, 257–59
    conspiracy theories. *See* Conspiracy theories
    direction of shots, 150–51
    Groden and, 226–27
    hunt for Oswald, 49–50
    Itek report, 255–57, 258
    reenactment, in *The Eternal Frame*, 259–67
    tenth anniversary, 233
    time clock, 142–43, 146–47, 148, 151, 158, 440*n*
Kennedy, John F., Jr., 399
Kennedy, Robert F. "Bobby," 139, 195, 269
Kern, Edward, 172–74, 178–79
Kessler, Helen, 28
Keylor, Art, 143–44
King, Alan, 331
King, Martin Luther, Jr., 195, 269–70
Kirby, Kathryn, 48–49
Kirkpatrick, Kathryne, 375
Kirkwood, James, 205–14
Knight, Wayne, 305–8
Kodak Laboratory, 46–49, 53–57, 90, 351
Kovel, Ukraine, 58–59
KRLD-TV, 106, 109, 111

Lamarre, Hervé, 220
L'Américain (film), 220
Landes, William, 384
Lane, Mark, 165–66, 200, 201, 234, 238, 268
Lattimer, John K., 281

Lawless, Anita, 276–78, 280, 281, 283, 286–91, 298, 299–301, 312, 317

Leavelle, J. R., 96

Lehrer, Jim, 375–78

Lelouch, Claude, 234

Lenahan, Edward "Pat," 231

Lesar, James, 294–95, 336, 337, 411

Lewis, Alan, 330

Libra (DeLillo), 357

Liebeler, Wesley J., 149–54, 182–83

LIFE (magazine). *See also* Zapruder film, Time ownership of
  Abe's sale of print rights to, 79–81, 82–90
  acquisition of all rights to film, 97–99, 105–6, 109–10, 112–13, 115–16, 152–54
  author's research in archives, 129–32
  JFK assassination edition (November 29, 1963), 77–79, 94–95, 97, 133–35
  JFK funeral edition (December 6, 1963), 135–36
  JFK Memorial Edition (1963), 136–39
  Josiah Thompson and, 171–74, 181–82, 190–93, 195–98
  A Matter of Reasonable Doubt (November 25, 1966), 170–74, 182–83, 201–2
  printing of film stills, 94–95
  return of film to Zapruder family, 246–53
  Warren Report edition (October 2, 1964), 158–62, 165

Lifton, David, 176, 281, 349–50

Limousine: Midnight Blue (Hecht), 416

Lincoln, Abraham, 393, 395, 396

Livingstone, Harrison, 348

Lloyd, Kate, 356–57

Lloyd, Robin, 217–18

LMH Company, 278–79, 284, 290, 291, 294, 296, 298, 317, 324–25, 328, 332–35, 345–46, 362–64, 397–98

Lord, Chip, 259–60, 261, 266, 377

Los Alamos Scientific Laboratory, 271, 281

Louis-Dreyfus, Julia, 306

Love Field, 47, 75, 133–34

Lower, Elmer, 194

Lubar, Bob, 236

Lubin, David, 167–68, 415

Luce, Henry, 78

Lynn, Ada, 2–3

Macauley, C. Cameron, 362, 366, 384, 389–94, 402

McCormick, Harry, 37, 41–43, 46, 49, 55, 85

McCrone Associates, 328–33, 371, 384, 388

McGwire, Mark, 393, 394, 396

McKnight, Felix, 105, 117, 123

McMahon, Homer, 142–43, 352–54, 451*n*

Mafia, 97, 274, 300–301

"Magic bullet" theory. *See* Single-bullet theory

Malcolm X, 269

Manchester, William, 1–2, 7, 100–101, 155–56

Mandel, Paul, 140–41, 143

Manhardt, Kirk, 382, 390, 392

Manhattan Effects, 195, 227

Manning, Gordon, 186

Mannlicher-Carcano rifle, 146, 147

Mantik, David, 348

Marcus, Stanley, 119

Marrs, Jim, 300

Marwell, David, 321–27, 333–35, 343–44, 348–49, 411–12

Metropolitan Museum of Art, 74

Michels, Doug, 259, 261, 265
Mike Douglas Show (TV show), 192, 193
"Mink Coat Mob," 32
Moore, James, 287
Moore, Philip, 362
Moorman, Mary, 35
Morris, Errol, 417, 418
Mort d'un président (film), 220, 234
MPI Home Video, 370–75
Muchmore, Marie, 35, 148, 243
Museum of Jewish Heritage, 321, 322–23

Nardis, 29, 67–70
National Archives, 13, 236–37, 238, 240–41, 278–79, 284–85, 287, 312–14, 320–21, 325–26, 332
National Lampoon, 265
National Nightmare on Six Feet of Film (Trask), 141–42, 163, 255, 258, 271–72, 274, 440n
National Photographic Interpretation Center (NPIC), 142–43, 352–53
Need to Know, A (Holland), 415
Neiman Marcus, 28, 119
Nelson, Anna K., 319, 338, 411
New Frontier, 72–73
NewsHour with Jim Lehrer (TV show), 375–78
Newsweek, 97, 147, 365, 415
New Yorker, 169, 418
New York Times, 8, 65, 124, 165, 220, 239, 251–52, 365, 408, 412, 414, 417
Nicholas II of Russia, 58, 177
Nix, Orville, 35, 148, 243, 261
Nixon, Richard, 308
No Ordinary Time (Kearns Goodwin), 376
Nulty, Tom, 56

O'Brien, Lawrence, 73
Oglesby, Carl, 268
Olan, Levi, 224–25
Olds, Greg, 215–17, 221–22
On the Trail of the Assassins (Garrison), 300
On the Trail of the JFK Assassins (Russell), 351
Orth, Herbert, 145
Oser, Alvin, 204, 210
Oswald, Lee Harvey
  HSCA and, 272
  hunt for and arrest of, 49–50
  murder of, 96–97, 140
  in police custody, 57, 79–80
  Shaw conspiracy and, 198
  Warren Commission and, 147, 165, 415

Packer, George, 418
Panzeca, Salvatore, 204
Paris Review, 357–58
Parkland (film), 417
Parkland Memorial Hospital, 24, 38, 41, 102, 120, 303
Passman, Sam, 105, 109–10, 111, 113–14, 116, 153–54
Patterson, Jerry, 384–86, 390, 395
Pattist, Pat, 54
Payne, Darwin, 39–40, 41–42, 85, 109
Peacock Jewelry, 50
Perle, Gabe, 235–36
Phillips, Dixon, 405
Phillips, Max, 57
Photomacrography, 330–33
Pictures of the Pain (Trask), 336
Pies, Roger, 312, 368–69
Playtone, 417
"Politics of Conspiracy, The" (conference), 238–40

Pollard, Dick, 82, 97–98, 131–32, 181, 189–90, 194, 215–17, 220–21, 222, 230–31, 279–80

Posner, Gerald, 411

Presbyterian Hospital, 223–24

Preston, Don, 169–70, 185

Preyer, Richardson, 270–71

Proctor, Jody, 259, 261

Quint, Bernard, 137–38, 160

Ramparts, 218, 221

Ramsey, Norman F., 275

Random House, 191–92

Rather, Dan, 105–13, 218, 257–58, 354–55

Redgrave, Vanessa, 166–67

Reeves, Harold, 363, 381–82

Richards, Michael, 305–8

Richter, Robert, 232–38, 245

Ries, Ernie, 288–89, 290, 296

Ries, Myrna, 5–6, 32, 59, 60, 151
  appearance of, 76
  day of assassination, 75–77
  death of Ernie, 289–90
  death of father, 224–25
  guardianship of film, 10–11, 382
  in home movies, 65–67
  legacy of film, 104–5
  move to Dallas, 68–70
  presidential election of 1960, 71–72
  screening of film, 20, 21

Rivera, Geraldo, 226–27, 241–45, 270, 280

Rockefeller Commission, 240–41

Rogers, Lillian, 21–22, 70–71, 156
  day of assassination, 28–34, 37
  Stolley and offer for film, 84–85, 89

Rolling Stone, 357

Rose, Ernest D., 362, 366

Rotoscoping, 229

Rotterdam, SS, 62, 323

Rowan, Roy, 78, 79, 94–95

Rowley, James, 57, 144

R.R. Donnelley, 78–79, 94

Ruby, Jack, 96–97, 119, 140

Rudd, Hughes, 440*n*

Rush to Judgment (Lane), 165–66, 201

Russell, Dick, 351

Russia, 24, 58–62, 63–64, 177

Sahl, Mort, 279–80

Salandria, Vincent, 169–70

Salvaged Pages (Zapruder), 321

Samuelsohn, Howie, 242

Saramago, José, 12–13

Saturday Evening Post, 57, 84

Schapovnik, Morris, 63, 66, 69, 126

Schoenman, Ralph, 241

Schwartz, Abe, 30, 70

Schwartz, Erwin, 60, 70–71
  day of assassination, 30, 33–34, 40–41, 43
  involvement in custody and development of film, 50, 54, 55, 56–57, 436*n*

Sciambra, Andrew, 204

Scott, Marvin, 174–77

Secret Service, 90–91, 92, 99–100, 352–53
  analysis of film, 141–43, 352–54
  assassination of JFK, 36
  duplicate film given to, 24, 39–42, 57, 81–86, 83, 92, 93–94
  screening of film, 83–84

Seiger, Ben, 74

Seinfeld (TV show), 8, 305–8

Selby, Gerard "Chip," 290–95, 298

September 11 attacks, 407, 420–21

Shaneyfelt, Lyndal, 144–45

Shanklin, Gordon, 91–94

Shapiro, Mike, 105

Shaw, Clay, 198–201, 204–15, 219, 268, 300, 302

Shipp, Bert, 46–47
Shooting Kennedy (Lubin), 167–68, 415
Silverberg, Jamie, 298
  JFK Act and, 309–14, 319–29,
    332–35, 363, 365, 367,
    371, 372
  Selby/Weisberg matter, 295, 298
Simon, Art, 339–42, 415, 443*n*
Single-bullet theory, 147–48,
    165–66, 184–85, 303, 306–7,
    308, 415
Sitzman, Marilyn, 22, 30, 33–34,
    35–37, 39, 175
Six Seconds in Dallas (Thompson),
    183–86, 190, 191–92, 195,
    202–3
Sixth Floor Museum, 174, 229, 413
Skadden Arps, 363, 373
Sklar, Zachary, 300
Sloan, Frank, 56
Smith, Bill, 353
Snyder, Tom, 251–52
Socialism, 63–64
Sorrels, Forrest, 37, 41–43, 46, 47,
    49, 57, 99–100
Specter, Arlen, 147–48
Sprague, Richard, 270
Stalin, Joseph, 294
Staszyn, John, 384, 390, 392–93,
    395–96
Stech, David, 78–79, 95
Stemmons Freeway sign, 106, 176,
    243, 255–56, 272
"Step-framed," 229
Stevens, Kay, 193
Stevenson, Adlai, 32–33, 106
Stokes, Louis, 270–71, 308
Stolley, Richard, 15, 77–81, 136,
    157, 248–49
  CBS and ownership of film,
    178–81
  first screening of film, 83–84
  purchase of film rights for *LIFE*,
    97–99, 105–6, 109–10,
    112–13, 115–16, 152–54
  purchase of print rights for *LIFE*,
    79–81, 82–90, 94
Stone, Oliver, 7–8, 299–308
Students for a Democratic
  Society, 268
Suydam, Henry, 144, 173
Swank, Patsy, 79–80, 82

Takings Clause, 314–15, 319–28,
    332–80
Technical Animations, 227
Tell Me a Story (Hewitt), 108–9
Telluride Film Festival, 418
Temple Emanu-El (South Dallas), 69,
    224–25
Tennessean, 375
Texas Observer, 215, 220, 221
Texas School Book Depository
  (TSBD) Building, 39, 41,
    42–43, 140, 240, 272
Thompson, Ed, 179–80
Thompson, Josiah, 168–70
  access to copies of film at *LIFE*,
    171–74, 181–82
  ARRB hearing, 336, 337, 338
  conspiracy theories, 173, 182, 350,
    355, 417
  Six Seconds in Dallas, 183–86, 190,
    191–92, 195, 202–3
  Time lawsuit against, 190–93,
    195–98
Thompson, Tommy, 78, 79
Time & Life Building, 78, 129,
    240–41
Time Inc. *See also LIFE* (magazine);
  Zapruder film, Time
  ownership of
  author's research in archives,
    129–32

Time Inc. v. Bernard Geis Associates,
192–98

Tippit, J. D.
 charitable donation to family from
  sale of film, 116–20, 122–25,
  152–53
 Oswald shooting of, 49–50
Toute une vie (film), 234
T.R. Uthco, 259–67
Trask, Richard, 163, 233, 336, 337, 339
 *National Nightmare on Six Feet of
  Film,* 141–42, 163, 255, 258,
  271–72, 274, 440*n*
Trien, Bob, 249–53, 280
Trien, May, 249–50
Trillin, Calvin, 169
Truettner, Bill, 411
"Truth Behind JFK's Assassination,
 The" (Holland), 97, 147, 415
Tunheim, John R., 319, 327, 334,
 337, 344–47, 396–97, 398, 411

Ukraine, 58–61
Underground News (TV show), 242
Underworld (DeLillo), 356–62, 421
Urban, Jerry, 291–93

Vågnes, Øyvind, 415

Wainwright, Loudon, 81–82,
 170–71, 180
Walker, Edwin, 32
Ward, Charles Ray, 219
Warren, Beth Gates, 384–88
Warren, Earl, 140
Warren Commission, 140–41, 143–46
 Abe's testimony, 149–54, 163–64
 screening of film, 144–46
 Sorrels's testimony, 42–43
Warren Report
 critics of, 163–66, 169–70,
  184–85, 275

images from Zapruder film in,
 162–63
JFK (film) and, 303–4
LIFE and, 158–62, 170–71,
 173–74, 182–83
Washington Post, 8, 365
Watson, Jay, 43–44, 46, 175
Watters, John "Jack," 186, 189–90, 221
Wegmann, Edward and William, 204
Weisberg, Harold, 163–64, 281,
 290–95, 411
Weitzman, Moses, 195, 227, 228–29,
 335–36
Welch, Jack, 405
Welch, Paul, 232–36, 238
Welch, Raquel, 241
West, Robert, 207
Wexler, Haskell, 230, 231
WFAA-TV, 43–45, 46–47
White, Theodore, 134
Willens, Howard, 143–44
Willis, Phillip, 35, 149
Willis, Rosemary, 271–72
Wilson, Don, 250–51, 251
Winfrey, Oprah, 281
Wolf, John, 257–58
Wolf, Sylvia Leonard, 384–85
Woodward, Richard, 417
World War I, 59, 60
WPIX-TV, 174–77
Wrone, David, 268–69, 292–93, 414
Wyatt, Inzer B., 195–98

You Are the Jury (documentary), 234

Zaid, Mark, 309, 366
"Zapruder," use of term, 416–17
Zapruder (band), 416
Zapruder, Abraham "Abe"
 appearance of, 66–67
 Bell and Howell camera purchase,
  50–51

bidding war for film, 85–87, 100
business interests of, 21–22, 28–30, 67–68, 70–71
cancer and death of, 219–20, 223–25
CBS TV interview, 187–88
charitable donation from sale of film, 116–25, 139, 152–53
day of assassination. *See* Zapruder, Abraham "Abe," day of assassination
descendants of, 6–7
duplicate film given to Secret Service, 24, 81–86, 92, 93–94
early life of, 24, 58–64
family life of, 65–66
financial considerations for film, 98, 100, 113–18, 152–54, 247–48, 355
first screening of film, 19–21, 77
home movies of, 21, 30, 65–67
initial sale of print rights to *LIFE*, 79–81, 82–90
internal conflict over film, 104–5, 113–16
LIFE's acquisition of all rights to film, 97–99, 105–6, 109–10, 112–13, 115–16, 152–54
Manchester's interview with, 155–56
move to Dallas, 67–70
Shaw trial testimony, 204–13
Warren Commission testimony, 149–54, 163–64
WPIX-TV interview, 174–77
Zapruder, Abraham "Abe," day of assassination, 35–37. *See also* Zapruder film
arrival at police department, 56–57
call to Henry, 37–38
development of film, 42–43, 46–49, 53–57
filming of assassination, 23–24, 35–36, 53

McCormick's interest in purchasing film, 37, 41–43, 46, 49
morning of, 27–28
Payne's interest in film, 39–40, 41–42
preparations to film motorcade, 22–23, 33–34
reaction to assassination, 36–37
reporter interviews, 24, 37, 39
retrieval of camera from home, 30–31
Secret Service and acquisition of film, 39–42
vantage point, 22, 23, 33, 34–35
WFAA-TV interview, 43–45
Zapruder, Chana, 58–62, 65, 67
Zapruder, David, 21
Zapruder, Henry, 2–3, 6, 18
admiration for JFK, 72–74
cancer and death of, 9–10, 219–20
courtship and marriage of, 73–74
day of assassination, 37–38
at Justice Department, 38, 74, 155–56
move to Dallas, 68, 69–70
Zapruder, Henry, guardianship of original film, 6–10, 16–17, 276–98. *See also* Zapruder, Henry, and JFK Act
copies, process for, 286–87
copyright issues, 278–80, 291–96, 337, 366, 380, 413
donation of film to National Archives, 236–37, 238, 240–41
fees, 281–82, 283–84, 288–89
Good Night America screening, 245–46
JFK (film), 299–308
letter to Ernie, 288–89, 295–96
licensing agreements, 279, 280, 281, 311, 338

Zapruder, Henry, guardianship of
     original film, (cont.)
   "profiteering" charge, 291–95
   refusals of use, 285–86, 296–97
   requests for use, 255, 279–86
   return of film, 246–53
   Selby/Weisberg matter, 290–95, 298
Zapruder, Henry, and JFK Act, 309–17,
     319–28, 332–47, 362–70
   arbitration agreement, 367–70
   arbitration hearing, 380–412
   ARRB hearing, 333–47
   drafting of JFK Act legislation,
     310–11
   eminent domain and Takings
     Clause, 314–17, 319–21
   just compensation, 314–15, 316,
     320, 327, 334, 336, 362,
     364–67, 369, 375, 380
   plan to remove film from National
     Archives, 312–14
Zapruder, Israel, 58–61, 65
Zapruder, Jeff, 21
Zapruder, Lillian "Lil," 5–6, 63–66
   Abe's cancer and death, 223–25
   appearance of, 126
   charitable donation letters and,
     120–21, 127–28
   day of assassination, 20–21, 25, 75
   death of, 317–18
   financial considerations, 247–48
   first screening of film, 20–21,
     24, 77
   Garrison trial and, 205, 208–9
   legacy of film, 125–28, 157
   move to Dallas, 67–70, 127
   personality of, 126–27
   return of film, 249, 250
Zapruder, Marjorie Seiger, 6,
     10–11, 223
   appearance of, 102
   courtship and marriage, 73–74

   day of assassination, 37–38, 102
   legacy of film, 101–3
Zapruder, Matthew, 2, 5–6, 8–9,
     126, 223–24, 254, 382
Zapruder, Michael, 2, 5–6, 8–9,
     12–13, 223–24, 254
Zapruder, Morris, 59–62
Zaprudered (Vågnes), 415
Zapruder film
   Alvarez analysis of, 201–4, 256–57
   alterationist theory, 111, 349–56,
     451n
   appraisals of value, 241, 312, 328,
     362, 366, 383–88
   authenticity of, 209, 258, 323–24
   author's history with, 1–2, 17
   breaking of social and cultural
     barriers, 160–61
   CIA analysis of, 141–43, 352–54
   copyright. See Copyright, of
     Zapruder film
   development of, 19–20, 42–43,
     46–49, 53–57
   edge markings, 313, 349, 352–53
   18 frames per second, 142–43,
     146–47
   inter-sprocket material, 52, 56,
     290–91, 293, 334, 349, 353,
     372
   in JFK (film), 302–3, 304
   missing frames, 95, 163–65, 173,
     176, 182–83
   sale of print stills to LIFE, 79–81,
     82–90
   Zavada study, 348–50
Zapruder film, cultural responses to,
     416–18
   Blow-Up (film), 166–68, 259
   The Eternal Frame (film), 259–67
   JFK (film), 8, 299–308
   Seinfeld's JFK parody, 305–8
   Underworld (DeLillo), 356–62

Zapruder film, duplicates of, 57, 90
  Abe and *LIFE,* 89–94, 112, 144
  bootleg copies, 131–32, 215,
    217–21, 225–29
  FBI and, 90–94
  Groden and, 225–29
  by Jamieson Film Company,
    54–56, 57, 89–90
  Secret Service and, 24, 39–42,
    81–86, 92, 93–94
  Thompson and, 172–74
Zapruder film, screenings of
  Assassination Information Bureau,
    268–69, 270
  confidentiality agreements, 110–11
  of Dan Rather, 111–12
  of FBI, 90–91
  Good Night America, 226–27,
    241–46
  HSCA, 270–75
  at Kodak, 53–54
  at "Politics of Conspiracy"
    conference, 238–40
  public debate about viewing,
    160–61
  of Secret Service, 83–84
  Underground News, 242
  by Warren Commission, 144–46
  by Zapruder family, 19–21, 24, 77
Zapruder film, Time ownership of,
  193–95, 223–53
  acquisition of all rights, 97–99,
    105–6, 109–10, 112–13,
    115–16
  CBS clashes with *LIFE,* 105–13,
    177–82, 186–88
  donation to National Archives,
    236–37, 238, 240–41
  Garrison and, 198–201, 204–15

Groden and, 238–40, 241–45
  issues concerning ownership,
    179–80, 183–88
  licensing agreements, 232–36
  LIFE's JFK editions, 133–39
  Olds and, 215–17
  proposal of sale, 222, 230–31
  return of film to Zapruder family,
    246–53
  Richter and, 232–38
  Thompson and Geis case, 172–74,
    190–93, 195–98
  Warren Commission and, 143–46
Zapruder Film, The (Wrone), 268–69,
  292–93, 414
Zapruder film rights, 104–28
  CBS and Rather, 105–13
  charitable donation from sale,
    116–25, 139, 152–53
  confidentiality agreements, 110–11
  financial considerations, 113–18,
    152–54, 326–27
  LIFE's acquisition of, 97–99,
    105–6, 109–10, 112–13,
    115–16, 152–54
  sale price, 112, 115–16,
    122, 124, 152–54
Zapruder frame 207, 164, 191
Zapruder frame 210, 148, 163–64
Zapruder frame 212, 164, 256
Zapruder frame 225, 148, 256, 272
Zapruder frame 313, 95, 137, 148,
  159–60, 160, 203,
  256, 272, 331
Zapruder frame 314, 164, 256
Zapruder frame 323, 159–60,
  161–62
Zavada, Roland, 348–50
Zelenko, Ali, 129–30

ABOUT THE AUTHOR

ALEXANDRA ZAPRUDER began her career on the founding staff of the United States Holocaust Memorial Museum in Washington, DC. A graduate of Smith College, she later earned her Master's Degree in Education at Harvard University. She is the author of *Salvaged Pages: Young Writers' Diaries of the Holocaust*, which won the National Jewish Book Award in the Holocaust category. She also served as the guest curator for an exhibition of original diaries at Holocaust Museum Houston. She wrote and co-produced *I'm Still Here*, a documentary film for young audiences based on *Salvaged Pages*, which was awarded the Jewish Image Award for Best Television Special by the National Foundation for Jewish Culture and was nominated for two Emmy awards. Alexandra has traveled around the country and spoken to thousands of teachers, students, and others about her work.

MISSION STATEMENT

Twelve strives to publish singular books, by authors who have unique perspectives and compelling authority. Books that explain our culture; that illuminate, inspire, provoke, and entertain. Our mission is to provide a consummate publishing experience for our authors, one truly devoted to thoughtful partnership and cutting-edge promotional sophistication that reaches as many readers as possible. For readers, we aim to spark that rare reading experience—one that opens doors, transports, and possibly changes their outlook on our ever-changing world.

12 Things to Remember about TWELVE

1. Every Twelve book will enliven the national conversation.
2. Each book will be singular in voice, authority, or subject matter.
3. Each book will be carefully edited, designed, and produced.
4. Each book's publication life will begin with a month-long launch; for that month it will be the imprint's devoted focus.

5. The Twelve team will work closely with its authors to devise a publication strategy that will reach as many readers as possible.

6. Each book will have a national publicity campaign devoted to reaching as many media outlets—and readers—as possible.

7. Each book will have a unique digital strategy.

8. Twelve is dedicated to finding innovative ways to market and promote its authors and their books.

9. Twelve offers true partnership with its authors—the kind of partnership that gives a book its best chance at success.

10. Each book will get the fullest attention and distribution of the sales force of the Hachette Book Group.

11. Each book will be promoted well past its on-sale date to maximize the life of its ideas.

12. Each book will matter.